MAGNUM OPUS

OTHER BOOKS BY JAMES GREENE, JR.

This Music Leaves Stains: The Complete Story of The Misfits
Brave Punk World: The International Rock Underground From Alerta Rosa to Z-Off
A Convenient Parallel Dimension: How Ghostbusters Slimed Us Forever

MAGNUM OPUS

The Unbelievable 15-Year Saga of Guns N' Roses' *Chinese Democracy*

JAMES GREENE, JR.

Backbeat Books
Bloomsbury Publishing Inc, 1359 Broadway, 12th Floor, New York, NY 10018, USA
Bloomsbury Publishing Plc, 50 Bedford Square, London, WC1B 3DP, UK
Bloomsbury Publishing Ireland, 29 Earlsfort Terrace, Dublin 2, D02 AY28, Ireland

Copyright © 2025 by James Greene, Jr.

All rights reserved. No part of this publication may be: i) reproduced or transmitted in any form, electronic or mechanical, including photocopying, recording or by means of any information storage or retrieval system without prior permission in writing from the publishers; or ii) used or reproduced in any way for the training, development or operation of artificial intelligence (AI) technologies, including generative AI technologies. The rights holders expressly reserve this publication from the text and data mining exception as per Article 4(3) of the Digital Single Market Directive (EU) 2019/790.

British Library Cataloguing in Publication Information available

Library of Congress Cataloging-in-Publication Data
Names: Greene, James, Jr., 1979- author
Title: Magnum opus : the unbelievable 15-year saga of Guns n' Roses' Chinese democracy / James Greene, Jr..
Description: [1.]. | New York, NY : Backbeat Books, 2025. | Includes bibliographical references.
Identifiers: LCCN 2025018390 (print) | LCCN 2025018391 (ebook) | ISBN 9781493074785 paperback | ISBN 9781493074792 epub | ISBN 9798765161630 pdf
Subjects: LCSH: Guns n' Roses (Musical group). Chinese democracy | Rock music–2001-2010–History and criticism.
Classification: LCC ML421.G86 G74 2025 (print) | LCC ML421.G86 (ebook) | DDC 782.42166092/2--dc23/eng/20250414
LC record available at https://lccn.loc.gov/2025018390
LC ebook record available at https://lccn.loc.gov/2025018391 For product safety related questions contact productsafety@bloomsbury.com.

The paper used in this publication meets the minimum requirements of American National Standard for Information Sciences—Permanence of Paper for Printed Library Materials, ANSI/NISO Z39.48-1992.

This book is dedicated to Minnie, my childhood dog.

CONTENTS

0 From the Gut   1

1 Veni Vidi Vici   3

2 The End of the Vogue   23

3 Axl's Been Researching You   43

4 Jimmy Said He Could Fix Everything   61

5 The Most Dangerous Guitarist Alive   83

6 La La Land   105

7 This Thing Is Never Coming Out   127

8 God Himself Cannot Eat It   149

9 You Can't Go Home Again   175

Acknowledgments   193
Notes   195
Index   251

0 FROM THE GUT

Honesty is the best policy, right? I'm not what you would call a die-hard Guns N' Roses fan. I was eight years old when *Appetite for Destruction* came out and it didn't really touch my life. What was I even listening to back then? "Weird Al," the Fat Boys. Also a lot of DJ Jazzy Jeff & the Fresh Prince. I think it's really important to emphasize here the fact that I was eight.

The hits from *Appetite for Destruction* were inescapable, though, and that was also the case when *Use Your Illusion* came out. If you'd asked me when I was twelve if I liked Guns N' Roses, I probably would have said, "Yeah, they have some cool songs." I would have said the same thing about Technotronic, Ugly Kid Joe, Soul Asylum, Heavy D, or any other band on the radio or MTV. I just liked music as an art form.

When I was in college, I picked up a copy of *Appetite* on a whim. It lived in my stereo for a while. You can't turn that album off once it starts. It's an adventure. The beginning is perfect, the ending is perfect, and there's a ton of killer stuff in between. It's like Beethoven's Fifth Symphony, but with more sex and drugs. That said, nothing Guns N' Roses ever recorded hit me the same way as the punk rock from a generation before. Dead Kennedys, the Germs, the Saints—stuff like that hit me in the solar plexus. Like, *Oh my god, another world is possible.*

Simultaneously, I couldn't help but be fascinated by the strange path Guns N' Roses was taking. No one really knew what was going on with them in the late '90s. Then they started adding all these left field players, like Josh Freese, Tommy Stinson, and Buckethead. Axl resurfaced with those Stevie Wonder braids. The next Guns N' Roses album, *Chinese Democracy*, was always almost ready to come out, but then a year or two would pass with no release.

In place of the album, we got weird rumors, tall tales. Oh, they had to build a chicken coop in the studio for Buckethead. Now he's out of the band, maybe. Oh, some guy from the New York Mets leaked a song, but very few people heard it, and the whole thing may have been a work. Oh, Shaquille O'Neal recorded a rap for the album. Supposedly it's amazing. Better than *Shaq Fu*.

Everyone loves a mystery, and this one was very compelling. What was really happening here? Was Axl Rose just lying in the fetal position under the mixing board?

I think the world resigned itself to *Chinese Democracy* never coming out. And then, incredibly, it did, in November 2008. I was living in New York City at the time. Often in New York, there are lines or mob scenes for things you wouldn't expect—like that British movie *The Trip* with Steve Coogan and Rob Brydon, which was sold out at the IFC Center for weeks. On the other hand, New Yorkers are Americans, and they buy into mainstream hype like anyone else. The lines for *The Dark Knight* were just as insane as the ones for *The Trip*.

I'll never forget riding the subway to Best Buy in Manhattan to buy *Chinese Democracy* the morning it came out, wondering what kind of scene would greet me. I felt it was my duty as a rock n' roll fan to be there on release day for this unicorn, but I was also writing for *Crawdaddy!* and I figured I could get an interesting piece of the experience. Well, I got to the Best Buy and I swear to God I was the only person there for *Chinese Democracy*. And they sure didn't have any giant banners up celebrating this thing. I wandered around for quite a while before I found it.

So I bought it, took it home, it didn't change my life, and that was the end of that. I guess my reaction was, *Well, Axl got it done. A lot of people thought he wouldn't, but he did.* You know, Auguste Rodin never finished *Gates of Hell*. He spent thirty-seven years working on that sculpture and then he died. Fran Lebowitz still hasn't written her third book. She's had writer's block for over forty years. Fran, we love you, but this is ridiculous.

Then again, *did* Axl get it done? Did he actually complete it, or was *Chinese Democracy* ripped out of his hands for still not entirely clear reasons? The mysteries surrounding this album feel ongoing, which is what really propelled me to craft the work you're currently holding, or looking at, or listening to on your mobile device.

I'm not a political writer, by which I mean politics has never been my primary beat, but writing this book taught me that Guns N' Roses is handled like a political subject. I'm guessing this is because, historically speaking, Axl Rose has been a litigious totalitarian. So this project had a lot of "you didn't hear this from me" and "I have to stay neutral, like Switzerland" and even "I have a statement prepared that I use to respond to such inquiries." Some of the interviews were a little contentious. Maybe not Isaac Chotiner interviewing Elliott Abrams contentious, but close.

Truth is stranger than fiction, and I tried to get as close to the truth as possible in this book. Hopefully, I've been equitable to this sprawling, inscrutable tale. In the highly dramatic words of Axl himself, "If my intentions are misunderstood, please be kind, I've done all I should."

1 VENI VIDI VICI

"They're completely insane. They know what it's like to be half-dead. They know what it's like to be completely wasted on drugs. They know what it's like to be happy, sad. They're not afraid to speak their mind."

Twenty-one-year-old Geoff Black was explaining the allure of Guns N' Roses as he waited outside Oasis Music and Video in Oakland, Pennsylvania. It was late in the evening on Monday, September 16, 1991, and the line to get into Oasis stretched down the block. At midnight, this record store would be one of over a thousand across North America opening half a day early to begin selling the second full-length effort from Guns N' Roses, *Use Your Illusion*. Although it was a double album, *Use Your Illusion* was being sold as individual units—*Use Your Illusion I* and *Use Your Illusion II*. The group's label Geffen Records took credit for the division, assuming that the predominantly teenage demographic who lived and died by these insolent, volatile hard rockers wouldn't be able to afford a $30 two-disc release.[1][2][3]

Excitement for *Use Your Illusion* had been white-hot all year. Ted Wenzel, manager at a Camelot Music in Ohio, said the daily phone calls inquiring about the albums' release date began the previous Christmas.[4] At another Camelot location in upstate New York, manager Kim Peterman reported that on some days over twenty-five people came in asking about *Use Your Illusion*.[5] Musicland, the largest music retailer in the United States, presold 100,000 copies.[6][7] *Use Your Illusion* had a nationwide record-breaking advance order of 4.5 million (2.25 million per disc).[8] As Dinky Rice of Boston's Strawberry Records put it, "This is like the second coming of the Beatles."[9]

Divine intervention was exactly what the record industry needed. Album sales in 1991 had fallen by 10 percent due to the recession and a dearth of marquee releases.[10] Could Guns N' Roses play savior? Brows furrowed when the band scrubbed the original May release date for *Use Your Illusion*. Then, over the summer, rabid response to "You Could Be Mine," a new Guns N' Roses song included on the soundtrack for *Terminator 2*, left experts agog. "When 800,000 cassette singles of 'You Could Be Mine' went out the door, without any campaign, we realized that they're bigger than we ever thought," said Geffen marketing head Robert Smith.[11]

Guns N' Roses were already pretty big. Their first album *Appetite for Destruction* was the most successful debut ever, having sold 14 million copies since 1987.[12] [13] Prior to smashing sales benchmarks, *Appetite for Destruction* was a word-of-mouth phenomenon that quenched a thirst for something more nihilistic and uncouth than rock's de rigueur.[14] Even critics who blanched at the lurid sleeve art (depicting a sexual assault) and the pornographic lyrics they heard within couldn't totally write off Guns N' Roses. "I wanted to dislike this album," Thom Duffy admitted in *The Orlando Sentinel*. "Strictly from a musical standpoint, I can't . . . this band is playing some of the most infectious hard rock I've heard in a while, without resorting to the simplistic chant-along choruses so common to metal pop."[15] And amid gritty salvos like "Welcome to the Jungle" and "Out ta Get Me" was "Sweet Child O' Mine," a power ballad put over by the multi-octave shriek of lead singer Axl Rose. "Sweet Child O' Mine" became a number one hit in September 1988.[16]

There was a style and intensity to Guns N' Roses that set them apart from other bands, but it wasn't hard to trace their influences—Aerosmith, the Stones, the Sex Pistols. Like all those forbearers at various points in their careers, people wondered if Guns N' Roses would survive long enough to make another album.[17] Acute belligerence, coupled with serious drug problems, made the group outlaws long before they had a record deal. The band members acknowledged their lack of civility. "People don't really like us," bassist Duff McKagan told *SPIN* in 1988. "They think we're dickheads from hell."[18] Naturally, that was part of the allure for cynical, disaffected kids. Those kids championed Guns N' Roses through countless instances of dickhead behavior. The most severe episodes were usually touched off by Axl Rose, whose nitroglycerin temper was unprecedented even in the field of out-of-control rock stars. Rose had zero qualms about punching fans, punching his band mates, trying to punch David Bowie (Bowie made a pass at Rose's girlfriend), disappearing for days on end, and answering to no one but himself.[19] [20] [21]

"If you put me under oath right now, I might say Guns N' Roses succeeded in spite of Axl Rose, not because of," says Alan Niven, who managed the band between 1986 and 1991. "I usually soften that with some equivalency by acknowledging his extraordinary vocal sound and delivery, his intensity on stage, his composing contribution . . . but as far as the other aspects of developing a career, he was often an impediment."[22]

One of Rose's most repugnant moments was "One in a Million," the racist and homophobic screed he forced onto the 1988 EP *GNR Lies* over the objections of everyone else in Guns N' Roses.[23] Noxious couplets included "police and niggers—that's right—get outta my way, don't need to buy none of your gold chains today" and "immigrants and faggots, they make no sense to me."[24] Geffen didn't want to release the song but they freely admitted that Guns N' Roses was too successful to upset. "[They] have a lot of power because they've sold a lot of records," said label representative Bryn Bridenthal.[25]

Rolling Stone gave Axl Rose a chance to defend "One in a Million" and everything he said was laughably pathetic. He complained about artistic boundaries while simultaneously explaining that he had to use the lyric "police and niggers" because "niggers" by itself was too offensive. He whined that Black people were allowed to repurpose the slur that had been used against them for centuries, but he (a white man who'd never had to deal with systemic racism) wasn't. As for homosexual men, they confused Rose; he wanted them to keep their lives private. And it was just easier to target immigrants as a whole instead of singing about the one bad experience Rose had with someone of foreign extraction.[26] None of this came close to being the death knell for Guns N' Roses. *GNR Lies* went triple platinum.[27]

Maybe *Village Voice* columnist Harry Allen was correct when he surmised that "the majority of the people who buy that album have used the word 'nigger' to describe black people" and that "the statements of Guns N' Roses, musically and philosophically, satisfy the diseased and racist tendencies of a diseased and racist culture."[28] Maybe most fans felt like Sinéad O'Connor, who couched her usually fierce criticism of bigotry with Axl Rose because she felt the Axl she saw in TV interviews was lovable. "You just want to bring him home and give him a bowl of soup," she said. "He's like a little kid, isn't he? He just seemed that he really needed some mothering or something."[29] In a separate conversation, O'Connor cited Rose, herself, and Roseanne Barr as beacons of hope for the downtrodden. "Really, we're just the same as everyone, we just happen to be so angry about it that we got ourselves famous so we could tell our stories."[30]

Ron Jones, a Black Guns N' Roses fan who was present for *Use Your Illusion*'s midnight release at a Tower Records in Philadelphia, admitted he'd been upset by "One in a Million." "I was offended, but I can look past it," he said. "You heard the expression 'be the first on your block?' Well, I'm the only one on my block. I just gotta have a taste of it."[31] That night, roving reporters from Boston to Anaheim recorded testimonials from the Guns N' Roses faithful as they congregated outside record stores. There was a lot of praise for the lead singer. "I love Axl Rose," gushed college freshman Catesby Major as she stood in the queue for Overland Park, Missouri's Movies at Home. "He's the coolest guy in the world."[32] Peter Mack, killing time outside a Peaches in Orlando, Florida concurred, dubbing Rose "our spokesman."[33] First in line at the Tower Records on the Sunset Strip was twenty-one-year-old Leathur Rose, who wore a photo of Axl around her neck and clutched a brand-new Walkman specifically purchased so she could listen to the *Use Your Illusion* cassettes as soon as she had them.[34]

Another early bird was Tom Velek, one of the first through Musicland's door at the Hickory Point Mall in Decatur, Illinois. Velek, a law school grad, was seriously injured the previous July when he got caught in the riot that broke out after Axl Rose stormed offstage at a concert in St. Louis. "I ended up with a big cut in my head, and a friend I was there with had to have arthroscopic surgery after they threw him off the stage," he said. And yet Velek's fandom hadn't wavered. "There are very few bands that can generate this type of excitement . . . [and] that's what rock n' roll needs, excitement."[35] Hickory Point Musicland was one of many locations that chose to open just an hour earlier on the morning of September 17 as opposed to midnight.[36] Some retailers couldn't do a midnight opening because their shipment wouldn't be in on time.[37] Others refused on the grounds that midnight openings were publicity stunts.[38] No matter; plenty of lines were forming at daybreak. "I guess it says something if somebody will get up at seven in the morning to buy a record," said Bill Kennedy, manager of a Peaches in Richmond, Virginia.[39]

By that time, *Use Your Illusion* had sold half a million copies.[40] The other half quickly followed; both discs went double platinum in less than two months.[41] [42] Sales might have been twice as large had *Use Your Illusion* been stocked at Walmart and Kmart. Those retail giants (boasting a combined 3,000-plus locations in North America) refused to sell *Illusion* due to explicit lyrics.[43] "It was a flat 'no' from Kmart," said Geffen sales chief Eddie Gilreath, "and [Walmart] would prefer to lose all that revenue based on the fear of a complaint from a parent."[44]

Use Your Illusion didn't contain any lyrics as incendiary as those in "One in a Million" but it was liberally sprinkled with profanity, including one instance where Axl Rose referred to his mother as "a cunt." That sour nugget prompted Evangelical columnist Cal Thomas to dub Guns N' Roses "The Band From Hell."[45] Geffen didn't feel there was any reason to court the Cal Thomases of the world with radio edits of *Use Your Illusion* songs. They were already selling every single Guns N' Roses album they could manufacture.[46]

The *Use Your Illusion* albums offered seventy-six minutes of music apiece, much of it in the same devil-may-care, dynamite-blast style that defined *Appetite for Destruction*. However, one could argue that the core of this project was a series of dramatic, grandiose ballads that proved Axl Rose wasn't lying when he cited Michael Jackson and Elton John as influences.[47] [48] The melancholia evoked by songs like "Don't Cry," "November Rain," and "Estranged" was further highlighted by equally somber and enormously expensive music videos. Those three clips cost over $1 million each and showcased a film style usually reserved for Hollywood blockbusters. In "Estranged," a dolphin swims out of an enormous block of water that is somehow being magically contained inside the belly of a jumbo jet; near the end of the ten minute video, Rose leaps into the ocean from the edge of a real oil tanker.[49] [50]

There was little consensus regarding the quality of these albums from reviewers. *Rolling Stone* awarded both *Use Your Illusions* four stars, praising the group for their artistic growth.[51] The *Chicago Sun-Times* wondered, "Where are the great songs?" and compared the project to a 300 page edition of *People* magazine's "Sexiest Man

Alive" issue.⁵² "The band lacks a tangible personality," wrote Don Mayhew in *The Fresno Bee*, "unless you're one of those who confuses immaturity with charisma, temper with passion, and self-importance with intelligence."⁵³ Cary Darling of *The Orange County Register* heard "some mesmerizing highs, disposable lows, and enough middle ground to show these guys still need a good editor."⁵⁴ *The Baltimore Sun* ran the headline "*Use Your Illusion* Proves Guns N' Roses is The Best Rock Band in U.S."⁵⁵ London's *Sunday Times* rolled their eyes, saying that all the *Illusion* albums proved was that Guns was "overbred, even inbred" and that their "whiter than white" rock had no substance or humor.⁵⁶

"One increasingly grating thing about the band is their inexhaustible capacity for self-pity," wrote Joe Queenan in *TIME* magazine. "Having been coddled from birth by their record company and MTV, and having been given a free ride by the rock press, the Gunners nevertheless cannot get off the whinemobile as they moan about the demanding life of a rock star. According to *Forbes*, the Gunners will earn $25 million in 1990-91. These guys don't know how to take 'yes' for an answer."⁵⁷ Bill Eichenberger of *The Columbus Dispatch* agreed: "There is nothing more irritating than a filthy rich rock n' roller whining about his problems."⁵⁸

One of Axl Rose's problems was journalists giving him a hard time. *Use Your Illusion II*'s "Get in The Ring" found Rose angrily scolding those journalists by name. "Bob Guiccione, Jr. at *SPIN*, what? Are you pissed off 'coz your dad gets more pussy than you? Fuck you, suck my fuckin' dick." Guiccione laughed when reached for comment, saying he'd gladly give Rose a bare knuckle brawl, adding that the singer was "like a child who should be spanked."⁵⁹

"Get in The Ring" wasn't the only song on the *Illusion* albums where Axl Rose vented his anger like that. The discs also contained a string of bitter, misogynistic diatribes about former lovers. Some critics felt these malicious entries curdled whatever beauty was achieved in balladry like "Don't Cry" and "November Rain" (a dichotomy of boiling hatred and earnest lovelorn pining was a hallmark of every Guns N' Roses release, and critics had taken the band to task over it before).⁶⁰ ⁶¹ But what did the average teenager on the street make of *Use Your Illusion*?

The Wichita Eagle convened a panel of high school music reviewers that October. "It's good that they try to mix mellow songs with upbeat songs," said Sam Fuhr, a senior at Wichita West High. "[But] we've been waiting for this for how many years? Was it worth it?" East High senior Dan Stevens didn't think so. "I expected more, it was kind of disappointing. I don't like the slow songs. They should stick with what they do best—thrash metal." The panel voted three to one against buying *Use Your Illusion*.⁶² ⁶³

Eight months after the release of *Use Your Illusion*, Axl Rose sat down with writer Kim Neely for a *Rolling Stone* interview. Commenting on the stylistic softening the albums presented, Neely said, "There are purists who prefer the raw vibe that bands like the Sex Pistols had and that Guns N' Roses had in the early days." Rose got defensive: "Yeah, well, there are people who like a girl that had the same haircut she had ten years ago, too. I understand that. I understand that a lot. But it's like, we're evolving, and it's us. . . . Maybe it would've been best for the purists if we'd died or broken up. Then they'd get to keep it the way they liked it."[64]

"The fact that we completed those albums is unbelievable," lead guitarist Slash commented a few years after the fact. "You might be able to go to a store and buy it and listen to it, but you'll never be able to understand the emotional turmoil that was going on from adjusting from being some piece-of-shit club band to all of a sudden being like, quote, 'the biggest band in the world' and having that attention thrown at you, and having the pressures that go along with it and all this ridiculous stuff."[65]

In terms of how the music industry operates, "all of a sudden" is a relatively accurate description of Guns N' Roses' success. Within a year of forming, they had a major-label deal and the third single from their debut album became a number one hit. These are milestones some musicians spend their entire lives chasing. Twisted Sister haunted the underground for nearly a decade before a major agreed to sign them. The Ramones issued fourteen albums over the course of twenty-two years and they never had a song break the top sixty.[66] [67]

This is not to say that Guns N' Roses always had an easy journey down the yellow brick road. "Welcome to The Jungle" was their breakout anthem, but MTV had to be cajoled into playing the video by Geffen Records namesake David Geffen, who had to be cajoled into making the phone call by Tom Zutaut, the A&R figure who signed Guns N' Roses. Geffen believed *Appetite for Destruction*, then stalling at around 200,000 in sales, had run its course. He was considering dropping the band.[68] *Appetite* had been out for over a year before *Rolling Stone* decided to review it; the album was given one paragraph in a three paragraph write-up also covering Metallica's *. . . And Justice For All*.[69]

The outlets that initially sneered at Guns N' Roses would quickly be hypnotized by them, and the true believers will tell you it was a fait accompli. There was simply no denying this band. The members of Guns N' Roses certainly believed that. "The moment that we fuckin' slammed into our first chord, there was something, and we all knew it," said Duff McKagan of the group's inaugural practice in May 1985. "We were only 20 years old, but we considered ourselves real veterans. It felt like, 'This is the band, this is it. This is what we've all been searching for.'"[70]

Dickheads from hell? Guns N' Roses, 1987. L-R: Duff, Slash, Axl, Izzy, and Steven.
Source: Photo by Paul Natkin/Getty Images.

They were right. The time had come for Guns N' Roses, a band that could rise above the *Road Warrior* meets *Swan Lake* aesthetic and brain-frying light speed guitar solos that were causing stagnation in metal and hard rock. There was something electric about the way Guns could take a carefully constructed song and make it sound loose or cavalier without sacrificing any of the emotional punch. And then you had the unmistakable vocals of Axl Rose, who could growl like a demon choking on sulfur and then explode into an ear-splitting air raid siren. Writers have had a field day trying to describe Rose's voice—it's been compared to a chainsaw hitting a railroad spike, a tomcat locked outside a fish market, a melting Farfisa, and an ostrich in heat.[71][72][73] Personality-wise, Rose was always "like that." As Guns N' Roses drummer Steven Adler once recounted, "The first week I knew Axl, he kicked me in the balls!"[74]

Like many rock stars, Axl Rose's life story contains realities that feel mythical, a few myths that are probably substituting for reality, and blankets of gray in between. Yes, he once paid a mystic $72,000 to give him an exorcism.[75] No, Rose was not a self-confessed poodle murderer, as one tabloid reported (what he actually said was, "Everything about poodles makes you want to kill them").[76] Another story about Rose shooting a pig at a barbecue remains unconfirmed, though it was plausible enough for the members of Depeche Mode to immediately terminate a friendship with the singer that had literally begun the same night.[77][78] If a Tampa area DJ is to be believed, Rose was once late to a concert in the city because he couldn't tear himself away from a hotel television showing *Teenage Mutant Ninja Turtles II: The Secret of The Ooze*.[79] [80] What about the night at the Troubadour where Rose allegedly started fighting a group of Marines and then went after the daughter of a "porno kingpin," tearing off all her clothes? A journalist asked him about it once but the singer said he honestly couldn't remember.[81]

Axl Rose was born William Bailey in 1962 in Lafayette, Indiana, into a family of foot-washing big tent Pentecostals who had him singing in the choir by age five.[82] [83] The Baileys spent so much time at church that William became an expert at scripture; before long, he was helping teach Sunday School.[84] This was a family where the television set was periodically sold off because parents Sharon and Stephen feared it was encouraging sin.[85] Rock and pop music were generally forbidden but William broke that commandment, smuggling them in any way he could. "I remember once my friend Dave called me and played Supertramp over the phone," he told one interviewer. "I just acted like I was talking to him so no one would know."[86] [87] [88]

Supertramp, Aerosmith, ELO, and their ilk offered refuge from the physical abuse William and his younger siblings Amy and Stuart endured from Stephen. Something as innocent as singing along to a pop song on the car radio could result in a fat lip (Amy has also accused Stephen of habitually molesting her over a twenty-year period).[89] [90] At school, teachers were charmed by William, though he did spend too much time talking about how he planned to be famous. It got so bad one day that his pals in the eighth grade taped his mouth shut.[91]

A bombshell hit William when he was seventeen. He stumbled across some insurance paperwork that revealed Stephen was not his biological father. Sharon and Stephen refused to discuss his actual father, William Rose, Sr. The shocked teenager decided to ditch the surname Bailey in favor of Rose.[92] [93] It was an attempt to establish his own identity but it was also the latest act of defiance from a kid who'd given up memorizing Bible verses in favor of wildly overstepping his bounds. William, known as Bill to his friends, started raining blows upon any authority figure who tried to discipline him. Once, a local mother asked Bill to stop cursing in front of her younger kids; he responded by thrashing her mercilessly.[94] [95]

Bill was arrested over twenty times around Lafayette on charges such as battery, trespassing, and delinquency.[96] Gina Siler, his girlfriend when he was twenty, said the violent tantrums were the result of Bill's impossibly high standards. "He is just a nit-picky perfectionist," Siler explained, "and when things don't go smoothly and to his liking he just loses it." Cops in Lafayette started keeping an eye out for Bill, a repeat offender they may have harassed regardless because of his long hair and effeminate features. Bill began wearing disguises when he left the house.[97]

Though he was never very confident about his voice, Bill enjoyed singing and wound up fronting a few bands on the local circuit.[98] He cribbed the name Axl from a band called Axl that he was never even in.⁹⁹ It wasn't the worst life he was carving out, but the small town doldrums did feel like shackles to Bill "Axl" Rose. He needed an escape. A path of sorts was laid out by his pal Jeff Isbell, who had been a part of Bill's first garage band. In 1979, Isbell crammed a drum set and all his hopes into a Chevy Impala bound for Los Angeles. Within three days of arrival, Isbell was in a band (though his drums were subsequently stolen; he switched to guitar). Bill materialized on Jeff's doorstep on Easter morning of 1980, soaked to the bone with only a backpack. "He'd been looking for me for about a month. He didn't know how big this place was."[100] [101]

Two years later, Gina Siler and Axl Rose traded the confines of Lafayette for Hollywood. She enrolled in college and found a job; he was going to try to make it as a musician. Rose was actually still transitioning from Bill to Axl at this point, which Siler felt had a measure of Jekyll and Hyde: "Some days he'd be Bill, some days he'd be Axl, some days I didn't know who the hell he was."[102] Their love didn't last, though they were reportedly engaged nine times.[103]

Guitarist Chris Weber knew Axl as Bill when Isbell, alias Izzy Stradlin, brought them together for a band tentatively called Axl (Rose's suggestion, naturally). That band morphed into Hollywood Rose and became intertwined with another group, L.A. Guns.[104] Rose sang for L.A. Guns for six months before a disagreement with the group's manager caused a fracture. Rose and guitarist Tracii Guns decided to rebrand as Guns N' Roses.[105] [106] Things were fine until a gig in San Pedro where Rose laid into Guns over a friend who hadn't been put on the guest list. The incident ruined the night for Guns. Then Rose was late to the next gig.

"That was the first time Axl was late to a show," Guns said, "and it was just waiting around, waiting around . . . So between then and our next rehearsal, which was on a Thursday, I had a lot of time to think, and I don't know, I just smelled trouble. I could see a very negative thing about to happen, and I didn't want to be involved in whatever that feeling was."

Guns blew off the rehearsal. Rose and Stradlin telephoned several days later, and as Guns recalled, "Axl was flipping the fuck out, like, 'What are you doing? What's your problem?' And I'm like, 'Hey, you know . . . *this*. The way you're talking to me right now. I'm not into this.' So we're going back and forth and finally he goes, 'Well, I'm just gonna call Slash.' And I'm like, 'That's a great idea!'"[107]

Lead guitarist Slash, born Saul Hudson, was a graduate of Hollywood Rose who had previously found it difficult to play in bands with a rhythm guitarist like Stradlin. He threw caution to the wind with Guns N' Roses (yes, Tracii let them keep the name, no hard feelings) because, as Slash put it, Axl was "the only guy on the whole L.A. scene who could sing."[108] Slash brought along drummer Adler, another ex-Hollywood Rose player who was also Slash's childhood pal from the streets of L.A. The upbeat Adler had a tan and a permanent smile; as *San Francisco Chronicle* writer Mick LaSalle noted, he looked like the only member of GNR who might be able to pass a physical. Bassist Duff McKagan was another transplant, coming from Seattle after cementing his punk credibility with such bands as the Fartz and the Fastbacks. By the summer of 1985, the quintet that would seize the world with *Appetite for Destruction* was setting L.A. ablaze. "We played our first show at the Troubadour and it was sold out," Adler recalled. "It was like we were rock stars, but just in Hollywood."[109][110]

Tom Zutaut caught one of their other concerts at the Troubadour and knew after only two songs that he'd be signing the band to Geffen Records. Zutaut was shocked when Rose demanded an exorbitant $75,000 payout for his group within a week. "Look, man," Rose threatened, "We told the A&R person at Chrysalis that if she walked naked down Sunset Boulevard from her office to Tower Records, we'd sign with her." Geffen ponied up, and everything was official by March 1986.[111][112] There were rumors a stipulation of the deal was that Rose had to get a therapist.[113] It is unclear if the band members' excessive drug use was similarly addressed in any way. Years later, Slash confirmed he spent nearly his entire portion of the Geffen advance on heroin.[114]

Slash was turned onto the drug by Stradlin, who was using and dealing it. "I remember the first time I took heroin very clearly," Slash said. "We were over at a friend's rehearsal studio and Izzy took me aside and said, 'Check this out,' so we went into the bathroom and did that whole thing. I thought, *Okay, I'll give that a go*. I've never really had a lot of common sense."[115] While drug addiction plagued several figures in Guns N' Roses, Axl Rose claimed it was impossible for him to become an addict because his goal-oriented mindset was too powerful. "I'll have done blow for three days and my mind will go *Fuck no*," he said. "I'll have the physical feeling of knowing my body needs it, and I'll just refuse to do coke that day. I'm not going to do it, because if I was going to do it, I know I won't be able to hit my goals with what I want to do with this band."[116]

Prior to their major label contract, the members of Guns N' Roses had been living together in a squalid 12-by-12 den of iniquity tucked behind the Sunset Grill. Known as Hell House, this loft was a booze-soaked, drug-infested void where an orgy or a fight could break out at any moment and often did. Disgraced Runaways Svengali Kim Fowley, who briefly courted GNR around this time, explained that the flophouse's nickname wasn't figurative. "You have to give them credit for cranking out all those songs in the middle of hell," he said. "I saw where they lived—it was horrible. It looked like Auschwitz."[117][118][119]

Life at Hell House hit a brick wall in December 1985 when rape charges were filed against Axl Rose and Slash by the parents of a fifteen-year-old colloquially referred to as Little Michelle (to differentiate her from Michelle Young, subject of the song "My Michelle"). There have been multiple conflicting accounts regarding this crime, the only consistency being that Rose had sex with Little Michelle and subsequently threw her naked and traumatized into the street.[120][121][122][123] In 2019, Little Michelle went public on social media, explaining that she's been pregnant with Rose's baby but miscarried. When she told him on the night in question, he erupted, attacking and raping her and then inviting the other band members to do so before kicking her out.[124]

Rose has only ever confirmed that there was a rape charge, though he did seem to voluntarily bring up the incident (or one similar to it) during a June 1986 *L.A. Weekly* interview when he emphasized the thrill he got from "going at it" with a different girl behind a stack of amplifiers at Hell House while the cops were looking for him.[125] [126] The singer had been accused of rape involving a minor before, back in Lafayette, so he understood the gravity of the situation.[127] Hell House was abandoned for the apartment of Vicky Hamilton, the manager of Guns N' Roses at that time, though occasionally Rose laid low by sleeping on park benches and under bridges. Little Michelle's parents had to drop the charges due to lack of evidence, freeing Guns N' Roses to move on to their next scandal. That may have been the $22,000 worth of damage they inflicted upon a house Geffen rented for them ahead of *Appetite for Destruction*'s recording.[128]

After that, there was a flap over album art. Geffen talked Guns N' Roses out of using a photo of the *Challenger* explosion for *Appetite*'s cover but substituting the Robert Williams painting that inspired the album's title was no more sanguine. Geffen's art department was so disgusted by the rendering of what was obviously supposed to be a rape that they refused to work on it. The project was farmed out to a freelance designer. Worried about consumer reaction, the band and record label agreed to only use the painting for the cover on half of the 130,000 *Appetite for Destruction* LPs they pressed.[129] [130] [131]

Guns N' Roses were called a lot of things in their heyday—rock n' roll saviors,[132] shameless trash,[133] Guns N' Poses,[134] Lines N' Noses.[135] Every so often, they were referred to as the most dangerous band in the world (a nickname that took on grim shades after two fans were crushed to death during the group's performance at the 1988 Monsters of Rock festival).[136] [137] Earlier generations paid them respect; "They are kind of a Stones of the '80s and '90s," John Fogerty remarked in 1993.[138] In the twenty-first century, writer Mick Wall dubbed GNR the "last of the giants" in his biography of the same name, rhapsodizing "the final stars still burning bright from an age and an industry now dead and gone."[139] *GQ*'s John Jeremiah Sullivan gave a more specific description in 2006: "[GNR] were the last great rock band that didn't think there was something a tiny bit embarrassing or at least funny about being in a rock band. There are thousands of bands around at any given time that don't think rock is funny, but rarely is one of them good."[140]

From that viewpoint, Guns N' Roses were fated to be usurped by grunge, a musical movement where embarrassment was a prerequisite and everything could be a joke. Mudhoney released what many consider the foundational grunge single in 1988, the scuzzy anthem "Touch Me, I'm Sick." By October 1989, they were preparing to release their debut album. "We're not as good as we used to be," singer Mark Arm announced during an interview with *The Bob*. "We've aged a year, a lot of energy has been drained out of us." Was Mudhoney's distorted, gravely sound part of a '70s rock revival? "I steal all my songs," guitarist Steve Turner quipped, "but not from the '70s." How long would this band last? When people asked Axl Rose that question, he'd talk about taking Guns N' Roses as an extension of his being.[141] Mudhoney wouldn't be caught dead saying anything like that. "Hopefully we'll quit when we think we suck," Arm replied. *The Bob*: "So you'll quit when you suck?" Arm: "No, no! We'll quit when we *think* we suck. There's a big difference. There's plenty of people who think we suck already!"[142]

Guns N' Roses experienced their first culture clash with grunge two years later when they chose Soundgarden as the support act for one leg of their *Use Your Illusion* tour. Axl Rose was a huge fan; "The singer [Chris Cornell] just buries me," he enthused to *Rolling Stone*. "The guy sings so great."[143] Few could argue against Cornell's soaring vocals, which made Soundgarden's inward undulations feel expansive and energizing. Aspects of mainstream hard rock and heavy metal could be heard in their music but the quartet generally scoffed at the shallow trappings of those genres.[144] There was an uncomfortable silence when Soundgarden's manager Susan Silver told her clients about the *Use Your Illusion* tour invitation.[145] Soundgarden accepted only because they recognized there weren't many other opportunities to get out of Seattle. "Musically, Guns N' Roses is more appropriate than any other tour we've really been offered," Cornell said.[146] Their base discomfort was tricky to mask, however. When a reporter asked drummer Matt Cameron during the tour if he actually liked Guns N' Roses, Cameron stammered. "Uh, um, yeah . . . pretty much. I liked their first album but I haven't heard the new one."[147]

"Our tour with Guns N' Roses? Yeah, not my fault," Soundgarden bass player Ben Shepherd groused years later. "I don't like that kind of music." Shepherd was quick to clarify that Guns N' Roses were "all really nice guys" but they played "butt rock" and he hated being in their world. "I'm not a rock star. I don't like rock stars, and I don't want to be around them. That word 'rock star' is really derogatory to me. There seems to be a malicious factor in calling someone that. It's a put down. The Guns N' Roses tour was a full on metal circus extravaganza. It was insane. I never wanted to play stadiums."[148] The "full on metal circus extravaganza" of a Guns N' Roses tour circa 1991–1992 included private jets, limousines, two enormous identical stages that were alternated between venues, and a road crew of over 200 people. There was also a subset of personal minders for Axl Rose, comprised of (but not limited to) three security guards, a masseuse, an herbalist, a chiropractor, a podiatrist, and a yoga instructor.[149][150][151][152]

Another staple of the Guns N' Roses experience was objectification of women. At the concerts, between bands, a video camera would scan the crowd and project women on the Jumbotron who were then subjected to chants of "Take it off!" Sometimes they happily complied; other times, they'd refuse and have to fight off male fans trying to shred their clothing. Venue owners were routinely uncomfortable with this practice but felt they had to comply to keep riot-prone GNR fans content.[153][154] No one wanted a repeat of St. Louis.

Pandemonium broke out at that city's Riverport Amphitheater in July 1991 when Rose left after three songs, livid over security's slow response to a fan illegally videotaping the concert. The rest of the band scurried away with him, the house lights went up, and angry crowd members started throwing rocks and chairs at roadies as they broke down the equipment. The roadies retaliated with spray from a fire hose. Fans somehow wrestled control of the hose away from the roadies and turned it on hundreds of invading police officers. There were sixty injuries, sixteen arrests, and $300,000 worth of property damage during the two-hour melee at Riverport. Police Chief Neil. F. Kurlander likened the scene to a Civil War battlefield.[155][156][157]

Soundgarden were so clearly unhappy on the *Use Your Illusion* tour that GNR's crew nicknamed them Frowngarden.[158] Not that everything in Guns N' Roses was peachy. They were no longer the same five outlaws who crawled out of the gutter to snatch the gold ring. Steven Adler had been fired in 1990 because addiction issues were allegedly affecting his playing. Adler argued that any impairments were caused by opiate blockers he was using to stay clean. He further accused management of tricking him into signing away his royalties, prompting a lawsuit. Matt Sorum from the Cult replaced Adler, which was like trading night for day.

Bryan Mantia, the Primus drummer who joined Guns N' Roses a decade later, spoke for many when he described the changeup: "I just loved Adler's greasiness. He brought a love to it. . . . This is his music. This is *him*. Sorum brought more of a metronomic style. He was more into, 'OK, my hair's gotta look good. I need to make sure my chains are hanging right.' Nothing against him. I'm sure he's a great guy. I just gravitated way more towards Adler because there was just this love screaming out of the drum set."[159]

Izzy Stradlin struggled with the drummer upheaval, and his own sobriety was making him realize life in Guns N' Roses was unfulfilling. He was also fed up with starting concerts three hours late because Axl was nowhere to be found. "I expressed my feelings to Axl," Stradlin said, "and the very next night on MTV I saw that I was going to be replaced by the guy in Jane's Addiction. So I took that as an indication that I'd really pissed him off." Stradlin quit GNR in November 1991 and moved back to Indiana.[160][161][162] Gilby Clarke was hired as Stradlin's replacement. Slash made Clarke feel at home by gifting the new rhythm player a rare guitar. "I'd only been in the band a couple weeks and Slash came up to me and gave me this beautiful red sparkle Les Paul," Clarke recounted. "This was so awesome. I barely knew the guy. Granted, he has a lot, but it was a guitar that he picked out because he know that I would like it . . . [it] was really cool 'cause there was a lot of stuff going through my mind at the time."[163]

Then came the sudden paradigm-shifting success of Nirvana. As one of Seattle's little brother bands, no one expected Nirvana to make much of a splash—until they finished their second album, *Nevermind*, an explosive blend of screaming punk rancor and clean Beatle-esque hooks. Nirvana's lyrics were an abstract poetry of idiom twists and non sequiturs; singer/guitarist Kurt Cobain delivered them with such conviction that whatever he was trying to express (discontent, embarrassment, nihilism) made perfect sense to listeners. *Nevermind* was released by Geffen imprint DGC one week after *Use Your Illusion*. Nirvana hoped it might sell one or two hundred thousand copies.[164 165] Instead, *Nevermind* went nuclear, selling millions, resonating deeply with almost everyone who heard it, a vanguard in rock n' roll catharsis.[166 167]

Cobain insisted he was no revolutionary, describing his band as nothing beyond "a '90s version of Cheap Trick or the Knack." Regardless, Nirvana was celebrated in every corner of the world, from the dense newsprint pages of *MaximumRockNRoll* to the thinly drawn lips of Axl Rose.

"I had an advanced copy of that record and it became my favorite," Rose told *Musician* in June 1992. "I would put it on repeatedly. Nirvana helped me do my job. I think that the world has gotten really bored, really fed up and really pent up with frustration, and that comes through in Nirvana. . . . And I'd like to do anything I can to support it. That's why we want them to play with us." Guns N' Roses had invited Nirvana to open their Summer tour with Metallica that year but Nirvana declined (they also turned down a chance to play Rose's thirtieth birthday party). "I just think they're having a lot of problems with who they are and who they want to be and trying to hold onto it at the same time," Rose explained. "At least Kurt is."[168 169]

In a sense, Rose hit the nail on the nead. Nirvana was a band with a social conscience. "I have a request for our fans," Cobain wrote in the liner notes for 1992's *Incesticide*. "If any of you in any way hate homosexuals, people of different color, or women . . . leave us the fuck alone! Don't come to our shows and don't buy our records." It's hard to imagine a statement that progressive appearing inside any other mainstream hard rock record from that year or the previous ten. Nirvana was proactive about their causes, especially concerning women's rights. The trio organized a 1993 concert that raised $60,000 for rape victims in Bosnia-Herzegovina; the same year, they played a benefit to aid the investigation into the rape and murder of Gits singer Mia Zapata.[170 171]

Getting involved with Guns N' Roses, a band Nirvana felt was actively combating their ideals (and whom they felt made shitty music regardless), was a nonstarter.[172] Guns N' Roses only seemed to lend their name to charity when they were invited by people so famous they couldn't say no (like George Harrison) or when they were ordered to by a court (a St. Louis judge demanded Axl Rose pay $50,000 to area charities after he was found guilty of several misdemeanors related to the July 1991 Riverport riot).¹⁷³ GNR's most discussed charity gig was one they never played; the band had their invitation to headline an AIDS benefit co-curated by David Geffen rescinded once staffers at the nonprofit doing all the ground work read the lyrics to "One in a Million."¹⁷⁴

Rose lost his patience with Nirvana when he realized they definitely wouldn't be joining the 1992 summer tour. He complained about them during numerous stops on that jaunt. "Your homeboys Nir-*van*-uh are just too good to tour with us and Metallica," Rose bitched onstage at Seattle's Kingdom. Then he made reference to Cobain's rumored drug problems and called Cobain's wife Courtney Love "an ugly bitch."¹⁷⁵ ¹⁷⁶ So began the most memorable rock feud of the decade, which climaxed with a confrontation at the MTV Video Music Awards that September. Backstage before the show, Love, who'd recently given birth to daughter Francis Bean, spotted Rose and jokingly called out a request for him to be the baby's godfather. Rose stormed over, threatening Cobain: "If you don't shut your bitch up, we're taking this down to the pavement." Cobain turned to Love, deadpan: "Shut up, bitch." Cobain kept his cool but was shaken by Rose's accosting. There were other incidents that night, like Duff McKagan trying to goad Nirvana bassist Krist Novoselic into a fistfight. Members of Guns N' Roses also started tipping over Nirvana's trailer. They only stopped when someone cried out that Frances Bean was inside.¹⁷⁷ ¹⁷⁸

And so it was—the corporate rock star sleaze bullying the righteous upstarts with cretinous behavior. Of course, the sleaze is in the eye of the beholder, and while Nirvana never tyrannized anyone in the same brutish way as Guns N' Roses, they'd certainly been accused of off-putting rock star bullshit. They were the first group to demand (drunkenly, angrily) a written contract from Sub Pop Records, the image-making indie label that released their earliest work.¹⁷⁹ Buzz Osborne from the Melvins has said Nirvana changed once they started getting some heat on the local level; they'd insist on headlining gigs over more established bands and get finicky about splitting money.¹⁸⁰ There was further dismay once Nirvana began surrounding themselves with the kind of crooked industry professionals who were the very reason underground music existed in the first place. When Mudhoney was thinking about signing with a major label, they quickly crossed Geffen off their list after one abysmal meeting with Nirvana manager John Silva.¹⁸¹

Another cliché Nirvana fell victim to was heroin. Cobain was indeed an addict at the height of his band's fame. He'd show up to photo shoots strung out; he'd overdose in hotel rooms. After Cobain almost died taking a strain called body bag in 1993, publicist Anton Brookes remarked to Love that her husband was turning into Axl Rose (the perception at that time being anyone as erratic as Rose must have drug problems). Cobain was furious when he heard about the slight. Brookes was afraid the singer was going to sock him in the jaw. "Nirvana were supposedly right on, weren't they?" Brookes said years later. "They were the voice of a generation . . . [and] Kurt mutated into everything he was against. He became your attitudinal rock star, with the tantrums and the plush hotels and everything.... Kurt was sucking corporation cock."¹⁸²

The actual similarities between Kurt Cobain and Axl Rose have often been remarked upon. Both were conventionally attractive and musically gifted figures whose still ended up outcasts in their backwater hometowns. Both had an interest in guns; Cobain felt he needed them for protection, whereas Rose used them for intimidation (Rose once bought an Uzi because a landlord was raising his rental price).¹⁸³ Rose may have recognized part of himself in Cobain. There's a story he said as much to Cobain once during an encounter backstage somewhere, before their feud. "You're everything I could've been," Rose allegedly told Cobain, which would be an odd remark from one of the biggest rock stars on the planet who achieved everything on his own terms. The source for this story is Courtney Love, who was known for fabrication ("Only about a quarter of what Courtney says is true," said Kat Bjelland, who has spent a long time refuting that Love was ever in her group Babes in Toyland).¹⁸⁴ ¹⁸⁵ ¹⁸⁶

In a 1993 interview with *The Advocate* where he also discussed his bisexuality, Cobain was asked if there was any aspect of Guns N' Roses he could appreciate. "I can't think of a damn thing," he replied. "I can't even waste my time on that band, because they're so obviously pathetic and untalented. I used to think that everything in the mainstream pop world was crap, but now that some underground bands have been signed with majors, I take Guns N' Roses as more of an offense.... They're really talentless people, and they write crap music, and they're the most popular rock band on the Earth right now. I can't believe it."¹⁸⁷

Axl Rose wearing a Nirvana hat in the early '90s. *Source: Photo by Independent News and Media/Getty Images.*

Kurt Cobain and Axl Rose shared one more commonality: they both wrestled lucrative rights away from their fellow band members. Nirvana came close to breaking up in 1992 after Cobain demanded that the even three-way publishing split between himself, Novoselic, and drummer Dave Grohl be retroactively amended in his favor. Novoselic and Grohl relented; they were more upset over the cutthroat way Cobain handled the situation.[188] A year later, Rose railroaded Slash and Duff McKagan into giving up their stakes in the Guns N' Roses name.

McKagan remembered this happening on July 5th during a concert in Barcelona. The opening bands had finished their sets and Guns N' Roses was preparing to go on when McKagan and Slash were summoned to a specific room by management. There, they were handed contracts that gave Axl Rose the right to continue as Guns N' Roses if they were suddenly unavailable. "You guys are not in good shape," a manager explained, referring to their drug habits. "If one of you dies, nobody wants to have to spend years in court battling your families." It was suggested Rose wouldn't go onstage until these documents were signed. Shocked, humiliated, but also exhausted and fearing another riot, McKagan and Slash complied. The idea of Guns N' Roses existing with anyone else seemed farfetched anyway. Slash in particular felt that, for all their problems, there was still so much magic when they all took the stage.[189] [190]

Magic or not, Guns N' Roses had proven an enormously profitable endeavor. It was reported in Steven Adler's lawsuit against the band that between 1988 and 1992 they grossed $57.9 million, an unbelievable amount for such a young group.[191] There is no way of fact-checking this figure; recording contracts have never been a matter of public record, and the amount of money a band might earn from touring is notoriously hard to track due to fluctuations in ticket prices, performance guarantees, general overhead, and merch sales (strictly a cash business during GNR's heyday).[192] However much Guns N' Roses earned, it was far more than anyone else in Geffen's eclectic stable, which included Donna Summer, Aerosmith, and Japanese composer Kitaro. "Guns were by far the biggest artist on the roster, period," says Bill Bennet, who was hired by Geffen in 1990 to head the DGC imprint. "And they would sell more records overseas as an American rock band. So as I sent my daughters to college, I appreciated them."[193] [194] [195]

Geffen stuck by Guns N' Roses through every trial and tribulation. Other less solvent artists weren't as lucky. Geffen agreed to distribute albums by Slayer and Danzig but left their logo off the jackets so they could avoid any negative publicity from Satanic heavy metal.[196] [197] In 1990, Geffen canceled the release of the eponymous major label debut from hip-hop group the Geto Boys because they believed the album went too far in its glamorization of violence, racism, and misogyny.[198] [199] [200] "I was simply unwilling to put out a record which talked about killing women and fucking the dead bodies," David Geffen told the *Los Angeles Times*. "You know, and cutting off their tits. I'm not going to put out records like that." The interviewer pointed out the hypocrisy at hand since Geffen had released and defended "One in a Million" by Guns N' Roses. "I don't think that because a person uses the word 'faggot' in a song, that makes them homophobic," Geffen replied. "They may have been insensitive at that time. But they're not homophobic."[201]

Following *Use Your Illusion*, Geffen reportedly advanced Guns N' Roses $10 million for their next album.[202] The label was probably expecting a disc of original material. What they got was a covers album primarily consisting of punk rock songs from the late '70s and early '80s. Many of the cover recordings were outtakes from the *Use Your Illusion* sessions; selections included "New Rose" (originally by the Damned), "I Don't Care About You" (Fear), and "Raw Power" (the Stooges). Slash commandeered this project, mixing, mastering, and putting together the artwork for what was eventually titled *"The Spaghetti Incident?"* "[I] made sure everything was going to be cool," Slash said. "So it didn't turn into a pop record and everybody is like, 'Oh, cute!'"[203]

"The Spaghetti Incident?" came out in November 1993; it was instantly engulfed in controversy due to the hidden final track, a cover of Charles Manson's "Look at Your Game, Girl." Cutting a tune from this deranged cult leader's songbook was an Axl Rose idea, another one he pushed through over everyone else's objections.[204] Rose's defense? He found the song engaging and enjoyed the irony of Manson criticizing someone else's mental illness. "Hearing it shocked me," Rose said, "and I thought there might be other people who would like to hear it."[205]

This wasn't an original idea. Red Kross put an unlisted Manson cover on their 1982 album *Born Innocent*. As a relatively unknown punk band living a stone's throw from the scene of the grisly Manson murders, Red Kross had legitimate fears that one of Charlie's followers might come out of the woodwork for reprisal.[206] For Guns N' Roses, there was sharper outrage from victims' families. Patty Tate, sister of Manson's most famous victim Sharon Tate, called for a boycott of Geffen Records and wanted "Look at Your Game, Girl" to be taken off *"The Spaghetti Incident?"*.

Tate also criticized Geffen for making it sound like they were doing something special by giving Manson's royalty cut to Bartek Frykowski, son of victim Wojiciech Frykowski, when in fact they were legally required to do so per a 1971 judgment. After just one week of *Spaghetti Incident* sales, Manson earned $60,000; Axl Rose claimed he'd been unaware of Manson's publishing deal and, prior to the enforcement of the Frykowski judgment, offered to donate those monies to an environmental cause. Tate herself refused any kind of payout: "It's like blood money." David Geffen said he agreed the song should be removed from the album but a contractual stipulation prevented them from doing so without the approval of Guns N' Roses, which, by that time, legally meant Axl Rose.[207] [208] [209] Rose decided the song would stay.[210]

Around this time, Rose was regularly spotted wearing a t-shirt with Manson's mug shot and the caption "Charlie Don't Surf." "You can't really see it without laughing," said Richard Lemmons, co-owner of Zooport Riot Gear, the company behind the shirts. "I mean, Charlie don't surf; he's in prison."[211] Rose said that he wore the shirt to make the statement that he was not Charles Manson (as the media had apparently led society to believe). It was a convoluted explanation.

Meanwhile, critics were dismissing *"The Spaghetti Incident?"* as contrived. Jim Farber of *The Daily News* accused Guns N' Roses of exaggerating their connection to punk because the genre was experiencing a renaissance. "Never did GNR take the risks of punk: the contempt for its own audience, its rabid uncommericality or its snarling anti-sexuality. . . . Guns N' Roses isn't doing these songs any favor by covering them. The band is turning anthems that people lived and died for into zippy singalongs for frat-house drunks."[212] *"The Spaghetti Incident?"* was one of 1993's biggest commercial disappointments as well, taking months to achieve comparable sales figures to *Use Your Illusion's* first week.[213]

Even that didn't mean anything anymore. A month before *"The Spaghetti Incident?"*, Pearl Jam, another grunge act noted for their moral integrity, released their sophomore album *Vs.*, which set a new record by selling 950,000 copies in its first week.[214]

Pearl Jam's success baffled many in the industry because the band acted like they were allergic to publicity. Singer Eddie Vedder refused to speak with *TIME* magazine when they put him on the cover; he later announced that he'd wiped his ass with the issue.[215] This wasn't snottiness so much as it was Pearl Jam trying to shield themselves from exploitation and overexposure. "I felt with any more popularity we were going to be crushed, or our heads were going to pop like grapes," Vedder said. Shortly thereafter, Pearl Jam stopped making music videos, a decision that would have been career suicide for most rock groups.[216]

If anything, Pearl Jam's popularity grew after they abandoned MTV, proving that the '90s would be, as writer Rebecca Jennings put it, "a decade defined by its obsession with authenticity and artistic purity." In this climate, principles mattered, and there was no greater scarlet letter for a musician than being branded a sellout.[217] *SPIN* magazine's 1993 reader's poll included a vote for "Most Principled Person;" Henry Rollins won. There was another vote for "Biggest Sellout;" U2 took that prize, but Guns N' Roses came in fourth (below the Red Hot Chili Peppers and Metallica but above Madonna).[218]

What made Guns N' Roses sellouts? The fact that they put out a tribute to punk rock that felt disingenuous, especially coming from a band that used private jets to get to their football stadium concerts where there was no guarantee they'd even play. From that perspective, it was difficult to argue with Peter Buck from alternative forefathers R.E.M., who called Guns N' Roses a "Benny Hill parody of what a rock n' roll band should be."[219] Slash realized his band needed to come back down to Earth. He figured a small venue tour in support of *"The Spaghetti Incident?"* might help. Axl wasn't interested.[220]

Although they were an iconic duo onstage—Slash, a mess of dark hair and leather throttling a guitar juxtaposed by Axl, the pale shrieking demon in bicycle shorts—the two most recognizable members of Guns N' Roses weren't ever close. This was especially true in 1993. "By that point, the support group I'd always enjoyed to help me deal with Axl was gone," Slash reflected. "Izzy was the last one in the band who was able to get through to him creatively. Between Duff and me . . . we just didn't have the proper tools to communicate with him effectively."[221] Perhaps, in this instance, Rose was trying to keep his schedule clear in case his acting career took off.

In December 1993, news broke that Rose was in final negotiations to play what the *Hollywood Reporter* described as "a warrior villain" in *Highlander III*. Director Andy Morahan was making his feature debut with this sequel; previously, he'd directed several Guns N' Roses videos. In addition to Rose's seven to eight days of shooting, the singer was considering recording new music for soundtrack.[222] "I had Axl ready to go," said Morahan, who noted that Rose was excited because his beloved Queen had worked on the original *Highlander*.

Then, without warning, everything fell apart. Rose refused to move forward until Mario Van Peebles, who'd been cast as *Highlander III*'s main villain Kane, was fired. Rose never specified his issue with Van Peebles, but as usual he refused to compromise. "So that screwed that one," Morgan lamented. "[The studio] wouldn't get rid of Mario. At the time, I thought it was more important to have Guns N' Roses!"[223]

Highlander III was given several different subtitles (*The Final Dimension*, *The Sorcerer*, *The Magician*), and not even the *Highlander* faithful could stomach the results. Fans were "hooting in derision" and throwing garbage at the screen during one Toronto screening in January 1995.[224] At least the *Highlander* devotees had something. All Guns N' Roses fans could do in 1995 was wonder if the band existed anymore.

2 THE END OF THE VOGUE

August 1993: As usual, the supermarket tabloids were chock-full of celebrity heartbreak. "LONI: BURT'S A DUD IN BED and his mistress can have him!"[1] "OPRAH IN SHOCK AS LOVER CALLS OFF WEDDING."[2] Among the tales that month was a story that seemed too corny to be true: a lovesick Axl Rose made one final play to win back his supermodel girlfriend Stephanie Seymour by dressing up like Roy Rogers. "He put on all the gear, including a ten-gallon hat and chaps, and shirt you could see for five miles," a tipster told *The Daily Mirror*. "Then he leapt on a horse . . . and galloped over to a startled Stephanie. Then he burst into a love song." It didn't work. Seymour told Rose to hit the dusty trail. Allegedly, she'd never even heard of Roy Rogers.[3]

Doug Goldstein, manager for Guns N' Roses at that time, corroborated the horse story, claiming he was there to knock on Seymour's door as Rose sat atop the white Arabian steed Goldstein himself procured for this stunt.[4] Seymour and Rose had broken up in March after a turbulent eighteen months together. Initially, Rose put up a calm front, saying, "It was fun. I wish Stephanie the best."[5] [6] Things changed after Seymour fell into the arms of publishing magnate Peter Brant. The pair were spotted sucking face at a screening of the Robert De Niro drama *This Boy's Life* ("hardly a make-out movie," *The Daily News* observed).[7]

Rose grew irate after the horse stunt failed. He demanded Seymour return baubles he'd gifted her, including an antique wedding band, a diamond necklace, and a poster for the film *Lolita*. Rose threatened to sue Seymour for abuse if she didn't comply. Seymour responded with a warning that she'd release photos of a black eye Rose had given her if he didn't buzz off. Rose filed suit in September for the $100,000 in gifts Seymour was withholding plus the injuries he'd endured after she allegedly assaulted him in 1992. Seymour countersued, claiming Rose was the abusive one and that he'd kicked her down a flight of stairs and dragged her through broken glass while punching and kicking her torso.[8] [9] [10] [11] [12] [13]

Seymour's counterclaim emboldened Rose's ex-wife Erin Everly to file her own suit in March of 1994, seeking damages for the sadistic and staggering abuses she suffered at the hands of Rose. Everly painted a picture that went beyond harrowing, detailing brutal hours-long beatings over anything and everything (including questions as banal as "What do you want to eat?"). When a friend of Everly's tried to intervene during one such episode, Rose threw a television at them and then threatened to kill Everly, her dogs, and himself if they told police the truth. Everly also accused Rose of routinely destroying her personal property, habitual sexual abuse, imprisonment, and grabbing her hand after one beating to physically force her to sign divorce papers. Rose also once picked Everly up and threw her over a wall at a friend's backyard barbecue.

The complaint takes an unexpected turn on page six: "Everly is informed and believes, and on that basis alleges, that Rose now professes to be spiritual, and is getting exorcised because he believes he is possessed. Rose consults regularly with a psychotherapist, Susie London. Rose requested that Everly visit Ms. London, who he claimed could help Rose and Everly reconcile. Ms. London told Everly that Everly's actions in a past life caused Rose to be violent in this life. Rose told Everly that, according to Ms. London, Everly and Rose's former girlfriend [Stephanie Seymour] were sisters in a past life and together had tried to kill Rose in their previous life. Rose told Everly that he wants her to 'break this pattern.'"

Axl Rose and Erin Everly, 1990. *Source: Photo by Vinnie Zuffante/Getty Images.*

This section goes on to state that Rose believed he was communicating with "spirits and extraterrestrials" and that in May of 1992 he hired a friend to break into Everly's house to steal pictures of her deceased dogs. Rose needed the pictures so he could use them to transfer the dead dogs' souls to living dogs. Understandably, all of this frightened Everly.[14]

It's telling that Erin Everly's complaint refers to Rose's psychotherapist as Ms. London, not Dr. London. The medical credentials of Susie London (who has alternately characterized her first name as Suzie, Suzy, and Suzzy) are difficult to verify. Research yields far more about her career as an entertainer. London came out of the womb singing and dancing back in Illinois, according to one profile of her theater work. In the early '80s, she fronted a band called Leggs. In 1986, she played a prison guard in the *Caged Heat* ripoff *The Naked Cage*.[15 16 17] A paragraph detailing London's experience in "energetic healing" floats around online. It says she holds a degree from the Sri Lankan school Medicina Alternativa.[18 19] The American Medical Association has said no one within their ranks had ever heard of Medicina Alternativa until 1995 when another one of their graduates, a dentist in Tennessee, was investigated for improperly treating his patients (one of whom died).[20]

When reached by phone, Susie London refused to discuss or clarify any of her credentials for this book. Regarding her treatment of Axl Rose, London said, "I've never spoken about that and I never will."[21] In his memoir, Guns N' Roses bassist Duff McKagan wrote about London without mentioning her by name. "[She] seemed to consciously feed [Axl's] megalomania . . . she was almost predatory in the way she handled him." Rose appeared to acknowledge McKagan's concerns when the two spoke about London, but ultimately the singer found his therapist's "talents" too intoxicating and persuasive to ignore.[22] After she guided Rose through regression therapy that allowed him to recover memories dating back to his own conception, Rose put London in the video for "Don't Cry." She played the part of Axl Rose's therapist.

Erin Everly's lawsuit made headlines, but the notions that Rose was seeking his own exorcism and talking to aliens didn't gain much traction. The news cycle that week was consumed with Nirvana frontman Kurt Cobain, who briefly fell into a coma after overdosing on sleeping pills and champagne.[23 24] It also wasn't exactly news that Axl Rose had become a little woo woo. In April of 1992, *Rolling Stone* published an interview where Rose spoke about his regression therapy, explaining that he and his birth father hated each other before he was born (and that his birth father kidnapped, drugged, and raped him when Rose was just two).

Rolling Stone pushed back on the validity of regression (which was growing in controversy due to the belief therapists were using it to plant phony memories in their patients): "Talking about being conscious of things that happened before you were born might throw a few people." Rose shot back: "I don't really care, because that's regression therapy, and if they've got a problem with it, they can go fuck themselves. It's major, and it's legit, and it all fits together with my life."[25]

Shortly thereafter, during Guns N' Roses' summer tour with Metallica, rumors began circulating that a psychic Rose kept on retainer was instructing him not to perform in geographical locations starting with the letter M. "There's no truth to that," GNR's management insisted, even though gigs in Minneapolis and Massachusetts were canceled with little to no explanation (the tour itinerary also excluded Milwaukee, Miami, and Memphis). Then, on August 8, Guns N' Roses, and Metallica tried to play Montreal's Olympic Stadium. Metallica had to cut their performance short after a misfiring pyrotechnic critically injured singer James Hetfield. Guns N' Roses went on early but Rose's voice gave out after five songs. He announced he was done and told the crowd to seek refunds. They rioted instead. Fires broke out, fixtures were uprooted, a police cruiser was overturned. As one concession stand employee reported, "Everyone was yelling, 'Kill them! We've got to destroy everything!'"[26] [27] [28] [29] [30]

Rose *was* regularly consulting with a psychic, one who did intermittently join him on the road. Her name was Sharon Maynard, and she vetted the auras of everyone surrounding Rose, usually after Rose provided her with photographs of those in question.[31] According to Geffen A&R man Jim Barber, Maynard also had Rose convinced that he was one of thirteen people who'd been sent to save the world. "That was her pitch to her wealthy clients," Barber explains, "although Axl never told me that directly."[32] This sounds like a twist on the eastern belief that there are a finite amount of enlightened people on our planet at any given time and we should turn to them for guidance (controversial spiritualist Frederick Lenz claimed to be one of twelve enlightened beings in 1988; when asked by *Newsweek* to name the other eleven, Lenz replied, "I'm not at liberty to say").[33] Perhaps this was Maynard's justification for holding seminars at her Arizona home where attendees could pay $2,500 just to breathe the same air as Rose.

Most people who are familiar with Sharon Maynard refer to her as Yoda. Former Guns N' Roses manager Alan Niven prefers "thief" or "charlatan." "She fucked a lot up," he says. "She and Axl met through his masseuse, as I recall. I didn't know about it." Niven explains that part of his job included protecting the band from anything that might hurt their image (which, in the case of Guns N' Roses, usually meant turning down photo spreads in high-end fashion magazines). Knowing Niven would toss out a psychic, Rose and tour manager Doug Goldstein kept Maynard in the shadows. This was part of "the coup," Niven says, wherein Goldstein, a figure who would cater to Rose's every whim, convinced the singer to fire Niven in May of 1991 and give him the top management position. Goldstein's story is he spent two years trying to stop Rose from firing Niven because he considered Niven a partner but relented after he heard Niven teasing Rose about the end of his relationship with Everly.[34] [35]

Sharon Maynard supposedly performed the exorcism that Axl Rose was seeking for himself. "She charged him $75,000 for that," says Niven. "Obviously it didn't take."[36] Rose was forced to testify regarding the details of the exorcism after Everly's case against him progressed; he claimed it only cost $72,000 and was performed by a man. "Mainly it involved getting some kind of herbal wrap . . . [and some] work on my skin." Begrudgingly, Rose admitted being exorcized was not the best use of his money. Everly also took the stand during these proceedings to describe further horrifying sexual and physical abuses she suffered from Rose and to specify that Rose believed he was possessed by the spirit of Led Zeppelin drummer John Bonham. The Seymour and Everly cases against Rose were settled out of court by 1996. No amounts were disclosed but rumor had it Everly's payout was over $1,000,000.[37][38][39]

Taking a surface glance, it's surprising that a violent hard rock misogynist like Axl Rose would commit his attention to New Age pursuits. Go deeper and you realize it was the perfect track for a rich, ego-driven rock star. A major tenet of New Age philosophy is that one cannot attain enlightenment without "abundance," which is a coded term for wealth, which Rose certainly had. Also, the concept that one can somehow better the world by simply recalibrating their own spirituality and the spirituality of those around them doesn't require the selflessness or proactive sacrifice needed to take part in truly progressive efforts like an anti-war occupation or on-the-ground humanitarian work in poverty-stricken regions. Shirley MacLaine, the Oscar-winning actress who mainstreamed New Age in the '80s through a series of books and lectures, explained that reality is dictated by one's own consciousness. "You are God," she told her enthusiastic followers. "Access that God energy within [yourself]."[40][41][42]

Sharon Maynard helped Axl Rose access his God energy for many years. Eventually, the singer had Goldstein turning over half of his own earnings to Maynard and her husband Elliott (who sometimes accompanied his wife to Guns N' Roses concerts and took pictures from the side of the stage). When they weren't tending to the needs of Axl Rose, the Maynards were running a nonprofit called Arcos Cielos, which was dedicated to the development of "co-evolutionary paradigms for the Third Millennium" and "Future-Science Technology."[43][44] In terms of tangible action, this meant Arcos Cielos sometimes helped buy computers for rural communities that otherwise wouldn't have access.[45][46] Elliott's career had more of an ecological bend before he met Sharon in the mid-'70s. As an aquaculture biologist with degrees from the University of Miami, Elliott had a hand in trying to reverse the agricultural fortunes of Florida's Seminole Native American Tribe by transforming their cow pastures into shrimp farms.[47]

Sharon was born Sharon Tanemura, not on the astral plane but in Penticton, British Columbia.[48] There was, according to Elliott, an immediate bond when he and Sharon first encountered each other in San Francisco.[49] They were married on March 26, 1977.[50] One year later, almost to the day, Sharon's parents were caught in the Tenerife airport disaster. Roy and Aya Tanemura, en route to a Mediterranean cruise, were aboard a stationary Pan Am jet when it was struck on a runway in the Canary Islands by a Royal Dutch Airlines jet that was attempting to take off. 583 people were killed; Roy survived, Aya didn't. One imagines such tragedy could have ignited a deeper spiritualism within the Maynards. Soon afterward, they enrolled in the consciousness-focused University of the Trees while simultaneously founding Arcos Cielos.[51][52][53][54][55]

As Elliott moved forward with Sharon, he left behind a young daughter named Wendy from a previous marriage. "Elliott was M.I.A. from my life after I was about three," Wendy says today. "I've spoken with him several times as an adult, especially after Sharon's death [in 2007], but haven't for many years. When I did, he spoke very highly of Axl Rose and seemed to consider him a friend. I got the sense that Sharon was the person Axl relied on, though."

And how would Wendy describe Sharon? She can't. "Sharon had nothing to do with me for the thirty plus years she and Elliott were married," she reveals. "I've never spoken to her."[56]

By the early '90s, the vinyl LP had been dethroned as the premier commercial music format, supplanted by the compact disc, a change that sacrificed fidelity for convenience. Even after a decade on the market, it was impossible for CDs to replicate the depth and warmth of vinyl. The same could be said for the digital recording techniques becoming standard in most studios. The computer chips that made everything easier simply couldn't capture music's true dimension. George Massenburg spent a great deal of time working against that. A renowned engineer in both the recording and electrical sense, Massenburg wrestled with digital for years, trying to optimize the new systems for less empty, clinical sounds. It's no surprise then that the Complex, the L.A. studio Massenburg co-founded with Earth, Wind & Fire in 1979 featuring consoles designed and handmade by Massenburg himself, remained one of the best-sounding facilities an artist could enter as the new millennium approached.[57] [58]

Linda Ronstadt, Neil Young, and Cher all spent time recording or fine-tuning their work at the Complex. In addition to music, the Complex was set up for television and film audio; a great deal of ADR for "The Simpsons" was recorded there. The Complex is also where Guns N' Roses decamped for roughly five years in the '90s as they tried to figure out life after *"The Spaghetti Incident?."* William Malouf, the studio's night manager between 1993 and 2001, remembers the group's tenure quite well. "They were there slightly before I came in," he says. "They had been there off and on. Right as I started, they took residency. They block booked the sound stage, which was a large area. Technically, it was *really* tedious. I mean, it was the Axl Rose Show. He was the king. I always said it was like the Billy Mumy episode of 'The Twilight Zone.' If anyone said anything Axl didn't like, he'd wish them into the cornfield."

"I think in the years I listened to them play, Axl only put his mouth in front of a microphone one time," Malouf recalls. "I mean, they spent a one and a half, maybe two years just working on Axl's guitar rig, and he's not even a guitar player! Like I said, it was just tedious. To put it in perspective, Stone Temple Pilots came in one night and they just started playing. And we were like, 'Oh yeah, bands can just start playing.' Although we had to keep the doors locked during that session because the singer had just sold his shoes outside to get a hit. Anyway, I don't even know if Guns N' Roses ever recorded anything [at the Complex]."[59]

Conversely, Complex engineer Chad Blinman remembers Guns recording enough material to fill two gigantic cabinets of ADAT tapes. "They were trying!" he says. "But it was so tumultuous with them in the studio. All of us were in a constant state of rolling our eyes."[60]

By the summer of 1994, Guns N' Roses had slipped into a morass. Rose had rejected numerous demos that the other members of the group submitted for the next album. The singer was no longer interested in oversexed, blues-based rock. He was now obsessed creating earnest, emotional material in the vein of Pearl Jam. This was a roadblock for Slash, who hated Pearl Jam. Soon he, Gilby Clarke, and Matt Sorum were figuring out a side project. Breakup rumors appeared in the press. Geffen issued a denial. Band management said Guns N' Roses were on hiatus but that work on the next album was supposed to begin the weekend of July 17.[61]

Clarke was away from the band at that time to promote his first solo record, *Pawnshop Guitars*. He planned on reconvening with them later that year. Unfortunately, Rose had never considered Clarke an official member of GNR and didn't want to continue with him. "[Axl] wanted to explore some other kind of writing approach," said Slash. "He's always had this vision of me teaming up with a guitar player that's going to stretch my boundaries, whereas I still come from the old Guns N' Roses school where I do what I do and he does what he does. Getting two lead players to meet eye to eye is difficult, not to mention overflowing the record with self-indulgent guitars."[62] Slash loved playing with Clarke, an affable guy who was also, in his eyes, a much better guitarist than founding rhythm guitarist Izzy Stradlin.[63] Clarke too felt an ease playing with Slash. "I was never once told what to play and not to play," Clarke said. "But I could always tell if it didn't work. Slash would just look over like, *What the hell was that? [laughs]*."[64]

Once again, Rose imposed his iron will, bringing aboard guitarist Paul Huge. Huge (pronounced Hew-gee) was Rose's scrawny, towheaded friend from Indiana who had already made a handful of songwriting contributions to the GNR canon. Rose hoped Huge could lend a hand in shaping the sound of the next album. There was just one problem: nearly everyone else in and around Guns N' Roses disliked Huge. It went beyond the fact he was a novice on guitar; Huge also allegedly possessed Godzilla-sized arrogance. Slash called off rehearsals at his home studio with Huge because the bad vibes were poisoning his entire residence. "I can't even have a beer with him," Slash told Rose. "Why do you have to have a *beer* with him?" Rose sneered in response. "You know what I mean," Slash tried continuing. "No, I *don't*."[65]

Asked about Huge, former Geffen employee Jim Barber lets out a sigh. "Paul Huge couldn't play a lick and he made everybody uncomfortable all the time."[66] "There are a lot of things I could say about Paul," William Malouf begins, "I'll say he wasn't very good. They'd work on his songs and they were dreadful. One of our guys at the Complex, Richard Burnett, every time he'd walk by while Paul was playing, he'd go, 'Dude, you're never gonna be in a band.' [*laughs*] Paul was just this dork hanging out with his buddy. He was not a guy you'd be intimidated by."

"And he spoke in this affected accent," Malouf adds. "I remember a conversation [between the band members] where Axl was trying to speak from the heart. 'There's nothing in my life right now that is material for a rock n' roll band. I'm living in Malibu. When we made *Appetite* we were living on the street.' He's making this plea for songwriting help. Paul goes, [*in surfer voice*] 'Say it on the *stage*, dude!' Just the dumbest response."[67]

For Slash and Duff McKagan, the Paul Huge situation was the latest aggravation in what had already proven to be a weird, unsettling year. Slash's house had been completely demolished by the Northridge earthquake in January. "That had to be the most shocking experience I've ever had," he said (thankfully, none of his family members or pet snakes were hurt).[68] In May, a lifetime of alcohol abuse caught up with McKagan when his pancreas exploded. The pain was so excruciating he begged the doctors to just kill him. About a month prior, McKagan had a strange experience when he turned out to be one of the last people to see Kurt Cobain alive. The two musicians were booked on the same March 31 flight from L.A. to Seattle. "He had just skipped out of a rehab facility," McKagan said. "We were both fucked up. We ended up getting seats next to each other and talking the whole way, but we didn't delve into certain things; I was in my hell and he was in his, and we both seemed to understand."

Cobain's body was discovered a week later at his Seattle home. He'd been dead from a self-inflicted gunshot wound for approximately four days. "I just felt numb," McKagan recounted upon hearing the news.[69] [70] Axl Rose was very shaken by Cobain's death and spent hours discussing it with Geffen Records publicist Bryn Bridenthal (Bridenthal called Rose as soon as she could after hearing the news because she was afraid he might be driven to self-harm). "[Axl] felt things really deeply," she said, "and he felt a real connection [with Kurt Cobain], even though there was no connection from the other side." Bridenthal likened the conversation to countless other intense dialogues she'd had with Rose. "One time, I got off the phone with him and my teeth were chattering and I felt like I was energy inside his head."[71]

That summer was marked by a number of upsetting events: the cold-blooded murder of Nicole Brown Simpson and Ronald Goldman by Simpson's ex, O.J. Simpson (which happened just a stone's throw from the Complex); the Rwandan genocide; the continuing wars in Bosnia and Yugoslavia. It felt like a good time for another Woodstock. That is to say, another three days of peace, love, and music. What came to pass was Woodstock '94, a highly commercialized event in August which only celebrated Woodstock as a brand. Kids were turned off by hundred dollar ticket prices, the long list of prohibited items (booze, outside food, cooking utensils, flashlights), and a lack of purpose. Even the artists hired to perform couldn't mask their cynicism. "It's going to be fun and everything, but it's nothing but these ex-hippies, or whatever they are now, making money that they were too high to make the first time," said Henry Rollins. Asked why Nine Inch Nails was playing, singer Trent Reznor was blunt: "We were offered a lot of money."[72][73]

The people behind Woodstock '94 (who were, surprisingly, the same people behind the original Woodstock) wanted Guns N' Roses on the bill and were saying as much even before they had secured the festival grounds in Saugerties, New York.[74] This provoked criticism from Aquarian die-hards who felt Guns N' Roses violated the principles of Woodstock.[75] Not that it mattered; negotiations with the band were fruitless, if they happened at all. "I really don't remember trying to get them to play," says John Scher, one of the concert's financiers who also occasionally worked as a promoter for GNR. "It's certainly possible I had some negotiations with Doug Goldstein but I don't recall any serious conversations."[76][77]

Ironically, Woodstock '94 didn't need Guns N' Roses to have Guns N' Roses style destruction. That's what happens when you trap thousands of people in a mud pit for several days with no access to basic amenities. "To tell you the truth, it was the closest thing to total chaos I've ever seen in my life," said Green Day's Billie Joe Armstrong. "The audience took over everything. I saw police and guards throwing down their badges, quitting on the spot, saying, 'I can't do this anymore.' Technically it was a human disaster. Everybody was living like dogs, pretty much."[78][79] Green Day was five songs into their set on the third day when a playful mud fight between the band and audience escalated into a riot. Bass player Mike Dirnt lost a tooth in the madness after being tackled by security, mistaken for just another face in the crowd.

The members of Nine Inch Nails slathered themselves in mud *before* they hit the stage, creating Woodstock '94's only indelible images as they captivated the masses like angry refugees from a postapocalyptic nightmare. This performance was a victory lap for Nine Inch Nails. Their latest effort *The Downward Spiral*, released six months earlier, had pushed the otherwise inaccessible construction site sounds of industrial rock into the mainstream. *Rolling Stone* hailed *The Downward Spiral* as "a new kind of loud," comparing the abrasive noise surrounding Trent Reznor's vocal hooks to Jimi Hendrix's mastery of guitar feedback.[80] There was also a theatrical element to Nine Inch Nails, a goth severity rooted in Alice Cooper, David Bowie, and Screamin' Jay Hawkins. "[Reznor's] scratching at the taboos of suburbia in a way grunge never will," wrote Darcey Steinke in *SPIN*, "linking anger and violence to a sexually-charged experience that suggests drag, camp, even homosexuality."[81]

Nine Inch Nails had opened for Guns N' Roses in the early '90s; Axl was a big fan.[82] Rose and Reznor talked about collaborating on new music, but nothing ever came to pass. "I feel a certain degree of compassion [for Axl]," Reznor told one interviewer in the mid-'90s, "just because he was thrust into something that was larger than anything else and a lot of weight was placed on him to carry the torch."

Offering a diagnosis on GNR's problems, Reznor said, "No one had the balls to say 'no.' As in, 'No, it's not a good idea to put out two double albums [sic] of mediocre material.' But if you said that you got fired. I think that's inherently the problem. I think the guy is talented at what he's doing."[83]

Many people doubted there was room in a post-grunge world for Guns N' Roses. The *Los Angeles Times* ran a piece shortly before Woodstock '94 that quoted several industry figures who felt the notorious rock band's ride was over. Axl's "spoiled rock star crybaby" image was anathema in a world of tortured idols like Eddie Vedder. One concert promoter who wished to remain anonymous said Guns had burned too many bridges behind the scenes. "You've got to pay a lot more dues than Axl has before you can do stuff like he does. He ain't Keith Richards."

"When Guns first came out it was fresh and exciting," said KNAC program director Bryan Shock. "But now Alice in Chains, Soundgarden, Stone Temple Pilots, and Pearl Jam are exciting things. If Guns N' Roses puts together a solid record with an hour's worth of great material, sure, there's gonna be interest. But if they don't, this could be it."[84]

Forget an hour's worth of material—first, Guns N' Roses had to complete at least one song. The stalemate broke in late October when they all agreed to take a stab at covering the Rolling Stones classic "Sympathy For The Devil" for the soundtrack to *Interview with the Vampire*.

There was a mountain of hype surrounding *Interview with the Vampire*. The film had been stuck in development hell for nearly twenty years, and several very famous people (John Travolta, Richard Gere) had tried and failed to get it off the ground.[85] Some felt the original novel was too complicated to adapt; some felt it was too overtly gay.[86] Things finally fell into place when David Geffen came aboard as a producer. He hired Neil Jordan to direct and hoped Daniel Day-Lewis would play the lead vampire.[87] Tom Cruise wound up with the part, co-starring with Brad Pitt. *Interview with the Vampire* author Anne Rice snorted at this, saying that hiring pretty boys like Cruise and Pitt was "like casting Huck Finn and Tom Sawyer in a movie."[88]

The big conventional modern rock song that was supposed to be heard in *Interview with the Vampire* was a ballad called "Who Wants to Go to Heaven?" by gothic glam band Gene Loves Jezebel. Rice was a fan and reached out to the group ahead of filming. "It's the first and only song that [Gene Loves Jezebel co-founder] Jay Aston wrote to order," says bassist Pete Rizzo. "It was the favorite for the soundtrack right up until the last moment. Guns N' Roses was a very late change. Of course, they were on Geffen Records and it was a Geffen picture. Such is life."[89]

Indeed, GNR were cutting it close, convening to record "Sympathy" just a few weeks before *Vampire*'s release. The only people thrilled with this idea were Axl

Rose, who had adored *Vampire* when he was given a sneak preview, and David Geffen, who recognized that Guns N' Roses was coming apart at the seams and understood they needed work in front of them. Slash only agreed to cover "Sympathy For The Devil" because he thought it might grease the wheels for the next Guns N' Roses album. The guitarist certainly wasn't motivated by any affection for the film. Whereas Rice reversed her position on *Interview with the Vampire*'s casting after seeing a completed print, Slash walked away hating every frame. "The movie is about a subject matter I'm very romantic about," he said. "[But] it was like this gothic Brat Pack thing." [90] [91] [92] [93]

Even though they had an entire setup going at the Complex, Guns N' Roses decided to cut "Sympathy For The Devil" at Rumbo Recorders. Perhaps they were trying to recapture a little magic; Rumbo is where they recorded *Appetite For Destruction*. Alas, the sessions, helmed by the group's usual producer Mike Clink, were anything but. As Slash recounted in his memoir, he, Sorum, and Duff McKagan toiled away, waiting for Rose, who didn't show up until a week after the instrumental was complete. Then Rose asked his people to tell Slash's people that Slash needed to re-record the solo to make it more like the original. "My first reaction, of course, was 'no,'" Slash said. "I stood behind what I'd done, because why would I copy Keith [Richards] if it was *our* version? The reply, through handlers, was, 'If you don't change it, I won't sing.'"

The guitarist relented, and he didn't think he could get any angrier about this situation. Then Slash found out Rose had brought Paul Huge with him to double Slash's guitar parts on a rhythm guitar track. Slash was beside himself. His work was being duplicated by someone he loathed, someone who wasn't even in his group, on a song he never wanted to record in the first place. For the sake of his sanity, Slash temporarily abandoned Guns N' Roses to focus on Snakepit, the side project he'd been working on with Sorum and Clarke. Summing up this experience, Slash semi-famously remarked, "If you've ever wondered what the sound of a band breaking up sounds like, listen to Guns N' Roses' cover of 'Sympathy For The Devil.' If there is one Guns track I'd like never to hear again, it is that one."[94]

Why wasn't Clarke present for the recording of "Sympathy For The Devil?" "Nobody told me about it," he said. "They did that while I was on the road touring for my solo record. . . . That was one of the last straws for me, because nobody had said anything to me and they recorded a song by one of my favorite bands. It was pretty clear I'm a big Stones fan, and they recorded the song without me. So I knew that was it."[95]

Actually, Clarke had to admit, it really felt like things with Guns N' Roses had ended the year before, in 1993, at their final show of the *Use Your Illusion* tour. "Axl was jokingly saying 'bye' to everybody, but he was really saying 'bye' to everybody. He even came up to me and said, 'Hey, enjoy your last show.' At that point, I thought he was being funny, but he wasn't being funny."[96] Clarke only knew he was done with the band for sure when the checks stopped coming.[97]

Interview with the Vampire opened on November 11 to big box office and favorable reviews. "I found myself admiring [Neil] Jordan's brave attempt to translate Rice's kinky fatalism to the screen," David Ansen wrote in *Newsweek*. "This is not a movie that holds up under daytime logic. It's about seduction, and either you succumb to its inky entrapments or you resist."[98] Reviewing the film for *Artforum International*, Greil Marcus was one of the few critics to remark upon the new Guns N' Roses version of "Sympathy For The Devil."

"The [original Rolling Stones] performance is so rich Jean-Luc Godard could build an entire movie around the emergence of its arrangement," Marcus said. "But here, at the end of a film that gets stronger—more menacing—as it goes on, instead of the thing itself there is, by Geffen Records' own, a horrible imitation: generic, cloddish, ham-fisted and, in Axl Rose's singing, hysterical, as if the end, the end of the vogue for his band, is all too plain."[99]

※

On Valentine's Day, 1995, Geffen Records released *It's Five O'Clock Somewhere*, the debut album from Snakepit, legally known as Slash's Snakepit. "My name's on it for two reasons," Slash explained. "I could tell Geffen was gonna be more supportive if I did. Since I consider this a new band, I needed that support so we could tour and do this thing. The other reason is that, all of a sudden, after the record was finished, some all-girl band in San Diego said, 'We're called the Snakepit!' We met them and everything. They were really upset about it. I said, 'I've had this name for two years. How long have you had it for?' 'Well . . . ,' they said. But I said, 'Listen, it's gonna be called Slash's Snakepit anyway, so don't worry about it.'"[100]

As a marketing gimmick, Geffen set up a camera inside one of Slash's actual snake pits to broadcast images of his reptiles on their website. "Every time you plug in, you'll see the snakes," Slash promised, using jargon illustrating our unfamiliarity with the Internet at that point.[101] [102]

It's Five O'Clock Somewhere needed all the help it could get. MTV didn't play videos by bluesy '70s-style rock bands like the Snakepit anymore, and radio was moving in the same direction. FM stations across the country were ditching Aerosmith and Van Halen for what the industry called "modern" or "active" rock—post-grunge bands like the Offspring, Collective Soul, and Better Than Ezra. That spring, Boston's traditional rock anchor WBCN shocked listeners by adding a slew of active rock to its rotation. If Slash's Snakepit had come out a year earlier, they might have had a comfortable home at WBCN. As it was, station program director Oedipus dismissed *It's Five O'Clock Somewhere* and its first single "Beggars and Hangers-On" as "not desirable to our audience." "It's old school," he continued. "It's not what's happening in music."

WBCN's area competitor WAAF followed suit. "Anywhere from 35 to 49 percent [of our format] is categorized as 'alternative,' although I don't know what 'modern' rock is," said WAAF general manager Bruce Mittman. "Quite honestly, it's comical, the definition. If it rocks and is guitar-driven, we play it."[103] Given that explanation, it is possible that Slash's Snakepit simply didn't rock enough. *SPIN* reviewer Chuck Eddy thought so, writing off *It's Five O'Clock Somewhere* as "tuneless boogie booger-picking" that was not indicative of Slash's talent. "The tracks all drag on too long, and I actually prefer Slash's lyrics to his guitars."[104] Critiques of the Snakepit's live show weren't much kinder. Multiple reviewers said their concerts were boring. Some pointed out that Gilby Clarke did a better job singing than Snakepit frontman Eric Dover ("[Dover has] a grasp of pitch like an archer with hiccups," said a *St. Louis Post-Dispatch* write-up).[105] [106]

Slash with his Snakepit. *Source: Photo by Mick Hutson/Redferns via Getty Images.*

While he was out pressing the flesh for the Snakepit, Slash repeatedly stated that some of the material on *It's Five O'Clock Somewhere* was originally intended for the next Guns N' Roses record until Axl Rose nixed it for sounding retro. Occasionally he'd mention that Rose changed his mind after some time and asked for the songs back. "Dude, the album is finished," an incredulous Slash replied. The rigamarole with Axl never seemed to end, but Slash insisted he'd never quit Guns N' Roses and that one of his top priorities was crafting a new Guns N' Roses album once all the stars for such an event aligned. To that end, he spent a little time rehearsing with Guns at the Complex just before the Snakepit tour, rehearsals that were notable due to the inclusion of Ozzy Osbourne guitarist Zack Wylde.[107]

Wylde was in the middle of recording Osbourne's *Ozzmosis* album when Rose extended an invitation to jam.[108] Rose was trying to fulfill his vision of pairing Slash with another dominant lead player. "We don't really sound like Guns N' Roses with Zakk in the band," Slash remarked. "It doesn't have the sort of looseness that Guns normally has. It's very tight. Zakk and I play the same parts, just because we're similar guitar players. It sounds sort of like Ozzy N' Roses. Interesting concept."[109] Guns N' Roses was committed enough to this idea that Sorum sat out the Snakepit tour to try and build a foundation at the Complex with Wylde; Brian Tichy, drummer for Wylde's band Pride & Glory, hit the road in Sorum's place. The Wylde experiment petered out, however, and Slash was less charitable about it later in the year when he referred to it as "that whole bullshit thing with Zakk." "It's nothing against Zakk," he clarified. "I love jamming with Zakk . . . but in Guns N' Roses it doesn't sound right."[110] [111]

Wylde has said there were multiple issues that prevented him from going beyond just a few jam sessions with Guns N' Roses. Pride & Glory had an album due for Geffen; there were no concrete song ideas to work on in Guns; most crucially, there were too many managers and lawyers sticking their noses into the musicians' business. "It was supposed to be a fucking rock band!" Wylde said. "I remember thinking to myself, *Even if we are making a shitload of cash, will everyone just shut the fuck up and relax?* [laughs] So it just went down the shitter."[112] Years later, Slash recounted a conversation he had with Wylde right after one of their GNR jams (one which Slash had enjoyed). "Listen man, that was alright," Slash remembered Wylde saying. "We could get this thing together, fuck it, that's cool. But you and Axl have to get the fuckin' *band* going, man. Get yourselves together and it get it fuckin' going again."[113]

That's what Slash tried to do once the Snakepit tour came to an end—or came to a halt, rather, because Rose decided he was really ready to begin serious work on the next Guns N' Roses album, prompting Geffen to cut Snakepit's funding. Slash was annoyed because he felt the Snakepit had more roads ahead of them, and he returned to the Complex only to encounter the same problems that precipitated his leave of absence in the first place. He couldn't talk to Axl, figuratively or literally; all communication was filtered through Doug Goldstein. They were still arguing about Paul Huge. Slash wanted Huge out so they could bring Gilby Clarke back. Axl refused. "My memories of [this period] are hazy at best because I did everything I could to forget," Slash said. "I do remember going down to the studio and rehearsing without direction. I just had too much animosity blocking my creativity." To ease the pain, Slash drank heavily.[114]

Slash was trying to power through the fall of Rome. According to some, the guitarist was absent not just in mind but also in body. "I think Slash was there maybe twice during the whole period," Complex night manager William Malouf says. "One time, he walked into the room then quickly walked out, chuckling to himself and saying, 'This sucks!' Then he got in his car and left."[115] An anonymous source later said that Slash would only turn up at the Complex when he knew the coast was clear from both Rose and Huge.[116]

Axl Rose may have been torturing his bandmates and grinding everything to a halt with his ego, but Malouf says the singer never gave *him* a hard time. "Axl was always super nice to me. I never went, but he'd invite me and my kid to his parties. Once he asked me if I wanted to hear some tracks he'd been working on. I said, 'You want the one guy who never bought any of your records to tell you what he thinks?' [*laughs*] He said, 'Actually, yeah!'

"He was like an innocent. I know that's hard for people to believe, but he'd be like [*adopts earnest voice*], 'Hey guys, do you want some sushi?' Like they were his kids and he had to take care of them. It's funny—Axl didn't have a driver's license back then, so his housekeeper would drive him down from Malibu. You could tell he'd been rehearsing the line he was gonna say when he walked in the whole way down. He'd walk in with that kind of grin on his face.

"You know, they were all pretty nice. Even Paul Huge never had an attitude with me. They had passes to see AC/DC once and they took a couple guys from the studio. It was Huge, [keyboardist] Dizzy Reed, and our guys. That was cool.

"And Axl always wore a bandana, so you didn't know what was going on upstairs."

The Guns N' Roses forecast continued to call for frustration and malaise. Matt Sorum and Duff McKagan found a reprieve in the Neurotic Outsiders, a punk rock cover band they formed after the co-owner of L.A.'s Viper Room Sal Jenco asked Sorum to put something together for a one-off charity gig. The lineup was Sorum on drums, McKagan on guitar, Duran Duran's John Taylor on bass, Sex Pistol Steve Jones on second guitar, and everyone except Sorum sharing vocals. "I asked John if he'd play bass because I'd always liked his playing in the Power Station," Sorum said. "Duff knew Steve from mountain biking. We rehearsed in the afternoon and did it that night. We thought it was cool, everything was good. Good karma."

That show in June 1995 went so well that the Neurotic Outsiders (or the Neurotic Boy Outsiders as they were actually first known) became the Viper Room's Monday night staple. Sometimes the Outsiders were joined onstage by special guests like Billy Idol, Iggy Pop, and Taylor's bandmate Simon LeBon. The popularity of these shows was astounding. "They were turning away like 800 people, 1,000 people at the door," McKagan said.[117] [118] The band eventually wrote enough original material to warrant record company interest. Madonna's label Maverick offered them $1 million to make an album. "That's when people had money in the music business," Jones said. "I mean, to think of that now, a million bucks to a bunch of jerk offs like us who are kinda putting a band together. It's crazy!" The Neurotic Outsiders took the deal.[119]

As Neurotic Outsiders got off the ground, Guns N' Roses brought in two other rhythm players to keep the seats warm. "Paul Huge asked me and [drummer] Sid Riggs to come in and fill in for Matt and Duff," says bass player Krys Baratto. He and Riggs had previously played together in the Real McCoys, a reincarnation of the band Johnny Crash (in which Sorum and Dizzy Reed were briefly involved). "Sid might have been in there a month or two before me. But me, Paul, Dizzy, Sid, and the recording engineer whose name I can't remember—he used to play in a band called Heaven—they would basically just hit record and we would come up with ideas and just jam on 'em. Usually when I worked with a band or a producer they'd tell you exactly what they want. Here they were like, 'Come up with some stuff.'"

"Then Paul would go up to Axl's house with the recordings and Axl would say, 'I like this' or 'I don't like that.' We did that for like a year. Axl was never there in the studio with us. I did see him at one of those parties he threw, up at his house. He said, 'I like the way the bass is sounding!' I was like, 'Okay, great!' And he made sure I was getting paid. [*laughs*] The setup in the studio was Matt's drums and Duff's rig. Duff would come down sometimes and we'd bullshit. He had no problem with me being there. The one thing I could never figure out was . . . there were hallways lined up with road cases, cases that were filled with ADAT tapes of these recordings. How you pick from that, I have no idea. We weren't writing full songs. We were recording fragments."

Baratto says the vibe was always very casual, there were no hard feelings when it ended, and there was never any pretense that he or Riggs might become full-fledged members of Guns N' Roses.[120] This hasn't prevented theories from emerging that Baratto and Riggs were part of a "shadow" version of Guns N' Roses that Axl Rose was assembling. As Riggs's former roommate and collaborator Jeff McDonough so eloquently puts it, "There's a lot of jackasses who talk outta the side of their neck who don't know fuck about fuck. Sid was never a member of Guns N' Roses. Don't say that he was or you'll get trouble from all sorts of people, including Sid."[121]

Meanwhile, the Neurotic Outsiders' self-titled debut, produced by Jerry Harrison, was released in September 1996. The disc was crude, simplistic, and loud, and it fared much better than Slash's Snakepit when it came to breaking onto FM airwaves. "I'm going and doing alternative radio," McKagan said, half-marveling. "None of us would have ever gotten onto alternative radio. These guys at alternative radio, in this day and age—man, they really have their nose up in the air. I can remember when alternative radio was exactly that: they played what wasn't on the Top 100. But now it's a big political thing. And it's so funny going onto alternative radio, meeting this guy who is really stand-offish, and who finally admits on the air, 'Okay, I've got *Appetite For Destruction*.' To me, it's really funny. I grew up playing in punk rock bands and in the real alternative. Dude, I had to move out of Seattle [in the '80s] because there was nothing going on there. I lived there. That's where I grew up."[122]

The critics were less kind to *Neurotic Outsiders*. "They need to stick with their day jobs," wrote Jane Stevenson in *The Toronto Sun*.[123] "Music fans have good reason to yawn," snapped Dean Smallwood in *The Huntsville Times*.[124] Not that it made much difference; the Neurotic Outsiders weren't built to last. Every member had responsibilities to tend to with their more famous bands. For Sorum and McKagan, Guns N' Roses suddenly demanded their attention just as they were preparing for the *Neurotic Outsiders* record release. "It seems like every time something good starts happening, I get a phone call from Axl, 'We're going to start rehearsing tomorrow.'" Sorum remarked. "When Axl heard that me and Duff had gone out and gotten this multi-million dollar record deal and we're going to go out on the road, he started getting a little nervous."[125]

"On this [Neurotic Outsiders] tour we're doing, Matt and I fly back from Toronto and then we do four days with Guns," McKagan detailed, "and then we head back out, so Matt and I are playing every single night with one or the other in September."[126] The bass player promised the next Guns N' Roses album would be out the following spring "at the very latest."[127] He talked up a two week stretch in August where all of Guns N' Roses was together, working every day from midnight until five in the morning. They'd whipped up forty songs and were narrowing them down to a "rockin'" twelve with zero balladry. There was added excitement, McKagan enthused, because Axl was now playing guitar, bringing a new dimension to their music. "It's an innocent guitar, not unlike Izzy was, but Axl's got a lot more musically than Izzy ever did."[128] [129] [130] Sorum concurred that things were great: "It sounds like the band again. Everybody's in good shape."[131]

Now, what the members of Guns N' Roses told the press in the late '90s and what was actually going on were two different things. In his 2011 memoir, McKagan admitted that between 1994 and 1997 the band hadn't written a single new song. GNR "barely existed" at that point, he wrote, little more than a name paying rent on an empty studio. "A press release went out in late 1996 announcing that Slash had officially quit Guns N' Roses," McKagan recounted. "It barely registered with me—I had long since come to grips with the fact that he was done."[132]

The press release in question buried the lede—Axl Rose had six other points to make in his October 30 missive, faxed directly to MTV, before he even got to Slash. "LIVE!!!! From 'Burning Hills,' California," Rose began. "Due to overwhelming enthusiasm, and that 'DIVE IN AND FIND THE MONKEY' attitude . . ."

> #1. There will NOT be a Guns N' Roses tour. #2. There will NOT be an official Guns N' Roses website. #3. There will NOT be any NEW Guns N' Roses videos. #4. There will NOT be any new Guns N' Roses involved merchandise. #5. There will NOT be a Guns N' Roses fan club. #6. There will be a new Guns N' Roses 12 song minimum recording with three original B sides. NOTE: If all goes well this will be immediately repeated. #7. However Slash will not be involved in any new Guns N' Roses endeavors as he has not been musically involved with Guns N' Roses since April 1994 with the exception of a BRIEF trial period with Zakk Wylde and a two week initial period with Guns N' Roses in the late fall of '95. [Slash] has been "OFFICIALLY AND LEGALLY" outside of the Guns N' Roses Partnerships since December 31, 1995. Nothing here is subject to change without A PERMANENT SUSPENSION of the "Pseudo Studio Musician Work Ethic." Sincerely, W. Axl Rose.[133]

Slash immediately issued a response confirming his exit. "Axl and I have not been capable of seeing eye to eye on Guns N' Roses for some time. We recently tried to collaborate, but at this point, I'm no longer in the band. I'd like to think we could work together in the future if we were able to work out our differences."[134] Geffen released their own statement saying this was a mutual decision between Slash and the band. A spokesperson emphasized that the next GNR album would be released sometime in 1997.[135] [136]

Slash would later explain that he felt suicidal the night before he called Doug Goldstein to quit the group. "I'd never felt that way before, I'd never wanted to snuff myself," he said. "For half an hour, I looked around my bedroom; I had nothing to do it with . . . if there had been dope lying around, I would've done it all in one hit and that would have been that." Instead, Slash stared at the ceiling and thought about his life and his band.

Whatever musketeer spirit Guns N' Roses retained after the *Use Your Illusion* era had been irrevocably shattered by Axl, Slash believed, not just by his general behavior but by an updated contract the singer presented that granted him the right to start a new version of Guns N' Roses without anyone from the original band (though Slash, Duff, et al. might have the opportunity to join as employees). This, according to Slash, dovetailed with Rose's stated desires to turn the next Guns N' Roses album into something akin to an Axl Rose solo record with a litany of guest performances from name musicians. Slash signed the new contract without weighing the legal ramifications. "I just wanted to move forward if we had anywhere left to go together."[137] [138]

They did not. And in another case of "tell the public what they want to hear," Slash insisted a few months after Axl Rose's fax to MTV that he was still in Guns N' Roses. "I haven't officially quit the band," he told *The Orange County Register*. "[I want to] let the smoke clear and maybe we can talk about it later, rather than try and force something unnatural and have everyone go, 'We waited around all this time for this?'"[139] There was no hiding the truth in private.

Engineer David Dominguez worked with Slash around this time on music for the soundtrack to Reb Braddock's *Curdled*. "This was two days before Axl sent that fax," Dominguez says. "Slash said, 'I won't be in this band in a month.' The way I heard him talk about Axl, I thought they'd never get back together."[140] The feeling was mutual. William Malouf remembers Axl getting mad one day at the Complex and shouting, "The only reason Slash was in this band is because he was the first guy who answered my ad in *The Recycler*!"[141]

In December of 1996, gossip columnist Liz Smith received an anonymous call clueing her in to the "total breakup" of Guns N' Roses. "The caller had a lot of names and complicated so-called facts on hand and sounded very personally involved. [They] ended the conversation this way: 'Whatever happens, it's management's fault, not Axl Rose's. He's gotten a bad rap.'"[142]

Management was Doug Goldstein, whose experience in such fields prior to joining the Guns N' Roses organization was minimal. Goldstein's primary gig had been concert security. The burly self-confessed "macho jock" protected the likes of Black Sabbath, the Rolling Stones, and Air Supply before leapfrogging his way up the Guns N' Roses ladder.[143] "He was a glorified security guy," said booking agent Barry Fey. "He used to do [GNR's] security, and he took over their management. But how do you manage manic depressive heroin addicts? That's a pretty good trick. I don't know how you do that."[144]

If you're Doug Goldstein, apparently you do it like a macho jock. Shortly after Goldstein took the position, in the summer of 1991, Guns N' Roses tried to secretly decamp to Chicago to prepare for the recording of *Use Your Illusion*. The press caught wind of their presence; Goldstein went on the attack. "Who the fuck do you think you're fucking dealing with?" he seethed at a reporter for *The Chicago*

Tribune. "If you fucking print anything that says they're there, you'll never talk to this fucking band. Ever. We don't have to talk about any of this. We turned down the cover of fucking *Newsweek*." *The Tribune* printed all of these remarks under the headline "If You See Guns N' Roses in Chicago, Just Remember: You Didn't."[145]

Slash has described Goldstein as an "ambush predator" whose fealty to Axl accelerated the band's death. The guitarist knew dumping Goldstein's predecessor Alan Niven was a mistake; Niven could go toe-to-toe with Axl and he'd steered GNR to international renown. Unfortunately, Slash didn't feel motivated to save Niven following a lewd remark Niven made to Renee Suran, Slash's eventual wife (a remark Niven vehemently denies making).[146] [147]

Duff McKagan realized what a grave error the band made allowing Goldstein to take charge the morning after McKagan signed away his stake in the Guns N' Roses name in 1993. The bassist asked Goldstein to straighten things out. "I manage Guns N' Roses," was all Goldstein would say in response. When it dawned on McKagan that Goldstein meant he only managed the person who owned the Guns N' Roses name (Axl), he became so angry he couldn't speak.[148]

One might wonder why McKagan hung on through that, and through the Paul Huge mishegas, and through Slash quitting. "Duff was in my office one time and I said, 'How can you stand all this?'" Malouf says. "He said, 'If this guy'—meaning Axl—'sings into a microphone, it means millions of dollars to me.'"[149]

3 AXL'S BEEN RESEARCHING YOU

As the twentieth century was drawing to a close, the Complex Studios in Los Angeles remained a top-flight facility for music, film, and television production. *James and The Giant Peach*, *That Thing You Do!*, *Austin Powers*, "King of The Hill," and "The Simpsons" were just some of the productions that utilized the Complex's unique rooms and equipment.[1] Celebrities of all standing came walking through their doors, celebrities who were often just as curious about what Guns N' Roses was doing holed up there as anyone else.

"One day I got a call—'We need to book some time for Shaquille O'Neal for Thursday,'" says former Complex night manager William Malouf. "'Well, we're booked that day.' 'Also, he needs an SSL console.' 'Well, that's easy, we don't have one.' So I hung up. I went into the studio and told everyone, 'We just got a call from Shaquille O'Neal.' I didn't follow basketball so I didn't really know who he was. Everyone in the room started freaking out. 'No way! Shaquille O'Neal?' They moved the schedule to get him in. I guess the SSL console wasn't so important. [*laughs*]

"He was on one stage doing a Taco Bell ad. In the other room was Guns N' Roses. That was a locked out room. There was a sign up that said 'No Entry.' Shaq went in there anyway. Who's gonna stop him? [*laughs*] He started singing with them and they were thrilled. He was saying, 'They've never seen anything like me!'"[2] That was absolutely true for keyboardist Dizzy Reed, who didn't recognize O'Neal at first and was alarmed by the incredible size of this unannounced visitor. O'Neal's hands were the size of frying pans, Reed said, and when the NBA All-Star sat down on a stool to shoot the breeze, the furnishing instantly splintered apart.[3]

This was April 1997, according to O'Neal's recounting of events. "I saw Guns N' Roses listed on the bulletin board in the lobby of the studio so I stuck my head in to check it out," he said. O'Neal was no stranger to the music world, having released three rap albums since his rookie year in 1992. And so this friendly hello with Guns N' Roses—which, on that day, was Reed, guitarist Paul Huge, and session drummer Sid Riggs—turned into a jam session.

"They asked me to join them, so I started freestylin' over their track," O'Neal recounted. "It was the first time I ever performed with a rock group, and it felt *good*."[4] Reed rhapsodized about this jam, describing it as an organic, magical moment that began with O'Neal plunking out a catchy sequence on the keyboard. The band built a groove around his riff for a few beats before O'Neal handed the ivories off. "[Shaq] and his buddies grabbed the mic and started doing this rap," Reed said. "Our engineer Tommy was rolling tape the entire time.... I mean, it was really cool."[5]

The press caught wind of O'Neal's hijinks with Guns N' Roses; it made for great copy. Maybe GNR would truly surprise us on their next CD. Of course, dyed-in-the-wool obsessives probably weren't holding their breath for an Axl and Shaq duet. Axl Rose himself later complained about the "media jerkoffs" who used this story to joke about O'Neal's legitimacy as a rapper.[6]

"No, I wasn't there when Shaq came in," says session guitarist Krys Baratto. "I also wasn't there when, uh—who's the guy from 'Star Trek' who says, 'Oh *my*?' George Takei. He just happened to be there one day. Everybody was bullshittin' with him, and either Dizzy or Sid asked, 'Can we just get you go to "Oh *my*!" so we can sample it?' They put it in the keyboard, just for fun."[7]

For most fans, the idea that Guns N' Roses would continue without Slash was, at the very least, wrongheaded. Surely there were zealots who considered it blasphemous. To that end, Doug Goldstein tried to convince Axl Rose to change the name of the group following Slash's exit. "I thought he should've called it . . . I don't know, Axl Rose, something with his name," Goldstein said. "I don't even know if I came up with something. I just said, 'I don't know if you should taint what you had in the original name by using it again.'" Rose was unmoved.[8]

Rose also wanted to begin experimenting with samples, loops, and other hallmarks of electronic music and its sub-genre techno. These techniques had been popularized in mainstream '90s rock by groups like White Zombie, Garbage, Ministry, and, of course, Nine Inch Nails (the most innovative act in that field and easily the most successful). "Pure" electronic enjoyed a newfound success in this era as well thanks to landmark works by the Chemical Brothers, the Prodigy, and Paul Oakenfold. Rose actually invited Oakenfold to remix Guns N' Roses material earlier in the decade. Oakenfold declined, his reasoning simple: "Axl Rose has got no soul."[9]

The story was different when Rose put the feelers out to Moby. The emaciated and practically hairless techno wunderkind behind 1995's vibrant rave disc *Everything Is Wrong* agreed to meet with Guns N' Roses in early 1997 to consider producing their next album. Moby's philosophy was unique among his peers: he believed it was wrong to dismiss any form of music. "It's easy to do, but I don't think it's healthy," he told *Option* magazine. "I was watching MTV and this Bon Jovi video came on and I just instinctively changed the channel. Then I thought, *No, I'm not going to do that. I'm going to watch the whole thing and see if there's something I can relate to.* This might sound dumb, but I think musical elitism is the same instinct that turns people into racists—you develop these snap decisions and you take them too seriously."[10]

Moby claimed it was his album-length foray into industrial rock, 1996's *Animal Rights*, that really captured Axl Rose's attention (U2 front man Bono and David Bowie were also fans of *Animal Rights*; Bowie hailed it as "amazing" and "very adventurous").[11] [12] DJ Shadow's *Endtroducing . . .* was another recent release living between Rose's lobes (according to Moby, at least).[13] An atmospheric instrumental album built from thousands of samples, *Endtroducing . . .* redefined hip-hop's possibilities (as *Vox's* Andy Crysell put it, "[*Entroducing . . .*] leaves the rest so far behind it's as if they're still searching for the 'on' switch in the studio").[14] [15]

Moby revealed his involvement with Guns N' Roses during a panel at South by Southwest that March. "They're writing with a lot of loops," he said, "and believe it or not, they're doing it better than anybody I've heard lately."[16] He later clarified that he'd spent less than a week in the studio with the band. In that brief stretch of time, Moby committed one major faux pas. "I asked the question I'm never supposed to ask. I asked, 'Oh, this [material] is great, but where are the vocals?' And everyone got very uncomfortable. [They'd] been working on the record for six years and they hadn't done any vocals."

It quickly dawned on Moby that this was not the project for him. "I just realized, like, 'Look, I'm not a producer. I can make my own records, but I've never produced a rock band in my life.' And I just didn't think that my first job as a rock producer should be producing Guns N' Roses." Moby bowed out with the expected repercussions. "Axl still hates me," he said in 2019. "He won't talk to me. I don't know why 'cause I actually found him to be kind of, like, an endearing, interesting character . . . [but] even now, I'll see him out and he won't talk to me."[17]

Axl Rose's enthusiasm for electronica dated back to the early '90s; he was probably the most famous person championing Nine Inch Nails when they only had one album to their name.[18] Still, Guns N' Roses drummer Matt Sorum felt his work with electro chanteuse Poe on her 1995 album *Hello* played a part in Rose's decision to integrate drum loops into their music.[19] Sorum also said he was the one who suggested Rose could find the group a new guitarist at the circus, a notion that sounded potentially ridiculous but turned out to be right on the money.[20]

The touring company of Cirque du Soleil at that time featured Robin Finck, a guitar player raised in suburban New Jersey whose style was informed by Santana, the Cure, and Bauhaus. "I was doing this circus thing for a year or more," Finck said, "and it was a blast and I really enjoyed my time there. But I would have been over the moon if even an usher from the circus show told me, 'Hey, I got a drum kit in my garage. You wanna go play some AC/DC?'" As fate would have it, when Cirque du Soleil swung through Los Angeles for a residency, Axl Rose bought tickets. Finck remembered Rose attending just for the hell of it, and the singer's interest in him wasn't entirely piqued until an associate leaned over and said, "That's Robin from Nine Inch Nails."

Indeed, prior to the circus, Finck was pulverizing audiences on the Self Destruct tour, a multi-year jaunt Nine Inch Nails undertook to promote their 1994 masterpiece *The Downward Spiral*. Finck cut an extraterrestrial figure onstage with NIN—lanky frame, missing eyebrows, a Richard O'Brien *Rocky Horror* hairstyle—and if there ever was a "classic" in-concert lineup of the group, he was a part of it. Performing with Trent Reznor was exhausting, though. The music was unrelenting and Reznor was a full-contact performer, hurling his body into everything and everyone onstage. Once the Self Destruct tour was over, Finck ran off for the big top.

The first phone call Finck received from Guns N' Roses was completely unexpected. "This was before cell phones," he said. "I had the curly-cabled telephone hanging on the wall in my kitchen. It rang and someone said they were a representative of Axl Rose, who wished to speak to me. Would I be at the number in 15 minutes?" Nervous, Finck asked for the caller's number to call back. After speaking with Rose later that day, Finck decided to start spending his days off from Cirque du Soleil with Guns N' Roses. When the circus left town, Finck stayed. Rose wanted him on the new album and in the band for the next tour.[21][22][23]

Sorum was excited that Finck was joining up, not just because it was his idea (allegedly) or because Finck was a versatile player. With Finck, Sorum believed Guns N' Roses finally had a reason to dump their rhythm guitarist, Axl's childhood buddy, the hated Paul Huge. Then, with a perfect foil in place, they could lure Slash back to the lead guitar vacancy and continue their legacy. Axl Rose felt differently. Rose wanted Finck to simply take Slash's spot; Huge would remain on rhythm. That's exactly what happened.[24][25] The wind fell out of Sorum's sails, but it hardly mattered. He was about to exit Guns N' Roses permanently.

"The night Matt Sorum got fired, the whole thing went down in my office," says William Malouf. "He came into my office and said, 'I'm gonna get fired tonight. You know, I'm one of the best drummers of the '90s.' He gave me a look and said, 'Just agree with me for argument's sake. I was out with my girlfriend for her birthday and they called me—"You gotta get down here, you gotta get down here!" I get here and they're tuning the piano.' Then, a few minutes later, I heard some yelling. Paul and Axl followed Matt into the parking lot. Axl was holding a guitar he just happened to be holding. Now he was holding it like a weapon. So they followed Matt out. When they came back in, I said, 'I'm just glad nothing happened to the guitar!'"[26]

Sorum said the fracas began after Huge made a cutting remark about one of Slash's recent talk show appearances. Sorum, indignant that a guitarist as untalented as Huge would criticize Slash, warned him to keep comments like that to himself. Rose leapt to Huge's defense and everything erupted. Sorum was fired. Huge allegedly tried to get Sorum back into the Complex once the action spilled into the parking lot. "I can't come back, he's fired me," Sorum protested. Then he asked Huge, "Do you feel good about breaking up one of the greatest bands that ever lived?"[27]

Sorum went home understanding that this fight was different from all the others he'd had with Rose. He was no longer the drummer for Guns N' Roses. As with Gilby Clarke, Rose had never considered Sorum a true member of his band. The time had come, Rose believed, to figure out a permanent drum situation. He started with another former Nine Inch Nail, drummer and programmer Chris Vrenna. It was spring 1997, and Vrenna was programming for the Smashing Pumpkins. One day, he received a mysterious voicemail. "It just said, 'Hello, this is Axl Rose. I'm looking for Chris Vrenna,'" Vrenna said. "And I just kept hitting repeat on the voicemail over and over and I thought, *My God, it really is him*."

"I got asked to go down and ended up sitting in [with Guns N' Roses] and the next thing you know six or eight months later, I was still there," Vrenna said. In what was becoming a familiar refrain with GNR, the drummer explained that the band had no new songs written at the time. "Every single thing that was played in the room got recorded just in case somebody came up with something good. It was nuts."

Vrenna added that Rose only showed up about once a week, but when he did, he was soft-spoken, polite, and always touching off friendly discourse about current events. Vrenna considered Rose to be the most well-mannered of the "notorious" lead singers for whom he'd worked. Unfortunately, Vrenna wasn't keen to get involved with what was looking like a very long term project. "If you've already spent eight years trying to make a record and you're only still doing this, then it could be another eight years."

Moby was still involved with Guns N' Roses when he was there, Vrenna has said, and the two would occasionally nurse coffees and shoot the breeze. Vrenna has also said he was the one and only drummer with Guns N' Roses during that period, a claim Dave Abbruzzese disputes. "I don't know why he said I came in after he was gone," Abbruzzese says. "I came in, auditioned, and he was there playing for the duration I was there. We were gonna have two drum sets. I was on acoustic kit, he was doing electronic stuff.

"I had drums set up down there for three to six weeks, and we only played for a couple weeks. But he and I definitely played some new music together."[28][29][30][31]

If you had to whittle down Pearl Jam's extensive discography to just two clutch releases, they might be 1993's *Vs.* and the following year's *Vitalogy*. Dave Abbruzzese was Pearl Jam's drummer for both albums. He felt the potency of the music as much as any fan, which is why it stung so hard when Abbruzzese was given his pink slip just before *Vitalogy's* release. "Dave was a different egg for sure," said bassist Jeff Ament, who went on to explain that Abbruzzese was more into "partying, girls, [and] cars" than the rest of Pearl Jam. Abbruzzese derided this assesment as "a crock of shit," pointing out that he drove a used car while he was in Pearl Jam and dated the same person for nearly a decade. The drummer has also refuted an oft-repeated story that he was actually fired for refusing to face up to Pearl Jam singer Eddie Vedder after accidentally breaking one of Vedder's vintage guitars: "[That] never happened. . . . I would never be so careless or so thoughtless."[32]

Abbruzzese's dalliance with Guns N' Roses began through his attorney. "Laurie Soriano was handling me after I got fired from Pearl Jam," he starts out over a video call. "She was Guns N' Roses' lawyer too. She was dear friends with Axl. They were basically family. She told me one day, 'Axl's been researching you.'" Abbruzzese pauses, recreating the look of confusion a dog wears when it hears a strange noise.

"'*Ohhh*-kay.' 'Now he's been told it's time, so he's interested in you joining the fold.' She explained that Axl had had my picture for a number of years and consulted his guru to know the right time to talk to me. My reaction was, 'I don't know.' The ending of Pearl Jam hit me hard. It got ugly really quick. So I said, 'I wanna talk to Axl first.'" Abbruzzese got in touch with Doug Goldstein, who said he had to play intermediary.

"I said, 'that's not gonna work.' So Doug, against his better judgment, gave me Axl's number. I'll never forget that call. His assistant answered. 'Hi, this is Dave Abbruzzese calling for Axl.' Silence. 'Okay, hold on.' Then Axl gets on the phone: 'Hello?' 'Axl, it's Dave!' 'Why are you calling me here?' 'I heard you wanna play!' [*laughs*] I went straight at him. 'I love music, I wanna play music. I'm not a big Guns N' Roses fan but I want to see what we can do.' It took a week or two of talking every other day for hours at a time, but he let his guard down and a friendship began. He had some far out notions, but we shared some of the same trust dynamics."

Odd man out? Dave Abbruzzese (center) with Pearl Jam at the height of their fame, 1992. *Source: Photo by Paul Bergen/Redferns via Getty Images.*

The regular phone calls with Rose went on for nearly four months before Abbruzzese even saw a drum kit. The singer was being cautious; he wanted everything "locked down on paper." When it came to such contracts, Abbruzzese was at something of a loss. "I spoke to Laurie—'I don't know what to ask for.' I didn't need the money. 'Ask for the fuckin' moon!' [*laughs*] Then, all of a sudden, I got a call from Laurie where she told me Axl had fired her. He was worried about the conflict of interest, and rather than me get another attorney, he severed the relationship. Wow, that was heavy. So anyway, I asked for the most absurd, ridiculous percentages and the most ridiculous salary." Abbruzzese was floored when all of that was approved.

The only issue was an addendum levying a fine of half a million dollars against Abbruzzese if he spoke publicly about Rose without permission. "I said, 'That's fine, I just want the same thing on the back end.' Axl didn't like that *at all*! [*laughs*] But we worked through it."³³

When the day finally came for Abbruzzese to start playing, he showed up early to the Complex; no one from the band was there yet. There was, however, a full crew toiling away, as well as a full rack of recording gear that was constantly going. "I thought, *Wow, they're spending a lot of money, they've had this going for years, and they've got nothing to show for it*. Then I noticed a Guns N' Roses pinball machine in the corner with a .357 magnum resting on top. *Okay, this is getting interesting*. So the band showed up, and at this point it was Duff McKagan, Dizzy Reed, Paul Huge, Robin Finck—and Robin, wow, I've met some people in my life but that guy was a *star*. When it came to my drums, it was my set up, and they were like, 'Do you have any bigger sizes?' The tech was stressed that Axl would immediately want bigger drums."

Eventually, Rose turned up, at which point, Abbruzzese says, the floor of the Complex turned to eggshells. The singer was cracking a lot of jokes at the top of the session, all of which the new drummer was laughing at. Suddenly, Rose began slowly stroking his chin. "Hey Dave," he said. "I notice you're laughing at all my jokes." An uneasy silence fell over the room. McKagan quickly disappeared; Reed pretended to focus on something with his keyboard. "I don't wanna get fuckin' fired," Abbruzzese quipped. "I just got here!" The tension racked up even further for a moment, only to deflate when Rose said, "Ahhh, that's a good one!"

"I thought we'd start playing some songs and see how it went," Abbruzzese recalls. "But Axl said, 'Hey Duff, why don't you and Dave play just the bass and drums together?' *Oh shit!* But it felt really good. You know, I made no bones about the fact I wasn't a GNR fan. I remember going to the store and saying, 'I need a cowbell,' because there's a lot of cowbell on *Appetite For Destruction*. The guy goes, 'What kind of cowbell?' 'Uh, the Guns N' Roses cowbell!' [*laughs*] I'd heard these songs so much on the radio I figured I'd know where to go once they started to play 'Welcome to The Jungle' or whatever. So Duff and I played together for a while and then Axl said, 'Wow, you really *do* hit harder than Matt!'

"Axl was showing up every day, which I guess was unheard of at the time. We were working on stuff that was really heavy and really good but they weren't Guns N' Roses songs in any way, shape, or form. I mean, this stuff was so heavy, very heavy and exciting music. It was akin to White Zombie. And no, Axl wasn't singing."

Things were going swimmingly until the day Abbruzzese decided to rearrange the room. As it was, the musicians were spread across the cavernous space Guns N' Roses was occupying at the Complex. "One day I came in and I saw Paul standing on the enormous stage, and the tech guys were on the other side of the room. Paul leans into the mic, calls his tech up, I see this guy walk 50 yards. Paul says, 'Can you get me a pick?' The guy just reached and got one off Paul's mic stand. 'Nuh uh,' I said. 'We can't do it like this.'" Abbruzzese had all the instruments pushed closer together in the center of the room, with everyone facing each other. The one instrument not put into this new communal circle was Axl's grand piano.

"I'd never seen him touch it," Abbruzzese protests. "But he felt offended that I didn't bring it into the set up. But it was also like he was poised to be offended by something. It hadn't happened in the previous six months but there it was. Like, 'It can't be this good! It can't be this smooth!' I kinda talked him outta that, too."

Did Abbruzzese get along with Paul Huge? "Yeah, he wasn't a bad guy. I have no bad words to say about him. You know, the problem was he was given the title of Guns N' Roses guitar player, it was really the first thing he ever did, and he was given that title by Axl Fuckin' Rose! [*laughs*] He was just thrust into a situation. Another thing was—I was 15 years old when an older musician told me to shut up and listen. Paul hadn't been told that yet."

At one point, Rose asked Abbruzzese why he was interested in all this if he wasn't a Guns N' Roses fan. The drummer explained that he loved the idea that Rose wanted to somehow make his band even bigger and better than it was, giving the world another "holy shit" moment, and he wanted to be a part of it. Then Rose blew Abbruzzese's mind. "He said, 'Dave, I'm the captain of this ship, but I can't be at the helm all the time. I want you to take the reigns and know the ship will be okay.' He'd never told anyone that before. I would steer the ship because I wasn't ego driven. Now, he wasn't giving me free reign—just steer the ship. It wasn't my ship."[34]

"Dave called me one day," says Jimmy Shoaf, Abbruzzese's longtime drum tech. "He said, 'Hey, I've been jamming with Guns N' Roses, things are going really well. You wanna get involved?' 'Yeah, that sounds like a pay bump.' [*laughs*] But then it didn't happen. I heard somebody was worried about what Dave was gonna wear onstage, which was really puttin' the cart before the fuckin' horse. Dave's not a Judas Priest leather clad spiked arm band guy. I've seen Axl wearing flannel, though. Anyway, that whole thing shocked the hell outta Dave. And then nothing was happening, so I took a gig with Rage Against the Machine."[35]

Abbruzzese says the real reason everything went south with Guns N' Roses was because of a conversation with Doug Goldstein. "He said to me, 'Dave, this [version of the band] is gonna fail, and it's gonna fail miserably, but you're in, and when it fails, that's how we get Axl to accept the original guys back. If you're there, that's all that matters. You'll be GNR's drummer when they reunite.' Because Axl didn't get along with the other drummers. Axl trusted me.

"Doug's whole trip was, 'Axl doesn't feel he needs those original guys, he doesn't realize he needs those guys.' The band was already so in debt, without a doubt if everybody got back together, they could have gone out and done big things before they ever had to be creative. The label, the managers, they decided the best thing to do was to let Axl do this and show him it's more valuable to be with the other guys. They couldn't say that to him or they'd be fired.

"'Just go along with it and you'll be in.' It broke my heart."

❧

Abbruzzese went back to Seattle with a heavy weight on his shoulders. He wasn't sure how to handle this situation. "I couldn't bring myself to call Axl. I knew once I heard his voice, I'd owe him the truth, but it wasn't my place to fuck him up like that." He faxed Rose a letter instead, one that explained he couldn't move forward with Guns N' Roses or he'd risk being swallowed up by the machine, which is how Abbruzzese often describes his experience with Pearl Jam.

Four hours later, Abbruzzese received a call from his friend Kim Neely, the *Rolling Stone* writer who often covered Guns N' Roses during their heyday. She asked if he was okay. "Yeah, I'm fine." *Strange thing to ask*, he thought. "I just got off a four hour call with Axl," Neely said. Abbruzzese's call waiting beeped during this conversation. It was Rose.

"I put the phone down on the table," Abbruzzese says, "and me and my girlfriend Sheri listened to the most incredible vocal range of expletives. He was talking about 'dark forces' and 'dark energies against me.' It was very serious. This was a hurt man. The camaraderie and friendship was gone. He screamed at me for an hour." The drummer started crying during Rose's tirade.

"I hope Axl reads this. I know he's like Eddie [Vedder], he reads everything that's written about him. I never got the chance to tell Axl why I backed out. I miss him. I looked forward to taking on the world with him. It just reached a point where my love for him. . . . I just could't be the one. I sacrificed our friendship because I didn't want him to stop."[36]

Complex night manager William Malouf recalls a slightly less emotional reason for Abbruzzese's departure. "Axl wanted Dave to sign an exclusivity contract where he couldn't play with anyone else," he says. "Dave said 'nah' and bailed. After Dave, they had that short guy with the tattoos. He looked like a weight lifter? Joey Castillo.

That's when they sounded the best, I thought, but it didn't gel. I can't give you an exact answer as to why. He just showed up for a few days and then off he went. I didn't know anything about him, just that he'd been in Danzig. To my ears, that's when they sounded the most like Guns N' Roses. When Joey Castillo was there."

"I came in and played for a couple days," Castillo confirmed during a 2022 podcast appearance. "Duff had called me and said, 'Hey, you wanna come play some drums for a couple days? Y'know, you get paid.' . . . Danzig was managed by the same managers as Guns N' Roses at that time. Doug Goldstein and everybody. . . . I had to sign something, like, 'whatever you play in here could be possibly used,' this and that. . . . And that was kind of it. [This] was while I was still in Danzig. I didn't bail—I was in Danzig, y'know?"[37]

Regardless of his employment situation, it's not surprising Castillo didn't jockey harder to move forward with Guns N' Roses. A self-taught Southern California punk who got his start in hardcore legends Wasted Youth, Castillo actually quit playing in the late '80s and took a job at the Los Angeles airport because he was so turned off by the hair metal scene. Castillo wasn't even familiar with Danzig's theatrical style of devil metal when he was asked to try out.[38]

Mike Penketh, a Complex employee and drummer in his own right, was occasionally invited to sit in with GNR when the stool was empty. It became a regular enough occurrence that Rose felt compelled to pull Penketh aside one evening. "Look, I don't want you to get the wrong idea," Rose began. "I know you're helping us out . . ." Penketh cut him off. "Dude, I don't want to be in your band. That would be a fate worse than death."[39]

In August of 1997, Guns N' Roses was suddenly without a bassist as well. Duff McKagan was about to become a father and felt himself needing more solid employment. By his account, he informed Axl Rose about his decision over dinner one night; they shook hands and went their separate ways. No tantrums, no hour-long diatribes about dark forces.[40]

Chris Vrenna has said that around this time there was another conversation with Rose about the band's name. "[I said] 'You know, you're changing the sound of the band and it's really just you and all new dudes and we all come from cool places. But have you ever thought of just saying, "Fuck Guns N' Roses, that name is dead, the band is over, we are now called 'blank?'"' And he goes, 'Yeah, you're not the first person who's told me I should probably do that. But Guns N' Roses is an international brand name. . . . I can't sacrifice the branding that's already been established.' And I got his argument. . . . But I also firmly believed in what I was saying."[41]

Music history is rife with famous groups re-emerging with practically all new lineups. Doo-wop legends Frankie Lymon and the Teenagers hit the oldies circuit in the early '90s as Frankie Lymon's Original Teenagers; this edition boasted only two actual original members, neither of whom were Frankie Lymon (Lymon died of a heroin overdose in 1968).⁴² A more pertinent example might be "the Clash Mark Two," a reconstituted version of the Clash front man Joe Strummer assembled for one final album, 1985's dismal *Cut The Crap*. Just a few years after *Crap*, Strummer admitted the whole thing was a mistake (though he shielded the musicians involved from any criticism because he felt his bad decisions shouldn't reflect on them).

"I was trying to prove I was the Clash and it wasn't Mick," Strummer said, referring to founding Clash guitarist Mick Jones, who'd split with the group in 1983. "I learned that it wasn't anybody, except maybe a great chemistry between us four, and I really learned that the day we sacked [our drummer] Topper [Headon in 1982].... You can't jigsaw puzzle it, take out a piece and put in another piece... it was something weird between four humans that when we played, it sounded okay, you know. And that's fairly rare. And when we knocked out Topper for excessive drug use, I don't think, honest to God, we ever played a good gig after that. Except for one night in New Jersey... but I reckon that was just by the law of averages."⁴³

Shortly before his death in 2002, Strummer was asked why the Clash broke up. He cited power struggles, but he also mentioned fatigue. "We put out sixteen sides of vinyl in five years. Maybe we said all we needed to say in a five year blast. We could have strung it out over 20 years, and we'd be on the fifth side of *Sandinista!* right now."⁴⁴

Maybe Guns N' Roses said all they needed to say in the four-year blast between *Appetite for Destruction* and *Use Your Illusion*. Maybe that's why they were already six years into making a new album. Obviously, Axl Rose didn't think so. Guns N' Roses would march forward, even it had to be completely redefined.

Bill Bennett is a gregarious storyteller who has many a rich tale from his lengthy career in the music industry. A significant chunk of that career was spent at Geffen Records.

"The first three or four years, I was really the head of... well, we didn't have titles back then," says Bennett, who was hired in 1990. "I was head of DGC. One of the first things we did was sign Nirvana. At any rate, I was there for ten years, Virtually every Monday morning, there was something left outside the door for Guns N' Roses. Books, love letters, candles, feathers. Madonna used to get the same kind of things when I worked at Maverick Records."

In 1996, Bennett was named president of Geffen.⁴⁵ He succeeded Ed Rosenblatt, who had held the position for the entirety of the label's fifteen-year existence (Rosenblatt moved up to Chairman/CEO after David Geffen exited to co-found Dreamworks SKG).⁴⁶ Bennett inherited a company whose headiest days were growing smaller in the rear view mirror. Nirvana was done; Aerosmith moved to

Sony; Guns N' Roses was frozen in carbonite. The newer acts Geffen was investing in, like Weezer and Elastica, weren't as lucrative as their predecessors. The label's top-selling CDs for 1995 were the Eagles reunion disc *Hell Freezes Over* and *Astro-Creep 2000* by White Zombie (who were on the verge of a break up).[47] Even worse, Geffen's independent spirt was suffocating thanks to a merger between parent company MCA and beverage giant Seagrams.

"After the [1995] merger, that was the first time we had a meeting with 'risk management,'" Bennett remarks sourly. "You could tell these guys had just taken their ties off the minute before they walked through the door. We had to go through every release on the schedule and evaluate it. It would start like this: 'Who's Peter Gabriel?' [*pause*] 'Well, he was in a band called Genesis.' 'You have him down for 1.5 units that'll ship for Christmas. Will that happen?' 'I don't know. We're going to see him in England next week.' 'So there's a chance that record might not come out this year?' 'Of course.' 'When will the record come out?' 'When Mr. Gabriel thinks it's ready to come out. That's one of the reasons we have great relationships with our artists.'

"This went on for two or three hours. 'When's the next Nirvana record coming out?' This was after Kurt was dead. So, you know."

Geffen's policy of not leaning on their artists to meet etched-in-stone release dates was part of the reason a new Guns N' Roses album didn't exist. Another factor, as Bennett puts it, is that Guns N' Roses had their own rules. "And those rules were established long before I got there," he adds. "They were like Ireland was to the UK." Even though he was president of their record company, Bennett did not feel it was his place to get personally involved in the push for new Guns material. "I never had a real relationship with Axl and not really with Slash, either. They weren't bad guys, they just had their own world. You know how you can't go to the Supreme Court without standing? I didn't have the standing to go in there and futz around."[48]

"There were only a few people who had a working relationship with Axl, if you can call it that," says Robin Sloane Seibert, who headed up Geffen's art department for most of the '90s. "One of those people was Tom Zutaut, the A&R guy who signed them. Anything with Guns N' Roses, he spearheaded. He made sure shit got done."[49] Zutaut had resigned from Geffen in January 1995 to explore new opportunities. He was the last of the label's legendary A&R figures to exit, behind Gary Gersch, who brought in Nirvana, and Aerosmith shepherd John Kalodner.[50] [51]

"Those three guys were massive," says Seibert. "They really controlled so much of the budgets pertaining to their acts. Once that structure changed, Geffen was a very different place."

"I had my hands full with [Courtney Love's band] Hole," Bennett explains. "I did send people into the studio [with Guns N' Roses], though. Producers. Scott Litt, Flood, I think there were a couple more. They'd be there for three or four days. I remember both Scott and Flood going, 'Well, there's tons of music, not tons of songs. There's tons of starts.' Everyone told me, 'There's this one song called "Prostitute" that's fuckin' brilliant but it doesn't start and it doesn't end.'"

I ask Bennett if Axl Rose's psychic guru Sharon Maynard caused any interference. "I've never heard that name before," he replies, "but Beta was often the source of not being able to get a hold of Axl."[52] Beta is Beta Lebeis, the Brazilian woman who was Rose's housekeeper. She'd worked in a similar capacity for Stephanie Seymour when Seymour was dating Rose. After the couple's split, Lebeis went to work for Rose, feeling that he'd been victimized by Seymour.[53] Lebeis gradually became Rose's answer to Erin Fleming, the woman Groucho Marx hired as his secretary toward the end of his life who ended up managing and reviving his career.

As with Fleming, there would be controversy regarding how firmly Lebeis implanted herself (and her children) into Axl Rose's life.[54] A person once close to Rose who wishes not to be identified can't say the name "Beta" without sounding like they're tasting poison. "She's the biggest pathological liar who ever lived," they tell me. "She would try to direct shit, start shit, try to keep her shit floating, and Axl was just too far gone to give a shit. The Beta shit is criminal. She and her kids did stuff you wouldn't even believe."

As Bennett sees it, this was all just par for the course. "Even by 1991, Guns N' Roses had become a long soap opera. But, you know, they literally made Geffen the rock label that it was. With a band like that, you never ask how much it's gonna cost or when it's gonna come in."[55] And yet, the new Guns N' Roses album had to come in sometime—the sooner the better, ostensibly. Geffen tried sticking employees on the Axl beat to coax the singer into finishing something releasable. Talent executive Todd Sullivan was on the task in 1997. Sullivan thought Rose needed to commit to hiring a specific producer for the album, so he asked him to pick somebody from a handful of CDs he sent over. Rose responded by running over the CDs with one of his cars. Sullivan was relieved of his Guns N' Roses duties after he dared to suggest to Rose's face that he bite the bullet and finish the song sketches he had sitting in the tank.[56]

Sullivan wanted to have a conversation with me before he committed to being interviewed for this book. "I didn't really do anything," he told me. "My one contribution was getting Robin Finck in the band." He didn't elaborate. We made plans to speak again.[57] Sullivan ghosted me at the agreed upon time and date. Despite repeated follow ups, I never heard from him again. No one else I spoke with can recall which CDs of Sullivan's Axl Rose crushed under the wheels of a car.

Five years passed without any kind of commercial activity from Axl Rose. He was no longer omnipresent on MTV, in magazines, or newspapers. The perception began to take hold that he was turning into the Howard Hughes of heavy metal, locked away in a studio, spending days and nights deliriously laboring over every piece of minutiae tied to making a rock album.

Rose undoubtedly had a few things in common with Hughes, the billionaire industrialist from half a century earlier (give or take). "Howard is the most utter perfectionist that ever lived," one friend remarked in 1962. "You can't hurry him. He does everything as though he expected to live 300 years. He can out-wait anybody."[58] Hughes had his own famously expensive, time-consuming boondoggle in the form of the H-4 Hercules, the jewel aircraft at the center of a fleet he and business partner Henry Kaiser were contracted to build for the war effort in 1942. Descriptions of the Hercules left people breathless—eight engine design, a 320 foot wingspan, and the theoretical ability to carry 750 soldiers (or several tanks, or an entire makeshift hospital).[59] [60] [61]

The Hercules and her sisters were still under construction when Japan surrendered in 1945. Two years later, Hughes finally finished the Hercules and managed to get her off the ground—only for a mile, though, and at an altitude of less than 100 feet.[62] Military interest had bottomed out by that point, so this behemoth plane spent the next thirty-five years entombed in its one-of-a-kind hangar at Long Beach Harbor in California. A crane liberated the Hercules in 1982 to place it atop a barge as a tourist attraction; that two and a half hour procedure was the longest the plane had ever been off the ground.[63] [64] [65] [66] [67] These days, the Hercules is better known as the Spruce Goose, a nicknamed coined in the '50s by AP writer Jim Bacon (Hughes wasn't fond of that moniker because it was inaccurate; he used pine to build the Hercules, not spruce).[68]

When people in the '90s were comparing Axl Rose to Howard Hughes, however, they were evoking the fastidious germaphobe Hughes became in the '60s, the one who walled himself up in a penthouse filled with purified air and a staff who couldn't handle anything without gloves.[69] Hughes was besieged by OCD; it's also theorized that, following a plane crash, he developed a neurological condition called allodynia wherein the slightest touch causes debilitating pain. Allodynia makes hygienic practices intolerable, which explains how the once strapping Hughes shriveled to a ninety pound wisp with eight-inch fingernails. When Hughes died of kidney failure in 1976, he was so unrecognizable that the medical officials who received his body sent his fingerprints to the FBI to confirm his identity.[70] [71] [72] [73] [74] [75] [76]

Axl Rose did not suffer from anything that severe and did, in fact, leave his house in the late '90s (although not as much as he used to). He was spotted at boxing matches, like Mike Tyson's August 1995 comeback match against Peter McNeeley (Tyson had just served three years in prison for rape; he beat McNeeley in about 90 seconds).[77] [78] Rose also attended soirees at the luxury homes of music industry moguls, as he did in the summer of 1996 when Jimmy Iovine hosted a get-together to try and convince up-and-coming musician Ben Kweller to sign to his label Interscope (Kweller said Rose didn't really talk to him but Dr. Dre was "totally cool").[79] And there was no mistaking Rose's visage when a new mugshot flew across the AP wire following an arrest for disorderly conduct at Sky Harbor Airport in Phoenix on February 10, 1998.

Rose was flying back to Los Angeles that Tuesday evening after spending some time in Sedona with Sharon and Elliott Maynard. Security screener Kim DeGeorge noticed "a dark unidentifiable object" in Rose's carry-on bag as he moved through one checkpoint. As DeGeorge began to search the bag by hand, Rose tried to grab it away from her; he was reprimanded, but then Rose tried reaching into the bag himself. The singer was hurling angry invective at DeGeorge the whole time. After calling for police, DeGeorge's supervisor Duane Welsh tried to intervene. Rose shook his fist in Welsh's face and shouted, "I'll punch your lights out right here and right now!" Rose complained to arriving officers that security was mishandling his items. The police warned Rose he'd go to jail if he didn't calm down.

Axl Rose's 1998 mug shot. *Source: Photo courtesy Bureau of Prisons/Getty Images.*

"I don't give a fuck," Rose sneered. "Just put me in the fuckin' jail. You are all a bunch of little people on a power trip!" Off Rose went for the night. In his report, Officer Dan Tarrazon wrote, "At no time did [Rose] converse with me during his transportation to jail."[80] [81]

Geffen Records publicist Bryn Bridenthal painted a different picture of the incident, saying that it was all a misunderstanding involving a gaggle of birthday presents Rose had in his bag, one of which was a delicate glass object. As a few of these objects began to fall off the security table, Rose simply reached out to catch them. "Who wouldn't want to catch their stuff when it was falling off the table?" she reasoned. Bridenthal was also forced to give an update on the state of Guns N' Roses. It certainly seemed like, from a creative standpoint, the band was on the balls of its ass. Bridenthal insisted a new album was just around the corner, arriving later that year, or the next. Were Matt Sorum and Duff McKagan still in the band? That she couldn't say.[82]

Though it's never been confirmed exactly what the object or objects were that Rose was trying to protect from airport security that night, there has been speculation that the item or items were similar to numerous two-foot sculptures of "future science art" that Elliott Maynard made in his role as a self-proclaimed "techno shaman." In a 2012 interview, Maynard explained that the sculptures have their own "embedded consciousness" and seemed to gloat when he noted that a "world famous rock star" who lived in Malibu kept one by his bedside.[83]

"Yeah, the Maynards were still a huge part of the story and a constant presence in 1998," says Jim Barber, the Geffen employee who was saddled that year with trying to get Rose to deliver his new record before the rapture. "Things would get delayed because he had to go to Sedona."

"He had a really specific vision about why the other people weren't in Guns N' Roses anymore," Barber says. "They were too wrapped up in their own egos. The new people who eventually came in, they were willing to let go of their personalities, they understood the bigger mission of Guns N' Roses."[84] This sounds vaguely cultish: did Guns N' Roses have a "bigger mission" than creating rock music and selling it? It feels worth pointing out here that Geffen's founder David Geffen has always been candid about his curiosity and involvement with various controversial "self-help" movements pegged as cults, and that spilled over into the culture of his record label.

"I remember touring Geffen and they all seemed EST-ed to me," recalled Louise Post, singer and guitarist for Veruca Salt. "They all seemed really weird and woo woo, and I remember saying to [my band mate] Nina [Gordon], 'They've all been to EST.' And, sure enough, they'd all been to Lifespring, which is the current day EST . . . they all said the same lines. They all said, 'You guys are so good! You're poppy with an edge.'"[85] [86] During interviews for this book, several former Geffen employees would, apropos of nothing, begin praising David Geffen, and speaking his name in hushed, reverent tones, as if he were an apostle.

Jim Barber seems a little more grounded, but he still defends Axl Rose's insistence that band members suppress their identities for his greater good. "When Axl and I would talk about it, the internal logic was, *Well, he really believes what he's saying.* It wasn't a power move," Barber says. "He wasn't using it as a goofy excuse. He thought Guns N' Roses had a responsibility to be the best. I can only imagine that Slash and Duff thought, *This guy is so full of shit.* But Axl wasn't doing this stuff to be a jerk.

"He was really trying to do the right thing. That made it a lot harder for people to call him out on it. That's also why giving him bonus checks didn't work."[87]

That's exactly what Geffen did, though, handing Rose $1 million in 1998 to finish the next Guns N' Roses album with a promise of another million if he handed it in by March 1, 1999. Bill Bennett says he "sincerely has no clue" how much had already been spent on the project by this point, which is exactly what he told reporters who called during that period seeking confirmation on rumored figures like $5 million or $7 million.[88] As previously stated, it didn't matter. Whatever Guns N' Roses released, surely it would be another blockbuster.

Such was the prevailing thought among many Geffen figureheads. It was wishful thinking at a time when the company was floundering.[89] They only had one new release break into 1997's top 200-selling albums—*Eight Arms to Hold You* by Veruca Salt, holding an embarrassing position at #193.[90] Who could blame a small nation for turning their lonely eyes to Axl?

Not everyone at Geffen was throwing their hopes behind Guns N' Roses. "I didn't hear a thing about them that I remember," says folk singer Robbie Fulks, who was signed to Geffen during this period. "As things were sort of crumbling in later 1998, with staff and artist layoffs and the absorption into Interscope, all I heard about was Hole and Rob Zombie. The survival of the label was pinned to hopes that those two releases would lift all other sinking ships.

"Ridiculous then as now."[91]

By the time of Axl Rose's Phoenix arrest, Guns N' Roses had vacated their residency at the Complex—mostly. "They were definitely doing things in different places simultaneously," says Chad Blinman, who worked both at the Complex and GNR's next studio destination, Rumbo Recorders. "Full on '80s, '90s rock star unlimited budget style, holdover of a dying era."[92]

Rumbo engineer David Dominguez vividly remembers Guns N' Roses' arrival at the studio. "I was actually about to quit," he says. "Mike Clink, he was my mentor. I told him I was about to quit and he told me to hold on a little bit because he had a band he wanted me to work with. A band that he really needed me to work with.

I'd heard some rumblings that they were coming in . . . so I asked, 'Is it Guns?' And he said, 'Just hang on, hang in there.'"

Clink sealed his immortality in 1987 when he produced *Appetite for Destruction* at Rumbo; he'd worked on every Guns N' Roses release since. "I would always ask Mike how he got that sound on *Appetite*," Dominguez says. "What it came down to is he made the band comfortable and they played. So I asked him if he was producing this new record and he said it hadn't gotten to that stage yet. They were still in talks.

"I didn't know who was in the band at that point. I was a staff guy, so my whole thing was just getting them set up. They were gonna have a MIDI room, a live room, and a computer set up. They had a PA in the main room and amps and that was split into an isolation booth. They got there and I wanna say it took two or three weeks to get everything set up. I think Axl came in on the third day. I got to meet him and the whole entourage. That's when I found out the band was gonna rehearse *Appetite* and re-record it."

As time went on, Dominguez realized Guns N' Roses had no primary engineer for this project. So he inherited the position. It turned into a long, strange eight months.[93]

William Malouf, night manager at the Complex, chuckles when he remembers Guns N' Roses leaving his facility. "I didn't think it could possibly go on any longer," he says. "Then they went to Rumbo. So much money had been pumped into this thing you knew it would never recoup."

Malouf reiterates that during the five years Guns N' Roses spent at the Complex, he only heard Axl Rose sing once. "One time, the band went into 'Welcome to The Jungle.' Axl jumped up and grabbed the mic and he just nailed it. Every single note was right on the money.

"It was impressive. We all thought he couldn't sing anymore."[94]

4 JIMMY SAID HE COULD FIX EVERYTHING

Josh Freese was already making headlines when he was just fourteen-years-old. Specifically, "Boy Drummer's on a Roll; He Hopes It's to Stardom" in the *Los Angeles Times*. It was 1987, and Freese had landed a gig drumming for a pop rock band called Polo who were so squeaky clean they regularly performed at Disneyland (where, coincidentally, Freese's father Stan had worked in a musical capacity for many years). This teenager's influences were on the esoteric side; his favorite drummer was Vinnie Colaiuta, best known for backing Frank Zappa. "I went up to talk with him when I was 10," Freese said, "and he taught me a lot of about drums. I was bewildered, and once in a while we would sit down [together at] a drum set."[1]

Freese was in demand a couple of years later. He turned down an offer to get involved with Private Life, a rock band Eddie Van Halen was producing, because he'd just committed to a six-month tour with Michael Damien (before that, he was with Stacy Q). Incredibly, Freese worked out a special deal with his high school where he was allowed to complete all his courses by mail. "The school has my itinerary, so they'll send the work to the hotel I'm staying at and I'll return it by Federal Express when I'm done." Ultimately, Freese said he hoped one day to front his own band, away from the drums. "I want to be in the weirdest, strangest band," he said. "Not a band that scares people, but one's that different."[2]

A chance to do something weird arrived when Freese was invited to drum for the Vandals, a group of punk rock jesters who revealed in kitsch as often as they mocked it (case in point: the quintessentially unpunk Kelsey Grammer appears on their 1990 album *Fear of a Punk Planet*).[3] Freese's charismatic style propelled the Vandals through zany displays like *Live Fast, Diarrhea*, and *Hitler Bad, Vandals Good*.[4] [5] While making the earlier comment about wanting to form his own strange band, Freese made specific reference to Devo. Lo and behold, Freese was hired as Devo's drummer in 1996 (this was probably not pure luck; Devo's Bob Casale produced *Fear of a Punk Planet*).[6] This was when Axl Rose took an interest in Freese's percussive talents.

"I got a call from their now ex-manager in 1997 saying, 'Guns N' Roses is auditioning drummers. They'd like you to audition,'" Freese remembered. "I was busy at the time playing with Devo and doing lots of Vandals gigs and working with Paul Westerberg, my hero from the Replacements. I was already really busy, not being a rich and famous rock star, but being cool . . . working with people I loved and really stood behind and making a good living. I wasn't filthy rich, but I wasn't broke. So, I was like, 'I'm good, man.' And I had a conversation with the manager, and he said, 'Why don't you just come down and meet Axl?' I said, 'I don't know.'

"And he said, 'Listen, who knows if you'd even get the gig, and if you get the gig, you don't have to say yes. Just come down.' I think, *What have I got to lose?* At that point, no one had seen Axl in five years. You heard rumors, 'I heard he's 350 pounds,' 'I heard he lost all of his hair.' . . . I was like, 'I should go down. Does he drive himself or does he take a limo? Does he show up with his sister? Does he show up with the porn stars? . . . Let me see how this dude rolls.'"

Freese discussed this opportunity with friends; most thought he was foolish to even consider it. The only person who encouraged him was Westerberg, who reasoned that since playing with Guns N' Roses sounded like the wrong move, it was worth trying. "What are you going to do, be in some totally cool alternative band?" Westerberg asked Freese. "Are you going to join the Foo Fighters or something obvious?" (Freese did join the Foo Fighters in 2023). "So I went down and met [Axl]," Freese said, "and I really liked him. He was really nice." On the subject of Devo, Freese was impressed that Rose talked up deeper cuts like "Gut Feeling." "He's not just saying he likes Devo and remembering that one hit from 1983. He knows his shit."[7]

"They auditioned drummers at the Complex for months, maybe years," says Dave Dominguez, the engineer who worked with Guns N' Roses when they started at Rumbo Recorders in 1998. "And then it was between Josh Freese and Michael Bland from Prince's band. The audition was, 'Hey, we're gonna play to a drum loop, listen to the loop and play it.' Michael Bland killed it except for one little part. Then Josh came in with his own drum kit, or maybe his own snare. The whole band's in there, Beta, the manager—there's a lot of people in the control room, and that part's coming up that Michael Bland had trouble with, and Josh did something very cool with it and everybody threw up their hands like, 'Oh, touchdown!'"[8]

Bland recalls being aware that Freese was already involved when he was asked to audition. "I got the impression that I was a failsafe," he says. "It was not my dream gig or anything. I just thought, *This could be interesting. A different adventure.*" Bland was in Italy in early 1998 when he received a voicemail from Paul Huge inquiring about an audition. "I was gonna be at NAMM anyway," he says, referring to the annual California-based industry event thrown by the National Association of Music Merchants. "So I was at NAMM and I ran into a bodyguard, Big Earl was his name, I think. I knew him from a tour I'd done with Westerberg. He said, 'Hey man, how you been? Axl wants to say hi! Come with me.' We go a little ways and I see a diminutive dude with a hoodie and wide leg jeans and Converse. I can only make out the jawline."

Rose told Bland everyone was very excited for him to come in and audition. "So I go to Rumbo and the first person I meet his Robin Finck. He said, 'Dude, I'm a big fan!' We got to talking. He said, 'Axl's gonna be a minute, let's get in there and kick some stuff around.' We played and everything felt pretty good. It was Paul, Robin, and the bass tech. We played for a little while. I developed a pretty good blood blister. We played for two and half hours, actually. 'Axl's not here yet, maybe you'd be interested in hearing what we've been working on and taking a pass at it.' 'Sure, show me something.' Some of it sounded like Massive Attack, some of it sounded like Fiona Apple." When it was clear Rose was no-showing, Bland decided to take off. As he was leaving, Rose appeared. "Sorry, man," the singer said. "I got held up."[9]

"Axl loved Josh's playing and that was it," Dominguez says. "So he joined, and he had to sign an agreement to stop session work. But he did other stuff anyway. He was secretly playing on Chris Cornell's first solo record. I'd come into Rumbo and he'd be asleep on the couch. He got there at two in the morning. 'I'm playing on Chris Cornell's record, don't tell anyone!'"[10]

Through Freese, Guns N' Roses cemented their new bass player, another unlikely candidate whose career started before he could drive. Tommy Stinson was only eleven when he hit the club circuit in the '80s with his half-brother Bob in the Replacements. Legends in their own time, the Replacements won over countless hearts by churning out exciting, honest, self-effacing rock n' roll rooted in punk insouciance (all while looking like they worked at a gas station). The group's behavior was insouciant as well. They'd purposely tank concerts by playing classic rock covers and tv themes. There are many colorful stories about the band trashing venues and studios, often the result of their favorite time-killer, "I dare ya." Once, when the Replacements decided they hated all their albums, they got loaded, raided their label, stole what they thought were the master tapes, and threw them in the Mississippi River.

The Replacements broke up in 1991. Stinson started a few other bands afterward, including Perfect. Restless Records spent $200,000 to record Perfect's debut album only to shelve it because they didn't think the music was marketable. Stinson was feeling low. "You work and you work and you work . . . and nothing," he sighed. "By the time the Perfect thing was falling to pieces, I was so fed up. I just wanted to go play bass with some band and hang out." Stinson called Freese, who he was chummy with, just to say hello. Freese wasn't supposed to talk about it, but he couldn't help himself—he told Stinson he was in Guns N' Roses and that they were working on "*the* record."

Freese also mentioned Duff McKagan had quit and Guns N' Roses needed a bass player. He suggested Stinson try out. "I was just joking with him, 'Oh, that would be a fucking hoot,' given my thoughts about Guns N' Roses at that time," Stinson recounted. "But I did it anyway just as a laugh, and it turned out pretty good. They didn't really audition anyone else. They liked me, and because Josh was doing it, it was a compelling notion."

Another compelling notion for Stinson was high-paying steady employment in his chosen trade. Just a handful of years earlier, the bassist was so broke he took a job as a telemarketer selling office supplies to make ends meet.[11]

※

For a while, it seemed like a foregone conclusion that Mike Clink would produce the new Guns N' Roses album. He'd worked on nearly all their other releases, after all, providing a clarity and focus that anchored a very chaotic band. Clink was calm, unaffected; he earned the nicknames Mild Mike and Mellow Mike when he was producing Megadeth's 1990 album *Rust in Peace*. There was a touch of drama, however, when Clink halted work on *Rust in Peace* to start *Use Your Illusion* for Guns N' Roses. "He fucking left," Megadeth leader Dave Mustaine groused in 2020. "In the middle of a project." Clink was adamant that the deal when he accepted *Rust in Peace* was that he'd be allowed to leave whenever *Use Your Illusion* began, which Megadeth agreed to, and that *Rust in Peace* was four-fifths of the way done when he did leave. "[And] it wasn't like I left the next day," Clink said. "There was a transitional period."[12]

Even in the midst of kvetching about this perceived slight, Mustaine admitted Clink was "a good cat" and a great producer. This is the general consensus throughout the industry. True to his reputation, Clink was exceedingly polite every time he turned down invitations to be interviewed for this book. The producer has never spoken at length publicly about his decision to walk away from the next Guns N' Roses album. "I never got a reason, either," says Clink's protege Dave Dominguez. "I'd always assumed he'd produce it. I don't know. He was always a part of it and then, for some reason, at some point he wasn't."[13]

Clink produced albums with a self-described tunnel vision; in the late '90s, there was still no light at the end of the GNR tunnel. In early 1998, it was rumored that GNR had amassed 300 hours of material spread across one thousand demo tapes.[14] [15] Even the most calm and collected individual would be overwhelmed hacking that mountain down to a fourteen song album.

The search for a producer continued.

"I was summoned to Los Angeles to meet with Axl Rose," recalled Steve Lillywhite, best known for working with U2. "We went for sushi and then we went to the studio to listen to some tracks and he played me some instrumentals. I thought, *I can understand why he'd want me to work on this*. And then I said, 'Do you have anything with vocals on it?' He said, 'Yeah, I've got one song.' I listened to it and I thought, *Oh my God, I'd forgotten how much I hate his voice.*

"I'm sorry! To some people, Axl Rose is royalty. To me, it's like fingers on a chalkboard. Now, he was a very nice guy. We finished the evening—he paid. The next morning, the manager called and said, 'Steve, you're in. He thinks you're fantastic.' I said, 'I'm sorry, I don't think I'm the right man for this job.' And that was it and I left it at that. I wouldn't be telling this story except the next issue of *Rolling Stone* came out and it said, 'Axl Rose turns down Steve Lillywhite!' I would have said nothing if he said nothing!"[16]

That wasn't what the blurb in the June 11, 1998 issue of *Rolling Stone* said verbatim, but close enough: "Axl Rose has anointed former Killing Joke bassist Youth as the producer of the next Guns N' Roses album. Youth, who was behind the board for the Verve's *Urban Hymns*, beat out the likes of Steve Lillywhite, Scott Litt, and Moby for the privilege."[17]

The stark, doomed post-punk that Killing Joke created in the early '80s was once described as "the sound of teeth gritting, blood pounding in the temples and nerves stretched to the snapping point."[18] They were an intense quartet, and the dynamic was such that bass player Youth (alias Martin Glover) was often a punching bag for the others.[19] [20] In 1981, a never-identified member spiked Youth's drink with LSD, prompting him to walk to the bank in his underwear, withdraw all his money, and set it on fire in the street. Youth was arrested and placed in psychiatric care. "With Killing Joke, we *hated* each other," he later said of the incident, "but we made great music, and I know at least that no matter what can happen to me in my life, it is *never* gonna be as bad for me as it was then."[21] So taking a job with Axl Rose probably didn't sound all that tough.

Like Tommy Stinson, Youth admired Axl Rose for ripping up Guns N' Roses and starting over. "He wanted to do something nobody had ever done before, which was really commendable, very cool," Youth tells me. "Swimming against the tide was heroic. Otherwise, it becomes Doris Day, doesn't it?" There's a twinkle in Youth's eye when he talks about how excited he was to be with Guns N' Roses at "the Captain & Tennille studio"—Rumbo Recorders was indeed built and owned by Daryl Dragon and Toni Tennille, the soft rock duo who were chart-toppers in the '70s. "I was buzzed to be there," he says with a big smile.

Youth estimates he was employed by Guns N' Roses for over a year and half, working in six-week increments over the course of two or three visits from his native England. Immediately, he wasn't thrilled that Rose was chomping at the bit to re-record *Appetite for Destruction*. "Today, everyone does [re-recording] to get around copyright issues, like Taylor Swift or Roger Waters. I could understand that reckoning but I didn't see the rational wisdom in there. Re-recording a classic album like that, you don't want to mess with that."

Convincing Rose to move forward with newer material was difficult. "Maybe Axl had a schedule in his head I wasn't privy to," Youth reasons. "He just wasn't ready. I respect that. Obviously there's a weight of expectation. The label were happy to let Axl do what he wanted to do, though. They didn't want to put too much pressure on the goose that laid the golden egg. They were the biggest selling rock band. They were still selling 6,000 a week, outselling Elvis by three to one. That band really connected."

When Rose did tackle fresh ideas, Youth marvels that it was "like seeing constellations being born." Ultimately, however, things were not progressing quickly enough for the producer. "I was losing patience. I wanted to nail the vocals down," he says. Moving the sessions to Rose's pool house for increased comfort didn't help. "After the pool sessions, I was pushing hard to begin recording these songs in earnest but I was told I was pushing too hard." Youth says he wasn't fired. "It drifted off into inertia for a while . . . then I read Roy Thomas Baker was helping."[22]

David Dominguez remembers differently. "I was there when Axl fired Youth over the phone. I was the only one in the control room when it happened. Oh yeah, Axl was mad. He wasn't screaming, but he had that tone of voice. Actually, it was me and an assistant named Kenny in the control room. Axl came in, the band was tuning up. He told me to turn it down in the control room, then he called and fired Youth."[23]

"It was an honor and a privilege to work with them," says Youth, regardless of how it all ended. "They're one of the legendary bands. And the new lineup was formidable." He has even greater praise for Axl Rose: "If this was 6,000 years ago, he'd be a shaman."[24]

In April of 1998, SPIN magazine ran an article on the state of Guns N' Roses titled "Appetite For Procrastination." Doug Goldstein was one of a few insiders quoted: "Axl isn't going to force an album because of commercial pressures. He'll keep trying different people and things, and when it's right—however long it takes—he'll be ready to put out a record." Geffen rep Bryn Bridenthal sounded a little over it: "It's entirely possible that Guns N' Roses will deliver an album by the end of the year. But I've been saying that for the past three years." Matt Sorum explained that Rose was "overanalyzing" every other popular rock act on the market and that the singer's obsession with going techno was a dead end. "Truth is, if kids want to buy a techno record, they're not going to buy Guns N' Roses."[25]

Rose was undeterred; he had the lounge at Rumbo Recorders turned into a room for Pro Tools, the digital production software that was suddenly making it very easy to record and manipulate audio on a computer. Eric Caudieux, an expert in the field, was hired to help out. "Eric was paid an outrageous amount of money," says Geffen's Jim Barber. "He was the only one who knew how to Autotune. They paid him $425 an hour. Now you can do all that stuff on your phone."[26]

According to Dominguez, Rose tried his own single-handed experiments at Nine Inch Nails-style rock, including a version of Elvis Presley's hit ballad "Can't Help Falling in Love." Not that Rose was always creating when he was sitting in front of a computer.

"He didn't have Internet at his house yet, so he'd come down to Rumbo and use the Internet on the computer in the control room."

※

"I was hired to be Axl's hidden weapon. He would say that. I liked being behind the scenes. I was just trying to make good product and trying to inspire him to work. That was hard to do."

Chris Pitman was a Los Angeles-based musician proficient on numerous instruments who had a loose affiliation with the progressive rock band Tool, touring with them for a stretch and playing in a handful of Tool side projects. One of those projects was Lusk, a dream pop outfit whose album *Free Mars* caught Axl Rose's attention. He'd heard it through Billy Howerdel, a former Tool guitar tech who was doing computer work for Guns N' Roses in 1998.

"Billy was a guitar tech to the stars," Pitman says. "He worked for Billy Corgan, he worked for U2, then he became Axl's right hand man. Billy's a complete genius. He was smart to get outta there not long after I arrived, and I curse him for leaving me there, stuck with it [*laughs*]. At first, Billy asked me to audition to play bass and I said, 'I have no interest in that.' Then a few months later Billy said they were looking for something more like a musical collaborator. I thought that might be interesting."

Pitman accepted an invitation to hang out with Rose at his Malibu home. "We spent a whole night listening to tapes," Pitman says. "He was in high spirits. He's a great salesman, you know? 'Hey, I already have two guitar players, a bass player . . . if there's some way to get you in here, I wanna find it.'" Pitman and Rose began working on songs together in Rose's home studio.[27] One day just a few weeks in, Rose was strumming two or three somber guitar chords as Pitman demonstrated a number of synthesized organ sounds. Something about the French horn struck Rose; This was the birth of "Madagascar," one of the few songs from this era that made its way into the set lists when Guns N' Roses began performing live again in 2001.

The lyrics of "Madagascar" seemed to find Rose announcing his own resurrection: "I won't be told anymore / that I've been brought down in this storm / and left so far out from shore / that I can't find my way back, my way anymore." He then adopts the tone of a priest to absolve his naysayers: "Forgive them that tear down my soul / and bless them that they might grow old / and free them so that they may know / that it's never too late."

"I took 'Madagascar' down to [Rumbo] for the rest of the band to learn and they said, 'Why isn't he down here with us?'" Pitman recalls. "I said, 'I don't know, call him.' I kept bringing material down and they'd be like, 'He hasn't been down here in three months.' That's how it was. There were a bunch of studio guys, a studio band, and there were guys like me, working directly with Axl." When I ask Pitman if Guns N' Roses ever felt like a real band during his tenure, he thinks for a moment.

"I wouldn't say it *never* felt like a real band, but . . . well, we didn't know how it was panning out. We were all just hired hands and we didn't know what was going on. We were all hopefuls, though, and we honestly thought there was gonna be a record or a band. But Axl's very autocratic. There's no hierarchy. It's him, and then everyone else. No one can delegate authority. That's why it was really difficult."

Pitman also started having health problems due to the vampiric hours Rose kept. "I tried doing the graveyard shift with him, but it was really unhealthy," he says. "I quit after three months. Then they switched it around for me. The hard part of my job, though, was all the instrumental stuff they'd do in the studio and send up to Axl's house. He'd say, 'Go through everything, pick out something that sounds good.' He'd filter through me rather than going through it himself. It's hard to make a judgment off instrumentals. They all kinda sound the same."

"And," Pitman adds, "there were other people sending material in from outside the band." He confirms these outside songwriters were big names but declines to identify any of them.

While Pitman shies away from any question regarding the money he was making in Guns N' Roses, Josh Freese has been candid about his paycheck over the years.[28] "Everyone's like, 'Dude, I heard you got paid one million dollars,'" the drummer said in 2013. "You want to put your pinky up like in *Austin Powers*—'One million dollars to join Guns?' Fuck no . . . It was good money and it was good money for me at the time being a single guy with no kids . . . [but] I didn't get a big signing bonus, you know, and I wasn't out shopping for Ferraris the next day or anything."[29]

Another former band member who speaks with me on the condition of anonymity confirms, "Guns N' Roses didn't pay that much. It wasn't as much as people thought. It was enough to get by in Los Angeles. At least my pay was. And I sure as hell didn't try to buy a new house or a new car, because what if it suddenly ended? Like, 'Aw shit!' [*laughs*] 'Got fired, fuckin' broke again!'"

Things went from bad to worse for Geffen Records that May when parent company Seagram bought Polygram Records for $10.6 billion. Seagram already owned the Universal Music Group, which included Geffen, A&M, and Interscope Records. The added earning potential of the Polygram deal instantly put Seagram in the same league as Time Warner and Walt Disney.[30] [31] A decision was made to fold Geffen and A&M into Interscope, the most successful of the three labels and the most talked-about in recent years thanks to a roster that included controversial acts like Nine Inch Nails, Tupac Shakur, and Limp Bizkit.[32] [33] [34] Everyone knew what this meant: layoffs. "We're trying to pretend there's nothing going on because there's nothing we can do about it," one anonymous employee told *The Daily News.* "We just wish they'd get on with it."[35]

They got on with it January 21, 1999—that day, Universal Music Group fired 170 people at A&M and 115 at Geffen, leaving thirty employees at each label. A large black memorial band was draped around A&M's famous sign as tear-streaked castoffs packed their cars with office accoutrements. At Geffen, there was a sense of relief, according to one anonymous employee: "No one's surprised. Honestly, it was like we came into work today to get laid off. Right now, everyone's out celebrating at the Rainbow Room across the street." The *Los Angeles Times* eulogized both labels: "At their peaks, A&M and Geffen represented the commercial and artistic potential of independent labels, which have been the proving ground for scores of musicians whose talents and vision did not fit into more mainstream labels."

Axed A&M head Al Cafaro was less wistful. "This isn't about Universal or Seagram," he said. "The record business is changing fundamentally. Don't think that there are calm seas on the other side of this threshold. If the quake that devoured A&M and Geffen is a 6.0 on the Richter scale, there is a 7.0 coming in this industry. It's a Wall Street world now. Get ready."[36] [37]

Interscope head Jimmy Iovine pledged to keep A&M and Geffen "exciting and vital." "Anyone who knows me knows how much I revere the legacy of those companies and the guys who built them," he said, adding that Interscope, which he co-founded eight years prior, was molded using philosophies that drove A&M, Geffen, and several other legendary outlets.[38] Talk is cheap, of course, and scores of acts on the labels being absorbed quickly found themselves in no man's land. A&M's Dishwalla was told there were no longer enough resources to promote their latest effort *And You Think You Know What Life's About*; the record tanked.[39] Days of The New had been on Geffen imprint Outpost, which was junked in the merger; Days were asked to re-record their third album even though they'd spent half a million on it, and Interscope refused to dissolve their contract when Rick Rubin tried to bring them to his American label.[40]

Aimee Mann was in the midst of recording her next album for Geffen when the merger struck. Her spring 1999 release date was scrapped and she was transferred to Interscope. "They actually said to me, 'You know, if you want to leave, you can leave,'" Mann recalled. "I even had one meeting with Jimmy Iovine—that he was late to—and when I told him [the record] was finished, he was like, 'It's not finished until I say it's finished.' And I was like, 'I'm outta here.' He was talking about Sheryl Crow and how her last record was a big disappointment that sold a million and a half records. So I'm like, 'Fuck this.' At that point I didn't care what happened. I was like, 'I'll sell this out of the back of a van. I don't give a shit. I don't wanna do this anymore.'"

One of the songs Mann intended to put on that record, "Save Me," landed on the soundtrack to the 1999 drama *Magnolia* instead; it was nominated for an

Academy Award and a Grammy. Mann eventually released her delayed Geffen album, *Bachelor No. 2*, herself in 2000. It wound up being the most successful record of her entire career.[41][42]

Jim Barber, who survived the Geffen layoffs and transitioned to a role within Interscope (where one of his more odious duties was the Iovine-forced dropping of Mann), attests to the lack of deference to the artist at his new home. "Interscope was like Atlantic Records," he says. "If it wasn't working, they'd throw you off a cliff."[43] Gavin Rossdale, whose grunge band Bush was on Interscope for a number of years, once summed up the label's philosophy toward their acts as "You've had a bunch of hits. You better have another hit."[44]

This approach was an extension of Iovine himself, the scrappy Brooklynite who'd been a hard-nosed producer squeezing everything he could out of Tom Petty, Stevie Nicks, the Pretenders, and countless others. Iovine was the kid with the golden ears when he first broke into the game. There's a telling anecdote from one of his first engineering jobs—John Lennon's *Rock n' Roll*. Iovine was futzing with a mix one day, admittedly still learning the ropes, when Lennon and his assistant May Pang sauntered in. Pang announced that she and John wanted coffee, expecting Iovine to jump up and fetch. Lennon turned to Pang. "You get the coffee," he said, "unless you can make it sound like that." Lennon said Iovine was realizing the material exactly as he envisioned it in his mind. Iovine's reaction? "My fucking head exploded."[45][46]

Mr. Golden Ears: Jimmy Iovine with Sheryl Crow, 2005. *Source: Photo by Jeffrey Mayer/ WireImage for Universal Music Group.*

Not every project was so smooth. Iovine had to chew tin foil to stay awake during the grueling and traumatic four months he spent working on *Born to Run* for Bruce Springsteen. The record was mastered ten times; when Iovine delivered the lavish, Phil Spector-influenced end product to Springsteen at a hotel in Baltimore, Springsteen listened to it once and then flung the LP into the pool. Iovine was crushed. He ate Valium like candy on the train ride back to New York. Luckily, Springsteen had a change of heart. *Born to Run* was released as it was and became one of rock n' roll's most celebrated records.[47] [48]

Patti Smith, U2, the Eurhythmics, and Dire Straits all hired Iovine to helm releases over the next decade. As he approached his forties, however, Mr. Magic Ears knew his vitality as a producer was fading. He wanted to start his own label. In 1991, Iovine struck a deal with Marshall Field's heir Ted Field to launch Interscope Records. Many who expected this venture to fail were bowled over when Interscope became the toast of the industry. They were music's most profitable label two years later, thanks largely to their investment in gangsta rap. Naturally, this garnered a lot of flak from conservative pundits who felt Interscope artists like Dr. Dre, Snoop Dogg, and Tupac Shakur were corrupting society. In the face of such criticism, Interscope was nothing less than defiant. "A lot of this is just plain old racism," said Field. "You can tell the people who want to stop us from releasing controversial rap music one thing: Kiss my ass."[49]

"Rap" was still a dirty word in many parts of the industry when Interscope began. Their tenacity played a significant role in hip-hop's cultural ascent throughout the '90s. By the time Interscope was swallowing up Geffen and A&M, there was no denying that rap had totally supplanted rock as the raw, exciting musical movement invigorating the nation's youth.[50] [51] [52] And the turn of the century's most invigorating (and controversial) rap megastar, Eminem, released his quadruple-platinum major-label debut on Interscope. This label didn't need the assortment of rock bands it signed exclusively pre-merger; it certainly didn't need to inherit so many from Geffen and A&M.

That said, Guns N' Roses wasn't just a rock band. They were, in so many ways, *the* rock band. It definitely wouldn't hurt Interscope to get their next album out pronto. Easier said than done, of course, even for a no-nonsense mogul like Jimmy Iovine.

"I never saw the renegotiated GNR contracts [from before the merger]," says Barber, "but I bet Geffen gave them approvals Interscope would've never dreamed of. Y'know, Jimmy said he could fix everything with them. Then the album didn't come out for another ten years."[53]

Jim Barber's involvement with the Guns N' Roses album had been an open-ended commitment before the merger. Once Jimmy Iovine took the wheel, Barber was off the project. That was in February 1999. Easy come, easy go, Barber says.[54] [55] According to Barber's co-worker Bryn Bridenthal, however, his departure wasn't so uneventful.

"Axl at one point told me that Jim came to the studio and Axl felt Courtney Love energy coming off of him and made Jim leave," Bridenthal said. "He couldn't work with that energy in the room. What I found out later, and what Axl didn't know then, either, is that Barber had taken up with Courtney. They kept it a secret from me and the company. So for Axl to feel Courtney Love energy coming off Jim Barber's forehead, not knowing that they had a relationship, was sort of like, Whooooo! . . . Jim's work on the album ended shortly after [that]. Because Axl thought that Courtney was evil and that her evilness would impact the record."[56]

"That is one million percent not true," Barber counters. "I'm glad I'm learning about this now and not then. That's nonsense. Because, you know, how could he not have known? I have many fond memories of working with Bryn and I'll just pretend she didn't say that."[57]

Before he left, Barber did help set a Guns N' Roses live album into motion. *Live Era: '87-'93*, released later that year, was a double-disc release of vintage concert tracks. Doug Goldstein once described the genesis of *Live Era*: "What it came down to literally was every single month I'd have to have a meeting with Jimmy Iovine, once Geffen was sold to the Interscope A&M grouping. And Jimmy would just rip my ass about why he didn't have [the new] record. And so he came to me and said, 'Look, you need to give me something . . . *something*!' And so I arranged where the live record counted against our album commitment and it also put something out that the label would be able to take a look at."[58]

"Doug came into my office," Barber remembers. "He said, 'The new record won't be ready this year, but Axl wants to do a live record.' Del James, who was one of Axl's right hand guys, he went through every *Use Your Illusion* [concert recording] and picked out the best versions. Del proudly presented me with this two CD set. The performances were outstanding, but they were flat mixing board recordings. They were doing stereo on the fly, it wasn't multitrack."

Needing recordings with more resonance, a good portion of *Live Era* ended up being sourced from previously released concert footage on official Guns N' Roses VHS tapes.[59] Intermediaries shuttled tapes between Axl Rose and Slash for their individual approvals. Slash later remarked that *Live Era* was one of the easiest projects Guns N' Roses ever tackled.

As GNR were preparing *Live Era* that summer, "Sweet Child O' Mine" re-entered the zeitgeist thanks to a folksy run-through by Sheryl Crow recorded for the soundtrack to Adam Sandler's latest comedy *Big Daddy*. Crow had fun with "Sweet Child" but felt iffy about officially releasing it. She was probably glad she did after the rendition won a Grammy for Best Female Rock Vocal performance.[60][61] Crow's version of "Sweet Child" was not exactly embraced by the populace, though. A 2011 *Rolling Stone* readers' poll placed it fourth on a list of history's worst covers (not as egregious as Madonna's "American Pie," but worse than "Imagine" by Avril Lavigne).[62]

Big Daddy featured another unique version of "Sweet Child O' Mine" over the closing credits. It's a live rendition by Guns N' Roses from the early '90s that segues into a studio re-recording by what was then the current lineup of the band. Naturally, the logic comes into question. If there's a live album coming down the pike, why not use the entirety of the live "Sweet Child"? Why not use the full re-recorded version to showcase the vibrance of the new players? Like so many decisions before and after, perhaps only Axl Rose knows for sure. *Big Daddy* music coordinator Wende Crowley is at a loss. "Honestly, this was so long ago that I can't remember," she says.[63]

A more important soundtrack opportunity loomed on the horizon. After dipping his toes in goofier cinematic waters (*Jingle All the Way*, *Batman & Robin*), Arnold Schwarzenegger was returning to the action genre that November with the religious thriller *End of Days*. The soundtrack fell to Geffen Records, and new president Jordan Schur believed this could be an instrumental step in revitalizing Geffen post-merger. "I'm a rock guy," Schur said. "I want Geffen to be *the* rock label again." Schur was known best as the brains behind Flip Records, which he claimed to have founded the day Kurt Cobain died ("I wanted to do something to help fill the void"); Flip's most famous act was Limp Bizkit, who they signed in 1996.[64][65]

Limp Bizkit, Korn, Powerman 5000, and several other nu metal acts were slated for the *End of Days* soundtrack, but the real selling point would be the inclusion of "Oh My God," the first original song from Guns N' Roses in eight years. Maybe Axl and Arnold could enjoy a comeback together. It was cultural and commercial kismet when they last paired, for 1991's *Terminator 2: Judgment Day*. Schwarzenegger was a fan—he chose the cold-hearted shit kicker "You Could Be Mine" for *Terminator 2* from six possible choices and volunteered to be in the music video.[66] The actor was not as involved with "Oh My God." Schur was the one who secured GNR's spot for *End of Days* while Jimmy Iovine picked out the track.[67][68]

"I spent a fascinating day in the studio with Axl [for that song]," says engineer Chad Blinman. "It was at the Complex in Studio C. I was minding an ISDN connection to New York where ['Oh My God'] was being mixed by Andy Wallace. Without any prompting, Axl opened up at length about the history of the band, troubles with the press, disputes with former band mates, arguments with Geffen— juicy stuff, details that I think journalists would have paid good money for, but that I would never repeat. It was kind of bizarre. I was struck by how friendly and kind and trusting he was. He was seriously one of the coolest people ever. I'd have encounters like this with him and I'd be thinking to myself, *Isn't this guy supposed to be a total asshole? [laughs]*"[69]

Producer and engineer Terry Date, known for his collaborations with Soundgarden and Pantera, was also asked to mix "Oh My God." "The label called me," Date explains. "I was scheduled to work with this other band, and at the last minute the label said, 'Nah, we'd rather have you do this mix.' I was called in after the song was quote-unquote done. I was there with Sean Beavan—he and I were friends. We hadn't seen each other in a long time, so it was a nice 'hey, how you doin'?' type of thing."[70] Beavan was the latest producer Rose was trying out and the latest Nine Inch Nails affiliate he poached; Beavan mixed the *Pretty Hate Machine* demos that got NIN their record deal and later worked on *The Downward Spiral*. Also, in the early '90s, he played bass in a rebooted version of Humble Pie.[71] [72] [73]

Date continues: "I started midday and we were working pretty much 'til midnight or so to get it done. At midnight, Axl showed up to take a listen. I think he liked it. He and I kinda grew up in the same area in Indiana, and I'd never met him before, so we talked a lot about bands we knew growing up. While we were doing that, people were laying down different versions of the mix. I think we were there 'til really late, or early in the morning."

"I had to catch a plane the next day," Date says. "I was at the airport and Sean called me. He said Axl wanted more low end. He wanted to record a new keyboard part. I said, 'Go for it, I'm on a plane.' You know, I was asked to produce their whole new record years ago, when I was first getting started, but I turned it down because I knew Axl took his time and I didn't want to spend a year doing a record. But I always wanted him to do well. I never had any weird feelings about him and he was super nice the night we met."[74]

Listening in a vacuum, one might never guess "Oh My God" wasn't recorded during the *Use Your Illusion* sessions or that the song was written by the band member with the least musical experience (Paul Huge). The enticing swagger and pushed-to-the-limit venting of classic GNR is alive and well here, albeit with a slight electro twist. Such accentuation does nothing to detract from the solar plexus punch of "Oh My God."

Rose probably could have let the song speak for itself. Instead, in September he issued a 400 word biography of "Oh My God," explaining that it was all about repressed emotions, "the appropriate expression of which," he wrote, "is often discouraged and many times denied." He also took shots at a few of his estranged associates. "Former member Duff McKagan as well as former employee Matt Sorum failed to see ['Oh My God's'] potential and showed no interest in exploring, let alone recording, the piece. When the demos were played for the new band, Josh, Timmy and Robin were, as they say, 'all over it.'"

Rose concluded with a few heaping mouthfuls. "The fight of good vs. evil, positive vs. negative, man against a seemingly undefeatbale [*sic*], undeterrable

[sic], unrevealed destiny, along with the personal and universal struggle to attain, maintain and responsibly manage freewill can be and often is frustrating, to say the least. In America, our country's constitutional right to freedom of expression gives us a better chance to fight for that expression than many in other countries enjoy. It can be a big gig, like kickin' the crap outta the devil!"[75]

❧

"I called all my friends [and] called in five years' worth of favors to make this record," Jordan Schur said of the *End of Days* soundtrack. "And it's a record that all these guys are happy to be on. We have brand new songs that are exclusive to this collection. They are all hits. There's not a throwaway track on this record."[76]

The *End of Days* album sold 77,000 copies when it debuted the first week of November, making it the third most popular soundtrack on store shelves. The collection spent a couple weeks in the number two spot but it would never top the chart. Astoundingly, the *End of Days* disc was shut out by the soundtrack to *Pokémon: The First Movie*, the best-selling soundtrack in America for seven consecutive weeks (*Pokémon: TFM* continually moved units in the six digit territory).[77][78][79] *End of Days* the film suffered a similar fate when it was released around Thanksgiving, unable to compete with *Toy Story 2* or the latest James Bond.[80] Roger Ebert gave *End of Days* two stars and called it "a head-on collision between the ludicrous and the absurd."[81]

Specific critiques of "Oh My God" were not exactly euphoric. "Megadeth meets Rob Zombie," declared Jim Farber in *The New York Daily News*. "Nothing original, in other words, but worse, nothing catchy."[82] Corey Moss of *Iowa State Daily* wrote that Rose "sounds powerless without Slash, like a crackhead doing L7 karaoke. [This is] Filter with C.C. Deville-like guitar solos."[83] In *The Orange County Register*, Ben Wener rejected "Oh My God" as bland "faux-weirdness" but was sure to note that it wasn't the worst song on *End of Days* (that honor was a two way tie between Creed and Powerman 5000).[84]

Guns N' Roses didn't film a video for "Oh My God," not that it would have made any difference. MTV had shifted away from their signature video block programming in the mid-'90s in favor of reality shows, game shows, and other nonmusical endeavors. There had also been a shift in power balance; modern rock radio had grown so much that emerging artists didn't need MTV to help break them. So the channel fell into a role of only playing videos that were already proven radio hits.[85] This dovetailed with the belief that music video as an art form was dead. There were no frontiers left to explore. And why would Guns N' Roses ever try to make another video after their epic *Use Your Illusion* trilogy? Well, they did try, filming a clip for 1993's "Since I Don't Have You" that comes across like a "Saturday Night Live" parody of a Guns N' Roses video.

MTV did grant "Oh My God" the only extended promotion it received in the form an an Axl Rose interview with MTV News fixture Kurt Loder. Loder opened with the obvious question: "What have you been doing for the last six and a half years, since, like, the last tour ended?" "Trying to figure out how to make a record!" a chipper-sounding Rose replied. "Ah, you already knew how to do that, right?" Loder countered. Rose explained that his original plans to make "a traditional record" were thwarted (these were strange remarks, considering the stories from former Guns N' Roses members who said Rose had no interest in carrying on the band's established traditions). "What prevented you from doing, like, a traditional rock record?" Loder inquired. The interviewer chortled at Rose's answer: "Slash."

On the topic of replacing Slash, Rose framed it romantically. "If you know somebody has a relationship, and there's difficulties in that, and Mr. or Mrs. Right doesn't kind of just stumble into their path, or they don't stumble across that person, they can't really get on with things." They couldn't find a replacement for Slash, Rose complained, but that's also not what they were really trying to do anyway. Rose agreed with Loder's suggestion that the *Live Era* set was a farewell to the original GNR. "It was a very difficult thing to do," Rose said, "as listening to it and the people involved . . . [it] wasn't the most emotionally pleasant thing to do." The singer insisted that he wasn't retiring these songs. "In fact, actually, I have re-recorded *Appetite* and—" Loder's eyes bulged at this. "You re-recorded *Appetite For Destruction*?"

"Well, we had to rehearse [those songs] anyway to be able to perform them live again, and there were a lot of recording techniques and certain subtle styles with drum fills and things like that that are kind of '80s signatures that subtly could use a little sprucing up . . . a little less reverb and a little less double bass and things like that." After Rose credited the new players on the *Appetite* re-recording, Loder asked about Duff McKagan and Matt Sorum. "That was their choice to leave. Everybody that's gone did it by choice. Matt was fired, but Matt came in attempting to get fired and told many people so that night. . . . They really didn't think I was going to figure out a way to make a record, [and they] didn't want to help really make a record."

Eventually the conversation turned to "Oh My God." Loder noted that it was "real, real different." He was curious about the evolution of Rose's musical approach. "Basically, [I'm] listening to everything that's out there, as far as music goes," Rose said. "That was a big difference between myself and Slash and Duff, is that I don't hate everything new that came out. I really liked the Seattle movement. I like White Zombie. I like Nine Inch Nails, and I like hip-hop. I don't hate everything. [And] I don't think everybody should be worshipping me 'cause I was around before them." Loder asked how many songs were prepped for the new album. Rose: "We've been working on, I don't know, 70 songs. The record will be about, anywhere from 16 to 18 songs, but we recorded at least two albums' worth of material that is solidly recorded." Later, Rose proclaimed that his vocals for the new album were 75 percent done.

There were tangents about Rose's love for Jane's Addiction (their guitar player Dave Navarro guested on "Oh My God") and a dissection of the term "hip-hop beats" ("There's actual, 'official' hip-hop beats and then there's 'Radiohead-style' hip-hop beats"). Asked what music has been "knocking him out lately," Rose mentioned Fiona Apple but was sure to emphasize that the *End of Days* soundtrack is "a lot of fun." The most vital part of this interview, however, was the reveal of the title *Chinese Democracy* for the forthcoming Guns N' Roses album (allegedly, working titles had included *2,000 Intentions* and *Cockroach Soup*).

"What is the meaning of [*Chinese Democracy*]?" Loder asked.

"Well, there's a lot of Chinese democracy movements, and it's something that there's a lot of talk about, and it's something that will be nice to see," Rose explained. "It could also just be like an ironic statement. I don't know, I just like the sound of it."

Rose hoped the album would be out early in the year 2000. Then there was the following weird exchange: "Have you thought about maybe taking the boys out and playing on New Year's Eve or something?" "Nah." "No? None of that?" "Nah!" "Why not?" "Na-nah-na-nah!"[86][87]

Playing any kind of show would be tough for Guns N' Roses. Lead guitarist Robin Finck had quit the band the previous August, returning to Nine Inch Nails.[88] "I was excited about the material," Finck told *Kerrang!* that December. "The band sounded good. But we'd get a song done to an extent and wait for Axl to write a lyric. . . . I couldn't work on songs with titles like 'Instrumental 34' anymore." *The Providence Journal* quoted Finck a few months later: "We wrote and rehearsed and argued about, and laboriously recorded, dozens of songs in L.A. for several years. Of those songs, two fistfuls are musically finished. Axl is, as far as I know, completing these songs sometime, but work there was done. . . . [There were] way too many Fridays going, Hmmm?"[89]

Rose told Loder that Finck's departure came as a surprise but ultimately worked out for the best as it allowed the rest of the band to "push some of the guitar parts a step farther." Auditions for Finck's replacement were ongoing.[90]

Live Era: '87–'93 was released on November 23, 1999, and its commercial success was a "glass half full, half empty" situation. There was a glut of twenty live albums from big-name acts in the final four months of the year. Only two—Metallica's symphonic experiment *S&M* and a Dave Matthews Band disc—were Top 20 hits. Though *Live Era* sold better than similar efforts from Marilyn Manson, Meat Loaf, and Sheryl Crow, its chart debut at forty-five was dismal for a band that once had armies of fans tearing apart record stores for *Use Your Illusion*.[91]

Artistically, *Live Era* was a staid and plodding patchwork, doing little to convey the white knuckle thrill of Guns N' Roses at full throttle. Gavin Martin from *Uncut* described the album's sound as "gargantuan firepower curdling into a metal mudslide, glistening jagged power chords dragged into the mire by a blunderbuss rhythm section."[92] For some, *Live Era* was too bittersweet a reality check regarding the current state of Guns N' Roses. "These guys had it all and blew it," sighed Dave Herman in *The Fort Worth Star-Telegram*. "[They] blew it bad."[93]

It's been standard practice for decades to sweeten live albums through editing and re-recording and *Live Era* was no different. Guns N' Roses were more blasé about it than their predecessors; whereas KISS and Cheap Trick tried for years to keep the doctoring of their famous live discs under wraps, at least one initial blurb about *Live Era* casually mentioned that Axl Rose and Slash would be contributing overdubs.[94][95][96][97] Sharp-eared fans who were well-acquainted with bootlegs from GNR's glory years easily figured out both the origins of *Live Era*'s tracks (which were not detailed in the liner notes) and what had been re-recorded. Per the latter, it was mainly Rose's vocals, which was mystifying since quite often his original vocal was very strong. In one truly strange overdub, Izzy Stradlin's backup vocals on "Mr. Brownstone" were replaced by a voice many identify as Robin Finck.[98][99][100][101]

"With perspective, I would seriously advocate now releasing what Del James originally brought in for that album, the stuff from the mixing board," says Jim Barber. "Actually, they should have released the Marquee show in London from before *Appetite* came out, but I don't think there was any way they could because of the deal they signed. Of course, you can watch the whole thing for free now on YouTube."[102]

Slash was praising *Live Era*'s authenticity a year after its release, saying "it sounds good and it's real," but expressed disappointment that, in terms of marketing, the album was "[shoved] down the toilet." "It would have been great if Guns, at that particular point in time, was together and were touring," he said. "That album would have been amazingly huge, but there was no reality to that . . . how [do you] work a Guns N' Roses record when the band's not together and Axl's on some trip—I can't really give you an answer."[103]

If this were any other band, the three or four month space between Robin Finck's departure and *Live Era*'s debut would have been plenty of time to find a new guitarist for a promo tour. Alas, it just wasn't coming together for Guns N' Roses. Michael Lee Firkins, a shredder whose specialty was a heavy metal bluegrass fusion, didn't get hired because Rose felt he was too liberal with his whammy bar.[104] Marilyn Manson guitarist Zim Zum was allegedly offered the lead spot but turned it down because he was already too fried from touring.[105] Rob Holliday, front man and guitarist for Sulpher, was invited to play on some material that year but has avoided discussing specifics, aside from saying Axl Rose was "genuinely a nice guy."[106]

Stevie Salas also auditioned around this time. "I think it was '99, but it could have been early 2000," he says. Salas was looking to make a transition; he was coming off ten years of being a hired gun for an eclectic range of names (Rod Stewart, George Clinton, Sass Jordan). "Matt Sorum, who was one of the first people I met when I moved to L.A. and was homeless, called me up and said, 'You should go down and see about playing with GNR!' I said, 'Really?'" Salas reached out. Guns N' Roses asked him to learn a handful of the classics.

"The studio was down in the Valley somewhere. I show up and to my surprise, it's like a cover band, or a tribute band. I don't know what it is. Josh [Freese], another guy I knew real well, he was there. Axl's friend Paul was there. He was a nice guy, don't get me wrong, but he wasn't a monster player at all. He wasn't in our league. It was kinda weird; this guy was a complete unknown, but he was running the show. Tommy [Stinson] was there, he was really, really cool. I had this square shaped Bo Diddly guitar and he freaked out. 'Play that one! Play that one!'"

Salas noticed there were cameras set up all around the room. "I was told Axl was on the other end of the cameras. I don't know if he was in another room or on the moon or some other planet or flying high above us in some kind of jet. [*laughs*] So we started jamming." Immediately, Salas was taken aback by the volume. "When I started with Rod Stewart, playing football stadiums, I had my Marshalls at five. Then, after a while, you relax, you can hear yourself better, it goes down to three. With Guns N' Roses, they were all up to eight. It was the loudest I've ever played and it was in a closed room! And it was fuckin' *loud*! It was the loudest shit I've ever fuckin' heard! 200 Marshalls on eight was unheard of."

"When you have everybody on 10, all that really does is make everyone zero," Salas says. "What they were probably doing was squashing themselves. I call it a guy with a 10 inch dick syndrome. If you walk into a room and take your 10 inch dick out for a second, everyone goes, 'What the fuck was that?' You take it out and leave it out all day, people get used to it."

Salas thought the jam sounded right on, but he couldn't escape the tribute band feel. "The other thing they kept saying was Axl was dying to find a guitar player who knew how to sweep pick. Trust me when I tell you, that's *all* they were talking about. They brought it up to me about 10 times. Jazz guys would sweep pick, then metal guys started doing it. I wasn't really a sweep picker. I was doing all this Chemical Brothers shit on my guitar that was pretty dope, and I didn't really want to learn how to sweep pick. Anyway, we played every song two or three times. Then Dizzy [Reed] grabs me to show me around, and that's when shit got really weird."

"It was the loudest shit I've ever fuckin' heard!" Potential Guns N' Roses guitarist Stevie Salas. *Source: Photo by Jim Steinfeldt/Michael Ochs Archives/Getty Images.*

Away from the main area in the studio, Salas says, there were a number of smaller rooms, each outfitted with a different person monitoring a Pro Tools setup. "They would jam for 10 hours, then go back and listen to it. Dizzy says to me, 'We find two bars of magic, erase everything else, and rebuild.' He wasn't saying it like, 'Oh man.' He was like [*hushed and awed tone*] 'It's a really courageous thing to try to do.' I thought, *Holy shit, this record is gonna cost $20 million*. I mean, when you have Axl Rose, all he has to do is sing, and it's magic."[107]

Salas chose the $20 million figure as a means of exaggeration, but Jim Barber says the bill for *Chinese Democracy* was approaching $20 million when he left the project in early 1999. Barber adds that classic corporate mathematics made that figure disappear. "When Seagrams did that merger and they shut down A&M and

Geffen, they were able to write down all kinds of shit from those companies as tax write offs. GNR was so far into *Chinese Democracy* that they wrote off what they'd spent and started over. God, imagine getting that off your books."[108]

Former Geffen president Bill Bennett insists he never knew how much Guns N' Roses was spending but says the $20 million figure is plausible. "They would have written off each year as unrecouped expenses," he says. "I remember when I worked at Warner Bros, I went to go see Dwight Yoakam and I decided I wanted to try to get him back on the label. So I called the label up and asked, 'Does Dwight Yoakam owe us any money?' And they said, 'Yeah, $6.5 million.' It had been written off incrementally, year after year."[109]

Speaking of money, the more time Stevie Salas spent with the Guns N' Roses members at his audition, the more he felt that some of them were just there to cash enormous checks, "like they were getting paid not to speak up." Salas was still interested in the gig, but he knew he'd have trouble keeping his mouth shut. "Anyway, I never went back," he says. "What happened was I had bought one of those Macs—you remember those Macs that were kinda chunky and came in different colors? I bought one of those and I went online and I noticed a *lot* of fuckin' people talking about me being there, with Guns N' Roses. Everyone knew. So I got on there and said, 'It was pretty cool jamming with the guys, but it's really just a tribute band.'

"That was *not* the right thing to say. [*laughs*] I heard through the grapevine that it pissed them all off. Well, I was rich already. I didn't care. Later on, a guy who worked for the band told me, 'You were super close. They were gonna hire you. But then Buckethead came in.'"[110]

5 THE MOST DANGEROUS GUITARIST ALIVE

"In '89 or '90, I was working as an editor at *Guitar Player*," says Joe Gore. "We got a lot of homemade tapes from players, like *a lot*. One day, one of my mentors, Jas Obrecht—probably the most admired guy in the field of guitar writing because he wrote the first big piece on Eddie Van Halen—he came into my office with a video tape and said, 'You *gotta* see this.'

"So Brian Carroll was a guitarist in this band called Deli Creeps, and they were just a rock band. My recollection is he was just Brian, himself, in Deli Creeps, but as a side thing, he made this joke guitar lesson VHS tape as the Buckethead character. Video tapes with guitar lessons were so big back then, everybody was making them. We'd never seen anything like the Buckethead tape. The technical skill was top of the order, and on top of that, it was such a sharp parody of 'shredding.' We were like, 'Yeah, Deli Creeps is fine, but this Buckethead thing is incredible.'"[1]

Gore wrote about Buckethead's video in *Guitar Player*: "A screaming, hatchet-wielding narrator introduced a teenage guitarist clad in a butcher's apron and a featureless white mask with an inverted KFC bucket on his head. The hatchet man explained that Buckethead, raised by chickens in a coop, was mute, his only passions practicing guitar and killing people who ate poultry . . . then the lanky guitarist began to play. It's hard to say which hit harder: his stupefying technical prowess or the bizarre originality that veered clear of all the usual shred-rock clichés."[2]

"I thought [the Buckethead persona] made sense with the way I play," Carroll said. "I play all this weird stuff, but if I just look like me, it just isn't going to work. But if I'm like this weird freak. . . . It opened up the door to endless possibilities." Through Buckethead, Carroll had the license and opportunity to combine all his disjointed influences: Disney, *Texas Chain Saw Massacre*, Asian pop culture, professional basketball. "Even though I'm wearing a mask and have a character, it's *more* real, more about what I'm really like," he went on, "because I'm too shy to let a lot of things out. Every reason I became Buckethead and am Buckethead has to do with the way I live. It's not because I thought it'd be successful."[3]

Buckethead's look was largely inspired by Carroll's life-long obsession with horror movies (his mother nicknamed him "Boo" at an early age). After seeing *Halloween 4: The Return of Michael Myers* in 1988, Carroll walked across the street from the theater and bought a knockoff Michael Myers mask. "That night I was eating chicken out of a bucket that my dad brought home," he said. "It wasn't a Kentucky Fried Chicken bucket either. It said 'Deli Chicken' on the outside. I was eating it, and I put the mask on and then put the bucket on my head and went to the mirror. I just said, 'Buckethead. That's Buckethead right there.' It was just one of those things."[4][5][6]

Gore gave Buckethead a column in *Guitar Player*. Even the guitarist's vernacular was unique. "Greasy offerings," one column began. "Some people say I'm a disembodied loaf, so I wrote this piece for 'em. Some big-big stretching shards in the right hand but mostly basic fingerpicking pattern, so forth, with disembodied chords for spice and season."[7] Buckethead didn't play riffs, he played "binge splinters" or "danglers." "Whoa!" he exclaimed while teaching an augmented fingering. "My head almost got chopped off again!"[8][9]

"He is the sweetest human ever to draw breath," Gore says, "but he is not a normal musician."[10]

Gore invited Carroll, a native of southern California, up to his home in San Francisco. During that visit, Gore brought Buckethead to meet his friends in funk rock band the Limbomaniacs, who were recording an album with producer and key avant-garde musician Bill Laswell. "Then Bucket became one of the central characters in the opera that was Bill Laswell records," Gore says. In 1992, Buckethead was the guitar hero for the *Transmutation (Mutatis Mutandis)* album by Lawwell's experimental supergroup Praxis. A *Daily Telegraph* review hailed Bucket as "probably the most dangerous guitarist alive."[11] *Vibe* said the "unpredictable liquid groove" of *Transmutation* "made the Red Hot Chili Peppers look like Vanilla Ice."[12]

Ironically, Buckethead tried out for the Chili Peppers, at Gore's suggestion. The story is typical Bucket; after Chili Peppers singer Anthony Kiedis picked him up from the airport, Buckethead admitted he'd never heard any of their songs. He auditioned with his usual rapid-fire fret board insanity. The Peppers eventually gave up trying to play with him and just started applauding.[13]

Bury him at Disneyland: the ever mysterious (and incredibly talented) Buckethead.
Source: Photo by Jeff Kravitz/FilmMagic, Inc via Getty Images.

"He seemed sweet and normal," said Chili Peppers bass player Flea. "He came in and started jamming, playing all this crazy shit, a lot of fast, crazy runs with lots of effects. That would be great, but we needed someone who could also kick a groove."[14] Commenting indirectly on this episode, Laswell said, "Most of this trip is such bullshit that he's not gonna be able to work with many people, so it's lucky that he's finding his way. He's in no hurry."[15]

"I met him when he was about 17, 18," Gore says. "He had his thing together from day one. What he was playing as a teenager is what he became famous for, that mix of traditional rock gestures and freaky atonality."[16]

Musically, Buckethead was deeply influenced by the Wagnerian style of Yngwie Malmsteen, the precision picking of Shawn Lane ("I've never seen anybody more efficient," he raved), and light speed virtuoso Paul Gilbert (from whom Bucket took lessons). He also devoured music theory. "I got a lot of mileage out of Slonimsky's *Melodic Patterns*," Bucket said. "There's a lot of really disjointed stuff in there, like far apart intervals and octave displacement."[17] [18] Buckethead was a devout student of guitar, but that ran neck-and-neck with his enthusiasm for Disneyland. "I want to be buried there. Parts of me in a It's a Small World, Haunted Mansion, and Pirates of the Caribbean, plus parts in Tokyo Disneyland, Euro Disneyland, and Florida Disney World. There are enough bones to go around."[19]

So here was the rare case of a guitar player who was at home on both *Arc of the Testimony*, a collaboration between jazz legends Tony Williams and Pharoah

Sanders, and the soundtrack to *Mighty Morphin Power Rangers: The Movie*.[20] [21] Buckethead also released a number of solo albums, including 1999's *Monsters and Robots*. "For some reason, that record was getting a lot more notice than previous Buckethead albums," says David Lefkowitz, former manager for the Limbomaniacs who spent fifteen years as a Buckethead friend and collaborator. "Supposedly that's how Axl Rose found out about Buckethead. He heard *Monsters and Robots*."[22]

A running joke had developed between Rose and Josh Freese regarding how Freese seemed to have a friendship with or connection to anyone Rose brought up. So there was no surprise the day Rose asked about Buckethead and Freese replied that he'd known the guitarist for years, having met him through Vandals band mate Warren Fitzgerald. Could he get a hold of Bucket? Freese knew Buckethead had recently been spending time with the members of Primus (some of whom played on *Monsters and Robots*). Primus came of age alongside the Limbomaniacs in San Francisco's thrash funk scene before breaking out nationally; Lefkowitz had been Primus's manager since the late '80s. So Freese called him.

"It's interesting, I discussed this subject with Josh recently," says Lefkowitz. "Bucket introduced me to Josh at a Primus show at the Palladium in '93. Two years later, I managed Slider, who Josh was the drummer in. They were led by Matt Winegar. Slider made an incredible record for A&M but it didn't go anywhere because Matt had a drug problem. Anyway, there's this famous interview where Josh talks about this, about calling me to ask about Bucket for Guns N' Roses. And what did I say? 'Yeah, I think he's tired of the starving artist routine. He's ready to make a living.' So that was interesting. I had sort of a minute there [*laughs*]."

"I could have never foreseen Bucket in Guns N' Roses," Lefkowitz adds. "Sort of the biggest challenge with Bucket is he can't deal with people, in general [*laughs*]. So to be in a high level band with sort of a strong leader didn't seem like anything he would be able to do. He always had visions of grandeur, but always on his own terms. Like Willy Wonka or Michael Jackson."[23]

One of the first public mentions of Buckethead's involvement with Guns N' Roses arrived in a *Rolling Stone* interview with Axl Rose conducted in November 1999 but published the following February. Buckethead was named among a "barrage of guitar players" contributing to *Chinese Democracy*, a list that included Rose's guitar teacher Gary Sunshine (who performed on the already released "Oh My God") and Rose himself. "What we're trying to do is build Guns N' Roses back into something," Rose told writer David Wild as he sat and listened to several new songs. "This *wasn't* Guns N' Roses, but I feel it *is* Guns N' Roses now."

The songs Wild heard had tentative titles like "Catcher in the Rye," "I.R.S.," "The Blues," and "There Was a Time" ("TWAT" for short). *Chinese Democracy* was also just a tentative title for the album, but GNR's manager Doug Goldstein claimed the music was 99 percent done, the vocals were 80 percent done, and the whole thing would be out by Summer 2000. "Imagine Led Zeppelin's *Physical Graffiti* remixed by Beck and Trent Reznor," Wild wrote, "and you'll have some sense of Axl's new sound. Song after song combines the edgy hard rock force and pop smarts of vintage Guns N' Roses with surprisingly modern and ambitious musical textures."

Still, since Rose was sole remaining original member, Wild, like many before him, wondered why the name was still Guns N' Roses and not the Axl Rose Band. Rose emphasized that he was no dictator, that the new band was an Algonquin roundtable where everyone had a say. "I contemplated letting go of [the Guns N' Roses name]," Rose admitted, "but it doesn't feel right in any way. I am not the person who chose to try to kill it and walked away." Paradoxically, Rose said he had to assume complete control of the old Guns N' Roses lineup so it could survive. "It is the old story that you are told when you're a kid: 'Don't buy a car with your friends.' Nobody could get the wheel. *Everybody* had the wheel. And when you have a bunch of guys, I'm telling you, you are driving the car off the cliff."

"The reality is, go buy those guys' solo records," Rose continued. "There are neat ideas and parts there, but they wouldn't have worked for a Guns N' Roses record."

When Rose spoke to Wild about Slash, the writer remarked that Rose sounded like a shellshocked husband following a rough divorce. The singer agreed, looking forlorn. "It is a divorce. The poverty is what kept us together. That was how we became Guns N' Roses. Once that changed. . . ." Later, Rose got very candid, revealing that Slash's artistic path away from Guns N' Roses had him crying "hot, burning tears" for the first time in his life. "It was because I am watching this guy and I don't understand it. Playing with everyone from Space Ghost to Michael Jackson. I don't get it. I wanted the world to love and respect him. I just watched him throw it away."

So what of the future? Rose hoped all the time and money spent on *Chinese Democracy* would yield two whole albums. The second one might delve deeper into techno soundscapes. "I'd like to take some of the old Guns fans along with me gradually into the twenty-first century."[24]

A decade earlier, when *Rolling Stone* would run an Axl interview, their Correspondence, Love Letters & Advice section in the following issue would usually be stuffed with readers expressing admiration for the singer. Not so in the year 2000. "Sorry, Axl, you've overstayed your welcome in my CD collection," wrote Caroline B. Wright. "There's just no room for any more washed-up megalomaniacs." Brian G. Loftus commented, "This guy is the rock n' roll version of a car wreck. He's been history for nearly a decade, and we still can't look away."[25]

The addition of Buckethead kept a lot of eyes glued to Guns N' Roses. Could this be a sign that GNR was entering a new frontier, one that required a more esoteric approach to the lead guitar? Buckethead's full-fledged membership in the band would not be confirmed until practically the end of the year, but as early as January he was telling his inner circle he was joining. There was a contract signing in March, allegedly, one that took place at Disneyland's Haunted Mansion, per Bucket's request. Axl Rose was there, happy to oblige this kooky but committed talent. That month, MTV News reported that Buckethead was a Guns N' Roses "collaborator" who was working on material with Rose but noted "he's not necessarily the band's new guitar player." Doug Goldstein insisted that GNR were still searching for Robin Finck's replacement.[26]

Other tides were turning. Ahead of Buckethead's Guns N' Roses audition, Josh Freese informed the guitarist he was planning to quit soon (Freese considered this a professional courtesy so Buckethead wouldn't feel abandoned if he joined and expected Freese to be his buddy on the inside). Like Finck, Freese's enjoyment of playing with GNR was being hampered by the fact that nothing was being completed. Would this record be out in a year? He couldn't say. Freese had another iron in the fire, one that was really heating up. It all started one day during a break when Billy Howerdel, who was working with Guns N' Roses as a studio tech, handed Freese a phone. Howerdel's roommate, Tool singer Maynard James Keenan, was on the line.

"Billy doesn't want to say anything because he's a shy guy," Keenan said, "but he's written some awesome songs. Billy is too insecure to play them for anyone, so don't even listen to what he says about them. I'm going to write some lyrics and I would love if it you would play drums." Suddenly Freese's weekends were being eaten up working on this project, which quickly grew into something very special. "This was much cooler than much of what [Guns N' Roses] were working on," Freese said. He, Keenan, and Howerdel fleshed out their new band with guitarist Troy Van Leauwen and bassist Paz Lenchantin and christened it A Perfect Circle.[27] Their debut album, *Mer de Noms*, was released that May to critical and commercial acclaim (*Mer de Noms* entered the Billboard 200 at #4, the highest position ever for a rock group's debut).

Freese summed up his Guns N' Roses experience by saying, "I had fun playing with Axl. He's a cool guy, but it got really frustrating just reporting to a studio and not playing out live. . . . I was in the studio with Axl for two years and I had to get out."[28]

Rose was deeply wounded when Freese and Howerdel left. He felt a real kinship with Howerdel specifically, who'd spent a few years working Pro Tools and other computer programs for Guns N' Roses. It didn't help that the pair were involved with Keenan. "Axl wasn't a big Maynard fan," Goldstein said. "There was stuff between them." That "stuff" was planted by Rose's psychic Sharon Maynard, who convinced him that Keenan was some sort of negative entity.[29]

Keenan hasn't said much about Rose over the years, though he did take a shot at him during a 2007 interview with *Revolver*. The magazine asked Keenan to name his favorite front people of all time. One of his picks was Bill Murray.

"He was recently busted for driving a golf cart drunk," Keenan said. "That's better than Axl Rose ever did. And Axl Rose wasn't in *Groundhog Day*, so fuck him."[30]

❦

As one might surmise, Buckethead was an introvert who cherished his privacy away from the bucket. One person he did enjoy palling around with was Brain, a.k.a. Bryan Mantia, the drummer he played with in Praxis who also backed him on a handful of solo albums and tours. How did they kill time together on the road? "We like to go to malls," Mantia once divulged. "We get some food, like some Mrs. Fields cookies, and cruise around.... We spend four or five hours in there just watching people. I'm embarrassed to say that. I wish I could say it was going to a museum and art, y'know, checking out real things, but no, I'm a mall guy."[31]

Mantia met Buckethead through Joe Gore—Mantia was drumming for the Limbomaniacs when Gore turned up to their rehearsal space with Bucket in tow. Mantia and Gore had been in a band together as well. "In the '80s, I was in Big City," Gore explains. "For a couple years, we were the big band in [San Francisco]. We were thinking about getting a new drummer, and one night, our opener at Slim's was this band we'd never heard of, the Limbomaniacs. They were all prodigies, and they were all teenagers. Brain was *astounding*, not just in the chops sense, but in the authority sense. He laid it down with complete confidence.

"We wound up stealing him from Limbomaniacs. He played with us for a bit, and it was stunning. Then things fell apart, he went back to Limbomaniacs, and they became very, very big."[32]

The Limbomaniacs signed to Relativity Records and their debut album, 1990's *Stinky Grooves*, got a nice write-up in *SPIN*, but that's basically where their ride ended.[33] They and every other thrash funk band in Northern California were eclipsed in popularity by Primus, whose eccentric backwoods style practically put the "alternative" in alternative rock.[34] [35] Mantia did a brief stint in Primus in the late '80s (Primus singer and bassist Les Claypool was one of Big City's roadies). "But I was still skateboarding," Mantia said. "Then I broke my foot. They ended up getting Tim Alexander. Tim worked out great. They went off and did their thing for years and years."

After *Stinky Grooves*, Bill Laswell invited Mantia to join Praxis, his fusion supergroup featuring Buckethead, funk legends Bernie Worrell and Bootsy Collins, and AF Next Man Flip from the Jungle Brothers. "I played on Steve Jordan's kit, and he was one of my heroes," Manta enthused. "I was like 'Oh my God!' . . . We literally just jammed that first album, *Transmutation*." The same year, Mantia connected with Tom Waits to play on *Bone Machine*. "I really didn't know who Tom Waits was," Mantia admitted years later. "When [Les Claypool] said, 'Tom

Waits is looking for a drummer,' I said, 'Okay.' He goes, 'No, dude. I don't think you understand. People would kill to play with this guy.' It's only now that I understand the magnitude of it. And when I played shows with him, I'd tear up at some of the songs in the middle of them."[36]

Mantia earned the nickname Brain from high school chums who couldn't believe he spent so much time studying classical music.[37] He obviously applied that knowledge to his drumming. "Brain is a fucking *loud* drummer," says Gore. "And so efficient . . . but he can also do stuff that's otherworldly. Once, someone asked him a question while he was drumming, and Brain just turned the volume down on everything he was playing to answer them, like it was a stereo system, without missing a beat or anything."[38]

Tim Alexander quit Primus in 1996 and Mantia was invited back into the fold. Mantia had his work cut out for him; Alexander was revered by the fans, and he enjoyed a unique chemistry with Claypool and guitarist Larry LaLonde. The changeup was noticeable on 1997's *The Brown Album*, which wasn't quite as snappy or vibrant as previous efforts. As one fan put it online: "I think [Brain] missed the salad days." Mantia was honest with the interviewer who brought this comment to his attention during *The Brown Album*'s promotion. "I think as far as being a strong band, I kind of agree," he replied. "As far as being able to headline our own shows and 5,000 people coming every night, yes, I think that's not happening right now. But I don't think the band was that happy when it was really popular . . . we're a happier band now."[39]

High spirits were fleeting. *The Brown Album*'s commercial performance was weak, and Primus's label Interscope started giving them grief. Claypool was also feeling dried up creatively. Primus announced a hiatus after 1999's *Antipop*, but that was just a cover for a total breakup.[40] [41] [42] Thus, Mantia was in the market for new opportunities when Buckethead called in early 2000 to talk Guns N' Roses. "Hey, Josh is leaving," Bucket said. "Do you want to come and play? Axl's an awesome dude, you should come check it out."

As was the case with numerous figures ahead of him in this narrative, Mantia was unsure he even wanted to try out for Guns N' Roses. It wasn't his métier. "I thought Axl was cool when he was throwing the mic around and going crazy just being a freak, but I [didn't] really listen to their music," he said. Regardless, Mantia decided to give it a chance. GNR rolled out the red carpet, buying him a first class ticket from San Francisco to Los Angeles and ushering him to their studio in a Mercedes. Axl Rose was there; Mantia thought he was cool. They chit-chatted for a while and then Mantia went home. Three months passed. Mantia assumed he'd lost the gig. Then Guns N' Roses bassist Tommy Stinson called.

"Hey man, we need a drummer. So what's going on? You wanna do this or what? You should come down and jam. Learn some songs and do whatever."

The enormity of what was on the table hit Mantia during his second visit with Guns N' Roses, when he saw his drums set up on a six foot riser in an absolutely enormous rehearsal room. "I'm just thinking, *Whoa, wait. This is kinda cool. This is like when you go to the 10th floor, this is 11. This is* it! *Shit, man. Maybe I've made it if I take this gig.*" Then a wave of dread washed over him. He'd ignored Stinson's request over the phone to learn a few Guns N' Roses songs before this audition. Mantia fumbled his way through the material. Stinson was confused. "I thought you were a good drummer," he wondered aloud. "What the fuck's going on?" Mantia's tail was between his legs. Then a phone in the rehearsal room rang. It was Rose.

"I hear Tommy and [Axl] going back and forth. And at that point I thought, *Uh oh. Now I'm turning out to look like a fuckin' douche.* So I said, 'Tommy, give me a day. Just give me a fuckin' day and we'll come back.'" Mantia knew part of the problem was the drum kit he was auditioning with, his usual fusion type of set up. It was too small. He asked a Guns N' Roses drum tech to set him up a larger, louder "all power" kit. Mantia spent the night at his hotel listening to *Appetite for Destruction*. "I went in [the next day] and just played so hard that four or five drums fell off the risers. . . . Tommy was like, 'Yep, he's our guy, that's it. Let's just do this.'"

Mantia may have been in, but he felt there was still a big intimidation factor with Rose. "I knew, *Uh-oh, this guy may snap on me*," he said. "But my main goal was to play with Miles Davis or Prince. Instead, it went to Primus, Tom Waits, and Guns N' Roses. So I didn't really think about him. I was like, *I'll go in there and talk about Wu-Tang*. I think he liked it. He thought it was cool. Axl has always been into different music. And because I went in naively, it kind of worked." Mantia also admitted that he was surprised by the musical complexity of Guns N' Roses.

"When I started listening to the old stuff, I started realizing, *Shit, this stuff is deeper than I thought*. [Steven] Adler kind of played like Alex Van Halen. He's playing the guitar parts on the cymbals, or he's playing the bass part. He's not just playing through it as a groove. There would be two bars here and a six-beat section. There were like A, B, C, D, F sections. I was like, *Shit, this is kind of complicated*."[43]

Josh Freese, Mantia's predecessor, wasn't surprised he took over the stool. "When I left, I could have told you that Brain was going to come play, because they had already auditioned a bunch of guys in L.A. and didn't like any of the the ones they'd found. I was the one they had settled on, and it was now two years later and I was like, *Are they going to audition the same ten dudes there?* And Brain's a great drummer, and he wasn't doing a lot, so it only made sense."[44]

The addition of both Brain and Buckethead got Chris Pitman excited for the future of Guns N' Roses. "I felt like the band could have been something new with them in it. We all talked about that for sure. The Bucket era was the only hope for that band.

"And Buckethead was so fuckin' hilarious. He had all these nicknames for his buddies. Like he called this one guy Throat Raker [*laughs*]. I was Mother Goose, and this was so long ago, I don't actually know if Bucket came up with that one. . . . I think he did. I was a big fan of Philip K. Dick, and he'd written this book *Valis*. There's a character called Mother Goose who wrote music that did shit to you, like psychologically. So I thought that was cool, that he called me that."[45]

※

Sean Beavan spent two years as the producer of *Chinese Democracy*. He also engaged with Axl Rose socially. Rose invited Beavan and his family to one of his blow out Halloween parties, the one where the singer wore a pig costume (Beavan's daughter took one look at Rose and declared she was going to turn him into a ham sandwich). When Beavan and his wife Juliette bought a new house, Rose showed up to the housewarming party and unleashed one of his hidden talents—mixing margaritas.[46]

"It was a blast working with Axl," Beavan said. "He was a really funny guy. That's probably the one thing that surprised me the most—just how funny the guy could be. When he'd come into do vocals, he'd warm up for like 45 minutes not by singing, but by telling jokes. He was just extremely funny and super nice."

Beavan was under the impression that *Chinese Democracy* was crossing the finish line in early 2000.[47] Interscope didn't see it that way. They felt the album was a few paces behind. The label ousted Beavan for producer Tim Palmer. "I'd recently finished the *All That You Can't Leave Behind* album with U2," Palmer says. "As you know, Jimmy Iovine has a very close connection to U2 and visited the studio quite a few times when I was mixing that album. He may well have suggested me to come in to the A&R person taking over *Chinese Democracy*. I think that was Mark Williams. At that point, they were looking for someone who could finish the record. I was under the impression from the label that we were really just trying to finish the vocals and start mixing." With a chuckle, he adds, "I know they tried this many times."

Palmer didn't have to submit his photo to Rose's psychic for clearance; he simply had lunch with the singer and Williams. "We had a good lunch and we talked about the record and we decided that we would give it a shot." Palmer wasn't thrilled when Rose said he preferred to work nights. "My wife Veronica was quite heavily pregnant with our first child," he says, "but still, I was up for it. I was sent some backing tracks with no vocals, and I thought the backing tracks sounded really good. So I thought, *Yes, this is definitely something I should do, let's go for it.*

"Axl wanted to meet at midnight at [the studio], so I turned up at 11:15 with my engineer, Mark O'Donoghue. There was a tense vibe in the studio. I found the staff to be very . . . not scared, that's not the right word. They were on full alert, that's for sure. Axl was due to arrive at 12 and we had a bunch of phone calls saying, 'Axl's on his way, he'll be leaving soon, he'll be leaving in 20 minutes, he'll be leaving in 30 minutes, he'll be leaving in an hour.' And he finally arrived in the car park at 2 a.m. Immediately all the assistants start dimming the lights and getting ready for Axl to walk in. I thought it was a bit over the top, personally."

Palmer and Rose spent the next several hours working on a song which, to Palmer's dismay, had no lyrics. "He had ideas for melodies, and he was singing lines of melody, of syllables, but no actual words. So I felt it quite frustrating because the obvious thing at that point for me to do was to let Axl work at home until he had finished melodies with lyrics, and then try singing them, and help him with the performance and give input. He didn't want to do it like that. He definitely seemed like he was very comfortable working with me and we were getting on quite well, but I can't honestly say I was enjoying the process."

Two or three nights went by like this. Palmer found himself driving home on the 405 freeway at the sun was coming up, wondering, *Do I really want to do this that badly that I'm prepared to punish myself this much?* Palmer realized this wasn't going to work out. "Rather than having telephone numbers for everyone in those days, we were all given a Blackberry pager," he says. "It was quite a unique thing at the time. So I got out my Blackberry pager, which I'd only had for a couple of days, and I wrote a long text to Axl explaining my situation and saying that I'm going to have to back out and I wished him well with the record and told him how much I enjoyed him.

"And he just replied to me and said—these are the exact words, I'll never forget—'Fuck you. Lose my pager number, you putz.' So that was it, really. But I must point out, I wasn't backing out because I didn't like the music. I actually thought the record was pretty good. This just wasn't the right thing for me to be doing at the time."[48]

After Palmer, storied producer Roy Thomas Baker was hired to breathe life into Guns N' Roses, an idea that is said to have originated with Interscope president Tom Whalley. This frustrated the band for a couple reasons. One, they'd been under the impression that at some point Iovine himself would enter the studio with them for x amount of time, lending them his magic ears. Two, Roy Thomas Baker exuded all the worst stereotypes of a record producer: weird, tyrannical, expensive.

Baker liked to luxuriate in a La-Z-Boy recliner at the studio console, an ice bucket of Dom Perignon at his side, listening to playback at deafening volumes.[49] He loved to brag that his wife Tere Livrano had briefly appeared in *The Godfather*.[50] Baker drove a white Rolls Royce with a matching white suit during the day; once the sun went down, he switched to a black Rolls Royce with a black suit.[51] You can get away with being like this when you've produced "Bohemian Rhapsody" for Queen and all those late '70s hits for the Cars.

The man who made "Bohemian Rhapsody:" Roy Thomas Baker in 2002. *Source: Photo by Kevin Winter/Getty Images.*

In a 1987 interview, Axl Rose mentioned Baker was on his band's shortlist to produce *Appetite for Destruction*: "[He's] supposed to be just crazy, kind of a psycho. I have been really looking forward to meeting him because of that."[52] And Baker was a Guns N' Roses fan. "When I think of 'November Rain' . . . and 'Welcome to the Jungle' . . . these are tracks that go down in history," he remarked when he was brought aboard for *Chinese Democracy*. "These are tracks that you remember exactly where you were when you first heard them. That's very, very rare that you ever get into a situation where you can actually remember what you were doing the first time you heard something."[53]

Baker arrived and the pages of the calendar flew off. By fall, Axl Rose felt *Chinese Democracy* was ready to be mixed. Was it, though? To that end, fresh ears were summoned in the form of Bob Ezrin. One of biggest hard rock producers of the '70s, Ezrin helped define the decade's sound on albums by Alice Cooper, Aerosmith, and Pink Floyd. Like Iovine and Baker, he was no pussyfooter. Ezrin screamed at Lou Reed to get the most out of him for *Berlin*, and he put KISS through hell to yield their most varied and accessible effort, *Destroyer*.[54] [55] More recently, Ezrin had swooped in to rescue *The Fragile* by Nine Inch Nails; the album was just "an abstract blob" in singer Trent Reznor's words until Ezrin helped sequence the songs and push the whole thing across the finish line.[56] Maybe Ezrin could do the same for Guns N' Roses.

"I agreed to go there immediately and listen to a bunch of stuff," Ezrin said. "I don't want to be insulting because [Axl] worked very hard on it—but what I heard was something that he had painted over too many times. So, by the time I heard it, the original content was lost and it was just a highly produced piece of something. . . . I went to see Jimmy Iovine and I gave him my perception of the situation, including the fact that they had to get out of Rumbo [Recorders] immediately— not because Rumbo is a bad studio, it's a wonderful studio—but because they needed to be closer to the scrutiny of the record company and Jimmy's team, so there could at least be some measure of control."[57] Indeed, when Rumbo was built in 1977, founder Daryl Dragon purposely chose to put it off the beaten path in a West Valley vacation spot, away from the distractions of L.A. proper.[58]

Axl Rose avoided seeing Ezrin one-on-one until it was absolutely necessary. Ezrin was having dinner at home when Iovine called to pry him away for the summit. "I told him, 'Okay, I will be there at 8PM and I will leave there at 8:30, whether Axl shows up for not,' because that was Axl. Because the last time we had an appointment at 10PM and Axl showed up at two in the morning. . . . I went to the restaurant at eight and a team of Axl supporters and hangers-on showed up and joined me at the table—and no Axl. Axl finally came about 8:25. [*laughs*] . . . When he sat down, he started saying to me that he has finished the record. And I said, 'Axl we are not ready to mix this record. . . . There are two great songs on it and I know you're capable of more, that's the reason why I'm here. You're such a great talent and I would do you a disservice if I didn't tell you the truth, which is that most of the songs aren't great. But I'm very happy to help you get there and I believe it's possible, if you would like to continue to work on the record, to make it better.'

"He said, 'I don't agree with that. We are ready to mix.' And I told him, 'You have my number, if you change your mind let me know, but I have a dinner party at home now and I have to go.' I left and I haven't heard from him since."[59]

Chinese Democracy was not mixed that Fall. Guns N' Roses did accept Ezrin's suggestion that they leave Rumbo Recorders, though (Toni Tennille, Rumbo co-owner, was thankful for their patronage; all the money GNR spent blocking out studio time allowed her to retire).[60] *Chinese Democracy* was moved to the Village, another exalted facility alternately known as the Village Recorder. The Village was a magical space where Bob Dylan recorded *Planet Waves* and where the monolithic seven-sided Studio D was built for Fleetwood Mac's *Rumors*. In the '90s, *Mellon Collie and The Infinite Sadness* and *Adore* by Smashing Pumpkins were both cut in the Village's Studio B, which had a bizarre set up.

"The control room faces a wall, so you can't see the musicians," explained the Band's Robbie Robertson, "and there's an elevator for the piano for no reason whatsoever . . . When I recorded in there, I set up some of my musicians in the bathroom, and we came up with some great stuff. Why it works is a bit of a mystery to everyone. The Village just has a lot of soul."[61]

"I was working on my own stuff when *Chinese Democracy* came in," says Matt Marrin, who started at the Village as a runner and worked his way up to second engineer. "That was kind of a unique project. There was a lot of discussion—'*How many* years have they been working on this stuff?' And there was a little discussion, like, 'Don't put me on it.' We all knew what it was. And it took a bit to deal with Roy. We had to deal with him previously as runners and assistants. You know, we had a Chili Peppers record and a Tom Petty record and a Rage Against the Machine record . . . there were a lot of crazy records going on. This came after some of those."

"At the time, I was traveling to New York," Marrin continues. "The studio manager Sharon Sue Lewis called me and said, 'We wanna put you on this thing.' I was a little reluctant. I had other things that I wanted to work on, and there was a fear that once you get on it, you're stuck on it. Well, I went on the gig for one day. [*laughs*] You know, it was probably a half day. [*laughs again*] The problem was between Roy and I, and it's really pretty funny. It's the only project I've ever been fired from in my entire life. I honestly don't know why. I've worked on a lot of big records, I've got a Grammy. . . . I don't have problems working with big names or producers. It was just an issue between Roy and I."

Marrin describes being thrust into a chaotic environment for his half day. "There was a lot of communication and requests coming in from different people upstairs, like Buckethead wanted certain tapes or whatever, and there were requests coming in from different people downstairs, and I was new. Roy came in, looked at me, and said, [*in thunderous tone*] 'What are you doing? Why are you touching that?' I said, 'So and so told me to get this tape.' So we were off to a weird start. The next incident that happened is that he was complaining about the draft from the air conditioning in the control room and, for whatever reason, my response was something he didn't like. I don't think it was particularly off-putting. I think he wanted me to say something like, 'Yes sir, I'll get that fixed right away, sir!' Then he asked me to leave the room.

"So I did, and I saw the owner Jeff Greenberg in the hall. I was like, 'I got canned. You need to get someone else on this.'"[62]

One of the most patently ridiculous facts about *Chinese Democracy* is that Bryan Mantia was forced to re-record every single drum part Josh Freese recorded for the album before him, beat for beat, note for note, in a meticulous and draining process that lasted eight months. It is hard to say what is more mind-boggling— that Mantia was asked to do this, that he did it, or that he did it without physically attacking anyone in the studio.

Axl Rose and producer Roy Thomas Baker were both in agreement that Freese's drums needed a do-over. Rose had hang-ups about retaining the work of someone no longer in the band; Baker thought the drums didn't sound organic enough. Mantia's looser approach certainly had a natural feel that seemed to elude Freese in his otherwise wizardly command of percussion. To that end, Rose initially asked Mantia to merely re-record everything in his own style.

Mantia, it should be noted, had nothing but admiration for Freese. "He's an amazing technician," Mantia said. "I saw him with Nine Inch Nails. It's one of the greatest things I've ever seen, just technically and how he can play something so fluid and perfect." Mantia discussing the differences in their respective styles as it pertained to *Chinese Democracy*: "There's one song where there's a bunch of 16th notes going by. Every time [Josh is] doing the fill, he keeps the kick drum going, doing eighth notes. It's the Keith Moon style. My style is way more Wu-Tang. When I did that beat, I did it like the GZA from *Liquid Swords*.

"[Axl] came back and was like, 'Uh oh. There's too much space. I don't think Brain doing his thing will work.' . . . [He] said, 'Why don't you keep your feel and what you do, but do all of Josh's parts.'"[63] Mantia was slightly incredulous. "So I'm like, 'So, I'm gonna have to transcribe every, like, 30-something songs?' I'm like, 'Pffft, oh man, I'm not getting paid enough for this.'" The drummer took two CDs worth of songs to the head of transcription at Sony Studios. It took them a month to write out note for note all of Josh Freese's drumming. In the meantime, Baker ferried Mantia all over town in his Rolls Royce to assemble the perfect drum kit.

Mantia has maintained that in the end he wasn't especially bothered spending almost a year surrounded by sheet music, painstakingly recreating Josh Freese's drumming. He seems to have had fun with the process. Early on, he moved his setup from the Village's main room to an allegedly haunted upstairs auditorium for better vibes ("You just had, like, Kenny G in [the main room]," he told Jeff Greenberg; "I can't have my shit sounding the same as a Kenny G album"). And

Mantia appeared to take pride in the fact that he holds the record for having drums set up the longest at the Village—four or five or six years, depending on who you ask.

The drums weren't the only instrument being re-recorded. In fact, *everything* was being re-recorded, per Baker's demand, until they found the proper sound. This was very irritating to Tommy Stinson, who later groused that Baker had to try "every Marshall guitar amp in a five state area."[64] Stinson was from the "use what you got" school, even if it's broken. When his old band the Replacements were recording their major-label debut *Tim* in 1985, front man Paul Westerberg played guitar through the whole album with at least one blown speaker in his amp.[65] And the Replacements sure didn't take kindly to overbearing producers. Stinson in particular rebelled with extra fervor when Tony Berg was hired to whip the band into mainstream darlings for 1989's *Don't Tell a Soul*. Windows were smashed, instruments were obliterated, Berg's hand was mangled after Stinson kicked a car stereo while Berg was changing the station.

Berg was finally fired after Stinson broke down in tears and told Westerberg he couldn't take it anymore.[66] Alas, there was no such camaraderie in the new Guns N' Roses. Stinson dug in and stuck it out, perhaps worried that without GNR he'd have to go back to telemarketing.

Buckethead was also not thriving under Roy Thomas Baker. The monotony of coming in day after day to keep recording the same pieces of music over and over again was wearing on him. And he never saw Axl, the guy who was supposedly most agog over his guitar playing and had to have him in the band. Bucket's breaking point was on the horizon.[67]

With all the re-recording going on and all the re-recording that *had* been going for years at various studios with so many different producers, engineers, and musicians, it's a wonder nothing from *Chinese Democracy* had leaked by this point. A miracle, practically, in the year 2000, when online file-sharing network Napster was running wild. Major labels were still trying to figure out how to create and market digital music files when computer science student Shawn Fanning read one book on coding and created Napster, a peer-to-peer program that allowed users to easily swap MP3 files with one another at no cost.[68]

The ethical debate over Napster exploded that April when Metallica hurled a $10 million lawsuit against the company for copyright infringement and racketeering. The band was angry that their entire catalog was being downloaded for free by hundreds of thousands of users, but the impetus was a brand-new unreleased song called "I Disappear" leaking out of their vault, onto Napster, and subsequently onto FM radio. Stations across America were playing "I Disappear" before Metallica even knew Napster existed.[69] [70]

It is of course entirely possible that material from *Chinese Democracy* was being passed around Napster and no one noticed—at its zenith, the service had an estimated seventy-five million users, and thousand of people could be using it at the same time.[71 72] Then again, if Metallica, Madonna, and even the Tragically Hip noticed their music had been leaked ahead of schedule, Axl Rose probably would have noticed too.[73 74]

※

A week before Halloween, there was a bombshell: Guns N' Roses would end their seven year concert drought by performing the following January at the third Rock in Rio festival in Brazil.[75] Reportedly, it took festival organizer Robert Medina six months of negotiations to cajole Axl Rose into signing the contracts. Also confirmed for the first time: Guns N' Roses had three guitarists: Buckethead, Paul Huge—now going by Paul Tobias—and the surprise return of Robin Finck. The prevailing logic, as Finck described it, was that GNR needed another lead guitarist who was less of a "stunt player" than Buckethead, one who could be relied on to keep the songs from going off the rails. The tension of having two lead guitarists probably served the angry, paranoid base of the music as well.

There was another surprise for Chris Pitman, Rose's songwriting partner who up to this point had played all manner of instruments for Guns N' Roses. "Axl came in one night with a drawing of the stage design, and he was like, 'You'll be up here on keyboard,'" Pitman says. "And I was like, 'What?' And you know, at first I thought it would be fun, but it turned out to be a lot of work. Being a keyboardist is exhausting."[76]

There had been a sign that GNR might be returning to the concert stage. The previous June, Rose made a surprise appearance at the Cat Club on Sunset Boulevard to sing a couple Rolling Stones songs with his former band mate Gilby Clarke, who was there jamming with his group the Starfuckers. Starfucker and Cat Club owner Slim Jim Phantom wasn't sure he believed the bartender when he pointed out that a nondescript figure leaning against the bar in a ball cap was Rose. "I took Gilby over and tapped the guy on the shoulder," Phantom recalled. "He turns around and Gilby says, 'That's not him!' But Axl grins and says, 'Hey Gilby, how're you doin'?'"

The crowd ate Axl up and the experience seemed to recharge his batteries. He was ready to get out there again. Before Rock in Rio, though, Guns N' Roses would ring in 2001 in Vegas.

"To tell you the truth, when they first called, I thought it was a joke," said Kevin Morrow, Senior VP of Entertainment for House of Blues. "I said to myself, 'There's no way this can be real.'" Sure enough, Guns N' Roses were contacting him in late November, adamant about wanting to book the company's Mandalay Bay location in Las Vegas for New Year's Eve. The venue had already been booked for that auspicious date, naturally, by the Goo Goo Dolls (with opening act Epstein's

Mother). Nevertheless, Guns N' Roses was accommodated; the Goo Goo Dolls would finish at midnight, GNR would start an hour later. "We'll see if they play," smirked Robby Takac, bassist for the Goos. He didn't mind Axl horning in on his action. "I'll be plastered by then."[77]

House of Blues made it clear that the Guns N' Roses performance was a separate event with its own tickets ($153 general admission, $253 for reserved seating; Goo Goo Dolls tickets were between $78 and $178). "After [the Goo Goo Dolls] play, fans will be ejected," *The Las Vegas Review-Journal* noted.[78] [79] Guns N' Roses attendees had a two-hour wait to get in once the Goos departed; Rose wanted every patron searched for cameras and tape recorders. The show didn't actually start until 3:30 a.m.[80] When it did, the introductory preamble included a crudely animated cartoon depicting Rose as the weird shut-in the world perceived him to be, saving his urine in jars and angrily demanding his bedpan from a servant.

Both *Rolling Stone* and *The New York Times* thought the two hour, twenty song show was great but felt that Rose and the band lacked confidence when playing new material (only four cuts from *Chinese Democracy* debuted that night—"Rhiad N' The Bedouins," "The Blues," "Silkworms," and the title track). In *Rolling Stone*, Richard Abowitz noted that Axl, still wailing like a banshee, appeared to be a changed man. "His once omnipresent cigarette was nowhere in sight, and he was good natured throughout the show, despite a few of the technical glitches that used to throw him into a rage; he also showed off the results of some serious weightlifting.[81] [82] Similarly, the *Los Angeles Times* suggested this could be the beginning of a new era for Axl, a la Aerosmith in the late '80s.[83]

"I have traversed a treacherous sea of horrors to be here with you tonight," Rose told the crowd at the start of the concert. On paper, that sentence sounds dramatic, but Rose's delivery was tongue-in-cheek. At another point, the singer joked about waking up from an eight year nap.

"I was nervous myself [for the first concert]," Mantia said, "because I was like, *Wow, this is a lot of music to remember. It's not really my style 100 percent.* There wasn't that freedom of Primus, where it was like jazz—we had no setlist. Les would just call off songs and we'd start playing them. With this, I got nervous about the technical side and if I could do well for this band. I didn't understand the magnitude of, *There's no more Slash or Duff. Shit. This is a big deal for Axl.* My thought was, *I'll just keep a beat.* That was my protection. I didn't let myself go there. It's only later I realized, *What the hell? I can't believe I went through that.*"

Rose confessed onstage in Las Vegas that he'd only rehearsed with the band once before the show, the previous Thursday, which was the first time he'd sung an entire set in eight years. Mantia seemed to dispute that long after the fact, saying the only time Rose showed up during the month GNR spent rehearsing for their January 14th appearance at Rock in Rio was the day before all their equipment had to be shipped to Brazil. And Rose didn't sing with the band that day; he sat on a couch and watched them. The band was well into an all-night rehearsal when Rose materialized. The atmosphere was even more surreal as these particular rehearsals were taking place on a massive movie studio soundstage.

"All I can remember is, I'm playing 'November Rain,'" Mania said. "They have the curtain of sparks bouncing off my cymbals, burning my face, getting on my shorts and shit like that. The [lot] door opens—it's *daylight!* You see people coming to work. . . . [Axl's] in the chair with his arms crossed, just watching. Bombs, fireworks, everything's fuckin' going off. We end with 'Paradise City,' do the fuckin'' shuffle [outro], they blew the confetti shit, the shit they do at the Super Bowl that goes all over, and has six inches off the ground of a football field, so you can imagine how much it filled this place up . . . in my mind, I'm just going, *Who's gotta fuckin clean the confetti? What are we doing? Some poor guy has to sweep fuckin six inches of confetti.*

"We hit the last note. [Axl] gets up, walks out. Never said a word, didn't see him. We just get up, everybody goes home, and the next time we saw him was in Rock in Rio."

※

Guns N' Roses played Rock in Rio II in January 1991, which kicked off the day after America started bombing Iraq as retaliation for their invasion of Kuwait. "The war is making everyone's stomach turn," Slash remarked, "but Saddam Hussein must be stopped at all costs."[84] Reggae star Jimmy Cliff opened Rock in Rio II with a different message, imploring Saddam Hussein and George Bush to seek peace in lieu of another Vietnam. The crowd roared with approval.[85]

Generally speaking, however, most Brazilians viewed this nine day event as pure escapism, in part because Rock in Rio II was designed that way. Coca-Cola poured $20 million into the festival; among the services on site were a bank and a post office; the hot dogs they sold there were called "rock dogs."[86] [87] By the time of Rock in Rio III, founder Robert Medina's perspective had shifted. He'd been kidnapped shortly after Rock in Rio II and held for ransom in a city slum. The poverty and desperation he witnessed left him dismayed.

And so Rock in Rio III had social objectives. The actual full name of the 2001 festival was Rio Rock Festival For a Better World. Medina started handing out scholarships to economically disadvantaged students, and he promised that 5 percent of the Rock in Rio gross (an estimated $6 million) would to to charity. Of course, he once again had a corporate sponsor, AOL, who ponied up $20 million. A who's who of acts were booked, including Guns N' Roses, Britney Spears, Sting, Red Hot Chili Peppers, Oasis, 'N Sync, FooFighters, Beck, and Neil Young.[88]

As with Rock in Rio II, Rock in Rio III was criticized for favoring international acts over domestic ones.[89] A number of high profile Brazilian acts, including the funk rock band O Rappa, decided to boycott the fest because the time slots and pay they were offered were not as favorable as what was given to the foreign players. It was a difficult call, because exposure of this size (in terms of both audience size and media coverage) might never come again.[90] Over one million people were expected to attend this seven day celebration; the home audience (Rock in Rio III was being televised throughout Latin America) was anticipated to be one billion.[91][92]

Guns N' Roses were slotted as the headliner for January 14th, Rock in Rio III's third day. Some questioned whether they were up for it. "If Guns N' Roses can defy the passage of time at the Rock in Rio festival, then so can just about anyone with a back catalogue and a microphone," sniffed *The Independent*. "The band, a caricature of hard-living rock stardom, was a throwback even in its vomit-stained glory days, the late 1980s. . . . What remains of the group is scarcely recognizable as Rose now heads an entirely reconstituted team and is the only member of the original lineup which found fame with the *Appetite For Destruction* album." The article this quote came from was a larger look at faded musical acts finding new fame overseas, like Deep Purple playing concerts in Lithuania and Boney M appearing in Pakistan.[93]

Oasis had just finished their set at Rock in Rio III when GNR's muscle had the backstage area completely cleared. Then the band arrived. Dave Buckner, drummer for Papa Roach, couldn't believe what he was seeing. "Is this Guns N' Roses or the Village People?" *Rolling Stone* described what happened next: "Moments after the sound of an incoming helicopter announced his arrival, [Axl] Rose strode backstage in striped sweatpants and an unbuttoned shirt, belying rumors of a late-period Elvis bloat." Before Guns went on at 2 a.m., they had video screens onstage flash ominous statements like "I believe in anger" and "I believe in pain."

"I believe in Buckets!" shouted Oasis guitarist Noel Gallagher, who was watching from the side of the stage. Once Guns N' Roses got rolling, Gallagher had to be honest: "It's actually fucking genius. It's the most disgusting, brilliant, outrageous thing I've ever seen in my life."[94]

In a report for MTV, Kurt Loder dramatically recounted the start of the performance: "Howling pyro fireballs suddenly erupted into the pitch black night, accompanied by a soaring air raid siren guitar note. The stage lights slammed on, and there they were—the new Guns N' Roses—ripping into 'Welcome to The Jungle' as if they'd just written it a little earlier that day."

There was a flash of the Axl of yore during the second song, "It's So Easy." Running out onto the lip of the stage, the singer spotted a fan holding up an offensive t-shirt. Reports vary as to what the shirt said—either "Where's Slash?" or "Fuck Guns N' Roses." After flipping the person the bird and staring them down, Rose blew his stack: "GET THAT GUY *OUTTA HERE*. THAT GUY RIGHT

THERE. ARE YOU LISTENING TO ME, MISTER SECURITY MAN? THAT GUY. *GONE.*" Everything was resolved without necessitating further action.

Rose had his share of between song diatribes, which lasted longer than usual; he was halting every few words for the benefit of his translator, Beta Lebeis. "I know that many of you are disappointed that some of the people you came to know and love could not be here today," Rose said. "Regardless of what you may have heard, people were working very hard—meaning my former friends—to do everything they could so that I could not be here today. I say, fuck that! I am as hurt and disappointed as you that, unlike Oasis, we could not find a way to all get along." Later, Rose defended his decision to play mostly older songs: "I have no intention, and never did, of denying you all something you enjoyed. And I thought it was only fair to you to see that this new band can play the fuck out of these songs." The singer also spent some time badmouthing the Internet, which drew frowns from assorted AOL executives.[95]

Overall, Rose seemed to enjoy himself at Rock in Rio, From one end of the massive stage to the other he dashed, unbuttoned shirt flapping in the breeze as he soaked in the adulation. He grinned and traded jokes with band members, putting his arm around them at various points to share vocals. There were heartfelt moments—introducing Paul Tobias, Rose said, "Without Paul, there would be no more Guns N' Roses." Finck showed his gratitude to Brazil during a solo spot by playing a rendition of the 1978 soul hit "Sossego." After the rousing finale of "Paradise City," Rose gushed over Lebeis, thanking her and her three kids for taking care of him for the previous seven years (Lebeis got choked up as she translated that for the crowd).

Guns N' Roses at Rock in Rio III was hailed as a rousing success by several outlets, though it was noted that the only act to actually fill the venue to capacity was the Red Hot Chili Peppers.[96] Neil Strauss, writing about GNR's performance for *The New York Times*, had something of a measured response (as he'd had for their preceding Vegas concert). "Guns N' Roses is now two bands in one. The first is a very effective Guns N' Roses cover band that happens to feature the original singer and keyboardist; the second is a very eclectic new band that if judged on its own merits would be one of rock's most interesting current acts."

"Rock in Rio was a really great show," Pitman says. "It was really insane. The Brazilians, music is like food to them. They were the greatest crowds ever. We had a blast there. Really, it was the best experience of being in the band. And so the next day, we were sitting around the hotel pool with all these reporters, and Axl said, 'We'll have a record out in six months.' And we all thought, *Cool, we'll have a record and get rolling.*

"We all thought it was coming out . . . and then it wasn't."[97]

6 LA LA LAND

"Guys, I'm having a fucking blast. Can we book a European tour for the summer?"

These were, allegedly, Axl Rose's words to manager Doug Goldstein and London-based agent John Jackson as they were coming in from the hotel pool the day after the triumphant Guns N' Roses performance at Rock in Rio III. "We can make that happen," Goldstein replied, and they did. A slew of June dates were lined up in Germany, the UK, Italy, Switzerland, Holland, Norway, and Belgium. Then, a few weeks before this *Chinese Democracy* tour was supposed to kick off, it all fell apart. Rose, according to Goldstein, was suffering from amnesia.

"Axl calls me up," Goldstein said. "I'm on my way home. He goes, 'I'm on my computer. What the fuck am I looking at, these European dates?' I said, 'Dude, what are you talking about?' He goes, 'I never fucking agreed to these.' I go, 'Axl, look, I'm walking back in from the Hotel Intercontinental pool in Rio with John Jackson . . .' Give him the whole rundown. And he goes, 'No. Never happened. I'm not going on the tour. It's all on you. Fuck you.' Click."[1][2]

An official announcement cited Buckethead's sudden health issues as the reason for the tour's cancellation. "Buckethead has suffered hemorrhaging and has missed rehearsals. . . . Doctors have been unable to determine the hemorrhaging's cause, though the guitarist is going through extensive testing in California."[3] Almost immediately, a conflicting report appeared in New York's *Daily News* claiming that Rose flushed the tour because he was upset with Interscope—they weren't allowing him to tweak *Chinese Democracy* any further. As one anonymous source complained, "The album has been finished to everybody else's satisfaction for over a year now. But Axl keeps going back to remix it and add vocals."

"There was never a scheduled release date [for the album]," countered Interscope publicist Lori Earl. "The tour wasn't meant to support the album. Jimmy [Iovine] and Axl are completely in sync on this album. When it's ready, it will come out."[4]

"I can't speak to Buckethead's health at that time," says the guitarist's friend Joe Gore. "Two things can be true, though. Maybe the situation was giving him an ulcer."

Guns N' Roses' European tour was rescheduled for December, but those dates were scrapped too, again because *Chinese Democracy* wasn't ready (allegedly). Goldstein fell on his sword. "Following the euphoria of Rock in Rio, I jumped the gun and arranged a European tour," he said in a statement, "as our plan was to have the new album out this year. Unfortunately, Buckethead's illness not only stopped the tour, but it slowed down our progress on *Chinese Democracy*. I am very sorry to disappoint our fans, but I can assure them that this is not what Axl wanted. . . . I made a plan, and unfortunately it did not work out."[5] Rose never forgave Goldstein for this touring miscommunication and fired him shortly thereafter.

It was true that Rose at this juncture did not feel *Chinese Democracy* was complete. And so the latest person burdened with going into the studio and chasing the singer into the end zone was the guy who brought Guns N' Roses to Geffen in the first place: Tom Zutaut. Zutaut was one of Geffen's three fabled A&R men during the label's championship seasons in the late '80s and early '90s, along with Josh Kalodner and Gary Gersh. Some, like former Guns N' Roses manager Alan Niven, scoff at the legend of this revered trio: "Josh Kalodner synthesized music for aisle 13 of the supermarket, Gary Gersh had the propensity to get lucky sometimes, and Tom Zutatut was lucky enough to know me."[6]

Zutaut was indeed fortunate that Niven agreed to take the position of Guns N' Roses manager in 1986 after much begging and pleading from Zutaut. No one else wanted the trouble (except Vicky Hamilton, who'd managed the band up to that point but was fired because Guns N' Roses thought having a woman manager made them look weak). It is also true that since Zutaut's departure from Geffen in 1995, Guns N' Roses had been unable to finish and release an album. According to Zutaut, this is exactly what Jimmy Iovine said to him during the initial February 2001 phone call that sucked him back into Axl Land.

At first, Zutaut, who was living in New York, would only agree to a meeting with Rose. He knew committing to this would put him on call 24/7. Could his marriage survive that? Zutaut flew to Los Angeles and had his face-to-face with Rose. "[Axl] was sitting on a sofa in the studio and I was sitting in a chair and he looked at me and he said, 'Before you and I can do anything, I have to know the truth about Erin Everly.'" The singer was referring to a pass Zutaut had supposedly made at Everly when she was still dating Rose in the late '80s.

Zutaut was resolute in his denial. Everly fabricated the pass, he claimed. She'd grown angry after Zutaut lectured her about always holding Rose liable for the problems in their relationship. She deliberately antagonized Rose, Zutaut told her. She had to recognize that or leave Rose. These are, of course, awful, victim-blaming statements to make to a woman whose boyfriend often beat her so badly she couldn't remember where she was. It was also part of the power structure protecting Rose, the famous rock star lining Geffen's pockets, from punishment; this conversation evidently took place right after one of the many times Zutaut intervened during an altercation between the couple, taking Everly to his own home to wait for Rose to cool down.

In fact, as Zutaut recalled telling Rose, his main concern was not that Everly would get hurt but that she'd get hurt, call the cops, and "things would get fucked up for the band and for you."

Zutaut was under the impression this grudge had evaporated in 1991 when Rose requested his assistance mixing the *Use Your Illusion* albums. "There's no one I trust with the sound and the vibe of Guns N' Roses more than you," the singer told Zutaut back then. "I think you probably did hit on [Erin], but I don't care, I'm not with her anymore and I need your help."[7] Was it really still bothering Rose in 2001? Erin Everly hadn't been his partner for over a decade; even her legal proceedings against him were over.

And by 2001, Axl Rose was said to be completely hung up on his other ex-sweetheart, Stephanie Seymour, so much so that every July on Seymour's birthday his already slack work ethic was scuttled entirely by depression. Most of *Chinese Democracy's* lyrics pertained to Seymour, Rose once admitted, and he hoped that one day Seymour's son, who was an infant when they were together, would listen to the album so he could learn "the truth."

Rose made Zutaut swear to God that he never hit on Everly. The two men then spent six hours discussing *Chinese Democracy*. "Here was the Axl that I met in 1985 again. A guy that had a vision and wanted to make the best record that had ever been made," Zutaut said. "And we talked and he said, 'I go to the studio, I tell 'em what I want, and they tell me that they've got what I want and then when I listen to it I'm bummed out. . . . Nobody seems to understand my language.'" Zutaut quickly proved he was fluent.

One specific frustration of Rose's concerned the drum sound on the album's title track. He wanted to mimic the powerful crack of Dave Grohl on Nirvana's "Smells Like Teen Spirit" but the engineers just couldn't get it right. Zutaut took a listen the next day; agreeing something was off, he did the sensible thing—he went to Tower Records and bought a copy of *Nevermind*. "I guess maybe they heard the Nirvana hits on the radio and they just thought they knew the sound," Zutaut said, "but none of them had thought to just go buy the album and listen to it."

Problem solved. When Rose heard the new mix, he was ecstatic. "I've only been asking for that for like six fucking months! You don't understand! I've been losing my fucking mind! I wish I'd called you a couple of years ago."

Rose told Interscope to pay Zutaut whatever he wanted—he was worth it.

For the time being, at least.[8]

Axl Rose viewed Tom Zutaut's arrival like a knight in shining armor. The way drummer Bryan Mantia tells it, Rose was alone in that opinion. "Nobody liked Tom Zutaut," Mantia said. "I'm not even sure I liked him. He was put in the band thinking he could save the band and project. He was kind of a punk to everybody. And I'm not saying I know Tom to where I can say these things. And he never bothered me."[9] Still, Mantia reserves a dash of ire for Zutaut, specifically for comments Zutaut made about Buckethead to *Classic Rock* magazine.

In February 2008, *Classic Rock* published a lengthy behind-the-scenes feature on the making of *Chinese Democracy* from Zutaut's perspective.[10] The album still wasn't done at this point, and Zutaut hadn't been involved with it for six years. Regardless, Zutaut offered a host of fascinating insights gleaned before he was fired in late 2001. The *Classic Rock* article, written by Scott Rowley and titled "Chinese Whispers," was the first time multiple individuals spoke on the record about the chicken coop that was built in the Village Studio's auditorium to appease wayward guitarist Buckethead, who'd left *Chinese Democracy* because there was no forward momentum.

Rumors had circulated over the years about the chicken coop. Some said the poultry-obsessed Buckethead demanded it.[11] Zutaut claimed he was the one who suggested the coop in a spur-of-the-moment brainstorm while trying to convince Buckethead to come back to the studio.[12] In response to a general inquiry sent requesting an interview for this book, Guns N' Roses guitar tech Curtis Laur wrote, apropos of nothing, "The only thing I'll say for the record now is the chicken coop was my idea." Laur declined to comment any further.[13]

Buckethead's coop had the accoutrements of the genuine farmland article, like wire fencing and straw on the floor, but Zutaut described it as more apartment-like, with a few pieces of furniture, a television, a DVD player, and of course a headless rubber chicken and some random doll parts for decoration. Zutaut told *Classic Rock* that Bucket requested the TV setup because he wanted to watch hardcore pornography while he recorded. Rose had no problem with the chicken coop but the singer was mortified when he discovered his guitarist was watching porn in the studio. "Axl is a firm believer that the energy or soul of everyone involved in the process comes through in the final artistic piece," Zutaut explained. Rose took Bucket out of the coop for a stern lecture, which, according to Zutaut, left Bucket feeling so awful he vanished for several days.[14]

"That's bullshit! That's bullshit!" Bryan Mantia replied when asked about the porn story. "That's just mean and rude." Mantia felt that Bucket became Zutaut's scapegoat for everything going wrong with Guns N' Roses. "Buckethead was just trying to survive. He was struggling with it in his own way. . . . They just tried to put Buckethead in a cage, no pun intended."[15]

Further investigation yields no conclusive answers. David Lefkowitz, longtime friend of both Mantia and Buckethead, says he definitely saw pornography inside Buckethead's coop the one time he visited the studio.[16] Guns N' Roses keyboardist Chris Pitman, who often sat in the coop to give Bucket feedback on his guitar solos, says there was zero pornography. "What he did have," Pitman explains, "were all these cut-outs from *The National Enquirer* and those types of magazines—he'd cut out pictures of Michael Jackson and Timothy McVeigh and hang 'em up. And he had a little TV that was always playing Japanese science fiction stuff from the 1950s."[17]

Tom Zutaut offered *Classic Rock* another tale about a puppy Rose brought to the studio as a gift for Zutaut's daughter that got into Buckethead's chicken coop and defecated. Allegedly, no one was allowed into the coop except Bucket, and when he arrived, he insisted the poop remain as he found it inspirational. Eventually the odor was too overwhelming and someone swept it up. Bucket came in the next day and was reportedly upset. "Where is my dog poop, man?"

Zutaut also claimed that, a month after 9/11, Buckethead hit the roof when a newscast showed a KFC on fire in the city of Karachi, Pakistan, collateral damage in citizen protests against the bombing of Afghanistan. "That's fucking *it!*" Buckethead allegedly screamed. "They've gone too far now! I'm joining the fucking army! They are not going to hit KFC, no fucking way!"[18]

During an Australian television appearance the same year as the *Classic Rock* article, Zutaut said Buckethead was making $50,000 a month as GNR's guitarist. Surprisingly (or maybe not so surprisingly), the band was spending even more on rented musical equipment each month, a large portion of which they never even used. Zutaut helped rein in that excessive spending, he said, while simultaneously helping to complete songs. "We were finishing tracks. Doing overdubs with Buckethead and Robin Finck and some stuff with Tommy Stinson." *Chinese Democracy* was coming together. Then Axl Rose went ballistic at a screening of *Black Hawk Down*.

Black Hawk Down was director Ridley Scott's action drama about the US helicopter that was downed during the Battle of Mogadishu. Scott had designs to put "Welcome to The Jungle" in the movie, so a screening was arranged for Rose. An earlier debate among the GNR camp about whether to let Scott use the original version of the song or to offer him a re-recording by the new band went out the window as soon as Rose arrived at the theater. The singer had been under the impression that this would be a private affair. It was not.

"Who the fuck are all those people in there? I was told this was my private screening and I don't know who these fucking people are! I can't believe you lied to me about this! You told me this was a private screening! You're fired!"

"Welcome to The Jungle" was not used in *Black Hawk Down*.

"By the time I left [*Chinese Democracy*], I felt that there were probably 11 or 12 tracks that just needed final mixes," Zutaut said. "We could have had a record out for September 2002. I don't think it would have been an issue. I would have given it another three months for a few more overdubs and three for mixing and, worst case scenario, out Spring of '03."

A few months after Zutaut's firing, in February 2002, Roy Thomas Baker was axed, another reportedly spur-of-the-moment decision by Rose.[19] Baker remained tight-lipped about Guns N' Roses in the years leading up to his 2025 death; he did not respond to multiple e-mails and phone calls for this volume. There are preexisting Baker quotes, however, that one might apply to the *Chinese Democracy* situation. "People need an identifiable sound," he told *Mix* in 1999. "When your song is being played on the radio, people should hear who that is, even without the DJ mentioning who it is. That's true with all the great bands, even the ones that have been around for hundreds of years, like the Stones.

"There are thousands and thousands of bands out there with these really smooth, great, generic-sounding records that nobody gives a toss about. Then somebody like Beck comes along and he hits a can and sings about being a loser and he gets a number one, and who knows what that was recorded on? [*laughs*] And who cares? I loved it! If you don't have that identifiable sound, you are getting merged in. If the DJ isn't mentioning who it is, then nobody will know who it is. It will be just another band, and nothing is worse than being anonymous."[20]

With *Chinese Democracy*, Axl Rose was trying to completely reinvent the identifiable sound of Guns N' Roses, an audacious move, and one that was clearly not easy to execute. An argument could be made, naturally, that a piece of music with Rose's vocals laid on top could be identifiable as Guns N' Roses. At the dawn of a new millennium, though, people were wondering—would any music featuring Axl Rose ever be released again?

Time heals all wounds, but not enough time had passed yet for Slash to even be in the same building as Axl Rose. The guitarist discovered this on December 29, 2001, when he found out about a Guns N' Roses concert in Las Vegas at the Hard Rock Hotel and Casino and tried to get in as an audience member. "I've never actually seen Guns N' Roses from that perspective," he said, "and I was curious. And I wanted to go in a supportive capacity as well." Not wanting to draw any attention to himself, Slash made arrangements to get himself on the guest list.

The secret got out and Guns N' Roses management sent a few representatives to Slash's hotel room to tell him that no former band members would be admitted to the show. Slash tried to negotiate, promising to just pop in the back for a small portion of the show. No dice. Then he found a security guard who would sneak him in; that plan fizzled when the promoter caught wind. Dejected, Slash thought about pranking Guns N' Roses by calling the venue's head of security and saying he was already there.

"It shouldn't have been a big deal," he said. "And if, even after all this time, if Axl had wanted to do a song, any number of our old GNR songs, it would have been way cool." In a statement to the *Los Angeles Times*, Doug Goldstein said, "We didn't know what [Slash's] intentions were. If nothing else, it would have been a distraction. Axl was really nervous about these shows." The gig Slash was turned away from was the first of two nights that weekend, and these two shows were only the second and third concerts Guns N' Roses had played domestically in eight years.

The show itself was plagued with technical difficulties. "I couldn't really hear Axl's voice," one attendee told ABC News, "but you know what? I've been waiting to see Guns N' Roses my whole life, so it was good times." Another fan wasn't impressed. "It's not the old lineup," they said. "I mean, the guys weren't into it. . . . It just wasn't Slash."[21] [22]

In 2002, the music industry was once again looking for saviors. 2001 had seen the first decline in CD sales in ten years, a depression caused by a lack of breakout talent and a handful of expensive flops. Michael Jackson's $30 million comeback *Invincible* went nowhere. Virgin Records signed Mariah Carey to a four-album deal for $100 million in April; she released the movie *Glitter* in September; *Glitter* was such an embarrassing bomb that Virgin bought Carey out of her contract for $28 million the following January. Record executives were trying to move forward, betting the house on theoretical new album revenues from Bruce Springsteen, Nine Inch Nails, Lisa "Left Eye" Lopes, N.E.R.D., the Rolling Stones, and Guns N' Roses.[23] [24] [25]

Demand for more Guns N' Roses was certainly there, at least according to the way *Appetite for Destruction* continued to put up strong numbers. SoundScan reported that roughly 5,000 copies of *Appetite* were selling every week in the summer of 2002. "It consistently sells a couple copies here each week," said Dave Swenson, assistant manager at Westlake, Ohio's My Generation record store, "which is pretty unusual for a 15 year old record by a band that essentially doesn't exist, and with a catalog that hasn't been re-marketed in any way."[26]

The world wouldn't get a new GNR album in 2002. However, there was enough activity for fans to presume they were close—namely, a surprise awards show appearance that more or less introduced America to the new Guns N' Roses and a North American concert tour marred by two good ol' fashioned riots. And before all that, there was a freshly minted Guns N' Roses feud.

Some time prior to May, Paul Westerberg called up Tommy Stinson to see if he'd be interested in accompanying him on a tour of the Midwestern cities Buddy Holly, Richie Valens, and the Big Bopper were scheduled to play on the Winter Dance Party Tour in 1959 before their fatal plane crash. Westerberg flip-flopped on whether or not this was meant to be a Replacements reunion ("I'm trying to find the highest offer for us *not* to ever play again," he joked at one point). At any rate, Stinson was onboard—for a couple of days. Then he called Westerberg back; Axl needed Stinson to stay home. "And I couldn't do it without him," Westerberg explained, "because he's the one guy who can read my mind musically."[27][28][29]

It has been suggested that Rose dissuaded Stinson from following Westerberg on the Winter Dance Party route because it was inviting bad karma.[30] Stinson's back out certainly put a cloud over Westerberg's head; the singer started taking shots at his old pal while he was promoting his dual releases *Mono* and *Stereo* that year. Sometimes he'd sneak teasing references to Guns N' Roses into songs at concerts.[31] When asked about Stinson's new gig during one interview, Westerberg said, "it's the most fun he'll never have. Look, I'm supposed to be the one who made money in the Replacements. And I didn't make any money, so he damn sure didn't make any. How can you begrudge him for making a living?"[32]

Westerberg's response was slightly more bitter in other instances: "People don't move to Los Angeles to be a musician or a songwriter. They go to be a star. That's what Tommy is doing, and I'm not the least bit surprised. It's what he's always been groomed for."[33]

Stinson eventually fired back. "[Paul's] gone out on a limb to say a bunch of nonsense that's made me look bad, that's made Axl look bad, that's made [Axl] feel bad . . . it's just lame. It's really unnecessary, for one. I don't appreciate it, and Axl doesn't deserve any of it." The bass player insisted he wasn't locked into anything contractually with Guns N' Roses and he was free to work with anyone else he wanted. However, he noted, "[Guns] is my priority, and my other priority is the rest of my life. It was never a possibility of doing a Replacements reunion while I was in Guns N' Roses, and I'm in this for a while. And I tell you right now, there isn't going to be one. As a matter of fact, there will not be a Replacements reunion ever. [Paul] blew it."[34]

The Replacements have reunited three times since Stinson made those comments—once in 2005 to record two new songs for a greatest hits compilation, once in 2012 to record a benefit EP for their ailing guitarist Slim Dunlap, and finally for an actual reunion tour in 2014.

The summer of 2002 was flecked with the occasional *Chinese Democracy* tidbit: *The Drudge Report* said it would be out in September; Indonesian concert promoter Tommy Pratama said November. Then, in August, without much warning, Guns N' Roses kicked off the *Chinese Democracy* world tour with dates in China, Japan, and Europe. Rose made sure to confirm via GNROnline, the band's official website, that this tour was nonfictional. "This is a collection of performances I've agreed to, that I have personally authorized, not someone else's good intentions gone awry or a reckless promoter's personal agenda. These shows are important to us . . . we'll be there."[35][36][37]

A batch of quotes from Rose appeared in the form of a press release on GNROnline the day of the first concert in Hong Kong. "It's a dream realized," he said of being in China. "A dream come true. The right time, the right place and the whole thing came about by chance." Rose did not elaborate on the circumstances surrounding the Hong Kong date, but he had jokes about who was currently in Guns N' Roses. "We have Mini Me and Nipsey Russell and Charles Nelson Reilly and Colin Powell." There had actually been a significant lineup change since Rock in Rio—rhythm guitarist Paul Tobias was gone, replaced by Love Spit Love guitarist Richard Fortus.

Naturally, before he could explain what happened specifically, Rose had to go on a lengthy defense of Tobias, one that highlighted Tobias's selflessness in wanting to help Guns N' Roses and Slash in particular. "[Paul] is, and this is the bottom line, a good man, and that's the reality behind things. That doesn't change what took place with old Guns. I feel that some of the recordings we did in that limited amount of time [when Paul and Slash were both in the band] had some of the best playing that Slash had done at least since *Illusions*. I was there, I know what I heard and it was pretty exciting."

Richard Fortus, the nicest guy in the world, 2012. *Source: Photo by Kevin Nixon/Total Guitar Magazine/Future via Getty Images.*

"The world tour wasn't really [Paul's] cup of tea, whereas he's much more comfortable in a studio setting," Rose said. "We're fortunate to have found Richard, who has this vibe kind of like Izzy [Stradlin], but with amazing feel."[38] [39]

Fortus said it was a no-brainer to join Guns N' Roses; Tommy Stinson was a dear friend and the band was sounding "pretty unbelievable." A self-described punk rock kid, Fortus was yet another figure who previously carried no torch for GNR. "They were one of those bands that was kind of marginal," he said. "You know, they had long hair. Certainly 'Welcome to The Jungle' is a pretty undeniable song, and I loved 'It's So Easy,' too. . . . But Guns N' Roses were so L.A., and I was a New York City kid. So it wasn't until much later that I really got into the band."[40] Elsewhere, Fortus admitted: "The money on this one was too good to turn down."[41]

How did Guns make three guitars work together onstage? "Well, Bucket comes out and does his Bucket-ness," Fortus said, "and we just make room for each other. When I go back and listen to *Appetite for Destruction* and the other early stuff, there are definitely three guitar parts there. There's Slash's rhythm parts and Izzy's rhythm parts, and then there's Slash's wanking over the top in between the vocals. That's what we're trying to do live. And I think that's why Axl wanted to go with three guitarists, because that was always missing from the live sound."[42]

There was dismay with at least one other member of Guns N' Roses regarding this lineup change, not because anyone felt animus toward Fortus, but because Paul Tobias didn't leave of his own volition. That's what this player, name purposely withheld, volunteers to me during one of our conversations. "I love Paul. He was amazing. It really sucked that he got kicked out of the band. That's when I saw the real ugliness, that even a childhood friend could get kicked out because people in the background were making noise. Some of the other band members didn't like the fact that Paul had access to Axl."

Chris Pitman disputes this account, sort of. "Paul didn't get kicked out—I mean, I don't think he got kicked out. I don't really know what happened, to be honest with you, because no one ever really told us anything. But Paul was a great dude." Pitman also downplays tension between various factions of the band. "If you work at a bank or a dentist's office, you're going to hang out with certain people and not hang out with certain people. We didn't have this war going on. But we all probably read it like, 'These guys don't like us.' I was encouraged to work with Bucket and Brain directly, so I did, and we bonded. Those other guys are all killer musicians too, Robin and Tommy."[43]

Ostensibly, the point of Rose's website posting was to publicize the *Chinese Democracy* tour and the merits of his new band. So it was a little strange that he spent one thousand words of this posting talking about the collapse of the original band—how he'd tried to appease Slash by focusing the new material around his guitar playing, but Slash was afraid of success; how Duff McKagan siding with Slash was inscrutable and "inexcusable;" how Matt Sorum was a lousy friend and "an obvious albatross." "For the fans to attempt to condemn me to relationships, even only professional, with any of these men is a prison sentence and something I wouldn't wish on my worst enemy," Rose concluded. "I'd say my parole is nearly over. I'm practically a free man and if you don't like it you'll have plenty of time to get used to the idea."

Rose also defended the new cast of Guns N' Roses. "You've got the haters out there but the guys in this band, it just rolls off their shoulders because they take a certain pride in their work. They're hungry and they want to do this for all the right reasons. They want to get this material out there to the people. Now that we feel that we have the clarity as to the album we're trying to make, we're wrapping it up." So was *Chinese Democracy* arriving in 2002? Rose said the songs had been chosen and sequenced and the cover art was ready. And yet he was quick to clarify: "If you're waiting... don't. Live your life. That's your responsibility, not mine. If it were not to happen, you won't have missed a thing. If, in fact, it does, you might get something that works for you. In the end you could win big either way. But if you're really into waiting, try holding your breath for Jesus 'cause I hear the payoff may be that much greater."[44]

For *Guitar Player* editor Joe Gore, the new Guns N' Roses was very surreal on a personal level. Two longtime pals, Buckethead and Bryan Mantia, were already in the band. The addition of Richard Fortus (whom Gore emphasizes is literally the nicest guy in the world) meant he knew three people in one of the biggest and most controversial groups on Earth. "My background was in classic music and punk," Gore says. "I was a little too old for the 'shred' thing and I had no interest in all the Sunset Strip rock n' roll. I didn't care about Mötley Crüe or Guns N' Roses. That was not my bag. Drugs, debauchery, sexism, explicit racism—those guys were the enemy. Then one day I woke up and realized, *Okay, three friends of mine are in this band I used to loathe. That's really weird.*

"No one ever talked to me, like, 'this is why I joined.' They were all paid well and treated well. They were all on a retainer—a yearly salary, and they got paid whether they worked or not. That was already becoming pretty rare back then. Now it never happens.

"I did tell Richard once, 'I've not forgiven Axl for his overt racism and homophobia.' Richard said, 'He's changed, give him another chance.' Richard doesn't have an enemy in the world."[45]

※

The second and third shows of the *Chinese Democracy* tour were at Japan's Summer Sonic Festival in Chiba and Osaka, respectively. The bill for both days included Weezer, Suede, the Hives, the Flaming Lips, Hoobastank, and Hanoi Rocks. Guns N' Roses were heavily influenced by Hanoi Rocks when they first got together in 1985; after GNR were on top of the world in the early '90s, they invited Hanoi singer Michael Monroe to croon a bit on *"The Spaghetti Incident?"*. "I never realized how much chemistry the original band had until I saw Axl with those hired guns," Monroe said of the Summer Sonic gigs. "They were just sort of lost onstage . . . and the guitar player [Buckethead] was just so mediocre. It was like watching a cover band, and they looked ridiculous. They had no connection with the audience."

Monroe also mentioned that Rose didn't want Hanoi Rocks playing the same stage as Guns N' Roses, so they performed on a secondary indoor stage away from the main event. "I checked it out with many different sources," Monroe said, "and he thought that the audience would react more to us than to him. That was a great compliment and a good favor too because it leaked to the press and people were like, 'Hanoi Rocks must be really great if Guns N' Roses are shaking in their pants.' I did get along with him and he was very nice to me. I didn't think we were that good of friends until he was nice enough to give us that kind of promotion."

"It was funny," Monroe went on. "When I saw [Axl] play he opened the show with 'Tokyo, do you know where you are?' Of course, we're in Osaka, so I said, 'Do you know where *you are*, motherfucker?' Then he realized he messed up and tried to correct himself. Then a few songs later he'd say, 'Alright, Tokyo!' Maybe he should cut down on the Prozac or whatever."[46]

Monroe may have been projecting. According to a Summer Sonic write-up in *The Japan Times*, during the Chiba concert, Hanoi Rocks addressed the crowd as Tokyo an egregious fifteen times, though writer Simon Bartz said the crowd was charmed by them nonetheless. Bartz only caught the very end of Guns N' Roses's set (Suede was playing indoors at the same time and he was more interested in that). "[GNR] sounded like the Red Hot Chili Peppers," he wrote, "except that Axl still screeched like a leprechaun being castrated at 78 rpm."[47]

The Daily Telegraph's Andrew Perry was more impressed when Guns played the London Arena on August 26, calling the new lineup "unprecedentedly good" at peeling off all the *Appetite* and *Illusion* classics. The new songs, however, were pegged as "uniformly drab." And Axl Rose's new braided hairstyle couldn't be ignored. "What sprang from under [Axl's] red headband appeared to be disentangled strands of brown carpet. When, during 'Sweet Child O' Mine,' he briefly removed the headband, there was a collective gasp at the densely woven hairline beneath." Perry was also amused by the t-shirts being sold that read: "Guns N' Roses: Freedom Through Musical Integrity." "[They] haven't actually made any music for almost 10 years."[48]

Following that gig, Guns N' Roses returned to the United States, specifically to Radio City Music Hall in Midtown Manhattan, for an unannounced TV appearance.

"You kept hearing, 'They've got new music coming out, they've got new music coming out,' and MTV is where people launched new music," says Salli Frattini, who was an executive producer for MTV's 2002 Video Music Awards. "One of our talent team kept hawking the idea of Guns N' Roses performing at the VMAs. When the subject came up with their record label, they were like, 'We'll try.' Honestly it was so tenuous as to whether or not they'd would show . . . it was really just days before that we were convinced they were gonna show up."

Normally, Frattini explains, the planning stage for this kind of thing starts months in advance. "You kinda put it out there with many artists, you try to come up with timely ideas relevant to your audience," she says. "The conversation about Guns N' Roses started maybe six weeks out? We had tried to get Axl a couple times before that, but he would never commit. So we kept everything top secret. There was literally only four or five of us who knew. The director knew, lighting knew. [VMA host] Jimmy Fallon didn't know. We told him once Axl showed up for the rehearsal. There was a closed rehearsal the night before. Of course, we had security issues, because Axl came in a way he wasn't supposed to, and we couldn't tell the cops."[49]

Law enforcement was already on high alert; the first anniversary of the September 11 attacks was right around the corner. To that end, a joint terrorism task force stationed itself throughout Rockefeller Center during the VMA ceremony.[50] Rose had trouble getting in that night as well. "I had to get out of the car, run past the police," he said, "and they're telling me I have to stop, and I'm like, 'I've gotta sing.' And the best part was, as I'm running down the street, I had to run past all the people lined up to get into the building, and they're going, [*affects dumb rock guy voice*] 'Hey, there goes Kid Rock.' I thought that was pretty funny."[51]

Frattini says there was some back-and-forth between MTV and Axl Rose about what he could or couldn't do. "Originally we gave him a five minute slot, [and] he ended up going ten," she says. "We ended up putting him on last because we knew we could take time out of the post show." It was unclear ahead of time what Guns N' Roses would be playing. "I don't think Axl knew what he was gonna do until the day before." Was there any kind of failsafe in case Rose disappeared or backed out at the last minute? "Well, we never announced it, so the backup plan was it was never supposed to happen. Nobody would have ever known."[52]

The 2002 Video Music Awards was the most-watched awards ceremony in MTV history up to that point, garnering nearly 12 million viewers.[53] The audience got their fair share of memorable moments. The crowd inside Radio City started booing Eminem after he called Moby a girl during his acceptance speech for Best Male Video. "Yeah, keep booing," the rapper huffed. "I will hit a man with glasses" (referring to a bespectacled Moby sitting nearby). The surviving members of TLC paid an emotional tribute to Lisa "Left Eye" Lopes, who died in a car accident the previous April. There were appearances by the

Olsen Twins, Ja Rule, Shakira, and former New York mayor Rudy Giuliani, who received a standing ovation.[54][55]

There was a supremely bizarre moment where Britney Spears (dressed like a dominatrix) presented Michael Jackson (dressed like a paramilitary leader from Mars) with a birthday cake and a treble clef tchotchke in honor of his recent forty-fourth birthday. "I consider him the artist of the millennium," Spears told the viewers. Jackson misunderstood what was happening; he thought he was receiving a brand-new accolade. "When I was a little boy in Indiana, if someone had told me as a musician I would be getting the Artist of The Millennium Award, I wouldn't have believed it," he said. MTV quickly released a statement saying Jackson hadn't been awarded anything.[56]

In the closing minutes of the show, the ever-excitable Fallon took to the stage. "I just want to say, please, it's been great hosting the VMAs here in New York City, this is the best city in the world, and if anyone lives here, you know how powerful it is, how electric and energetic—the greatest city in the world. For those of you who don't live in New York, welcome to the jungle. Ladies and gentlemen, GUNS AND FUCKING *ROE-ZAS*!"

The performance did not live up to that introduction. Rose was pitchy and out of breath mere seconds into "Welcome to The Jungle," which was an abbreviated rendition to begin with, as Guns N' Roses decided to perform a three-song medley. The second song was "Madagascar," their new mournful ballad. Rose didn't sound much better as the rhythms cooled off; just as the kids up front started pumping their fists to the ponderous "Madagascar," the band made an extremely awkward transition into "Paradise City." A comical amount of confetti began falling, nearly obscuring the entire band. Rose was caught on camera picking confetti out of his mouth.

"He couldn't have been more winded if he'd been running up Heartbreak Hill with a piano on his back," Renee Graham wrote in *The Boston Globe*. "It's too late in the day to revive Axl's career. Running around the stage at Radio City Music Hall, he was like man trying to distance himself from his memories—and ours."[57] Reviewing for *The Chicago Sun-Times*, Jim DeRogatis called Guns N' Roses at the VMAs "one of the all-time anticlimaxes."[58] *Grand Rapids Press* scribe John Serba was meaner: "Like a horrible, body-mangling accident, we couldn't look away."[59]

"We had Kurt Loder in the wings," Frattini says. "We were supposed to go into the post show [immediately], the show and the post show were intentionally connected to keep the viewers engaged, one right after the other. Kurt was on the side of the stage because of that. When Axl came off the stage, he started walking toward Kurt, and we were screaming, 'Kurt! Get Axl! Interview him! Interview him!' If you had asked Axl beforehand, 'Kurt Loder is gonna interview you after the performance,' you know what he would have said."[60]

Loder intercepted the still out of breath singer. "Axl Rose—he's *back*!" Loder declared, eliciting a chuckle from Rose. Their conversation, though good-natured, did take on the tenor of a teacher gently prodding their student about an overdue assignment. "What's going to happen now? Is *Chinese Democracy* going to come out? Are we going to see it soon?"

"Ummm, you'll see it," Rose replied, "but I don't know if 'soon's' the word." The singer seemed to be disassociating as he spoke. "But it will come out, and we'll go back, do some more recording, and then we'll start an American leg of the tour and see how it goes from there."

"This has taken a *long* time . . ."

Rose interrupted with a brief rebuttal: "It's also how do you rebuild something that got so big and replace virtually every person on the crew, every single thing? And how do you make a whole buncha guys that are somethin' else into somethin' that already was? I don't know if it's exactly been done like this. And not with the intensity of these players wanting to play the material."

The dynamic changed when Loder ended the interview gushing like a teenager. "This was one of the great performances, congratulations. You really—this is a great band."[61]

Vancouver is a city with a rich history of civil disobedience. Often, it was for a just cause, like the 1918 general strike protesting the murder by federal police of labor activist Albert Goodwin, or the sit-down strike of 1938 that was a response to the government cutting social programs.[62] [63] There have been a few sports-related disturbances. 400 revelers were arrested after the 1966 Grey Cup Parade descended into chaos (one arrestee of note was seventy-five-year-old logger Axel Wallin).[64] 200 people were injured in 1994 when a staggering 70,000 hockey fans invaded downtown Vancouver following the Canucks' loss of the Stanley Cup to the New York Rangers; cops shot tear gas into a surging mass that was breaking shop windows and allegedly looting.[65]

On November 7, 2002, Vancouver added Guns N' Roses riot to its incident list. The band was scheduled to kick off the North American leg of the *Chinese Democracy* world tour that night at GM Place. 8,000 fans showed up early, but Axl Rose was still in Los Angeles, stuck on a plane that couldn't take off (GNR management blamed the weather, but the tour promoter Clear Channel said there were mechanical issues).[66] The throngs outside GM Place started chanting "bull-*shit*! bull-*shit*!" when doors remained shut after the scheduled 6:30 opening. About an hour later, an announcement was made via loudspeaker that the show was canceled. Within fifteen minutes, livid concertgoers began smashing venue windows.[67] [68] [69] [70]

"Five minutes before the show it was like, 'Axl cancelled, he's not showin' up,'" recalled Chad I. Ginsburg, guitarist for CKY, the hard rock band Rose personally chose to open the *Chinese Democracy* shows. "Then the riot started, and we were like, 'Oh shit!' By the time we were alerted and able to get back on our bus, [the fans] didn't know whose buses were whose, and they were rioting at our bus as well. I mean, you gotta know that the cheap bus isn't Guns N' Roses, but they were thrown' bottles and stuff, and our techs were terrified to load the trailer."[71]

GM Place only had eight police officers on site when the riot began. Overwhelmed, they called for backup, and every on-duty cop in Vancouver responded. That was 100 officers, and they were greeted with a hail of rocks and at least one Roman candle. Billy clubs started swinging with reckless abandon. One of them whacked twenty-two-year-old attendee Alysha Stephanischin. "Oh my God, this hurts so much," she cried. "I don't blame the officer, there was so much going on, but we weren't doing anything. I really wish we didn't come tonight, I didn't even want to."

As another unidentified fan put it to a CBC news crew, "I've paid $82 just to get maced."[72][73][74][75]

Deputy Chief Gary Greer pledged that Vancouver police would review complaints about their use of excessive force to quell the riot, though in his next breath he rationalized assaults on bystanders. "One of the problems you have with these large kinds of incidents is you have a minority who are very active and violent and everybody else who stands around watching, thinking that this is street theater and it's not. The reality is once you have an unlawful assembly, once we have this kind of violence, just your presence standing there becomes problematic." Greer made dubious claims about rioters breaking off chunks of GM Place's outside ashtrays and plant stands to hurl them at officers. He also said it took exactly one minute for the riot to erupt. "It went, at 7:35, from a crowd milling about, at 7:36, it was a full blown riot."[76][77]

"Shock and dismay" was the reaction guitarist Richard Fortus had to the concert's cancellation. "I didn't even know what the hell was going on," he said. "Tommy and Dizzy were doing an interview backstage with Kurt Loder from MTV, and they heard the announcement that the show was cancelled coming over the PA system in the arena. No one could believe it. And it was Robin's birthday, too. It was such a drag. Apparently Axl had no idea either, because he was on his way there. His plane was delayed, and we knew he wasn't going to make it to soundcheck, but there was never any question that he'd be there in time for the gig. Apparently, the venue just pulled the plug. It was pretty disappointing."[78] Fortus said it was easy for the band to slip away from the mayhem: "Nobody knew who we were."[79]

Guns N' Roses fans rioting outside GM Place in Vancouver on November 7, 2002.
Source: Courtesy estate of Ashley Maile.

Rose commented on the fracas a few days later while being interviewed on Seattle's KISW. "[We were] fully able to meet our commitments and we don't really understand what happened right now, why the show was pulled. We have a legal team looking into it to get to the bottom of it." Harvey Jones, operations manager for GM Place, said, "a decision to cancel this show was made when it was recognized that the band could not take the stage at a reasonable time."[80]

The basic facts left some scratching their heads. "This was the tour opener," remarked *Pollstar* editor Gary Bongiovanni. "Why wasn't [Axl] there a day early? It's almost unconscionable for him to try to come into the country so shortly before show time.... And the bad weather coming to California had been forecast for days. This was not a surprise storm."[81]

The riot caused over $100,000 in damage to GM Place (some sources ballooned that figure up to $400,000). Bridges were also burned with longtime fans. "That's it, I'm trashing all my GNR stuff," Dana Claydon announced at the scene. "I've been waiting for this since '93 when Axl cancelled the last time. What a jerk."[82][83][84] The riot also kneecapped momentum for the *Chinese Democracy* tour, which was suffering weak ticket sales outside major markets like Chicago and New York.[85] Sales were certainly sluggish for the November 8 show in Tacoma, Washington. Even after dropping some tickets to $10, the 22,000 plus seat Tacoma Dome was only half full for the GNR show.[86][87][88] Guns played a full concert that evening with no tumult (aside from a woman who was arrested for poking a security guard in the eye).[89]

Sound problems dogged the band as they crawled across the country. The primary issues revolved around Rose—his microphone would cut out, or his vocals were too low in the mix, smothered by the seven member assembly.[90] Several readers of *The Idaho Statesman* wrote in to complain about the sound during GNR's stop in Nampa. "It was the worst concert I've ever been to," said Ray Giles. Some people felt this new iteration of Guns N' Roses just didn't cut the mustard. *St. Paul Pioneer Press* writer John Nemo's review of the Minneapolis gig reads like a requiem. "Like millions of teenage boys in the late '80s and early '90s, I worshiped Axl Rose and his band," Nemo wrote. "But the revamped, bizarre version of Guns N' Roses that showed up on Thursday was painful to witness."[91] [92] [93]

Mixmaster Mike, the Beastie Boys DJ who Guns N' Roses brought along as their mid-card act, was routinely booed and flipped off by the hard rock crowds. There were also embittered old school GNR fans who wanted to see Slash next to Axl. A cadre of these fans started jeering at the Auburn Hills gig in Michigan when Rose introduced Buckethead. Anger turned to laughter when Buckethead held aloft a Colonel Sanders bobblehead as a peace offering.[94] Another moment of levity on the tour came when Guns N' Roses played Columbus, Ohio's Nationwide Arena. The day before, college football fans in the city had run amok celebrating Ohio State's win over Michigan, a melee that resulted in nine cars being set on fire.[95] "A riot?" Rose joked from the stage. "I saw it on TV and I said, 'Hey, am I late already?'"[96]

At Madison Square Garden, Rose took a moment before "November Rain" to bring out a box of Krispy Kreme donuts, saying they were for Conan O'Brien. "I read a little while ago that he was on a diet," Rose explained. "And now and then, y'know, you need a break from a thing like that, so I brought him some donuts.... Axl's White Trash Bistro Catering." This bit was the singer's response to a joke O'Brien cracked two months earlier on his "Late Night" program about Guns N' Roses changing their name to Chubby McGoo and the Guys Who Aren't Slash. Some people laughed as Rose sauntered around with his donuts; others shouted, "Fuck you, Axl! Play some music!" Rose tossed the confections to the front row, then sat at the piano to rattle off a few bars of a ragtime ditty calling O'Brien an asshole.[97] [98] [99]

Rose's tomfoolery didn't matter; Guns N' Roses bowled over the sell-out crowd at MSG that night. *The New York Post* hailed this concert as "the turning point" for the resurrected hard rock leviathan: "Axl was greased and the band was terrific," Dan Aquilante wrote. "It was an amazing transformation from the group that stunk up the MTV Awards earlier this year. GNR played a crisp concert worthy of a punk-metal band that had as big an appetite for destruction as it had 15 years ago."[100] Similarly, Jim Farber in *The Daily News* praised the "slick, professional set" GNR played, though he was bothered by the lack of rapport between the musicians and Rose. "Essentially, these players operated as a top-shelf tribute band."[101]

Ironically, drummer Bryan Mantia said the MSG concert was the first time this iteration of Guns N' Roses felt like a real band. "I remember even talking to Bucket and everybody and Mother Goose, and we were all just kind of hanging out and we were kind of like, 'Shit, it's working.' Like, you know, 'This is kind of cool.' Like, 'That was a cool show we just played.'

"Like, I think for any real band to gel and become something, you really got to get out on the road, play a bunch of shows, grind it out, start really feeling each other, and how they play and how it works."[102]

Unfortunately for Guns N' Roses, grinding it out was about to grind to a halt.

❧

"You name it, it was thrown. Even a Christmas tree was thrown."

Guns N' Roses fan Joe Pudla was describing the scene inside Philadelphia's First Union Center on the evening of Friday, December 6. The clock was approaching midnight, and the capacity crowd of anxious Guns N' Roses devotees (who'd been waiting ninety minutes since the second opening act) had just heard a muffled announcement that GNR would not be performing due to "health issues." A shower of bottles, chairs, clothing, and binoculars filled the air along with chants of "Axl sucks!" Some said they saw TVs being thrown from the luxury boxes.[103 104 105 106 107]

Axl Rose was in New York City when all this was happening, holed up in a hotel room, refusing to leave for unspecified reasons. First Union staff smelled trouble when Rose was still out of state as doors opened (the rest of the band was in the right city, though rumor has it they also spent the entire night at their hotel). At one point, Rose requested a helicopter, but when it arrived in New York, he reportedly refused to get off the sofa. Was he seriously ill, or was he too wrapped up in a televised basketball game?[108]

"The basketball game story is bullshit!" Rose's bodyguard Earl Gabbidon said. "We stayed in New York until the last minute, that's true. But it had nothing to do with a Knicks game. Axl had some personal things that would have kept him from giving the fans their money's worth. I personally told our tour manager at 6:30 that we weren't coming. The promoter in Philly chose to drag it out."[109]

First Union and the tour's corporate sponsor Clear Channel began serious contingency planning after 9:00 p.m.; that's when alcohol sales were halted. Two hours later, when it was understood that Rose wouldn't be materializing, security reinforcements took their place, bracing for reaction to the cancellation announcement, which was prerecorded. "An announcement earlier would have made it better," said an anonymous off-duty police officer who was at the concert as a fan. "That was way too long—I'm not sure they had the best interests of people at heart." Clear Channel insisted that they communicated the cancellation as quickly as possible.[110]

On the whole, the testy crowd exited First Union without incident; authorities categorized the unruliness as a "minor civil disturbance." Yet five audience members were taken to the hospital for neck and back injuries, and *Philadelphia Inquirer* writer Tom Moon returned to the parking lot to find that a garbage can had been thrown through the windshield of his Toyota Camry. "It shattered the windshield, but the safety glass did its job," Moon said, describing a "yucky" mosaic of beer bottles, paper, and garbage water, all frozen in place by the chilly temperatures. "It took me an hour to defrost it enough to drive home."[111] [112] [113]

"This is another example of what I call mayhem marketing," industry safety consultant Paul Wertheimer said of Axl's latest no-show. "This is a band that has [disappointed] fans in the past, and when these things happen it gets them international publicity—which, it should be noted, this tour was not getting on its own."[114] Guns N' Roses may have been making headlines, but there was no new album in stores to capitalize on that, and everyone with a financial stake in the *Chinese Democracy* tour suddenly saw their profits evaporating. A second show Guns N' Roses was supposed to play that weekend at the First Union Center was canceled.[115] On Monday, December 9, Clear Channel canceled the remaining fifteen dates of the tour.[116]

The *Chinese Democracy* tour had taken almost two years to plan. Rose was given a $1 million advance to make sure he'd show up. Allegedly, the band's guarantee every night was $750,000, which meant Guns N' Roses lost over $11 million on the shows that were axed. Time marched on, but Axl Rose remained Axl Rose. It was maddening for many behind the scenes, like Andy Hewitt, a promoter who partnered on the band's Idaho date. "[Axl] managed to cancel the dates that were doing well [at the box office], and when they didn't, he showed up," Hewitt lamented. "We did a show in Boise that did horrible business, and he showed. I wished he didn't."[117]

Some were unfazed by Axl's trip. "If this guy has a hit record, he's back," Irving Azoff suggested. "Rock n' roll has always been anti-establishment. Part of Axl's anti-establishment is pulling this shit."[118] CKY bass player Vern Zabrowski called it "perfect fucking symmetry" that the *Chinese Democracy* tour began with a riot and ended with one, adding that his band had fun journeying across the continent with Guns N' Roses. "Axl fucking rules. He was way, way cooler than I could have possibly imagined. . . . If we weren't getting equal billing and everything, he'd yell at his manager to get some shit done. He was pulling for us."[119]

Music journalist Nick Kent offered a succinct and biting analysis of Axl Rose in his piece "Meltdown," which *The Guardian* published the following January. "The crass, consumer-crazy 1980s have left behind a toxic wasteland of cultural debris for us all to steer around, but one of its most dismal legacies has to be the preponderance of fading superstars from that era who simply can't accept that their golden years are now behind them. The most obvious is Michael Jackson claiming to be the King of Pop, while his face, fanbase, and personal fortune collapse before a largely indifferent world. But even he seems sane compared with Axl Rose, the politically incorrect Eminem of the 1980s, the tattoo-encrusted, kilt-wearing Liam Gallagher of La La Land.

"What is this bizarre individual doing to himself? Alan Niven hazards a guess: 'Maybe Axl requires hate to drive his muse. David Bowie once told him that this drove his creativity and the comment made a big impression on Axl.' Rose, meanwhile, could face more criminal negligence charges in U.S. courts for his recent no-shows—he was convicted, fined and put on probation in 1992 for 'incitement to riot' after a concert in St. Louis. Still, Axl should look on the bright side: a bit of jail time might uncork that muse again, and finally put an end to one of the longest cases or writer's block in the history of popular music."[120]

Rose was never charged with anything connected to the unrest in Vancouver and Philadelphia, probably because in both cases he was hundreds of miles away at the time. Vancouver police did seek charges for unlawful assembly and mischief against numerous concertgoers, whom they tried to identify through a special website. A handful of these suspects, teenagers from the neighboring city of Chilliwack, were turned in by their mothers.[121]

Civil suits were also launched against the Vancouver Police Department for "oppressive, malicious, reprehensible and unconstitutional conduct" relating to their riot control. Forty-one-year-old Robert Parent was just trying to get home from GM Place when he was cross-checked in the parking lot by baton-wielding Constable Reg Forster; Parent lost two teeth, and six more had to be pulled after the attack. Detlef Schroeder, fifty-two, was knocked down and so severely beaten by Forster and Constable Ryan D'Onofrio that he suffered brain damage.[122][123][124]

There was video footage of both incidents, including a moment when Schroeder's twenty-two-year-old daughter was pushed to the ground after she tried to help her father up..[125][126] The cops argued that there was more to it than what the video showed and that they felt helpless during the riot (one constable testified that he took stress leave afterward and never returned to the force).[127][128] In 2004, complaint commission adjudicator Ross Collver ruled that Forster and D'Onofrio did not use unnecessary force on Parent but said the opposite was true in Schroeder's case. Regardless, Collver did not recommend the offending officers be disciplined in any way.[129]

The Vancouver PD could have saved a lot of time, money, and bad publicity if they'd simply apologized to Parent and Schroeder. That was all the pair were after in the first place. According to Parent's lawyer Phil Rankin, there was "not one word of apology" from the authorities. "Zero."[130]

7 THIS THING IS NEVER COMING OUT

There was a point in music history when two years was considered an egregious amount of time to spend recording an album. Carl Wilson from the Beach Boys spoke about that in reference to his group's famous lost album *Smile* (recorded between 1966 and 1967). "Two years before, [the label] wanted three albums a year," he said. The Beach Boys got halfway through *Smile* when group mastermind Brian Wilson realized he couldn't, in Carl's words, "thread it all together."

Brian and Carl readily admitted that copious amounts of pot and hash played a huge factor in *Smile*'s impediment. "I mean, we had to lie on the floor with the microphones next to our mouths to do the vocals," Brian said. "We didn't have energy." Instead of trying to push through, the Beach Boys gave up, simplifying all the songs and releasing them as *Smiley Smile*. "I've always said *Smiley Smile* was the bunt, and *Smile* was the home run," bemoaned a rueful Carl.[1][2] The Beach Boys soldiered on for decades, but general consensus holds that the *Smile* fiasco was the end of their golden years.

Sly and the Family Stone's 1973 LP *Fresh* came out just a couple of years after its predecessor, but Epic Records was so incensed by the delays that at one point they suspended the band's contract. Sly Stone was an unwavering perfectionist; he was also out of control on hard drugs. A chilling confrontation over the *Fresh* master tapes took place between Stone and Record Plant manager Michelle Zarin. Stone arrived at the studio one night with gun-wielding flunkies. "Give me my fuckin' tapes!" he screamed. "Go ahead, motherfucker, shoot me," Zarin replied. Stone left empty-handed. The Family Stone broke up in 1975; Epic dropped Sly in 1978.[3]

It was a stunning turn of events for Sly Stone, previously hailed as a Pied Piper, fostering racial harmony through his high-powered, hit-making funk.[4] Stone, radiating with joy and life's beauty on the cover of *Fresh*, transformed into an emaciated, paranoid recluse with no band, no label, and no family. "When we were starting out, Sly Stone had the power to control 80,000 people with his eyes," said Family Stone sax player Jerry Martini, "but in '93 [at our Rock & Roll Hall of Fame induction], he couldn't even look at me."[5]

For most artists, there was a price to be paid for testing patience, overstepping bounds, and ignoring deadlines. Axl Rose was not most artists. By 2003, he'd been working on the new Guns N' Roses album for ten years and, for all anyone knew, it might be another ten years before the thing saw the light of day. Was this because the people who could cut him off were afraid to because of his vicious temper? Were they clinging to a belief that *Chinese Democracy* would somehow turn a profit? Were there contractual barriers allowing Rose to continue unabated?

Whatever the case, it appeared Rose had stumbled into the situation every artist dreams about—unlimited time and money to realize "the vision." And in the grand scheme of things, even a tab north of $20 million for *Chinese Democracy* was trivial compared to what was going on at the top of this food chain. In 2000, Interscope's parent company Universal was absorbed by the French consortium Vivendi. In 2002, Vivendi CEO Jean-Marie Messier was forced to resign after it was discovered he'd been hiding a company debt of €35 billion. Messier took €20 million in severance on his way out; he was later convicted of embezzlement, which resulted in a suspended jail sentence and a paltry €150,000 fine (Messier's reputation was far from ruined—he moved to New York and successfully rebranded as a merger consultant).[6][7]

While the Universal Music Group was an undeniably valuable component of Vivendi-Universal, it wasn't the conglomerate's primary source of revenue. This multinational raked in their highest windfalls from a controlling stake in French mobile phone company SFR.[8] Profits from SFR tended to offset the losses Vivendi experienced elsewhere, so it's not as if financial fates were hanging on the entertainment divisions' successes.[9]

That said, the people closer to the ground at Interscope were reaching a point where something had to change with the Guns N' Roses situation. So they started taking charge . . . sort of.

"When the record's coming together, you try to seriously think of a title for ten minutes and then everyone in the band jokes around for the next two hours. . . . One day, somebody suggested *Chinese Democracy* and we couldn't stop laughing about it."

Dexter Holland, lead singer of the Offspring, was detailing the genesis of his punk band's joke announcement in 2003 that their seventh album would be called *Chinese Democracy*. "Axl ripped off my braids, so I ripped off his album title," Holland wrote at the time on the Offspring's website (referring to the hairstyle Holland sported a decade earlier when the Offspring first experienced mainstream success). "You snooze, you lose."[10][11]

"I think that once we said we were going to do it, the joke was already out there," said the Offspring's guitarist, known professionally as Noodles. "And we kind of got the mileage that we were going to get out of it. You can take a joke too far. It we had called it *Chinese Democracy*, it wouldn't have made any sense except as a joke."[12]

Reportedly, the Offspring received a cease and desist from Guns N' Roses, prompting copyright lawyers like Greg Victoroff to weigh in: "Trademark law does not come into existence unless the title is used in interstate commerce. [Right now], they're just two ordinary words. Under that analysis, it would seem that Guns N' Roses have no right to that title and the Offspring are free to use it in any purpose they wish."[13][14]

The seventh Offspring album was eventually named *Splinter*. In a coincidental twist, drumming on *Splinter* was provided by former Guns N' Roses drummer Josh Freese, who stepped in just before recording after longtime percussionist Ron Welty exited the band (under circumstances neither side discussed at length publicly until Welty's 2020 lawsuit against the Offspring; that's a rabbit hole worth falling down one night).

"Working with Josh on the record was phenomenal," said Noodles. "We've known him for a lot of years and the chemistry was there from the word 'go.' Whenever we'd go in to do basic tracks they were done so fast."[15]

Meanwhile, nothing about the real *Chinese Democracy* was moving fast.

Greg Morgenstein was an engineer working on a host of albums at the Village Studios when he was recommended for *Chinese Democracy*. "I was working on it after Roy Thomas Baker," he says. "I actually ran into Roy before that, while I was at the Village working on something else. He was at the front desk and one of the assistants was Xeroxing sheet music. I was like, 'Guns N' Roses know how to read sheet music?' I was surprised. He said, 'Yeah, Brain can read music.' Then he and Axl had a tiff, about what I don't know, and then I came on."

"I initially got hired to edit Buckethead's guitar solos," Morgenstein continues. "Another word for editing guitar solos is comping. It's getting the best parts, the best components, for a solo. The first day, I sat down, and there was something like 83 guitar solos. I remember that number specifically. It was supposed to be just me and Axl on guitar solos. The first two weeks, he didn't want to work. He just watched the Discovery Channel and shopped for Ferrari shoes. He's a big Ferrari guy. He loves that brand. I didn't even know they made shoes." Morgenstein says he was glad to spend that down time with Rose, chewing the fat and talking about the music at length. "I was lucky enough not to have to deal with any of his bad moods."

Morgenstein was already a fan of Buckethead—working with him was one of his career goals—and esoteric music in general. "Axl, who I liked, and Guns N' Roses, I loved growing up. . . . I wasn't sure how much talent Axl had, to be completely honest and open. I went into this wondering how much Axl was produced on the old stuff and if he still had it. When we started recording, I was blown away. He can really sing. I thought he was better in person."

"When Buckethead came in, it was just chaos and fun. I got along with him really well," says Morgenstein. "I was so enamored with him. Bucket's the kinda guy who likes shock value, and anything weird he can do, he does. So he would open the door, walk up the hall, and throw a life size doll into the room and not walk in after it. And he'd walk into the studio with a doll head tied to his head. That was common, very common. He never really had the bucket and mask on, but he wore other weird masks and weird clothes."

As for the chicken coop, Morgenstein was unaware that it was alleged sacred ground. "Yeah, I walked into it. I guess I was one of the people allowed in it," he says in a mock important tone. "Y'know, Buckethead got along with everyone and anyone, pretty much, at least when I was there, from what I saw. Well, he got along with everybody except Axl and some of the band members, or that's what I heard. There was friction between Buckethead and Axl."

Morgenstein is one of many individuals interviewed for this volume who describes Buckethead as playful and childlike. "He'd buy KFC merch off eBay. And I remember—he parked his van out front, and one day they sent someone to fetch something out of it, and when they opened it a ton of McDonald's wrappers fell out."[16]

2003 saw the emergence of the figure who would wind up sharing the ultimate production credit on *Chinese Democracy* with Axl Rose. Caram Costanzo was an engineer at the Village who worked on a few of the most popular rock albums of the '90s, including Pearl Jam's *Vitalogy* and Rage Against the Machine's *Evil Empire*. Even so, it was not entirely clear, even to other people working with Guns N' Roses, how Costanzo ended up in charge. As one Village employee who wishes to remain anonymous told me, "Caram only got the job because he was in the right place at the right time. And I think he thought he was gonna lose his job any day."

An e-mail invitation was extended to Costanzo to participate in this book. He wrote back a one word reply: "Omertà." Omertà is the code of silence to which the mafia adheres.[17] [18]

"He was very serious about everything," says Morgenstein of Costanzo. "He was always like, 'Okay, Axl's coming in today, everybody be on your best behavior.' Then Axl wouldn't show up. And everyone was tip-toeing around, making sure not to say Slash's name."[19]

Speaking of, a new chapter began for Slash in 2003. That May, following an exhaustive search, the fledgling group he'd formed with Duff McKagan, Matt Sorum, and old friend Dave Kushner announced they'd found a singer. "Yeah, I'm in the band," Scott Weiland told *Rolling Stone*.[20] Weiland was best known as the wiry heart of alternative rock darlings Stone Temple Pilots. That band went their separate ways the previous year after Weiland and bassist Dean DeLeo got into a fistfight onstage.[21] Addiction issues were unfortunately a part of Weiland's story; the week his union with Slash, McKagan et al was announced, he was arrested for narcotics possession.[22]

Forging ahead, the new band christened itself Velvet Revolver. Their debut single, the anthemic throwback "Set Me Free," was heard exclusively on the soundtrack to one of the summer's most anticipated tentpole films, Ang Lee's *The Hulk*.[23] "This has to be the best idea Slash and his former bandmates have come up with in a long time," surmised *The Garden City Telegram*. "No one will ever be able to replace Axl, but having someone in there like Weiland who actually is talented and has a powerful, commanding voice is welcomed."[24]

Velvet Revolver perform at The Roxy Theatre in Los Angeles, 2004. *Source: Photo by Jim Steinfeldt/Michael Ochs Archives/Getty Images.*

"[Weiland] is just awesome," Slash gushed. "We've been writing new songs. He's a great singer, and he's a great arranger. The music just sounds unique. . . . We just fit together as a band. There's not this weird subconscious pressure going on that something's not right." The guitarist said the group was taking their time before trying to get a record deal. "In light of the way the music business is right now, you want to put out a record that's going to be cost-effective and distributed properly. If you're going to make a deal, you want to make the best deal you can possibly make, and if you can afford to do it yourself, it's even better."

David Codikow, one of Velvet Revolver's managers, was a little less vague. "People are talking to us, and in the next 60 days or so we're going to figure it out. If radio embraces this band the way that we all hope, who's to say that you couldn't drop ship records to record stores and download them . . . even if you sold less from an economic standpoint, you'd still make money."[25]

Velvet Revolver wouldn't get their debut album out in 2003. A brand-new Guns N' Roses song snuck onto radio on Labor Day Weekend, however. Its means of distribution was unbelievable.

New York Mets catcher Mike Piazza was elected to the Baseball Hall of Fame in 2016, and he'd certainly put up the stats to earn it: twelve All-Star Game appearances, ten Silver Slugger awards, and 427 home runs, the most ever hit by a catcher.[26] [27] There's one achievement you won't find on Piazza's plaque at Cooperstown, though. He's the first National League right-hander to leak a song from *Chinese Democracy* on a syndicated heavy metal radio show.

Piazza, who liked to play the drums when he wasn't crouched behind home plate, was a well-known metal freak. Van Halen, Ratt, and Dokken were some of his big obsessions (occasionally, for a palate cleanser, he'd throw on Miles Davis or Sade).[28] [29] Every so often he'd co-anchor "Friday Night Rocks" or "Saturday Night Rocks," syndicated radio shows broadcast out of New York by former Megaforce Records veep Eddie Trunk.[30] Close to midnight, on Friday, August 28, 2003, Piazza arrived for Trunk's show with a mysterious CD-R labeled "New GNR."

Piazza claimed the disc, which contained approximately six songs, arrived with his mail three weeks earlier boasting no return address. He had no idea if this CD-R was real but encouraged Trunk to give it a spin anyway. Trunk agreed, airing the first track at 12:15 a.m. Trunk's audience heard "I.R.S.," a genuine and new Guns N' Roses song. "The phones went nuts," Trunk said. "[It] sounded like *Illusion* era GNR with a few modern touches. . . . I like GNR, but I'm not a fanatic, but I must say, the song was really good."[31]

Trunk and Piazza knew for sure "I.R.S." was a *Chinese Democracy* leak when Guns N' Roses management called them during the show to issue a verbal cease and desist. Trunk complied, scrubbing the segment from replays of "Friday Night Rocks" and turning the CD-R over to GNR management before the weekend was out.[32] The deejay did give the rest of the disc a quick listen before relinquishing it. "It sounded like a total of three songs, with instrumental versions of each of the three, making a total of six tracks, I think . . . [the last track was] a great rocker, with tons of shredding guitar from Buckethead. I don't know what the title was, but I kinda wish I had the chance to play that one as well."[33]

When *Rolling Stone* ran a news brief about the leak, they included what they claimed was an exclusive response from Axl Rose: "I've always been a Yankees fan. Go Clemens!"[34] Rose was referencing Roger Clemens, the New York Yankees pitcher who beaned and concussed Piazza with a nasty inside fastball during the regular season in 2000. Clemens and Piazza were also involved in a strange incident at the World Series that year wherein a Clemens pitch shattered Piazza's bat; Clemens caught one of the shards and threw it in Piazza's direction, prompting the benches to clear as Clemens shouted, "I thought it was the ball!" at a confused Piazza.[35] [36]

Piazza regretted leaking "I.R.S." once he realized it was real, but the Clemens taunt ruffled his feathers. "That's disappointing," he said of Rose's remark. "It shows you how out of touch he is."[37] A number of Guns N' Roses fans weren't buying any of this, and why should they? Trunk wasn't allowed to replay the segment. No fan recording surfaced online in the wake of "I.R.S." hitting airwaves. "I think that both [Axl's and Mike Piazza's] comments are made up," one person wrote on a GNR message board. "I also think that IRS doesn't exist." "Piazza is full of crap," another wrote. "If he has IRS then prove it. Release five seconds of it, and stop being a fraud."[38]

Trunk himself suggested this whole thing could be a work to drum up publicity for *Chinese Democracy*, which was now being promised by year's end.[39] [40] If we take Piazza's story at face value, who sent the CD-R? There are theories based around some interesting circumstantial evidence. A month or so before Piazza and Trunk went live with "I.R.S.," Axl Rose offered a preview of a few *Chinese Democracy* songs at Las Vegas strip club Crazy Horse Too. In 2004, Crazy Horse Too opened a branch in Philadelphia; the deal was facilitated by Piazza Auto Group owner Vince Piazza, Mike's father (Mike was raised in the Philly suburb of Norristown).

Vince became the owner of the new Crazy Horse but insisted he wanted to sell as soon as possible ("This is not my type of business," he said). He also downplayed any connection to original Crazy Horse owner Rick Rizzolo. Rizzolo was under federal investigation for racketeering and links to organized crime; the inquiry was set off by a 2001 incident at Crazy Horse where goons broke a patron's neck over an $90 tab.[41] Court records show that Vince and Rick Rizzolo were pretty tight in the sense that Piazza helped Rizzolo hide money from creditors as late as 2011.[42]

At any rate, the theory is that the strip club DJ on duty when Axl Rose came in to play some tracks at Crazy Horse Too in July 2003 secretly copied the disc and sent it to the metalhead son of his boss's "legitimate associate," who just happened to be famous baseballer Mike Piazza.

Mike Piazza and Eddie Trunk got to hash things out with Axl Rose in 2006 when Rose made a surprise in-studio appearance on an episode of "Friday Night

Rocks" that also featured Rose's buddy Sebastian Bach from Skid Row and Anthrax guitarist Scott Ian. Rose got in a few funny jabs but ultimately sounded forgiving as Trunk and Piazza (who was calling in from San Diego) apologized for the "I.R.S." leak, professing that they didn't really know what they were doing.

"Axl, dude, I just want to say, man, we love what you are doing and, uh, we hope you do more of it, man," Piazza said. "I mean, I've been a huge GNR. . . . I got GNR way before it hit, you know, the charts—"

"Yeah, I know," Rose cut in, to a round of laughter.[43]

⁂

"Every year there's been a new reason why Axl is not done with the record. Had he delivered this record like he promised seven years ago, this would not be happening right now."

That was an anonymous source explaining to Reuters in April 2004 why Geffen Records had just released, in lieu of *Chinese Democracy*, a Guns N' Roses greatest hits compilation, simply titled *Greatest Hits*.[44] Axl Rose, Slash, and Duff McKagan filed an injunction against the release of *Greatest Hits* on the grounds they hadn't been consulted regarding song selection, artwork, or remastering (Rose had his own separate complaints about *Greatest Hits* interfering with *Chinese Democracy*). A judge tossed the injunction and *Greatest Hits* arrived as scheduled.[45]

Greatest Hits debuted at #3 on the Billboard 200 and slid around inside the top ten for about a month.[46][47][48] Sales were great but the reviews weren't. "This greatest hits disc is an inevitable chronicle of decline," wrote Chris Greenwood in British paper *The Evening Press*. "It must have been tempting to include all of that first album."[49] Flora Liveras of Australia's *Northern Territory News* called the 14 track offering "anorexic": "Extras such as a DVD with some behind-the-scenes footage or some unreleased, rare or hidden tracks would have made this album a collector's item."[50] Alabama *Press-Register* scribe Lawrence F. Specker said *Greatest Hits* was "reeking of futility" and too sanitized, omitting many of GNR's most controversial (and popular) tracks. "And when you sanitize dirt, there ain't much left."[51]

Ahead of the *Greatest Hits* release, a reporter asked Slash if he'd ever reunite with Guns N' Roses. "I haven't talked to [Axl] since I quit," the guitarist replied. "I don't really see a reunion happening. The things that are keeping us apart are so much tougher than money."[52] Money was a part of the problem, though. Shortly after the *Greatest Hits* injunction was tossed, Slash and McKagan sued Rose for not roping them in to decisions regarding the licensing of their old music (specifically to film productions like *We Were Soldiers* and *Old School*).[53] This was the start of a protracted legal back-and-forth between the former GNR members and Rose over a host of issues pertaining to the classic Guns N' Roses catalog.

All wasn't well within the new Guns N' Roses, either. Buckethead severed ties with the band permanently at the end of 2003. The whole scene had become too much for the guitarist.[54]

"Bucket was a true musician in that he just wanted to play," Guns N' Roses drummer Bryan Mantia explained. "He'd be like, 'Why does it have to be so hard? Why can't the album just come out?' I was basking in it. 'That's part of the gig, dude.' He wasn't feeling it. We had a little bit of a falling out. He was like, 'It seems like they're just getting off on this.' I was like, 'It's not that I'm getting off on it. I'm just trying to let it be what it is. I'm not going to be able to change it, obviously. So I might as well get what I can out of it.'"[55]

"He was frustrated through the whole process," says Greg Morgenstein. "He quit so many times. I don't think he liked the process very much. I don't think it was as creative as he likes. He has a session mentality, but not structured like a session player. He likes an audience, but he has no interest in being in the spotlight and working on a pop song." The scale of *Chinese Democracy*, both literal and figurative, may have been daunting to Buckethead as well.

"When you have a big budget, you feel responsible for doing something big," Morgenstein says. "It wasn't just the budget, it was the personnel, the history. You come up with these concepts, like . . . we were trying to make the most in-tune album ever. Like, you listen to Soundgarden, and all the guitars are out of tune. And I'm not saying that's the exact case with them, but it's like, 'Okay, let's take this one step further.' I think that was Caram's concept."[56]

Prior to his final goodbye, Buckethead would express his dissatisfaction with Guns N' Roses by disappearing for long stretches of time. During one of these periods, someone from the Guns N' Roses organization hired a flatfoot to tail the guitarist. "They put a detective on him," says one anonymous source. "Then he caught the detective. They were outside his house and he went out there with a big axe, and he was going, 'AHHHHH! WHY ARE YOU FUCKING FOLLOWING ME?' The detective goes, 'There's some very important people who want to know what you're doing.' That's really uncool. Bucket was getting offers from a lot of people to play in their band back then. I don't really know the full truth. All I know is when he finally quit, I'd never seen a happier guy ever. He was dancing around, singing, 'I'm fuckin' done!'"

Bryan Mantia has touched on the detective story in interviews, revealing that the detective or detectives eventually deserted the tail. Mantia has also discussed how Buckethead's insistence on doing "the puppet thing" earned the ire of all the business professionals surrounding Guns N' Roses.[57] "The puppet thing" was Buckethead's common gimmick of only communicating with people via a grotesque-looking hand puppet named Herbie. There are unverified accounts of last ditch meetings where the lawyers who were trying to save Buckethead's position in the band grew infuriated that he only spoke through Herbie.

"They were so desperate to hang on to Bucket that at one point they said they were gonna turn part of Universal CityWalk into Bucketheadland, just to appease him," says another anonymous source. "They were showing him these plans they'd drawn up. Who knows if they meant it."

"I kept Buckethead in there as long as I could," sighs Chris Pitman. "They'd be like, 'Hey, go talk to Buckethead,' and I'd try. It would have been great if he was the only guitar player, or if it was just Paul [Tobias] and Bucket. That woulda been perfect. When Robin came back, that started some friction. It got too ugly for Bucket. And once Bucket was gone, things got real dark and heavy, and we never really recovered. It was a long, slow finish."[58]

Buckethead's departure forced Guns N' Roses to withdraw from their headlining slot at the 2004 iteration of Rock in Rio (which, for some odd reason, was being held in Lisbon, Spain). "During his tenure with the band, Buckethead has been inconsistent and erratic in both his behavior and commitment, making it virtually impossible to move forward with recording, rehearsals, and live plans," Axl Rose said in a statement (surely drawing chortles from anyone familiar with Rose's own career). Rose also accused Bucket of merely using his stint in GNR to secure his own solo deal with the Sanctuary Group, who'd bought out GNR's management in 2001. David Lefkowitz, who was now Buckethead's manager, came to the guitarist's defense: "Rose's accusations are false—and wrong. And with all the drama surrounding this matter, I'd better leave it at that."[59] [60]

"I was aware from my communication with Bucket that he was no longer gonna do Guns N' Roses," Lefkowitz says today, "and I knew that seemingly a long time before Axl knew. Like, a year. But as far as I knew, Bucket had quit and the whole thing was over. So there was a Bucket piece that ran in *SPIN* and they had reached out to me to set up an interview with Bucket. And I was like, '. . . Buckethead doesn't have a voice.' [*laughs*] They were like, 'Can we ask you some questions?' 'Okay.' They were like, 'Is he still in GNR?' 'No, he quit last year.' Supposedly, and I could be wrong, that's how Axl found out Bucket had really quit."[61]

Buckethead went back to his smaller but stable solo career after Guns N' Roses. He's released (as of this writing) twenty solo albums since then, as well as a staggering 380 mini-albums he calls "pikes." Bucket was afforded a great deal of exposure during his *Chinese Democracy* years and while it certainly earned him a lot of new fans, existing at that level of notoriety had its price. Longtime friend Joe Gore says Buckethead has been cagey about his exact whereabouts since quitting GNR; the speculation is that younger devotees have tried to invade his privacy.

Bucketheadland was rocked in 2017 when Brian Carroll guested on the "Coming Alive" podcast and gave the most out-of-character interview of his career. Not once did he refer to Buckethead in the third person, like he was a separate individual;

not once did he use terminology like "binge loaf" or "scoop rack." For an hour, haltingly, gently, Carroll discussed life, art, and his mind with host Barry Michels. It was here that Carroll revealed that he suffered from an irregular heart beat that had recently racked up in intensity. "I just, like, tried to deal with it and let it do what it did and then eventually it would stop," Carroll said, "but it got really intense, so I went to the doctor, and they said, 'Oh, you're on the verge of having a stroke.' And I'm like, 'Oh no, I didn't—' 'Cause I felt so good prior to having it."

Doctors performed an ablation on Carroll's heart to no avail. "I take medication, which is tough 'cause I've never took any of them my whole life," he said. "So it's been really difficult because it's scary and it comes on and it's like I feel like I lost half of my, like—even walking across rooms is difficult. . . . [I'm] thankful for [the medication] because it's kept it, you know, from going berserk, but it's still . . . it's pretty intense." In terms of his guitar playing, Carroll said the heart condition was prompting him to slow down and play lightly, which he found relaxing.

Carroll also spent a great deal of the "Coming Alive" podcast thanking Michels for being his therapist. "I'm just amazed at how there's really nothing I've ever asked you that you didn't have an answer for," the guitarist effused. "Even if I didn't understand at the moment, it did eventually come around to being. . . . You're one of the greatest people I think there is, for sure."[62] Michels was one half of an unconventional therapy duo with Phil Stutz; the pair embraced a philosophy of direct action and boundary-crossing, buddying up to their patients to say, "Stop being such a fucking baby" and "Do what the fuck I tell you, you'll feel better." Traditional psychologists viewed their approach as unethical, but big time stars like John Cusack and Jonah Hill swore by them.

In 2012, Stutz and Michels authored *The Tools*, which outlines Stutz's "miracle" visualization exercises of the same name.[63] [64] Carroll referenced *The Tools* throughout his conversation with Michels. One specific Tool Carroll and Michels touched on was "dusting," wherein a performer or public speaker can overcome facing a large crowd by imagining said crowd is covered in a thick layer of dust. "It's almost like they're dead," Michels explained. "What it does is it renders the outside world non-emanating, there's nothing coming from them, because they're covered with dust . . . once you've dusting the audience, [you] just see a fountain of light, but it's inside of you, it's inside your heart, and your job is to go into the room and light up the room."

The dusting talk was prompted by a very obvious question from Michels, a question probably asked by every single person who'd ever seen a picture of Buckethead. "It's hard to understand how you can even play guitar. Did you have eye holes or something?"

"If you just use your hands," Carroll tried to explain. "If you do it, you sort of get used to it."[65]

The Guns N' Roses *Greatest Hits* album released in March 2004 was originally planned for the previous Christmas. Axl Rose protested, promising *Chinese Democracy* by 2003's end. When that didn't happen, Interscope/Geffen had a "last straw" moment. They cut funding to the album and told Rose any further costs were his personal responsibility. Guns N' Roses' residency at the Village Studios was also ended, which was a relief to Village head Jeff Greenberg.[66]

"Jeff was definitely getting fed up with them," says Greg Morgenstein. "You want Guns N' Roses to use that space, but you also want Elton John to be able to come in and use it. When I came on to that album, they were already saying, 'Wow, this has gone on so long.' Yeah, of course we felt pressure to get it done, but you're bound by Axl. He's bipolar and you can tell. You never know which Axl you're gonna get."[67]

Guns N' Roses were moved to Interscope's own in-house studio. Bob Koszela worked there as a staff engineer and studio manager. "It was a dual role, evening shifts," he says. "I moved stuff around in Pro Tools. I worked for Jimmy Iovine, which meant any day I showed up for work I could be fired. I'm not trying to bag on the guy. He just demanded the best.

"So in 2004, we get this call that Guns N' Roses is coming. I say, 'Thank God!' I'm a fan. Caram [Costanzo] and Eric [Caudieux] sent a scouting crew ahead of time to get the lay of the land. We had all these big photos on the walls of all these different singers. One of them was Bob Marley. They see the Bob Marley photo and they say, 'Does this have to be here?' 'What?' 'Axl *hates* Bob Marley.' I say, 'Yeah, sure,' but I'm thinking, *Oh god, am I not gonna like this guy before he gets here?* Then it's, 'Can we replace some of these lights with red lights? Axl *loves* red lights.'"

Geffen president Jordan Schur was overseeing things with *Chinese Democracy* at this point. "I never got along with Jordan," Koszela says. "He was kinda full of himself. He gave me his cell number and he told me, 'The second Axl shows up, you call me before you call anyone else. I don't care what time it is.' Axl didn't show up for the first two nights. Then a month goes by. No Axl. This was costing $1,995 a day. So one day, Jordan says, 'If he doesn't show up today, we're pulling the plug.' Then security called me. 'Mr. Bob? Mr. Axl is here. We have a problem.'"

Rose drove a Lamborghini to Interscope's studio that day, and the vehicle had gotten stuck on the ramp descending into the parking garage. "So they let him park up top in front of the label and they stuck a security guard there to watch the car," Koszela says. "Axl came in with the braids, looking like a million bucks. He was a little bigger, but that's okay. He walked right out to the balcony for a smoke. We started talking about local bands, bands he'd seen on the road, undiscovered talent . . . then he asked, 'Can you get me on the roof?' He wanted to see this meteor shower. So we sat up there for two or three hours, waiting to see a meteor.

"After that, he went back downstairs and started talking to Caram. He never set foot in the studio. He called Nobu, ordered $2,500 worth of sushi, and had it delivered to Interscope. Then he left, but as he was walking out the door, the last thing he said to me was, 'I think you have a phone call to make.' Jordan was spitting mad."

A few days later, Koszela was present for a meeting between Schur, Rose, and Iovine. "Jordan was barking about when this thing will be done and how much money it'd cost. Axl never took his eyes off Jimmy. When Jordan was done, Axl said something like, 'I don't want to ever hear from this fucking idiot again. I don't want him anywhere near my music.' Jordan walked out. The next day, *Chinese Democracy* was on Interscope."[68]

When reached for comment about Axl Rose and *Chinese Democracy*, Jordan Schur wrote, "As a rule I do not discuss my private experiences with the artists I have worked with."[69]

Guns N' Roses were at the Interscope studio for roughly a month and a half. Despite Costanzo and his team coming in every evening like clockwork, Koszela says nothing was ever recorded (though he does point out that GNR already had forty songs in the can). "No one seemed to have as clear a vision as Axl," he adds. "He knew what he wanted, but he also felt like he was being 'disrespected' by the label, that they were preventing him from doing what he wanted . . . at some point it becomes this personal thing where he doubted himself."[70]

Another studio employee who wishes to remain anonymous describes a difficult moment during a mixing session: "Axl used [the audio program] Logic, and one time he sent over audio that he created at his house up in Malibu for me to put in the session. Like I had to actually mix this audio into the session. I was working with Caram and we were both like, 'This doesn't sound good. It's weird, it's dissonant—' when I say 'dissonant,' I'm being very polite.

"We put it in because we had to, but we put it in so low you couldn't hear it. That was the first time something like that had ever happened to me."

Not that it seemed to make a difference. As the anonymous employee puts it, "We all felt like, *Yeah, this thing is never coming out.*"

Jeff Leeds was a staff reporter for *The New York Times* in the mid-2000s who generally covered the music industry. "I was interested in stories about business excess," he says. "In that period, the industry was undergoing what felt like a secular decline, and it felt like everything was shrinking, including the role of, or the presence, of pop much in culture. I knew that there was this sense of, at least among some veterans of the business, this sense of longing for something to change that trajectory. There was also a sense of nostalgia for what was.

"I think there were people who were hoping against hope that certain white whales could still be caught. People wondered, *Was there a chance Rage Against the Machine could come back and do more?* There were a number of these projects that people believed could still happen. And *Chinese Democracy* was the most infamous of those."

So Leeds decided to tackle *Chinese Democracy* in what he says was always meant to be "a cover story type" story. "I don't think there was a specific deadline. I think there was an understanding that it might take a while. It wasn't anything anybody thought would be done in a week. I worked on it on and off for more than a year. With stories like this, you want to make sure the level of drama warrants the time and space you're investing. What was amazing about this was it didn't require sensationalization. You didn't have to reach to make this seem wilder than it was. This is a great example of why people say truth is stranger than fiction."[71]

On March 6, 2005, an article written by Leeds was published under the headline "The Most Expensive Album Never Made." It cited Geffen documents that stated over $13 million had been spent on *Chinese Democracy*. Leeds reported an internal cost analysis from 2001 that showed the band was burning up $244,000 a month (the guitar techs alone were being paid $6,000 a month; the software engineers were making four times as much). All the expected fence posts were hit otherwise in Leeds' unraveling of this unprecedented saga—the rotating cast of producers, the endless re-recording, the chicken coop.

"And at the center of [*Chinese Democracy*] is the confounding figure of Axl Rose himself," Leeds wrote. "A magnetic talent, a moody unpredictable artist, a man of enormous ideas and confused follow-through, he has proven himself to be an uncontrollable variable in any business plan."[72]

"This was a long time ago, so my perceptions of these things maybe have changed," Leeds says today, "but I do remember being impressed at the way the meter was allowed to run [for Guns N' Roses]—to have blocked out studios, equipment, people for months on end at this kind of cost was somewhat shocking, particularly given the day to day reality of the industry at that point was everyone else was scrambling for scraps."[73]

Merck Mercuriadis, CEO of Guns N' Roses' management company the Sanctuary Group, penned a lengthy response to Leeds's article. "I find it remarkable," Mercuriadis began, "that *The New York Times*—a newspaper of some repute—has chosen to run an article on the making of the forthcoming Guns N' Roses album *Chinese Democracy* without even bother to talk to anyone who has actually been involved in the making of the album. You quote five people on the record, all of whom, with the exception of Tom Zutaut, have been out of the picture for between six and nine years, and like the author of your article, have never even heard the album!"

Mercuriadis said that Leeds reached out to Sanctuary two weeks before publication. "I explained that it was not possible for him to write such a story," the CEO wrote, "as he had not spoken to the band, our two engineers, myself, or most importantly, Axl, all of whom have been working on the actual album for the last two years and enquired how he could write an investigative report with any integrity without doing so. I also asked why, if he was reporting on the 'process' [of making the album], why we were the last people he was contacting, as it was obvious from the discussion that he had been working on this for a number of weeks."

It was a "blatant lie," Mercuriadis declared, that Leeds was told Axl Rose couldn't be reached for comment for his story. Leeds was actually told that an interview request couldn't even be considered until Rose and/or Sanctuary knew who else Leeds had spoken with for the piece. "We were not going to lend credibility to an article that was based on hearsay from people that have not only had nothing to do with the album but whose only agenda was to recapture their 15 minutes of fame in an industry that had cast them aside and left them unemployed many years ago," Mercuriadis spat out. Leeds refused to divulge his other sources. Mercuriadis asked for an extra twenty-four hours past the deadline to discuss the issue with Rose, which was denied.

"It should be mentioned," Mercuriadis added, "that during our initial conversation the writer was offered the opportunity to hear the album in the studio when it was finished and talk to people who were directly involved and declined in favour of the article you have chosen to run."

Mercuriadis ended grandly: "As one of the few people involved in the making of this album I can tell your readers the following: W. Axl Rose is not interested in fame, money, popularity, or what *The New York Times* or any other paper for that matter might think of him. His only interest is making the best album he is capable of so that it can have a positive effect in 2005 on people who are enthusiasts of music and interested in Guns N' Roses. His artistic integrity is such that he has chosen to do so without compromise at great personal sacrifice, which makes him a soft target for the sort of rubbish you have chosen to print. I believe he will have the last laugh."[74]

Mercuriadis's letter may have been addressed and sent to *The New York Times*, but it was not printed by the paper. Instead, it was posted on Guns N' Roses fan sites like *Here Today, Gone to Hell* and heavy metal news websites like *Blabbermouth*. *Blabbermouth's* readers, known for their viciousness in the comments section, did not spare Mercuriadis. "My head really hurts after reading that verbal diarrhea." "You goddamn retard, why aren't you at some hospital getting treatment?" "WELL, TRASHL—AXL, HAS SENT HIS BALLSNIFFER TO SAY WHAT HES TO [sic] CHICKENSHIT TO SAY . . . AXL . . . U R A FUCKIN PANSY ASS TURD WHO HAS AN EGO THE SIZE OF RUSSIA, AND A MENTALITY THE SIZE OF A GREEN PEA."[75][76]

The New York Times did print a response letter from Tom Zutaut, who was quoted sparsely by Leeds in the original piece and said nothing untoward. "Axl Rose was one of the only artists I ever worked with who was never motivated by money," Zutaut wrote, clearly forgetting how he'd blanched at Rose's demand for $75,000 before signing with Geffen in 1986. "He consistently put the quality of his artistic output above all. Whether you consider him to be a musical genius on hold, a poster child for the misunderstood, or a narcissist, all of his actions are motivated by a pure desire to make every recording count as a true reflection of his own high standards.

"In a sea of musical mediocrity and generic voices processed into greatness by computers, Axl Rose achieved the American dream in music without compromising his integrity for the sake of fame or fortune." Another way of looking at this is that the first Guns N' Roses album made certain people at Geffen so much money in the late '80s that Axl Rose subsequently released a song angrily complaining about "niggers" and "faggots" and only received more label support instead of the necessary career-ending repercussions.

"I am sure that Axl's new Guns N' Roses will impact popular culture with the same vigor and vitality that made *Appetite for Destruction* a part of musical history."[77]

Original Guns N' Roses drummer Steven Adler had a different perspective. "We all know [Axl] is great, but he has his moments," Adler said in an interview that June. "He's a jackass, basically, a fucking weirdo, and he can kiss my ass. If he puts [*Chinese Democracy*] out, he thinks he'll sell 20 million copies. Well, maybe he's lucky if he goes gold. There's no hits on it, it's crap."

Adler was asked if he'd ever reunite with Rose. He would, on one condition: "I have to punch him in the face. I have to get one good shot at him first. The fucker has waited so much of my time, so much of people's times."[78]

Some serious reunion gossip was floating around in 2006. In fact, on April Fool's Day that year, a spokesperson for Axl Rose released a statement denying that Rose had entered discussions with Slash, Duff McKagan, and Izzy Stradlin to embark on a Guns N' Roses tour together that summer. Simultaneously, there was chatter that Slash had quit Velvet Revolver and moved all his equipment out of the band's rehearsal space.[79] The seeds of these rumors probably went back to the previous October, when Slash made a surprise visit to Rose's Malibu home.

Slash and McKagan were suing Rose over fraudulent changes the singer allegedly made to Guns N' Roses' ASCAP publishing copyrights. All Slash would really say about his unannounced appearance on Rose's doorstep was that he never saw or spoke with Rose and he left a note with someone concerning the lawsuit.[80] [81] When Rose countersued, included in his complaint was a story about Slash showing up at his home and venting about the other guys in Velvet Revolver.

McKagan was "spineless," Scott Weiland "a fraud," according to Rose's recounting of Slash's diatribe. Slash also allegedly told Rose he hated Matt Sorum.[82]

It all sounded like a middle school love triangle. Scott Weiland responded in kind, eviscerating Rose on Velvet Revolver's website. "Get in the ring or go to the gym, motherfucker, or if you prefer, get a new wig, motherfucker . . . you fat, botox-faced, wig wearin' fuck! . . . How many albums have you put out, man, and how long did it take the current configuration of this so-called band to make this album? How long? And without the only guys that validated the name. How dare you! Shame on you! How dare you call our bass player spineless. . . . What we're talking about here is a frightened little man who once thought he was king, but unfortunately this king without his court is nothing but a memory of the asshole he once was."[83]

The truth was things weren't going so well in Velvet Revolver, in part because Weiland would fly off the handle and post angry Internet missives like this. The other band members also believed Weiland was paranoid about a Guns N' Roses reunion ending their venture. Weiland argued the real problem was that Velvet Revolver spent too much time on tour, and that certain members' wives were too meddlesome in their affairs. After some public bickering, Velvet Revolver fired Weiland in 2008.[84 85 86] Seven years later, the singer died from a drug overdose. Reflecting on everything in 2018, Slash was candid: "Velvet Revolver was no fun. I have nothing positive to say about that experience except that we did write some cool stuff."[87]

Oddly enough, in the middle of their 2005–6 warring, both Axl Rose and Slash spoke fondly of one another to the press. "I love the guy," Rose admitted to *Rolling Stone*. "I always wanted everyone to know how great he was." Slash, building on a remark Rose made about new material in 2006, announced *Chinese Democracy* would be out that March. "I'm really excited," he said. "[It] sounds great."[88] In a different interview, Slash insisted there was no "bad blood" between himself and Rose. Both men admitted they hadn't spoken in ten years (coincidentally, Rose had pleasant run-ins in 2006 with both Matt Sorum and Steven Adler).[89 90 91 92]

Guns N' Roses management refuted Slash's words, saying that no release date had been set for *Chinese Democracy*.[93] March wouldn't have been an awful time to release the album. In late February, there was considerable buzz after three new recordings, all ostensibly from *Chinese Democracy*, leaked online. Rose's chainsaw voice was unmistakable on "Better" (a strong, sneering rocker with techno flourishes), "There Was a Time" (a power ballad), and "I.R.S." (a catchy mid-tempo rocker that starts like a power ballad).

Radio jumped on the tracks; K-ROCK put all three into rotation forty-eight hours after the leak (assistant program director Jay Lawrence admitted to downloading them, assuming the worst that would happen was Geffen would demand their removal).⁹⁴ ⁹⁵ *Rolling Stone* issued a brief but favorable review of the songs. "Hey, Axl, put the thing out," writer Brian Hiatt pleaded. "It already sounds better than Velvet Revolver."⁹⁶

This wasn't a suggestion Rose liked hearing, at least according to Sebastian Bach, the blonde hellion from Skid Row who accompanied Guns N' Roses on tour that spring and summer. "When we were first hanging out . . . we were just standing around a bunch of people," Bach said. "I go, 'Axl, do you think you might get the record out? It would be a great time, now that we're on tour and everything.' He goes, 'Oh. Great! Everybody! Sebastian has a great idea here, man. Guess what? Sebastian, should I put out a record? Maybe it would be a good idea for me to put out a fucking record! Hey everybody, listen to this! I never thought of that!' . . . I felt like Fred Flintstone in Mr. Slate's office."⁹⁷

The *Chinese Democracy* tour of 2006 was notable for a several reasons. Guns N' Roses got through the majority of the concerts without incident. They completed the tour without releasing *Chinese Democracy*. The tour marked the debut of new guitarist Bumblefoot, alias Ron Thal, a native of New York City whose style of shred was reminiscent of Buckethead, if Buckethead had been raised in the Catskills by Paul Shaffer.

Thal had actually been on GNR's radar for a couple of years already. Shred legend Joe Satriani recommended Guns hire him in 2004. "[Joe] sent me an email letting me know that in case they reach out that it's not some weird prank or anything, it's legit," said Thal. "A few hours later I heard from one of the guys in the band and we spoke for a couple of months." Busy with his own musical career (as well as an adjunct professor position at SUNY Purchase), Thal decided to pass. "They reached out again [a year and a half later] and I still didn't want to do it," he said. "I just didn't think I was right for it for a lot of reasons."

When Thal asked a mutual friend to decline again on his behalf, the friend encouraged him to at least have another conversation with Guns N' Roses. "And I'm being a brat saying, 'No! No! No!'" Thal recounted. "'For me, just talk to them.' And I was like, 'Alright.' So I went down. They were rehearsing in New York and I just brought my guitar, I figured we'd jam a couple of songs that night." One night of jamming turned into two, then seven. Bumblefoot was in Guns N' Roses.⁹⁸

While Thal was resisting Guns N' Roses, some members of Guns N' Roses were resisting Thal. His addition was last minute before a string of shows at Manhattan's Hammerstein Ballroom that were kicking off the tour in May. The instrumentalists had grown comfortable with just two guitars following Buckethead's departure, and some didn't think putting a third one back into the mix was such a great idea. Allegedly, both Bryan Mantia and Tommy Stinson told Axl Rose they'd quit if he hired another guitarist. "Who cares?" Rose was said to have responded. "We'll just get Duff and Matt." A retort followed about getting Slash too, and Rose grew livid.⁹⁹

"It didn't matter what anybody else thought," chuckles keyboardist Chris Pitman about this donnybrook. "It was all Axl. When Buckethead quit, some of us pointed out, 'Somebody else has to play Buckethead's shit. God, who can do that?' And Bumblefoot was fuckin' awesome! Some of the other guys didn't like that."[100] Thal once said he had to "get a little violent" with the rest of Guns N' Roses to earn his place, a comment he slightly walked back (or at least deleted from his Wikipedia page).

"I think it was just more of a situation like a new family member was brought home without the other siblings' consent," he said with a laugh, "or to their surprise . . . So it took a good minute for us to get to know each other . . . [but] I don't know if we ever did. I don't know if we ever got to really know each other, to be honest. I feel like the environment I was in never gave me a chance to just comfortably be myself and not feel guarded."[101]

Regardless, the Hammerstein shows were considered victorious. A scuffle afterward made the real headlines. Rose and fashion designer Tommy Hilfiger locked horns at the Plumm Club, where GNR performed an acoustic set for Rosario Dawson's birthday party. The fight was set off after Rose moved a drink belonging to Hilfiger's girlfriend.

"As the punch-up escalated, Hilfiger introduced Rose to some 'November Pain' with a blow to the cheek," *The New York Post* reported. Witnesses said Hilfiger flew off the handle, physically egging Rose on, but the singer wouldn't take the bait. "Axl was a gentleman and had the good sense not to retaliate," said Plumm owner Noel Ashman. It was also reported that Kid Rock was trampled by a small herd of people as the melee began.[102]

Rose was less of a gentleman on June 27 while Guns N' Roses was visiting Sweden. At half past seven in the morning that day, a security guard at Stockholm's Hotel Berns overhead a commotion in the lobby. Clear as a bell, he heard someone shouting obscenities in English. It was Axl Rose, who was drunk and, after being shown numerous rooms, dissatisfied with the offered accommodations (another report said Rose was upset because there was no "big party" to welcome him to the Berns). The guard asked Rose to lower his voice. Rose responded by knocking the guard off balance with a shove to the chest. The guard grabbed ahold of Rose's braided hair and yanked the singer to the ground. Rose then sank his teeth into the guard's leg, causing a blood blister.

Moments later, Rose snatched a vase and hurled it into an eighteenth-century mirror. The police were called. "You have to help me," the Berns guard pleaded with Rose's personal bodyguard. Rose threatened to fire his bodyguard if he so much as moved. Baton-wielding officers arrived and immediately arrested Rose (who suddenly calmed right down) on charges of probable cause, suspected violence against an official, and vandalism.[103] [104] [105]

Rosario Dawson gives Axl a smooch at her birthday party, 2006. *Source: Photo by Kevin Mazur/WireImage via Getty Images.*

Rose was detained at Kronoberg Prison for twelve hours. Ultimately, he was fined 40,000 Swedish kroner plus 10,000 kroner to the security guard plus an additional 500 kroner for a "victims of crime" fund. After his release from Kronoberg, Rose flew to Oslo for the next Guns N' Roses concert; reportedly, a great deal of his luggage remained at the Hotel Berns, along with his unpaid bill. After landing in Oslo, Rose refused to deplane, deciding instead to host a party for several hours as the plane sat on the runway. At one point, he had ice cubes delivered.[106]

Shortly after this episode, Bryan Mantia took some time off from the *Chinese Democracy* tour to be with his newborn daughter. Frank Ferrer, Richard Fortus' band mate from Love Spit Love, substituted but ended up as the new Guns N' Roses drummer when Mantia decided he didn't want to come back. "I still liked the vibe," Mantia said. "I still liked the people. I got along well with Tommy. I don't feel like there was ever any weirdness with Robin [Finck] or Dizzy [Reed] or anyone in the band. It really was, for me . . . the fun of Axl and the attitude kind of went away.

"I found myself like, 'Here I am playing "Nighttrain," doing the cowbell part. There's something else left for me in music, and it's not this.' Everyone is always like, 'What happened? Were they jerks?' No. Mainly for me, it was that I wanted to do something else with my life."[107]

On December 14, 2006, Guns N' Roses dot com posted "An Open Letter From Axl Rose" in which Rose announced the cancellation of four upcoming concerts in California and Nevada. "Because of the scheduling of these particular shows, valuable time needed by the band and record company for the proper setup and release of the album *Chinese Democracy* would have been lost," Rose wrote. "Rather than delay the album yet again, all involved have decided to remove these shows from GN'R's schedule. We hope our fans understand and we apologize for any inconvenience this may have caused."

After two subsequent paragraphs that touched vaguely on the "endless and seemingly insane amount of obstacles" Guns N' Roses had endured while making the album, Rose got closer to the heart of the current problem. "When I agreed to do our recent North American tour, I did it with the understanding that my manager, Merck Mercuriadis, and I were in full agreement regarding our strategy and touring plans and, most important, that any and all things needed to release the album by Dec. 26 at the latest were in place. Unfortunately, it turned out that this was not the case, and I regret to say that the album will not be released by the end of the year."

"Although many things went extremely well and were very exciting, there were, in our opinion, unnecessary and avoidable complications on our tour having to do with the tour routing, scheduling and album and video plans that wreaked havoc on all involved. This was compounded by an overall sense of a lack of respect by management for the band and crew and each individual's particular expertise that has resulted, unfortunately, in the end of both Guns' and my managerial involvement with Merck Mercuriadis."

Rose accused Mercuriadis of baiting concert promoters for the current Guns N' Roses tour with loose promises that *Chinese Democracy* would suddenly appear on store shelves at some point by the end of the year, with no advertising lead up. Rose denounced this as unfair, stressful, and an "utterly insane thing to do to our fans." Then Rose unearthed his buried lede: "This is not a promise, a lie, or a guarantee, but we do wish to announce a tentative release date of March 6. This is the first time we have done this publicly for this album. Others have made up all the other dates for their own reasons. We would like to assure the fans that everything in our power will be done to meet this date. Once it is finalized and official, you will be notified.

"If we are delayed for unseen reasons, you also will be notified as soon as possible in regard to a new date, and the album will be released as shortly thereafter as is possible. We thank you for your patience.

"In the end, it's just an album, but it's one that I, the band, our record company and all involved believe and feel is a true Guns N' Roses album. Ultimately the public will decide, and regardless of the outcome, our hearts, lives and our passion has been put into this project every step of the way. If for no other reason, we feel those elements alone merit your consideration."[108]

Mercuriadis issued his own open letter in response, where he outlined a situation where *Chinese Democracy* was being held hostage by Axl Rose's erratic, unpredictable muse. Ultimately, Mercuriadis stood behind Rose: "While some of Axl's letter is disappointing—as John Lennon once asked of Paul McCartney, 'How Do You Sleep?'—until you have walked a mile in his shoes you cannot begin to comprehend the pressure he is under. I know I sleep well at night in the knowledge that when *Chinese Democracy* hits the streets in March that is it large part down to my efforts over the last almost five years."[109]

The decision to invoke Lennon/McCartney was curious, and it remains unclear if Mercuriadis considered himself Lennon or McCartney, or how this comparison was even applicable (unless he secretly co-authored the lion's share of the Guns N' Roses catalog).

As it happened, *Chinese Democracy* was not released on March 6. *Chicago Tribune* writer Mark Caro tried to get to the bottom of things. "I called Interscope/ Geffen, the band's supposed label," he wrote, "and a rep said she had no information and referred me to Merck Mercuriadis. He was the band's manager until he became yet another jettisoned member of the GNR team in December. In other words, the label thinks the guy canned three months ago has the answers.

"Promptly responding to my e-mail inquiry about the album, Mercuriadis wrote, 'Sorry, Mark, but I cannot help you.' . . . As for when the finished version of *Chinese Democracy* will be available, the GNR site claims that 'all of the recording for the album has been completed,' but 'there is no official release date.'"[110]

Recording had not, in fact, been completed. Rose was still tinkering with *Chinese Democracy* at various studios. Dror Mohar, an in-house engineer at the world-famous Electric Lady Studios in New York's Greenwich Village, remembers Rose coming in for vocal and guitar work in 2007. "I definitely got the sense that we were like, 'we're down to the finals,'" he says. "I don't know that I knew that it was, 'Yes, it's literally coming out next year,' but this felt like the home stretch. It was no longer, 'Who the fuck knows?'"

Mohar says he mainly worked with Rose and Bumblefoot, and that Rose was always totally professional and never lost his cool. "Also, I appreciated the fact that, when Axl went to sing on a track, every time, he'd be trying to get into it. You could see that he was always really trying."

"I really liked a lot of the songs," Mohar says, "but by the time it got to me, so much of the work had been done, they could have put out this record six times. It was complete and more complete and re-complete and completed again. I didn't have a sense like I do on other records where the conception is—like, there's nothing there, and then there's something."

"It felt like we were throwing babies around."[111]

8 GOD HIMSELF CANNOT EAT IT

Former Guns N' Roses manager Alan Niven tells me he once had dinner with Sean Beavan, one of the many producers who worked on *Chinese Democracy*. This bread-breaking took place in early 2008, as Niven recalls, near his home in Phoenix. Beavan happened to be passing through and a mutual friend connected them.

"He asked me, 'How did you manage to make *Appetite for Destruction* sound so dangerous?'" Niven reports. "And I said, 'I cannot believe you are asking that kind of question and using that kind of idiotic language. I think you mean how did we make it sound live and full of vitality. Dangerous? Let me take you to another part of this city where people are in the shadows and they're armed. That's dangerous. Rock n' roll bands are not inherently dangerous.'

"And I'm thinking to myself, *No wonder this fucking record is taking so long.* I mean, this whole project was like a dead zone. It was a career black hole."

Niven had another chance meeting that year with a more infamous Axl Rose associate. "My wife Heather and I were invited to a gallery opening in Sedona. I was standing with our host when this primped up dandy came over and started to brag about how he had traveled the world with Axl Rose. Fuckin' steam started to come out of my ears. It was Elliott Maynard. I spun on my heels and walked away before I committed a social faux pas and decked the ass right there."[1]

Elliott Maynard was, of course, the "techno shaman" who'd been married to Rose's spiritual advisor Sharon Maynard. Sharon died in January 2007, succumbing to a heart attack while undergoing open heart surgery. Death wouldn't end their partnership; Elliott later revealed that before she died Sharon arranged for a psychic to channel her voice from the afterlife. Elliott eventually remarried, to a woman who could also commune directly with Sharon.[2]

It is unknown whether Sharon Maynard has kept in touch with Axl Rose since her death.

Today, people might know Chris Kooluris best for his occasionally controversial presence in the world of competitive pinball. Sixteen plus years ago, he was Vice President of Disruptive Media, a unit working within the Ketchum Public Relations firm. "I was just trying to find cultural opportunities for these brands," he says. "Dr Pepper asked for an opportunity in music to get music fans interested in Dr Pepper. At the time, Dr Pepper's marketing campaign was asking people to drink it slowly so you can enjoy the 23 ingredients. I started thinking, *What else is happening slowly? Axl is spending time to get the right ingredients*."[3]

"We'd been doing stuff like if an NFL team scores 23 points, every team member will get a free Dr Pepper," says Greg Artkop, who was Dr. Pepper's Vice President of Corporate Communication. "We did a kiss the can thing, like hands on a hard body, but it just wasn't breaking through. When they suggested giving everyone in America a free Dr Pepper if *Chinese Democracy* came out, I thought it was genius. I am a fan of GNR, I understood what was going on here."[4]

Kooluris was given a budget of roughly $10,000. "I told the executives, 'No way is this album ever coming out. We will never have to fulfill this,'" he says. "They said, 'Okay.'"[5] Kooluris wrote up a press release, which was issued in March of 2008: "Tired of a world in which Americans idolize wannabe singers and musicals about high schoolers pass as rock n' roll music, Dr Pepper is encouraging (ok, begging) Axl Rose to finally release his 17-year-in-the-making belabored masterpiece *Chinese Democracy* in 2008. In an unprecedented show of solidarity with Axl, everyone in America, except estranged GNR guitarists Slash and Buckethead, will receive a free can of Dr Pepper if the album ships some time—anytime!—in 2008 . . . We know once it's released, people will refer to it as 'Dr Pepper for the ears' because it will be such a refreshing blend of rich, bold sounds—an instant classic."[6] [7]

Before the press release went out to the media, Kooluris posted it in various Guns N' Roses Internet forums. "They all thought it was an April Fool's joke. 'Why would Dr Pepper even care about GNR?' Because I had no budget, I set up a Blogspot. It's just this lo-fi, shitty—everyone is like, 'There is no way a company like Dr Pepper should put up a shitty website like this.'"[8]

"We put out the press release, and nothing happened," says Artkop. "Nobody talked about it. For a little over two weeks, it floated around to different media outlets. Finally it made it to *The New York Post*." Artkop pauses for dramatic effect. "It blew up. It *blew up*."[9]

Kooluris included his office phone number in the press release. "So I'm in my office the day this *Post* story goes out, March 26th, and my phone rings. 'I'm Axl Rose's lawyer. I'm about to take this to Axl. What's up?' I go, 'I'm a huge fan, I've been following the band all my life'—which was true—'if the album comes out, let's make it sweeter!' I'm thinking, *Shit, I'm gonna get fired because we're using all their IP*. The phone rings again. It was somebody saying, 'You gotta go to GNR dot com!' Axl had a response up."[10]

"We are surprised and very happy to have the support of Dr Pepper with our album *Chinese Democracy*," Rose said. "If there is any involvement with this promotion by our record company or others, we are unaware of such at this time. And as some of Buckethead's performances are on our album, I'll share my Dr Pepper with him."[11]

"Once he came out and endorsed it," Kooluris says, "it was the golden goose. 'He's not gonna sue us!' Then my phone rang *again*, and it's Bumblefoot. 'I just wanna say thank you for showing the band support. No one's been giving us much love.' Holy shit!"[12]

It was the perfect stunt—almost.

"We didn't know the album was actually going to break loose and come out," says Artkop. "I don't think anyone could have anticipated what happened. And I'm glad that social media didn't exist," he adds with an enormous laugh, "because it would have been all anyone talked about."

With his long black hair, intense gaze, and mischievous smile, it's easy to believe Kevin Cogill was once an enfant terrible. Cogill, also known by his online alias Skwerl, helped facilitate the most significant leak of music from *Chinese Democracy*. "To see a document that says, 'United States of America vs. you,' that's pretty fuckin' nuts," he says. "The check I wrote my lawyer is the biggest fucking check I ever wrote in my life."

It was Wednesday, June 18, 2008. For a few years, the Los Angeles-based Cogill had been running the music blog *Antiquiet*, which he describes as "a glorified livejournal" where he and his friends took a no rules approach to posting. Around 1:00 p.m., Cogill was pinged by an industry contact he identified as Steve. Steve was curious if Cogill was a Guns N' Roses fan.

Anyone who read *Anitquiet* knew that he was. Two weeks prior, Cogill posted a missive detailing his love for GNR and how desperately he wanted *Chinese Democracy* to be released. "Just release the fucking album," he wrote. "The more you dick around with the details, the most likely the album is to leak on the internet, spoiling whatever big plans you're cooking up anyway."[13]

Suddenly, Cogill was receiving an album-sized file from Steve. It was nine songs from *Chinese Democracy*: "Better," "Chinese Democracy," "I.R.S.," "Madagascar," "The Blues," "There Was a Time," and three untitled tracks. Many of these songs had leaked before, but to Cogill's ears they'd never sounded quite so good. Steve said he got them from a courier who'd simply walked into Jimmy Iovine's office at

Interscope Records and grabbed a CD. "I believed that," Cogill says. "I've been in Iovine's office, it is *not* high security."

"I knew the album was done, that the mixes were done. It was sitting around because they didn't know how to release it," he continues. "'How do we make our money back?' I knew that before I got the album. If this leak was intentional, I don't think it was organized. I could see Iovine purposely leaving it out . . . or I could see it the other way, like somebody stole it."

After confirming that the songs were authentic, Cogill posted them on *Antiquiet* via a streaming player, because that's what *Antiquiet* was for. It didn't take long for the website to buckle under the traffic. Cogill had to disable numerous features on the site, including the streaming player with the Guns N' Roses songs, just to get it running again. It was nearly 3:00 p.m. when Cogill received a call from Fernando Santos, son of Axl Rose's point woman Beta Labeis. Santos dished out a terse interrogation; Cogill didn't take it seriously. A couple hours later, Axl Rose's lawyers e-mailed Cogill. Cogill explained that the files had been deleted and offered an apology.

An FBI investigation was opened, with which Cogill cooperated. "The Feds wanted to take down some crime boss who didn't exist," he says, rolling his eyes. "We gave them the name of the courier. I don't know the guy, I wish him no grief. They talked to him but it went nowhere."[14] [15] Cogill was arrested on August 27 and became the first Californian charged under a new law that made distributing copyrighted works prior to their release via computer a felony. Cogill was facing three years in prison and fines of $250,000.[16]

"I had been arrested before," he says. "I'd had guns pointed at me before, I'd been to court before, so when I arrived for my first day at court and they saw I wasn't some typical nerdy shut-in blogger who was pissing his pants—I was like, 'Hey, I've been here before! What's up?'—they saw they couldn't scare me . . . well, even though they *did* scare me."[17]

Guns N' Roses immediately issued a statement: "Presently, though we don't support this guy's actions at that level, our interest is in the original source. We can't comment publicly at this time as the investigation is ongoing." Former guitarist Slash minced no words about Cogill, grousing, "I hope he rots in jail." Corynee McSherry, an attorney with digital rights nonprofit the Electronic Frontier Foundation, disagreed with Cogill's arrest. "Bringing the hammer down on an individual music fan strikes me as entirely inappropriate," she said. "Taxpayers should be concerned that they are picking up Hollywood and the music industry's legal costs, particularly when you are going after an individual like this."[18]

The music industry had been bringing the hammer down on fans like this since the Internet became a public tool. In 1997, the RIAA orchestrated a copyright lawsuit against three "archive music [web] sites" on behalf of A&M, Capitol, Geffen, and numerous other labels. A settlement was reached wherein the labels agreed not to collect their millions in damages so long as the site owners agreed not to violate copyright ever again.[19] The RIAA sued Napster in 1999, seeking damages of $100,000 per song traded on the peer-to-peer network. Metallica sued Napster for $10 million shortly thereafter. According to drummer Lars Ulrich, Napster gave them a flip answer when they asked for the names of every user swapping their songs, so Metallica gathered 335,435 names themselves, printed them out across 60,000 pages, and had a weird publicity stunt where they delivered them to Napster headquarters.[20][21][22]

The lawsuits against Napster were settled in 2001 after German media giant Bertelsmann AG bought into the company.[23] Apparently, Napster was always hoping their service would grow so large in both users and venture capital that all the record labels would be forced to partner with them.[24] If the labels were smart, that's what they would have done, because in terms of easily and rapidly distributing music online, there had never been and never would be any service as good as Napster. Unfortunately, there was too much resentment and too much old world thinking plaguing the industry. After all, the RIAA even dragged Diamond Multimedia, makers of the first portable MP3 player the Rio, to court, trying unsuccessfully to block its release.[25]

And so the labels tried creating their own MP3 services, all of which were too confusing, too expensive, and junked up with too many unnecessary safeguards.[26] "Make music easy to get for a reasonable price" was a concept the industry couldn't crack until Apple launched iTunes in 2003. Charging ninety-nine cents per song, iTunes sold 2 million songs in its first two weeks.[27][28] The caveat was that iTunes files were only compatible with one portable MP3 player—Apple's iPod.

Thus, online piracy continued, and the industry continued trying to put the squeeze on singular people. By 2006, over 26,000 lawsuits had been filed against Internet users for sharing songs illegally. Jammie Thomas, a single mother in Minnesota, was the first among these cases to turn down a settlement of a few thousand dollars, maintaining her innocence. At trial in 2007, she was ordered to pay $220,000 for the twenty-four songs she'd allegedly posted online.[29] The judge asked for a second trial, where Thomas's fine went up to a staggering $1.92 million.[30] Another federal judge later lowered that figure to $54,000, but a third trial landed on $1.5 million.[31][32] Obviously this was all egregious. As Thomas's lawyer put it, "She may have engaged in the conduct. That doesn't mean they can take her head and stick It up on a pole."[33]

Digital music theft was a problem (only about 10 percent of songs acquired online during this era were purchased legally), but globally it paled in comparison to CD piracy, which was costing the industry billions every year. The International Federation of Phonographic Industries released a report in 2005 stating that one out of every three CDs sold the previous year had been pirated, and in thirty-one countries, bootleg discs were handily outselling the genuine article. 85 percent of all CDs sold in China were illicit copies; 99 percent of Paraguay's CD market was pirated. There wasn't much press about this Stateside, as pirated CDs only accounted for a sliver of the domestic market. And little would probably ever be done about CD piracy as the IFPI sourced all the major operations to deadly organizations such as the Russian mafia and the Chinese Triad.[34] [35]

As noted, the US government was hoping to peel back the layers of Kevin Cogill's *Chinese Democracy* leak and find another Al Capone. Alas, Cogill, like most online music sharers, had no ties to organized crime. And he was confident he wouldn't end up behind bars. "There was a time when my lawyer wouldn't have wanted me to say this publicly, but it's been so long," he begins. "If we had gone to trial . . . so, the government's position would be [Guns N' Roses] were cooking this big production and we ruined it. Our defense would have been you can't prove that because it sat there for so many years. It just sat there, deadline after deadline sailed by."[36]

Interestingly enough, a couple of weeks before Cogill's arrest, *Billboard* reported that Guns N' Roses were in negotiations to release *Chinese Democracy* as an exclusive to a big box retailer like Best Buy or Wal-Mart.[37] This was no hoax; a month later, sources close to the situation confirmed that Best Buy would be releasing the album by the end of the year.[38] Another month passed; just before Cogill entered a not guilty plea, news broke that *Chinese Democracy* would be available in Best Buy stores on November 23, 2008.[39] [40]

❧

Guns N' Roses first approached Best Buy in 2006, according to Best Buy Senior Entertainment Officer Gary Arnold. "The phone rang and it was Axl's manager, who said, 'I think the record is done, and we want to launch it in a really big way,'" Arnold recalled. "I said we would of course be interested in selling it, and my first question was, 'Can I hear the music?'" Several months later, Arnold was granted that privilege. Then, nothing happened until the summer of 2008. "There was a group of people around [Rose] who—after he believed it was ready to come out—jumped into action. The ball started rolling fast, and then there was no stopping it."

Arnold believed that big box exclusives like this one were "a logical step, given the challenges of breaking out from all the noise that exists in the marketplace. As technology and entertainment products proliferate, I think artists are trying to look for ways they can be as successful as possible."[41] This was certainly true for legacy artists. In 2007, Walmart advanced the Eagles a reported $30 million for the right to release to their album *Long Road Out of Eden*. "[Walmart] can't possibly be worse than a major record label," said Eagles figurehead Don Henley. "There aren't many places where 60 year old men, no matter good their record is, can get this kind of promotion and widespread retail coverage."[42] *Long Road Out of Eden* sold over 700,000 copies in its first week; it ended up one of the best-selling albums of that year.[43] [44]

The Eagles were represented by Irving Azoff's Front Line Management, who brokered a similar deal for Journey's triple disc release *Revelation*.[45] Azoff, a music industry legend best known for heading MCA Records, had taken Guns N' Roses on as clients in March of 2008, deciding to co-manage the band with Andy Gould (former manager of Pantera and Lionel Richie).[46] [47] Apply Occam's razor here (in which the simplest explanation is likely the truth) and you have the fact that *Chinese Democracy* was still languishing until the Cogill leak set its release into motion so the defendants would have a case at the potential trial.

There's another theory, however, regarding the album's launch. Axl Rose's business affairs were messy when Azoff and Gould became his managers. Two big issues were an outstanding debt (allegedly seven figures) with the singer's former management company Sanctuary and the ongoing legal spat with Slash and Duff McKagan that began over publishing rights but now also included band merchandise. As fate (or dumb luck) would have it, a year earlier Sanctuary was swallowed up by the Universal Music Group, longtime parent company of Guns N' Roses' record label Interscope/Geffen. Supposedly, Azoff worked out a deal with Universal bigwigs to wipe Rose's slate clean if he turned over *Chinese Democracy*.[48]

It's entirely possible both scenarios are true, intertwining to bring this album's fifteen-year saga to a conclusion. What we know for sure: Slash and McKagan's complaints against Rose (as well as all counter and cross complaints) were dismissed after *Chinese Democracy's* release was announced.[49] [50] As for Cogill, he originally entered a not guilty plea but wound up pleading guilty by December.[51] [52] His felony dropped to a misdemeanor and ultimately he was sentenced to a year's probation, including two months of home confinement and "subject[ing] his computers to government scrutiny." A public service announcement he was also sentenced to appear in on behalf of the RIAA was never filmed.[53]

Some people have always believed the *Anitquiet* leak was a coordinated hoax that Cogill was in on. They point to the fact that Cogill once worked for Universal as a graphic designer. Cogill addressed this on *Antiquiet* shortly after the leak: "Many news outlets are alleging that the songs were given to me by either the record label, or the band's management, and that it was all part of a publicity stunt to drum up hype for *Chinese Democracy*. . . . While I acknowledge that this has been the most believable and legitimate publicity the album could have possibly gotten after so many false alarms, I assure you that there's no collusion. How fucked would that be, if they slipped me the album to leak, and then sent the FBI to mess with me?"[54]

"Overall, it was a pain in my ass," Cogill says today. "I didn't like the attention, the fame. I had people in my bushes. People would show up to the court dates to needle me. I'm hesitating to say I regret it, though. I don't think I do.

"Well, okay—I wouldn't do it again. Just because of the stress."[55]

※

On October 22, Guns N' Roses released the first single from *Chinese Democracy*, which was the title track. It was Rose's angry rebuttal to someone, full of weird syntax ("it would take a lot more hate than you / to end the fascination") and references to Chinese culture (the Great Wall, the Falun Gong). And yet there were also self-effacing moments; "I know that I'm a classic case," Rose sings at one point with almost facetious inflection. "Chinese Democracy's" sneering refrain ends with the pointed, tongue-in-cheek declaration "all I've got is precious time."

More than one reviewer noted similarity between the song's stammering opening riff and the Scorpions hit "Rock You Like a Hurricane." And there was praise for "Chinese Democracy's" blazing guitar solos, even though no one was sure who was playing them. "This is not a typical radio hit," *Billboard* mused, "as it's not built around an obvious melody or hook like so many Guns N' Roses classics. But that hasn't hindered massive early airplay at several rock formats, and fans are clearly responding favorably to their first (authorized) taste of new GNR music in nearly a decade."[56] [57]

Was this song worth the decade or so of waiting? "No," said Randy Hawke, program director for Madison, Wisconsin's WJJO. "I do like the song, though. I think had it come out in the early '90s it may have been groundbreaking. Now it has more of a retro, Rob Zombie feel to it. That is a core sound of JJO, though, so the fit is good. As for the audience, they want to hear it. Everyone wants to hear it." Listener reposes was also positive in New Jersey, according to WRAT's Carl Craft. "Even among those who aren't too impressed, they seem open-minded about possibly needing to hear it a few times to let it grow on them and are still interested in hearing more from the full album. . . . There's excitement on the phones about this record."[58]

Slash heard "Chinese Democracy" while he was being interviewed by WBCN in Boston. "That sounds cool," he said. "It's good to hear [Axl's] voice again, y'know?"[59]

"Chinese Democracy" peaked at #5 on *Billboard's* Mainstream Rock chart. More importantly, the song's release was the strongest signal yet of its namesake album's materialization. This put Chris Kooluris on edge. He'd already spent much of the year worrying that the top brass at Dr. Pepper weren't taking his *Chinese Democracy* promotion seriously. "Months go by and they're still not really working on a contingency plan if the album actually comes out," he says. "They didn't get it. I had this strange suspicion that they weren't gonna fulfill the [free soda] offer."[60]

Dr Pepper Comms VP Greg Artkop pushes back on this. "Chris would have had no insight into that, into our preparation," he says. "But again, I don't think anyone could have anticipated what happened. We were hearing over the summer from [Guns N' Roses] management that it might be released. They reached out and we were talking about some promotional support, which never came to fruition. To be fair, I don't know that anything that [they] said we took as one hundred percent fact, because of all the previous release date promises."[61]

Kooluris insists that the beverage executives were totally disconnected from the reality of the situation. "We put together a sizzle reel of all the media coverage and they were flabbergasted. This was the same year they invested all this money into the new *Indiana Jones* movie. They were like, 'What the fuck? This $10,000 press release is trumping *Indiana Jones*?'"[62]

Around the time of the "Chinese Democracy" single's debut, Dr. Pepper explained how their giveaway would work. Americans were instructed to log on to Dr. Pepper's website on November 23 to redeem their coupon for one free twenty oz. soda. "Coupons will be available for 24 hours," the company said. "Allow 4-6 weeks for coupon to arrive. Coupon will expire on February 28, 2009. Limit one coupon per person."[63] "It's going to be real easy," one spokesperson assured.[64]

Another person stressing during the run-up to *Chinese Democracy's* release was artist and graphic designer Ryan Corey. Corey worked for Smog Design, the company hired to create *Chinese Democracy's* artwork. "Nothing with *Chinese Democracy* followed any procedure that I knew," Corey says. "It was definitely a roller coaster. We got it because we had done a bunch of work with Irving Azoff. He set us up with the point man for *Chinese Democracy*, Del James. And Del came up with the bicycle image that's on the cover.

"We did a whole bunch of stuff with the bicycle image. There was a whole lot of back and forth on it, even down to the type design. I had a custom type design I made and threw on there. Axl liked it, but there were a bunch of problems with it, like how it was spaced. I tried to show him other types, but he had his heart set on this specific one. Anyway, Del left after a while and then we were dealing with Beta [Lebeis]. This is just conjecture on my part, but I think there was some strife in the Axl camp. Strife between Del and Beta, maybe, like who's in charge. There was a lot of weird stuff going on in the background."

Corey describes Lebeis as a demanding client who didn't respect his privacy. "She would call my house at 11 at night and I wouldn't answer. Then she would complain to my boss about it. So that was difficult." Regardless, there were moments of levity, such as the time Lebeis forwarded Corey a rambling, stream of consciousness e-mail from Rose. "I think she was supposed to edit it down, but I got the whole thing. He was trying to figure out all this art, and the whole thing was like, 'What does this mean? What if we put a squirrel here?' That was funny."

Corey and the team at Smog worked on the cover for about a month. "Then, for the rest of the art . . . [usually] we have a week or two to put it together," Corey says, "but once the cover was ready they needed everything else the next day. And the directive was basically, 'put something together.' So I worked overnight. I slept for an hour in the morning and went back into work. We were just trying to satisfy Axl at that point. Everything you see in that package I did in one day. I don't know if I should say this, but all that Chinese imagery came from me. I had 24 hours to put together an album called *Chinese Democracy* and that's what I put together.

"So we turned in the original package, and we think we're done. 'Thank god that's over.' But then we had to do the art version, which we didn't realize was happening. I had been reporting to Beta and contacts at Universal. Beta was saying, 'Keep sending me stuff.' I was wondering why. The record company told me to ignore it. 'We're not doing another version.' But Axl was insistent. They did a small run in the end . . . the record company didn't really care because they had the original package for the release date."[65]

The liner notes were naturally extensive; surprisingly, they included the names of several people who did not actually work on *Chinese Democracy*. "After it came out, people were calling me up, asking, 'How'd you get that credit?'" says Bob Koszela, who was the manager at Interscope's in-house studio where Guns N' Roses spent a month and a half not recording anything in 2004. "'Jimmy's pissed! He's only in there once, you're in there three times!' I asked Caram Costanzo about it and he said, 'We know how hard you work.'"[66] David Dominguez, an engineer who worked with GNR at Rumbo Recorders in the late '90s, says this wasn't unusual. "They gave me a credit on *Live Era* even though I didn't do anything on that one. Axl just liked me."[67]

Guns N' Roses had wanted the *Chinese Democracy* artwork to include a piece by Beijing visual artist Chen Zhuo that depicted Tiananmen Square as an amusement park. The band offered Zhou $18,000, and he was very flattered, but after reading the lyrics to the album's title track, he declined. "We have to take political risks into account as artists in China," he said.[68]

Believe it or not, Guns N' Roses were considered a political band in China. Their music was embraced by Chinese youth in the '80s who felt Orthodox Communism was failing them. An ocean of these kids spent weeks occupying Tiananmen Square in the spring of 1989, pleading for democracy (the government answered with bloodshed, deploying the military, who murdered protestors by the thousands). Regardless of controversy, in 2007 Guns N' Roses was voted China's eighth most beloved rock group during a presentation on state-controlled China Central Television. There was a big audience in China for *Chinese Democracy*, but the title was radioactive.

Pro-democracy demonstrators in Tiananmen Square, May 1989. *Source: Photo by The Asahi Shimbun via Getty Images.*

China's government dissuaded retailers from stocking *Chinese Democracy* while simultaneously blocking the album's website and any related Internet searches (fans tried searching "Chinese Democraxy" and "Chi Dem" instead). Strangely enough, Chinese Internet users had no difficulty accessing the Myspace stream of the entire album that launched on November 20.

Global Times, the Chinese government's official newspaper, denounced *Chinese Democracy* as a venomous attack and another attempt by the West to impose their will on the world. A fax sent to China's Foreign Ministry by the Associated Press asking a series of questions about the article was ignored. "We don't need to comment on that," said one anonymous spokesperson. No one at China's Culture Ministry and State Administration of Radio, Film, and Television could be reached for comment, either.[69]

Meanwhile, Chinese citizens debated *Chinese Democracy* online. "I feel GNR has [a] mocking, misunderstanding and disdainful view of our country," one user named Tiffany from Guangzhou wrote on social networking site Douban.com. "You are judging it just from the album's name," responded a Mr. Lee from Guiyang. "Did you ever try to listen to it, understand it and think about it?"[70] There were those who savored the fact that a new Guns N' Roses album was irritating the establishment. As one citizen put it, "Rock n' roll, as a weapon, is an invisible bomb."[71]

What about Chinese fans who actually heard the music? Nicreve Lee, a student who ran a GNR website, offered his immediate thoughts on the first single: "This is an anti-China song." After a few more listens, he said, "I gradually began to understand what the song wants to say. Perhaps Axl Rose doesn't know China well, but at least he is on the right track."[72]

❧

Eager to engage the fans, Best Buy hosted nine *Chinese Democracy* listening parties across the United States the week before the album's release. Fortune cookies and finger cuffs were among the party favors Minneapolis's Fine Line Music Cafe put out for the soirée on November 18. Once the album was played, a reporter on the scene described the reaction as "generally favorable but rarely fawning." One listener, Scott Farrell, didn't think *Chinese Democracy* was poised for greatness. "It's not the real Guns N' Roses," he said.[73]

On November 20, Bostonians gathered for a listen at the city's Hard Rock Cafe location. "The air was anything but electric," wrote Joan Anderman in *The Boston Globe*. "People sat politely at tables, milled at the bar, and chatted as the songs blared." WAAF DJ Mike Hsu emceed the event. "I don't know how it's going to do," he said. "I'm of the school that believes this isn't really Guns N' Roses, not without Slash and Izzy and the other guys, and that's an obstacle. If people can let go of the old concept of GNR then they might love it. It is not boring."

The headline news out of these listening parties was Tom Zutaut's ejection from the L.A. event at the Roxy. Zutaut, the storied figure who signed Guns N' Roses to Geffen Records in the '80s, claimed he was asked to leave with just three songs remaining to be played. "I did stand on the sidewalk and hear the last three anyway," he said. Zutaut had plenty more to say about this incident, rattling off a diatribe that sounded like a teenager trying to process a bad breakup. "It is sad and disappointing to me that those around Axl would lie to him to fuel his hatred towards me with imaginary events used to drive a wedge between us. I love him deeply, will always love him and wish only the greatest success to one of the world's last true creative musical sparks with a god-given voice. I am proud of my contributions to his career and am always there for him should he one day become enlightened to the truth of what surrounds him. . . . I wear his hatred like a badge of honor as it would be far worse for him not to care at all."[74]

It's unclear if Axl Rose was at the Roxy that night. In fact, it's unclear where Axl Rose was at any point during the final sprint toward *Chinese Democracy*. He certainly wasn't doing any press or media to promote his brand-new album. Was he holed up in his Malibu mansion? Partying in Vegas? At least one report placed Axl Rose at a bagel shop that week in Sin City. Rumors circulated about friction between Rose and his management team.[75][76]

In lieu of Rose, the press settled for people in Rose's orbit. "There is no one as meticulous as Axl," said Guns N' Roses bass player Tommy Stinson. "He wants to get everything right. I can't argue with that." Per *Chinese Democracy's* lengthy gestation period, band co-manager Andy Gould added, "When they asked Michelangelo to paint the Sistine Chapel, they didn't say, 'Can you do it in the fourth quarter?' Great art sometimes takes time." Sebastian Bach, who was kind of a satellite member of Guns at this point, loved being the hype man: "Wait until you hear this album. This version of GNR rocks. There is some incredibly heavy stuff on the album. Axl sounds amazing. It's a classic album that you won't forget."[77] [78]

Rose did grant at least one interview prior to *Chinese Democracy's* release, an e-mail exchange with noted music journalist Gary Graff, but their conversation wasn't published in *The Oakland Press* until the following March. Rose explained his publicity conundrum: "If I talk, I need to 'shut the fuck up.' If I don't talk, it's much worse." Graff asked if the gap between albums was frustrating or if the process was its own reward. "Ha! Last thing anyone wants to read about are *my* frustrations!" What was Rose's creative goal with *Chinese Democracy*? "No.1 was just to be involved in what I felt was a good record that I could stand behind with confidence, with no shame artistically, to know that I gave the public our best efforts with no compromise and no holding back."

When did Rose know the album was finished? "Working with Bumble's fills, [Frank Ferrer's] additions and various intro bits etc, a lot happened in our final month of mixing as well as in mastering." Did Rose have a good time making the album? "No, not really, but I like the people [involved] and what we were able to accomplish. It was much better than previous lineups, and if not for the ugliness around us and the circumstances I'm sure it would've been much more fun." How did Rose think the world viewed Guns N' Roses in 2008? "I'm not so sure the world at large cares one way or the other."[79]

A fascinating subplot was brewing that week, and it involved a national coalition of independent record stores called Music Monitor, who were doing everything they possibly could to fight big box exclusives. Buying in bulk from overseas distributors, the coalition was able to get albums like *Chinese Democracy* and AC/DC's *Black Ice* (a Walmart exclusive released that October) into mom and pop stores. That's how Utah's Graywhale chain managed to start selling *Chinese Democracy* five days before its release. Graywhale co-owner Jonathan Tueller said this wasn't about money—they were trying to make a statement about business survival. "Our whole drive is that if you're a fan of music, and there's an artist you want, we want to have it," he explained. "We need to find a way to get this into our stores."

"It's unethical for [the record labels] to not make [the albums] available," complained Steve Duncan, head of purchasing for southwestern chain ZIA. Duncan, like many others, was upset because the labels wouldn't be able to break newer artists without the support of their stores. So why shouldn't ZIA and Graywhale and countless other indies across the country be allowed to stock sure-fire sellers from big-name artists? AC/DC's label Columbia turned their back on small retailers, Duncan said, but still expected them to promote AC/DC's back catalog.[80] The situation was particularly galling with *Chinese Democracy*. This was the first Guns N' Roses album in several decades, a disc some estimated could sell 600,000 copies in its first week (the previous week's #1 album, Taylor Swift's *Fearless*, sold 592,000).[81]

Best Buy refused to comment on Music Monitor; Walmart threatened legal action.[82] Neither of these companies would dare to acknowledge an ethical line drawn by a certain segment of the population. "Some people are just not ever going to go to a Walmart or Best Buy," said Bob Fuchs, who managed the famed Electric Fetus store in Minneapolis. Electric Fetus bought a stock of the previous year's Walmart exclusive Eagles CD; the discs were marked up by a few dollars but Fuchs said that dozens of people were thanking them for stocking the album.[83]

Unfortunately, independent record stores were losing the war against corporate chains. 3,000 standalone shops had closed since 2002, and as *Chinese Democracy* was being unleashed, Walmart and Best Buy were in fact the nation's two largest retail music sellers.[84] This is what drove essayists to declare *Chinese Democracy* the last old world music release, the conclusion to an era that had probably actually concluded years before.

"To an extent, I didn't care about *Chinese Democracy*," says Stevie Rachelle, longtime vocalist for Tuff and creator of tongue-on-cheek heavy metal news website *Metal Sludge*. "But I will say this—on release day, I went to Best Buy in Reseda and that's the first time I bought a record on release day in probably a decade, maybe more. That was also the last time I ever did that."[85]

Orthodox Guns N' Roses fans made a point of showing up hours before Best Buy locations opened the morning of Sunday, November 23, but their numbers were a far cry from the hordes that descended upon record stores seventeen years earlier for *Use Your Illusion*. Only two fans milled around outside a location in Buffalo, NY.[86] Ron Selander was the only person waiting for the Best Buy in Axl Rose's hometown of Lafayette, Indiana to unlock its doors. "I'm pretty psyched," he was quoted as saying. "They're just a great American rock band."[87]

The real frenzy that day was on Dr. Pepper dot com. Chris Kooluris knew the company hadn't allocated enough server space to handle the number of people who might want to claim their free drink. "They were like, 'Only 90,000 people are gonna log on,'" Kooluris says. "I was like, 'Guns N' Roses sold 90 million records. You need to get the servers ready.' Well, a hundred thousand people logged on in the first hour. The website was down for two days."[88]

In addition to the immediate crashing of their website, Dr. Pepper's phone lines were jammed with callers trying to get their soda. "Dr Pepper," "dr pepper chinese democracy," and numerous variations on those phrases flooded Google's search terms.[89] That night, Dr. Pepper extended the promotion until the following evening.[90] "People are passionate about Dr Pepper," said Marketing VP Tony Jacobs. "The response has been greater than anticipated and we want to do everything we can to ensure Dr Pepper fans get their free coupon."[91]

On November 25, attorneys representing Guns N' Roses fired off an angry letter to Dr. Pepper condemning their actions. Initially, the letter was credited to Alan Gutman, and in part it read: "Our clients are outraged at your treatment of their fans and the American public in general. The redemption scheme your company implemented for this offer was an unmitigated disaster which defrauded consumers and, in the eyes of vocal fans, ruined the day of *Chinese Democracy*'s release. . . . It turned out that Dr Pepper did not define 'everyone in America' the same way as 'everyone in America' defined 'everyone in America.'"

A demand was made of Dr. Pepper to issue a full page apology in *The New York Times*, the *Los Angeles Times, USA Today*, and *The Wall Street Journal*. GNR's attorneys also wanted "appropriate payment" for "the unauthorized use and abuse of their publicity and intellectual property rights." A lawsuit was threatened if Dr. Pepper failed to respond appropriately.[92] [93] [94] Laurie Soriano, another lawyer for Guns N' Roses, told CNN she'd actually authored the letter, complaining, "When you go on the blogs and you read the responses from the fans, they associate Axl with this promotion . . . and blame him for the fact that they didn't get their free soda."[95]

"We received that fax the Tuesday or Wednesday before Thanksgiving," Dr Pepper's Greg Artkop says. "In all honesty, it was probably meant to get more exposure for the record over the holiday weekend."[96] Dr. Pepper was not conciliatory. "We are disappointed that GNR's lawyers are turning a fun giveaway into a legal dispute," the company said in a statement. "Axl even expressed support for our efforts earlier this year. . . . For those who contacted us in the week after the giveaway about difficulties requesting the coupon, we continued to offer free coupons to address any problems they may have encountered. This was the largest response we have ever received for a giveaway. We wish Guns N' Roses the best with their album."[97] [98]

During an online chat with fans that December, someone asked Axl Rose if suing Dr. Pepper was still something he was considering. "Sure," the singer replied, "but the actions taken so far had nothing to do with me and I was taken off guard as I had specifically told our team who fucking cares, [right] now we have a record to deal with. My feelings are after their public response. It was cute. Maybe the guy who got it rolling originally meant well but it turned out sour and maybe it's just me but he seems like maybe he wants a bit too much attention so."[99]

Kooluris does like to tell people he helped get *Chinese Democracy* released. It's on his LinkedIn profile; it came up in a 2014 *New York Daily News* story about a relationship-ending argument he had with his fiancée over turning their bedroom into an '80s style arcade.¹⁰⁰ Kooluris does also claim that he tried to get Dr. Pepper to do the right thing and get everyone in the country their free soda, to no avail. "They were trying to spin it, and I was like, 'Get the site up! Get the coupons out!'" he says. "They took the bad way out and never really fulfilled the offer."¹⁰¹

"I don't know the final number," Artkop says when asked how many coupon requests Dr. Pepper actually fulfilled. "I know when the site crashed, Dr Pepper continued to give out coupons to anyone who asked." Could he ballpark a figure? "I'm sorry, I don't know."¹⁰²

It is entirely possible Dr. Pepper only sent out a comically low number of coupons. They did send them out, though, starting in mid-December. "The Dr delivers our promise," the mailer containing the coupon read. "Remember to drink it slow." No references to *Chinese Democracy*, Guns N' Roses, or their iconography were present on the coupons.¹⁰³

"When you look back at it, we had seven months of smart and seven days of stupid," says Artkop. "Was this the most challenging thing I had to do? Yes. Is there no such thing as bad publicity? Absolutely. The flip side of that is how much attention are you willing to endure? And if there's a key lesson here, I'd like it to be this: everybody loves Guns N' Roses."¹⁰⁴

In many respects, James Joyce was the Guns N' Roses of avant-garde Interwar era writers. Joyce's 1922 novel *Ulysses* attracted controversy because he eschewed literary convention for a feverish ramble that left readers wondering if they were holding a book or a 700 page joke.¹⁰⁵ ¹⁰⁶ There were also debates concerning the work's decency. "[*Ulysses*] is not pornographic," Arnold Bennett stated in an essay for *Bookman*, "But it is more indecent, obscene, scatological, and licentious than the majority of professedly pornographical books."¹⁰⁷ Cincinnati newspaper *The Billboard* denounced *Ulysses* as "printed fecal matter."¹⁰⁸ The book endured a decade-plus ban in the United States after a New York literary magazine printed an excerpt that was ruled to be too sexually frank by a court of law. The offending passage is milquetoast by today's standards. Modern readers of *Ulysses* would be more bothered by Joyce's repeated use of the word "nigger."¹⁰⁹ ¹¹⁰ ¹¹¹

On the other hand, some people hailed *Ulysses* asunprecedented genius; even Arnold Bennett admitted Joyce's writing could be "dazzlingly original" and that the best segments of *Ulysses* "are immortal."¹¹² ¹¹³ Devotees had to wait seventeen years for Joyce's next novel, the murkier and even more baffling *Finnegans Wake*. Joyce took his craft to the next level in this book by weaving together an impenetrable thicket of foreign languages (including those of his own creation). *Newsweek* called *Finnegans Wake* "the nightmare of a man who has read and learned too much."[114] A reviewer for *The Spectator* lamented not having an entire month to unravel Joyce's intent.[115] A cottage industry grew around trying to understand *Finnegans Wake*, the foundational text of which was the 1944 guide *A Skeleton Key to Finnegans Wake*. Max Lerner of *The New York Times* praised that volume: "If you try to read *Finnegans Wake* without [*A Skeleton Key*] . . . you will soon hang yourself from the rafters of your study."[116]

Axl Rose's hysterical sincerity prevented *Chinese Democracy* from becoming as inscrutable as *Finnegans Wake*. Regardless, it was probably the most Joycean work released by a major label rock band in 2008. As such, the album bemused and exhausted many professional critics. "*Chinese Democracy* isn't a masterpiece—it's more curious than actually great—but it's never dull," wrote Allison Stewart for *The Washington Post*, "encompassing everything from classic rock to prog rock to actual rock, with nods to *Phantom of The Opera*, hip hop, industrial, Putumayo's world music compilations, and countless other things that should never, ever go together."[117] In *The New Yorker*, Ben Greenman said, "Most of the songs are as modest as a rococo cathedral. That style can drag down the hard rock compositions, which traffic mostly in paranoia and resignation; even the stronger ones ('Better,' 'There Was a Time') are short on clean pop hooks." Still, Greenman celebrated Rose as "one of the most compelling rock singers out there" before jabbing him: "He certainly is out there."[118]

Chicago Sun-Times scribe Jim Derogatis likened *Chinese Democracy* to famously unsatisfying sequel *The Godfather III*. "The biggest problem," Derogatis noted, "is the same one that marred the band's last batch of original material, the two *Use Your Illusion* discs released in 1991 . . . Determined to be hailed as more than just a 'mere' hard rocker, [Axl] Rose began to worry entirely too much about his reputation as an artiste, incorporating diverse experimentation in other genres for which he had little feeling or talent. . . . About half of the 14 songs here wear out their welcome shortly after you're done marveling at all of the filigree. . . . [*Chinese Democracy*] is redeemed in part by its most straightforward, hardest-rocking and simplest moments . . . though even these require us to accept that 'simple' can describe a song with five or six studio guitarists shredding simultaneously."[119]

"Like light reaching the Earth years after its originating star has burnt out, *Chinese Democracy* is finally among us," wrote Robert Everett-Green in *The Globe and Mail*. "The central error of this record is that Rose thinks you can make epic music simply by adding more layers and jamming longer. Even the ballads tend to billow up into pompous overstatement. There's a lot of good playing on this record—too much, in fact. As Rose & Co. noodle their way in the direction of yet another elusive catharsis, you remember that it was because of this kind of thing that punk rock was invented."[120] And yet, for all that layering and jamming, a handful of reviewers complained that *Chinese Democracy* sounded thin and poorly mixed, with no bottom wallop.[121] [122]

Rob Harvilla of *The Village Voice* felt otherwise. "*Chinese Democracy* marks the death of something," he opined, "some combination of the music industry, 'the album' as a unit of cultural import, old-guard rock stardom, irony, sincerity, free-market capitalism, hip-hop, the spread offense . . . [but] what has really died here is the word overproduced. It will no longer suffice. So dense, so suffocating, so paranoid-android synthetic, so ludicrously engorged is Axl's magnum opus that you will have absolutely no problem believing it took dozens of people millions of dollars and nearly two decades to complete it. This is the mythical burrito microwaved by God that's so hot, God himself cannot eat it . . . it's a deeply unpleasant experience. You'll warm up to it. Maybe. Cling to Axl's voice. He's still got it, that deranged shriek-to-moan bazooka of lust, contempt, pathos, and megalomania that made us love him."

Harvilla's bottom line was, "You can fall in love with the idea of this album and eventually teach yourself to love the album itself, but nothing packs a tenth of vitality and exhilaration of, oh, let's say, 'It's So Easy' . . . ['It's So Easy' is] an objectively perfect song, and though objectively perfect songs aren't effortless, per se, they sound that way—the effort, the craft, the forethought, the money, the time, and the personnel they require is the least interesting and prominent thing about them. *Chinese Democracy* is the inverse: a hilariously painstaking attempt to synthesize that lightning, a lost cause taken to delirious extremes, a fascinating catastrophe inspiring equal parts awe and pity. A would-be Hollywood blockbuster upstaged by its own credits."[123]

Pitchfork, the music review website that became a major taste-maker in the new millennium, awarded *Chinese Democracy* a 5.8 out of 10. Reviewer Ian Cohen felt the album was salvaged by the talent involved, though ultimately the whole thing was hobbled by Axl Rose's creative direction. "Even if *Chinese Democracy* had dropped a decade previous, it would still sound dated," Cohen wrote. "1996 appears to be the cut-off point for sonic inspiration, a time when the height of electronic and rock synergy in pop music involved having an acoustic guitar and a drum machine on the same track. Fans deserve better than hearing Axl trying to fight with post-NIN nobodies like Stabbing Westward and Gravity Kills for ideas." Cohen was also puzzled by the fact that the bulk of the lyrics on *Chinese Democracy* seemed to be about the creation of *Chinese Democracy*.[124]

Chuck Klosterman noted this as well in his write-up for *The AV Club*, surmising that more than half the album outlines Rose's quest to bring this project to fruition. "The rest of the vocal material tends to suggest some kind of abstract regret over an undefined romantic relationship punctuated by betrayal," he wrote, "but that might just be the way all hard rock songs seem when the singer plays a lot of piano and only uses pronouns." Klosterman also wondered if samples from Martin Luther King, Jr. speeches woven into the soundscape of "Madagascar" were Rose's way of apologizing for the noxious racism of his 1988 song "One in a Million." Dr. King's words share space with dialogue from films like *Braveheart, Casualties of War, Mississippi Burning,* and Rose's old favorite *Cool Hand Luke,* and the basic gist is one of tolerance. The lyrics Rose sings could be construed as a bigot questioning everything they've been taught.

Of course, as Klosterman pointed out, "the most compelling question is never 'What was Axl doing here?' but 'What did Axl *think* he was doing here?'" Klosterman, a culture writer renowned for trying to ascribe deep meaning to every single thing Axl Rose ever did, awarded *Chinese Democracy* an A- and summarized by saying, "I find myself impressed by how close *Chinese Democracy* comes to fulfilling the absurdly impossible expectation it self-generated, and I not-so-secretly wish this had actually been a triple album. . . . The final truth is this: [Axl] makes the best songs. They sound the way I want songs to sound. A few of them seem idiotic at the beginning, but I love the way they end. Axl Rose put so much time and effort into proving that he was super-talented that the rest of humanity forgot he always had been. And that will hurt him. This record may tank commercially. Some people will slaughter *Chinese Democracy,* and for all the reasons you expect. But he did a good thing here."[125]

Ann Powers of the *Los Angeles Times* put forth the theory that the years spent on *Chinese Democracy* were all about Axl Rose's "fight to become and remain an auteur in a pop world increasingly hostile to such individualists." "Making this album has transformed Rose from a hungry contrarian to a full-blown desert prophet," Powers wrote, "howling mightily in protest against a pop industry that encourages its stars to innovate only within the realm of what sells best. At the same time, he's resisted the nostalgia that would have sent after a purer time or sound, preferring to invest in a foggy future. Purity is the opposite of what Rose seeks on *Chinese Democracy*. Convolution is everything as he spirals toward a total sound even he can't quite comprehend. . . . Lovers of 'edgy' music may find it too melodic and rooted in the blues, while fans seeking simple catharsis may rue the many shifts in tone and tempo."[126]

Naturally, Axl Rose's contemporaries weighed in on *Chinese Democracy*. "I have to say that I pretty much love it," enthused Jane's Addiction guitarist Dave Navarro. "The way I have been describing it has been 70% awesome and 30% really weird, but after a few listens the weird becomes awesome again. I don't know if it's the songs or the fact that I just enjoy hearing that guy's voice or both, but I am a fan."[127] Metallica drummer Lars Ulrich was also a big fan, even agreeing to appear in the video for his favorite song from *Chinese Democracy*,

"Better," which was ultimately never released. Ulrich listed *Chinese Democracy* as one of his favorite discs of the past decade, alongside such works as Green Day's *American Idiot*, the Sword's *Age of Winters*, and the Arctic Monkeys' *Whatever People Say* (his top pick).[128] [129]

Former Guns N' Roses rhythm guitarist Gilby Clarke said *Chinese Democracy* was "very good and very creative" but added, "There are too many slow-to-midtempo songs on it for my taste and some of the solos are a little overdone; they don't match the song. [Also] some of the lyrics are a little redundant."[130] Asked if he enjoyed the new album, founding Guns N' Roses drummer Steven Adler replied, "Not one bit. I didn't recognize Axl's voice on it. There's occasional parts where he does his loud scream but I didn't even know it was him."[131] Meanwhile, other former Gunners Izzy Stradlin and Matt Sorum both expressed appreciation for *Chinese Democracy*.

And what about Slash? "It's a really good record," he said. "It's very different from what the original Guns N' Roses sounded like, but it's a great statement by Axl. Now you understand where he was heading all this time. It's a record that the original Guns N' Roses could never possibly make. And at the same time it just shows you how brilliant Axl is."[132]

Six guitarists are credited on *Chinese Democracy*—Buckethead, Bumblefoot, Robin Finck, Paul Tobias, Richard Fortus, Chris Pitman, and Axl Rose—and there are numerous songs where five or all six are playing together. One notable guitarist was cut from the proceedings, however. Brian May from Queen made several contributions to the album in 1999, including a solo for the song "Catcher in the Rye," that disappeared before *Chinese Democracy* hit shelves. May learned he'd been cut when a fan send him a leaked copy of the liner notes.

"Ah . . . well, I did not know this!" May wrote on his website. "Well, it is a shame, perhaps. . . . I did put quite a lot of work in, and was proud of it. But I could understand if Axl wants to have an album which reflects the work of the members of the band as it is, right now. I do have the mixes of the tracks with my guitar on, work tapes at the time, but they will remain private, out of respect for Axl."[133]

Rose offered a typically convoluted explanation as to why May had been taken off *Chinese Democracy*, during which he insinuated that May had only provided the "Catcher in the Rye" solo and briefly veered off topic to complain that too many fans were still asking about Slash. Rose eventually explained that he and producer Sean Beavan had edited together May's final solo from numerous takes and that May objected to what he heard. "I remember looking at Brian standing to my left," Rose said, "and him staring at the big studio speakers a bit aghast, saying,

'But that's not what I played.' Sean Beavan and I were not in any way trying to mess with Brian, we just did what we do and then try and do our best to stand up for our decisions."

Ever the gentleman, May responded: "It's very simple, really. . . . Axl is making his record, and he can do whatever he wants! After all these years, I'm still a huge fan. It was such a long time ago, it tends to recede into the mists of time . . . [but] I certainly don't remember anything about disapproving of any 'comping' Sean Beavan had done. . . . I had actually comped it up with him myself. Of course, soon afterwards, Sean was taken off the project, although I have to say I thought the tracks were overall sounding bloody good at that time!" May also acknowledged that a version of "Catcher" had leaked with his solo intact, but that he wasn't to blame. "I kept [my rough mixes] private, because that's the professional way to be."[134]

The warm, rich tone May made famous in Queen is easily recognized in the leaked version of "Catcher in the Rye," and it compliments the breezy melody nicely. May, of course, had some degree of influence on Slash, and in a hypothetical situation where Brian May didn't exist, one might guess Slash was actually playing on "Catcher."[135] Maybe this was Axl Rose's way of trying to obtain a Slash-like feel without Slash. Maybe May's solo was ditched because it was too close to Slash. It's a moot point since this guitar solo was deemed non-canonical.

Chinese Democracy sold 261,000 copies its first week of release, falling well short of estimates that forecasted a number anywhere between 300,000 and 800,000 units. The measuring stick was AC/DC's *Black Ice*, which, released as a Walmart exclusive a month earlier, sold a robust 784,000 its first week. The major handicap for Guns N' Roses was that Best Buy only had 950 locations versus Walmart's 4,200. Walmart also threw their weight behind *Black Ice*, creating special AC/DC mini-stores in each location where fans could also purchase AC/DC merchandise and the group's back catalog (92,000 copies of older AC/DC albums were sold that first week as well). Meanwhile, many consumers who visited Best Buy for *Chinese Democracy* had a difficult time finding the album. *Billboard* writer Ed Christman said he did two circles around a Best Buy in Queens, checking the Guns N' Roses section in the CD bins, and still didn't see it. Employees eventually guided him to a small cardboard kiosk at the end of the center aisle.[136] [137]

One would think Best Buy would have done everything possible to move *Chinese Democracy* considering they bought 1.3 million copies on the condition that no unsold stock could be returned to Interscope. It was standard practice for retailers to return unsold CDs and LPs to record labels for refunds or future purchase credit. The discs themselves might be resold as discount stock or destroyed and recycled (millions of copies of *Rudebox*, the 2006 bomb by Robbie Williams, were apparently ground up for pavement and street lights in China). Thieves working along the supply chain might also pilfer CDs for the foreign black market. Best Buy executives probably wished thieves would ransack their *Chinese Democracy* stock as they watched sales drop 78 percent in the second week of sales.[138] [139] [140] [141]

Chinese Democracy's failure to take off was especially embarrassing because classic fist-clenching heavy metal was making a comeback. It wasn't just AC/DC, whose *Black Ice* was a million seller within two weeks' time, but Metallica, who came roaring back that September with the acclaimed *Death Magnetic* after God knows how many years in the weeds.[142] The asterisk here was both AC/DC and Metallica had been actively making music for the past two decades, a timespan where Guns N' Roses remained a big question mark. As *Billboard's* Keith Caulfield put it when forecasting *Chinese Democracy's* success, "This entire project exists outside the normal universe of expectations about what something should sound like or what it should sell."[143]

Interscope tried at least one unconventional marketing technique. Two songs from *Chinese Democracy* were added to the *StripJoints* compilation, a CD packaged with *Exotic Dancer* magazine, a publication that circulated among 2,500 of America's "sexually oriented clubs."[144]

Axl Rose stayed off the grid into December. "People have been trying to contact Axl for two months and he's completely AWOL," an anonymous source told *The Sun*. Allegedly, Interscope/Geffen hadn't heard from the singer since he delivered the final cut of *Chinese Democracy*. "It is frustrating," the source said, "because the album would have had a much better chance of going to number one if he had only been prepared to show his face. You would have thought after spending all those years on an album you might do a few weeks of promotion."[145] *The New York Post* reported that Rose had secretly been diagnosed with anthropophobia (a fear of people).[146]

Rose broke his silence mid-month when he submitted himself to inquiries from various Guns N' Roses fan websites. One fan did ask why he wasn't doing more press for *Chinese Democracy*. "What I have to say a lot of people have no desire to hear," he replied. "With our team we were able to negotiate [through] a mountain of issues to be able to release the album. Within those negotiations I believed I had secured agreements, commitments and assurances that would have allowed a promotional strategy to be implemented that obviously I've had a fair amount of time to consider. Unfortunately those things never happened and once the record was closer to release the biz went about things in their standard business as usual mode."[147]

The following February, another anonymous source gave a different explanation to *Rolling Stone*. "When Geffen sat down with [Axl] and said, 'OK, are you going to be around with this? Are you ready?', he said yes. But then he said no to everything."[148] The same week, *Billboard* published a Q&A with Rose where he went into detail about his issues with Interscope/Geffen. "Unfortunately I have no information for me to believe [that] there was any real involvement or effort from Interscope. I'm not saying there wasn't. But in my opinion, without Jimmy Iovine's involvement, it doesn't matter who anyone talks to or what they say—virtually nothing will happen from their end.... That's not to say they don't work for other artists and make things happen. I feel they work very hard for whatever it is they truly want to sell."[149]

Rose went on, saying that Guns N' Roses felt Interscope's investment in them did not extend beyond "a throw it at the wall, see if it sticks, no real ground work, something to take advantage of, last quarter, cook the books, write-off, fuck this headache, hoping to get lucky scam."[150] He wasn't the only artist unhappy with the Interscope experience. The Brian Setzer Orchestra were as big as a swing band could get at the turn of the century; Setzer was flabbergasted when the label did nothing with their 2000 album *Vavoom!*[151] Post-hardcore group ... And You Will Know Us by the Trail of Dead left Interscope after four years in the mid-2000s because they felt totally ignored.[152] Weezer's Rivers Cuomo was frustrated being on Interscope circa the same stretch of time because the in-house mantra was "rock is dead." "They had no interest in even putting out our records," Cuomo told *Rolling Stone*.[153]

Josh Homme from Queens of the Stone Age heard the same thing once when Queens were on Interscope—rock was dead. He came close to punching the executive who said it.[154] Homme described Interscope as "a constant battle" and was specifically annoyed with the label's lack of tech savvy. "I can't download my music from the Interscope website," he pointed out, "because they gave that power away to iTunes.... Sounds like a bunch of fucking idiots to me."[155] [156] Trent Reznor had similar feelings about Interscope bungling his art in the digital age: "The Internet had decimated their business, and they still don't know how instant messaging works." Reznor and Nine Inch Nails ended their 13-year relationship with label in 2007.[157]

It was, of course, obvious just from a glance that Interscope always had more interest in their hip-hop and pop acts, but Weezer, Trail of Dead, Queens et al. did get multiple records out on the label before realizing the situation wasn't ideal. Guns N' Roses, on the other hand, spent ten years trying to release just one work on Interscope. This, despite the fact, as Rose said, that they fell into a cycle where every few months an unbearable tension mounted because Universal Music started putting pressure on Interscope to start putting pressure on Guns N' Roses to wrap *Chinese Democracy* up (somehow, Iovine would step in and fix it every time).[158]

Obviously, Rose kept a schedule that wasn't consistent with anyone else's reality, but consider the brick wall that was Iovine, who refused to release albums until the songs met his personal standards. He said it himself: "If the songs aren't there, you're dead. You must do whatever it takes to get the right—as much time, as much pain."[159] This begs the question: Why, if he and the band were all sick of Interscope, didn't Rose terminate the contract and take *Chinese Democracy* to another more rock-friendly label at some point between 1999 and 2008?

Maybe his psychic Sharon Maynard told him Interscope had the proper metaphysical energy. Maybe Axl Rose simply placed his trust one too many times in Jimmy Iovine because of Iovine's superstar hit-making track record—Patti Smith, Bruce Springsteen, Tom Petty, Dr. Dre, Snoop Dogg, Eminem. And perhaps Iovine hung in there with Axl because he wanted to be on the ground floor of the inevitable reunion of the original Guns N' Roses lineup. That's a belief held by Tommy Stinson, who has suggested Iovine sabotaged *Chinese Democracy*.

"I think [Iovine] never gave it a chance. I think he was like, 'OK, I'll sponsor this, and then the band will get back together, and I'll have that.' I think he was always waiting for that ball to drop.... There were a lot of missteps [with *Chinese Democracy*], and they were all record company related, which had everything to do with the failure of that record."

Stinson has also said that Interscope "ripped [*Chinese Democracy*] away" from Rose before it was actually complete, which might give credence to the theory that the disc only saw the light of day as a bargaining chip to absolve Rose of all his financial and legal woes.[160] Chris Pitman isn't so sure of that; in his view, lawsuits were a constant problem for Rose, and there never was any magic way out. "He did say, 'They stole it from me!'" Pitman clarifies. "We were like, 'Dude, do something! Get behind it!' He was really precious about it, but no one else was."

Pitman is also grateful that renowned producer and engineer Andy Wallace stepped into do the final mix of *Chinese Democracy*. "It didn't sound anything like the record you hear today. Andy did a lot of creative stuff to save it. Axl loved, like, hundreds of tracks on a song. He'd get emotionally invested in six guitar solos at once. Andy took that out. He did an incredible job."[161]

Jimmy Iovine only made one public comment on *Chinese Democracy*, during an interview with *Billboard*. "Axl delivered a great Guns N' Roses album. Period. He did. It took him a long time for whatever reasons.... Bottom line is, he did it. It's hard to say if something is worth the wait, because how the hell do any of us know? I judge it based on what it is. Does it sound better than 99% of the rock records out there? Yes. I'm just thrilled for him."[162]

Punk sounds better on vinyl, but what about this? A Chinese Democracy LP. *Source: Grzegorz Czapski / Alamy Stock Photo.*

"Sometimes, at a label, the stuff is treated like a pair of shoes," says Robin Sloane Seibert, who spent many years in the '90s heading Geffen Records' art department. "Everything with *Chinese Democracy's* release sounds so random, like there was no plan, no thinking about it. Maybe Interscope just thought the record stunk."[163]

9 YOU CAN'T GO HOME AGAIN

Not in this lifetime: Axl Rose, 2016. *Source: Photo by Paul Morigi/Getty Images for BT PR.*

Chinese Democracy did not gain a foothold in the culture. It failed to reignite society's love affair with Guns N' Roses in the new millennium, proving no match against the rise of Taylor Swift, the fluctuations of Kanye West, or the sustained grip of Beyoncé.

There were a lot of contributing factors. For starters, the songs were good, not great, invoking the famous Oscar Wilde quote about humanity taking revenge on mediocrities with indifference. Of course, in the deeply saturated and lightning-fast twenty-first-century media landscape, art doesn't have much time to breathe. *Chinese Democracy* was derided as a bomb just a few weeks after release; industry experts started talking about what could be done to salvage its failure.[1] Once upon a time, 20 years earlier, Guns N' Roses were granted an entire year to break *Appetite for Destruction*, which they did, to unprecedented success.

The iTunes-ification of the music industry had also strengthened the singles market in the 2000s. Individual songs were doing bigger numbers than full albums. 2008's most popular song, "Bleeding Love" by Leona Lewis, sold over three million digital copies; the top-selling album for the year, Lil Wayne's *The Carter III*, only had combined sales of 2.87 million.[2][3] Rita Wilde, program director for southern California's KLOS-FM, believed *Chinese Democracy* contained winning material but felt the disc had no hope commercially thanks to its lousy lead-off single. "[The first single "Chinese Democracy"] just didn't have it," she said. "When you wait so long for something, you want to make sure it has it. We played it, and people went, 'Eh.'"[4]

That long wait also worked against the album. *Chinese Democracy* had to compete with what every rock listener and rock critic had imagined it to be for more than a decade. In that sense, it was like every *Star Wars* movie made after 1983; scores of fans rejected *The Phantom Menace* and *The Last Jedi* because these latter-day works conflicted with their own head canon. With *Chinese Democracy*, it seems die-hards dreamed up a disc that was leaner, meaner, and more in your face, like classic Guns N' Roses.

"That record tends to be a bit adult contemporary," observes former Guns N' Roses keyboardist Chris Pitman. "And you want it to rock." Pitman's use of the term "adult contemporary," which at this point feels a little lost to history, is very astute.[5] The *Chinese Democracy* story has echoes of Van Halen's abrupt transition from the wild, uninhibited David Lee Roth years to the button-down sounds of Sammy Hagar. "POST-LOBOTOMY VAN HALEN GO ON WITH HALF A MIND," *Musician* shouted in their review of *5150*, the first album with Hagar on vocals. The media began referring to this quartet as Van Hagar in an attempt to protect the sanctity of Van Halen.[6][7]

This is the common intersection of fan psychology, art, and commerce. To wit, there's a wide swath of Guns N' Roses fans who consider *Chinese Democracy* to be the Axl Rose solo record. It's not an incorrect argument, and it does tie in with another big problem facing Guns N' Roses in 2008: they lacked identity. No one knew who was in the band, and they had no story. This was not a group of underdogs united by poverty or ideology. They didn't all hang out at the same bar. In 2008, GNR's biography was "the singer of the most famous hard rock band in the world put a bunch of musicians on retainer and they dicked around the studio for 15 years."

People couldn't hook into this narrative. Now, the saga of the original Guns N' Roses, five dangerous mutants from the sewer who made unimpeachably great rock n' roll, that was a tale for the ages. No one could get over that legend. This was proven when Axl Rose eventually engaged with the media to promote *Chinese Democracy*. Repeatedly, he was asked if he'd ever get back together with Slash, Duff, and the other guys.

"I could see doing a song or so on the side with Izzy [Stradlin] or having him out [on tour] again," Rose told *Billboard* in February 2009. "I'm not so comfortable with doing anything having more than one of the alumni. Maybe something with Duff, but that's it. . . . In regards to Slash, I read a desperate fan's message about, what if one of us were to die and looking back I had the possibility of a reunion now, blah blah blah. And my thoughts are, 'Yeah, and while you're at the show, your baby accidentally kicks a candle and burns your house down, killing himself and the rest of your family.' Give me a fucking break. What's clear is that one of the two of us will die before a reunion and however sad, ugly or unfortunate anyone views it, it is how it is."[8]

Rose gave another interview that month to *Spinner*, one that was published under the headline "Axl Rose Insists Original Guns N' Roses Lineup is Dead and Buried." This interview was lengthy but contentious, a surprising fact since it was conducted by Del James, a trusted friend and associate of Rose. "Did you break up the old Guns?" James asked. "It is my belief that the commitment to end old Guns came long before the band started in the heart and soul of one man," Rose answered, ostensibly referring to Slash. Rose went on to say he felt "lucky to have survived" the original Guns because so many others in the band were trying to dominate him.

Why so many guitars on *Chinese Democracy*? "Why not?" Rose shot back. James pressed him. Rose basically explained that he was trying to add more flavor to his songs. Would he consider a reunion with the *Appetite* or *Illusions* lineups? "No." Again James pressed: "Why not?" "A lot more reasons than I'll get into here now," Rose replied before saying that Slash would have to ambush him be in GNR again. The singer added that he couldn't deal with the "ambulance-chasing attorneys" Steven Adler would bring along, plus his "nightmare of a mother."

James wouldn't let it go: "Wouldn't you make more money?" "If the music was there," Rose said. He didn't think, based on the material all the other members had put out since their heyday, that it was. As an addendum, Rose said, "There is the distinct possibility that having his intentions in regard to me so deeply ingrained and his personal though guarded distaste for much of *Appetite* other than his or Duff's playing, Slash either should not have been in Guns to begin with or should have left after *Lies*. In a nutshell, personally I consider him a cancer and better removed, avoided—the less anyone heard of him or his supporters, the better."

Near the end of their chat, James asked Rose when the next album was coming. "Have no idea and don't care." How much material did they have? "Really, it doesn't matter. If things go well enough, we'd like to get another out at some point in our lifetimes."[9]

In March, Guns N' Roses announced a new lead guitarist—DJ Ashba, taking over for Robin Finck, who'd finally departed the band for good. Ashba had the tattoos, piercings, and eyeliner that made him look like a generic "rock dude" character who just stepped out of *Guitar Hero*. Previously he'd collaborated with Mötley Crüe's Nikki Sixx. "[DJ] brings a fresh approach to our particular brand of mayhem," Rose assured fans. "Once DJ's name was in the hat, the hat disappeared!"[10] Speaking of hats, Ashba was often seen wearing a misshapen leathery top hat, one that evoked too many unfair comparisons to another famous top-hatted shredder.

※

Flash forward to December 2011. The *Chinese Democracy* era, as it was, continued. Guns N' Roses were on tour but only to help settle a lawsuit.[11] Front Line Management had sued Rose in March 2010 for $1.87 million in unpaid tour commissions. Rose countersued for $5 million, accusing Front Line's head honcho (and the band's former co-manager) Irving Azoff of various nefarious acts—mainly, sabotaging the release of *Chinese Democracy* to force Rose to reunite with the original GNR lineup. Azoff's alleged underhanded acts included purposely messing up the liner notes to the album, setting up a bad exclusivity deal with Best Buy, and somehow being behind a few Internet leaks of *Chinese Democracy* songs.[12] [13] [14]

The lawsuits took about 17 months to settle and the proceedings had their moments of high drama. At one deposition, Azoff grew so irate over a line of questioning from Rose's lawyer that he started throwing papers around before ripping off his microphone and storming out of the courtroom.[15] [16] [17] During this test of legal wills, Guns N' Roses hired Doc McGhee to be their manager. McGhee was known for ushering Mötley Crüe through their championship years; he'd done the same for Bon Jovi. And he was no stranger to GNR. Back in the '80s, McGhee put the band on their first big tour, the one where Rose punched a cop in Atlanta and had to go to jail.

"That's before the zeroes," McGhee asserted in 2020, referring, apparently, to GNR's riches. "I got 'em after the zeroes. Okay? So it was very disjointed and trying to be more calculated than what you needed to be . . . just [a] completely different band from what started."[18]

In February of 2011, *Metal Sludge* reported that McGhee was on thin ice with Rose because he was dropping the ball on a plan to relaunch *Chinese Democracy*. A reissue with new artwork and a bonus disc was allegedly being prepped for a March release. Simultaneously, a tour was supposed to launch, but the band wasn't receiving any concrete information. Bloomingdale's was rumored to be one of the sponsors of this tour, which, along with the *Chinese Democracy* reissue, didn't happen. Amid this gossip was speculation that Azoff, at that time still battling Rose in court, was somehow responsible all of this going down the toilet (the *Metal Sludge* piece also included an aside about *Classic Rock* magazine offering prominent GNR song leaker Mister Saint Laurent six figures for a thumb drive that allegedly contained Axl Rose's memoirs).

McGhee was fired ten months later. According to various unnamed insiders, McGhee audited the Guns N' Roses organization and uncovered "a lot of shit," including the resale of high-end cars by Axl's Girl Friday Beta Lebeis and streams of money being sent to her native Brazil. McGhee brought this malfeasance to Rose's attention in the hopes he could expel Lebeis from the singer's life. That didn't happen. "They paid Doc off," one source says. "I don't think anyone actually gets fired from those guys, they just kinda keep fucking you over until you leave. Well, Beta probably fired Doug Goldstein. Axl's not that kind of dude. He'd rather have someone else do it."

McGhee's replacement, Peter Katsis, lasted a month. "All these managers, they all believe in one thing: sell a reunion tour and get the commission," Rose told the *Los Angeles Times*. "It's just a phone call. It's a half a day's fucking work, or however long they want to keep the bidding war going. They get their commission and they don't care if it falls on its face." After Katsis left, Lebeis and her children, Fernando and Vanessa, became the new management team. According to another unnamed source, "No one would ever get paid when they were in charge. 'You gotta wait for the next tour,' they'd say. You wouldn't get paid for a year."

Los Angeles Times reporter Randall Roberts was warned not to bring up Slash when he spoke with Rose that December during the lawsuit settlement tour, but Rose launched into a diatribe unprompted. "The fight with me and Slash started the day I met him. He came in, popped my tape out and put his in and wanted me in his band. And I didn't want to join his band. We've had that war since day one."

This kind of stuff was probably always on Rose's mind, but it had newfound relevance as Guns N' Roses were about to be inducted into the Rock and Roll Hall of Fame. Would the original lineup reunite to perform at the induction ceremony? Rose had mixed feelings about the Hall, but he didn't want to ruin the evening for anyone by appearing in some kind of protest against his own history. "There is no plan yet," he told Roberts.[19]

A few days before the induction ceremony in April 2012, Rose sent an open letter to the *Los Angeles Times* announcing that he wouldn't be attending and requested that he not be inducted in absentia. "Please know that no one is authorized nor may anyone be permitted to accept any induction for me or speak on my behalf." This was only the second time anyone had refused the Rock Hall's induction; in 2006, the Sex Pistols turned the honor down in a handwritten note that called both the Hall of Fame and rock n' roll itself "a piss stain."[20]

"I don't think any of us wanted to be a part of it initially," said Slash. "I didn't think any of us were going to go. It was a thorn in everybody's—well, at least a thorn in my side—because I was busy doing other stuff." The guitarist said that all changed once Rose pulled out. "I thought, *Well, shit, maybe we should do it.* [*laughs*] And I'm glad that we went. It was very Guns N' Roses, what can you say?"[21] Slash, Duff McKagan, Matt Sorum, Gilby Clarke, and Steven Adler all attended the ceremony, where Rose was inducted against his will (when Rose's name came up, a chant of "Fuck Axl!" kicked off in the audience). As is customary for this event, there was a brief performance from each of the inductees; Adler, McKagan, Sorum, Clarke, and Slash performed a three-song set with friend and collaborator Myles Kennedy on vocals.[22]

Slash added that his frosty relations with Rose weren't something he liked to dwell on. "I don't even like to make comments because you end up with quotes that sometimes exacerbate the issue," he added. "It's not really at the forefront of my mind."[23]

There have been angrier dust ups at Rock and Roll Hall of Fame induction ceremonies. When Creedence Clearwater Revival was enshrined in 1993, bassist Stu Cook and drummer Doug Clifford were expecting to play a few numbers with Creedence singer and guitarist John Fogerty. They were shocked to learn upon their arrival that Fogerty would be performing their songs with ringers like Bruce Springsteen and Robbie Robertson instead. Cook and Clifford confronted Fogerty backstage. "I'm not ever going to play with you again," Fogerty told them. "I hate you."[24]

The animus festering between these players had been well documented in the years leading up to this; Creedence's bitter feuding was almost as legendary as their music. The issues rested primarily with Fogerty, who held such a grudge against Cook and Clifford that when he embarked on a solo career he refused to play any Creedence songs in concert. Eventually, there was a thawing. Fogerty married a woman named Julie, whom he credits with bringing him a newfound happiness. So when *Rolling Stone* asked him in 2011 if he'd ever consider a CCR reunion, the singer said, "Ummmm, yeah . . . If you feel good and you get busy, especially if you're in love, your heart heals. You're not carrying a bunch of baggage."[25]

Unfortunately, Fogerty's heart didn't heal quickly enough. In response to the reunion chatter, Clifford said, "It might have been a nice idea 20 years ago, but it's too late."[26]

It wasn't too late for Slash and Axl Rose. There's one version of their reunion story that mirrors Fogerty's case—a woman behind the scenes easing the tensions. Following his 2014 divorce from Perla Hudson, Slash rekindled a romance from decades prior with Meegan Hodges. Hodges, as it happened, was close friends with Erin Everly, Rose's love and inspiration during the *Appetite for Destruction* era. It's unclear why Everly would ever want to speak with Rose again in light of the repugnant abuses she accused him of in her 1994 lawsuit, but speak again they did, allegedly, thanks to Hodges.

Some have said that Slash's divorce from Perla was itself enough of a door opener for Rose. Perla was not well-loved inside the world of Guns N' Roses ("bitchy" was the term one publicist used).[27] Concurrently, there were a couple of notable exits from Rose's version of Guns N' Roses. Bassist Tommy Stinson left the group in 2014, citing personal reasons. Initially, Stinson said there was no ill will between himself and Rose. He later amended that, revealing Rose held him in contempt for taking off to spend more time with his daughters following his divorce. "It was one of the hardest decisions I had to make," Stinson said. "[But] I really had to do it."[28] [29]

Guitarist Ron "Bumblefoot" Thal also made an exit, though he was reluctant to get into details. "Anything I say will end up turned into something bad that's gonna hurt people that I don't wanna hurt," he remarked. "And it just happens that way. . . . I could say, 'The sky is blue,' and somehow it'll get turned into something when it comes to that subject. . . . All I could say is you reach a time when you just know it's time to move on."[30]

On the whole, Guns N' Roses had been struggling. "We were just barely getting booked after *Chinese Democracy*," says one former band member who asks not to be named. "We'd do a residency in Vegas, but it was a small theater, and sometimes it was only half-filled. There was no vibe to it, no one cared. Everybody in the band was off doing their own thing." By 2015, this figure says the only people left in Guns N' Roses were Axl Rose and keyboardist Chris Pitman. "The band had really fizzled out."

Rose and Pitman spent a portion of that year in the studio, working on various mixes of outtakes from *Chinese Democracy*. "They were D-list tracks," says another unnamed figure. "Chris was chopping all these songs up for Axl. Axl didn't really do anything, to be honest. He said he was going to build a new vocal booth for this project, but he didn't. While that was going on, the [Guns N' Roses] original guys were offered crazy money to play the 2016 Coachella festival. Axl was in a bad way financially at that point, and . . . I don't know. People were encouraging him to do it, but it was kinda sad."

Insiders say it was clear from the start that the Guns N' Roses reunion at Coachella (and the subsequent arena tour they scheduled) would be a hybrid act featuring Axl, Slash, Duff, and some of the *Chinese Democracy* players. Even so, there was some ugliness to this restructuring. As another anonymous source puts it: "When it came time for the original guys to rehearse, they were trying to shortchange all the newer guys, the guys who'd been there for, what, eight to ten to fifteen years? They were cutting all their pay and trying to get them fired. It was shitty."

"And also? Honestly? With Slash, that's like having two Axls in the band," the source continues. "For real. He's a dick. You go up to him, you're the only two people in the room, you go up and say, 'Hey, what's up?' And he acts like you aren't there. That made it easier for some of the newer guys to quit and be like, 'Go fuck yourself.' [*laughs*]"

Metal Sludge founder Stevie Rachelle remembers hearing through the grapevine that Slash and Duff McKagan really went to bat for Steven Adler to be the drummer for the reunion. "Axl was like, 'If you wanna give him a chance, I'm willing to go with it,'" Rachelle relays. "'But this is *your* call,' meaning, if Steven fucked up, it would be on them. So Slash and Duff backed down."[31] There were stories that Slash and McKagan also fought to get Matt Sorum behind the kit. Rose preferred to keep *Chinese Democracy* drummer Frank Ferrar.[32]

In a September 2021 interview *Rolling Stone* conducted with Sorum to promote his forthcoming memoir *Double Talkin' Jive*, a snippet of the book was excerpted wherein Sorum recalled a conversation with McKagan about the reunion. "Axl wants to use [Frank]," McKagan allegedly told Sorum, "but the guy can't even play drums. I've got to talk to Axl and say I really can't play with this guy." Sorum agreed that McKagan couldn't waste any more time. Then, as if he was just remembering, McKagan said, "Oh man, I already signed the deal."

Sometime before the March 2022 publication of *Double Talkin' Jive*, *Rolling Stone* edited the above exchange to remove McKagan's comment that he didn't think Ferrar could play drums. This was also stricken from the book, along with a few other tidbits (according to a version of the book that leaked ahead of time).[33][34][35] Sorum was obviously hurt not to be included in the GNR reunion, but by 2024 his perspective was different.

"I had that moment with the band," he said, "and it's really shaped and formed my life and a lot of doors have opened because of it. So I look at it with a lot of gratitude. When people ask me, 'Oh, you're not included in the new tour,' and I've said, in the beginning, it was a little weird . . . [but now] I look at it like. . . . I'm not supposed to be there. I got a child, I got a beautiful wife. The old me, the old Matt . . . if I got up there, I don't know what would happen to me."[36]

Izzy Stradlin, the founding Guns N' Roses rhythm guitarist who many cite as the original band's secret songwriting weapon (and who occasionally appeared onstage with the band during the *Chinese Democracy* era), reached a financial impasse with the other members regarding this reunion. "That's life," Stradlin wrote in a statement to *The Wall Street Journal*, of all places. "Sometimes things don't work out."[37] Richard Fortus remained in Stradlin's place.

Naturally, primary keyboardist Dizzy Reed was included; it would take an act of God to separate Reed from Axl Rose. Chris Pitman was replaced by Melissa Reese, a classically trained player who'd been working closely with former Guns drummer Bryan Mantia on incidental music for television and video games.[38] Pitman fell out of GNR's good graces following a social media post where he dismissed the Guns N' Roses reunion as "a money grab" (Pitman sued Rose not long after, seeking over $163,000 in unpaid wages; the case was settled out of court).[39][40]

The partially reconstituted Guns N' Roses booked a few warm-up shows before Coachella. The first was a "secret" gig at the Troubadour in Hollywood on April

Fool's Day. While tearing through "Mr. Brownstone" that night, Rose slipped on something, breaking the fifth metatarsal in his left foot. He underwent surgery and was ordered not to put pressure on his foot for four weeks. "This is what happens when you do something you haven't done in nearly over 23 years," Rose wrote on Twitter. This was a quizzical statement, considering Rose had famously spent a huge portion of that time leading a different version of Guns N' Roses.[41]

At the next gig in Las Vegas, Axl Rose materialized onstage seated in a familiar-looking circular throne bearing the Guns N' Roses logo. That logo was removed at one point, revealing beneath it the Foo Fighters logo, confirming that this throne was in fact the same one Foo Fighters singer/guitarist Dave Grohl utilized after breaking his leg during a 2015 tour. Rose thanked Grohl onstage and later expressed his gratitude by sending Grohl a pricy guitar from the early '60s. Grohl rhapsodized that it was "the nicest fucking guitar I have ever played in my life."[42] [43]

Maybe there was some element of shock to this story, considering the bad blood between Guns N' Roses and Grohl's former band Nirvana in the early '90s. Then again, it was gestures like this that earned Grohl a reputation as the nicest guy in rock. He volunteered at food banks, he invited kid music prodigies to play with him, he had a good relationship with his mother, etc.[44]

Interestingly enough, by the time of this writing, there's been a little role reversal between Dave Grohl and Axl Rose. Rotten stories about Grohl started piling up—he re-recorded all of William Goldsmith's drum tracks for the second Foo Fighters album without telling him; he regularly cheated on all of his girlfriends; in 2024, he sired a child out of wedlock.[45] [46] The most serious issue with Grohl is that he and the Foo Fighters spent years supporting an AIDS denial group called Alive and Well AIDS Alternatives. Alive and Well's influence was blamed for scores of deaths in South Africa; their founder Christine Maggiore died of AIDS, as did her infant daughter.

Sanda L. Thurman, director of the Office of National AIDS Policy under President Bill Clinton, called the Foo Fighters "extraordinarily irresponsible" for championing Alive and Well, likening the organization to a Flat Earth Society. The Foo Fighters gave up their support of Alive and Well at some point, but they've never issued any apology, and they've apparently done all they can to scrape news stories about this troubled connection from Google search results.[47]

Meanwhile, Axl Rose became more involved with social justice in the twenty-first-century. In 2015, he wrote an impassioned letter to Indonesian president Joko Widodo pleading for the lives of several drug offenders who'd been sentenced to execution.[48] Shortly after that, Rose dubbed Iranian sports journalist Mehdi Toutounchi the "Civilian Douche of the Year" for refusing to let his wife Niloufar Ardalan leave Iran to compete in a soccer tournament. Rose was especially critical of Donald Trump's first term as US president. In 2018, he denounced Trump for having "no regard for truth, ethics, morals or empathy" and called for America to "put an end 2 this nonsense now." This was on Twitter, which Rose regularly used to tear into Republicans for their racism, corruption, and cronyism.

In May 2020, as COVID's tightening grip grounded international travel, Trump's secretary of the treasury Steve Mnuchin encouraged Americans to take domestic vacations, even though the threat of COVID infection remained high within US borders. This prompted Rose to tweet: "It's official! Whatever anyone may have previously thought of Steve Mnuchin he's officially an asshole." Mnuchin replied: "What have you done for your country lately?" Rose unloaded: "I'm not responsible for 70k+ deaths n' unlike u I don't hold a fed gov position of responsibility 2 the American people n' go on TV tellin them to travel the US during a pandemic."[49]

This was the rise of "Woke Axl," as the media dubbed him, a pure hellion turned voice of reason during troubled times. It was a turnaround that shocked anyone who lived through Rose's vintage years. Some felt "Woke Axl" wasn't enough to absolve Rose of his past transgressions. "What's Milkshake Duck but the duck already wrote one of the most racist songs of the 1980s and put it on a hit album?" wondered social scientist Trey Menefee (Milkshake Duck being the term for any viral star on the Internet who is quickly revealed to have an unseemly, disgusting past). Menefee got more to the point later, calling Rose "a terrible human being."[50] [51]

This raises a worthy debate: if a terrible human being is making an effort to stop being terrible, should we not give them the chance? Are we just supposed to throw bad people away, or do we try to invest in their rehabilitation and encourage them when we see kernels of change?

Former White House staffer Bill D. Moyers once told a story about Lyndon Johnson that may very well be apocryphal, but it's a pleasant thought. It was the mid-'60s, and a reporter caught Johnson off guard by asking him to explain his sudden passion for civil rights. It hadn't ever been a leading cause for Johnson, a very Southern Democrat. "The question hung in the air," Moyers recounted. "I could almost hear his silent cursing of a press secretary who had not anticipated this one. But then [Johnson] relaxed . . . [and] he said in effect: Most of us don't have a second chance to correct the mistakes of our youth. I do and I am."[52]

Axl Rose probably needed to do the big Guns N' Roses reunion tour with Slash and Duff not just for the cash flow but for mental health reasons as well. That's another unnamed insider's account. "I could tell he was losing his marbles before the reunion," they said. "I don't know, I guess it was just the fact that he was aging. Losing his hair, getting larger. Nothing was happening with his version of Guns. And he was really getting into some Howard Hughes shit for real.

"I gotta tell you this, man. They called me up in like 2012? 2013? Beta said, 'Axl wants to work in the studio again, revamp it, buy all new gear.' I thought, *That sounds weird*. I go up there and I'm writing down what we need to replace. An hour goes by and Beta sticks her head in. 'Has he showed up yet?' 'No.' Another hour goes by, she comes back, same conversation. Then *another* hour goes by and this time it's her daughter. 'Have you seen him?' 'No! Why, what's going on?' She goes, 'We haven't seen him in three months.' She meant *inside the house*! She goes, 'We put his food on the floor and knock on his bedroom door and leave. We don't know if he has a Rip Van Winkle beard or what.' They hadn't seen this guy in his own house in three months!"

Rose emerged from his cocoon and Guns N' Roses were treated like conquering heroes on their humorously named "Not in This Lifetime . . ." 2016 reunion tour. Reviews were mixed (*Entertainment Weekly* hailed their Coachella show as "mostly excellent"; *Vice* disagreed, saying "the slanders of age have laid assault to both [Axl and Slash]") but commercially the jaunt was very successful.[53] [54] In fact, "The Not in This Lifetime . . . " tour lasted until 2019, grossing $584 million, making it one of the highest-grossing music tours in history.[55]

And, for those invested in the bromance, Slash has said that he and Rose worked out their differences at the start of the tour. "It was a real simple, relatively short conversation that we had," the guitarist said, and that was all it took to erase the hate. "In all these years that we've been apart, [Axl's] become super fucking professional. . . . So it's been great."[56]

One or two selections from *Chinese Democracy* were usually included in Guns N' Roses' set during the "Not in This Lifetime . . . " tour. *Rolling Stone* asked Slash how he felt about that. "Um, I mean, it's fun playing them," he said. "There's nothing weird about it. It's not like I'm playing something out of my comfort zone. I'm very conscious of maintaining the integrity to the recordings, but still doing it the way that I would approach it." Slash also praised Richard Fortus as "an amazing guitar player" who was "very, very easy to work with." When asked about "the vibe" with Frank Ferrer, Slash replied (with a laugh), "He's been doing for longer than I was ever in the band. So he's got his thing on lock, yeah."[57]

Meanwhile, there was still a subset of fans waiting to hear more from the *Chinese Democracy* era. They called themselves Five Percenters because they knew they represented just a sliver of GNR's fanbase, and they knew there was an embarrassment of unreleased music. They knew this because at various points during the album's gestation band members had teased *Chinese Democracy* as a double or triple album. They knew because they were familiar with the stories of Guns N' Roses holding down the record button all day and night for weeks, months, years on end to capture any stray ideas. In 2019, the Five Percenters experienced a miracle.

That March, the contents of two storage units at a CubeSmart in Culpeper, Virginia, were auctioned off because the renter, former Geffen Records bigwig

Tom Zutaut, fell too far behind on his payments. Storage flipper Robert Bird won the unit that contained a pot of gold, or maybe a Rosetta Stone—19 CD-Rs of never-before-heard Guns N' Roses material recorded at the Village Studio circa 2000–2001. Pure mania erupted among the *Chinese Democracy* faithful.

A lawyer in New York named Levi Lipton bought the CD-Rs from Bird and promised never to leak them. Lipton never promised not to tell people he had the discs, so he told a person only identified as Mario, who in turn told Rick Dunsford.[58] Thirty-something Dunsford, a Mississippi native, had been a GNR nut for most of his life, and he became a very familiar face at their concerts in the 2010s on both sides of the stage. "I had access to Axl Rose," Dunsford bragged. "I'd sit in Axl Rose's dressing room while he's in the shower, a door from him. If you're liked by [management], that's how you meet [him]."[59] A zealous Five Percenter with numerous *Chinese Democracy* tattoos, Dunsford was willing to pay $20,000 for the CD-Rs. After that offer was declined, Dunsford tattled on Bird and Lipton to Guns N' Roses manager Fernando Santos. "Don't want to see this stuff leaking until band is ready for us to hear it," he wrote.

Dunsford, however, was still trying to hash out a deal with Bird and Lipton and was also posting about the CD-Rs online. Bird finally agreed to sell Dunsford the music for $15,000. Dunsford only managed to scrape up $12,000, but Bird accepted it when they met up in a Panera Bread parking lot that July. An ecstatic Dunsford leaked a couple songs that night to the investors who'd help make him solvent while simultaneously posting cell phone video snippets online. Santos saw these clips and realized Dunsford wasn't as committed to stopping any leaks of this material as he'd professed. The legal saber rattling began.

In August, Dunsford and Guns N' Roses reached a settlement: the band would reimburse him for the money spent on the CD-Rs plus VIP tickets for two concerts on the proviso he turn in all the music, refuse to share it, and rat on anyone he'd already hooked up with the unreleased tracks. Before the ink was dry on that agreement, the music started leaking online. By October, it was all out there, all 124 songs. Guns N' Roses turned on Dunsford, blaming him for the leaks, demanding their money back, and banning him from all future concerts.

Dunsford was actually waiting in line for a Guns N' Roses show in Wichita, Kansas on October 7 when he received the e-mail informing him of the ban; he was quickly ousted. Then a scary letter from Universal Music Group arrived in Dunsford's mailbox threatening him with fines of $150,000 per leaked song. The conglomerate never exercised this threat, but Dunsford filed for bankruptcy anyway, assuming he was about to be destroyed by legal fees.[60]

When *TMZ* reported on this story in January 2020, they received a statement from Guns N' Roses: "It is tremendously disappointing, sad, and unfortunate that a record executive involved with the band in their early years found it appropriate to auction off the unreleased materials owned by his former employer."[61] This, of course, isn't what happened. Tom Zutaut didn't decide to auction off his Guns N' Roses wares, the proprietors of CubeSmart did after Zutaut was late with his rent. There certainly were questions regarding Zutaut's culpability in this situation, as well as the culpability of Interscope Records for not keeping tabs on their intellectual property, but those questions fell by the wayside as the more clear cut rule-breaking involved the leakers.

Guns N' Roses meant business with Dunsford's concert ban, which he discovered when he tried to attend a 2021 gig at Chicago's Wrigley Field. Even in a hat, sunglasses, and COVID-shielding face mask, Dunsford was identified. GNR security head Gio Gasparetti descended upon him just before showtime. Interestingly enough, Dunsford claimed Gasparetti never asked him to leave; he just started throwing punches (giving Dunsford a black eye) and twisting Dunsford's arm to shake loose a phone he was using to livestream the incident. Gasparetti denied any of this took place. Dunsford left Wrigley rattled. "They really are out for blood," he commented.

In December 2022, *Rolling Stone* published a lengthy, engrossing feature on the Dunsford affair and all its players, written by David Peisner. Peisner spent months working on the story, during which Dunsford routinely denied any role in leaking music from the CD-Rs. Then, unprompted, two figures identified as Kyle B. and Craig contacted Peisner to confess their parts in a series of leaks from September 2019 known as "The Chairman Leaks" (these leaks were accompanied by cryptic, Riddler-esque poems credited to "the Chairman"). Kyle B. and Craig implicated Dunsford as the mastermind behind those specific leaks. Confronted by Peisner, Dunsford fessed up.

"I felt like I did everything I could to help them," Dunsford said, referring to the Guns N' Roses organization and the August 2019 leaks (in which he insisted he had no involvement), "and [I] was stabbed in the back by Fernando. It was after that, when they took away the VIP tickets and decided to pursue me for the money, that's when I started getting with Craig about it."[62] Peisner took stock of his primary interview subject: "Even though he's consistently played fast and loose with the truth, I find it hard to dislike Dunsford. He's a guy who has essentially been getting his ass kicked since he was a kid because of his inability to moderate his zeal."[63]

Now Dunsford is an outcast among outcasts. "I can't go on the [Guns N' Roses] message boards anymore without being attacked," he said in 2024. "So, those message boards that have been a part of my life for 20 years, I no longer post on 'em or even log in." Still, he remains a vigilant Guns N' Roses fan. He even managed to sneak into a concert in Nashville in 2023 (or so he claimed). And he continues to thirst for what might be left in the vault.

"If there's a way I can get some more unreleased *Chinese Democracy* stuff, dude, I'm going to put together a team and I'm going to get it. If I find out who has it, I'll get it."[64]

All the money that was paid, all the threats and invective that were hurled, all the drama over the storage locker leaks that spilled across numerous Guns N' Roses message boards and legal filings from the band—it was all for naught. Today, most of the unheard songs can be instantly accessed on YouTube. Specific uploads may get taken down once Universal Music notices, but then someone else just uploads it again. So now anyone can judge these mystery recordings.

Axl Rose probably still considers these songs works in progress, but many sound as radio ready as anything else on the airwaves. The years and years of overthinking that hang over the final *Chinese Democracy* album are also absent in these recordings. There's exuberance, vibrance. "Mustache," for instance, has a quirky snap accented by Buckethead's unmistakable pyrotechnics. It's easy to imagine it blasting from a passing car's stereo (at least in the year 2000, when it was recorded). Rose is only bleating out syllables in "Quicksong" but it's catchy, and there's an inviting punch to the hard rock bed beneath it.

Obviously, not every song from the storage locker CD-Rs is gold. "REAL DOLL.com" suffocates under a thick cloud of Limp Bizkit vibes. "State of Grace" sounds like Rose is trying to rewrite several Faith No More songs at the same time. Unfortunately, the song labeled "Curly Shuffle" is not a cover of Jump 'n the Saddle Band's infectious 1983 novelty hit about the Three Stooges.

One of the most outstanding pieces unearthed from the storage locker leaks was "Hard Skool," another sneering kiss-off to someone who violated Axl Rose's trust. "Hard Skool" conjures up the classic Guns N' Roses slam dance street swagger and Rose tears into the vocals like piranha. The song allegedly dates back to the '90s; the working title was "Jackie Chan," tying into reports from that time frame suggesting Guns N' Roses had been asked to write music for a Jackie Chan film. Rose, Slash, and Duff McKagan recognized "Hard Skool's" value—a reworked version became the centerpiece for the first new studio release featuring the trio in 28 years (a slow, maudlin intro was ditched for the thunderous rumble of McKagan's bass).

The *Hard Skool* EP was released in January 2022, and its other "new" offering was a stuttering song called "Absurd," a *Chinese Democracy* era composition originally called "Silkworms." "Absurd" was actually the lead-off single from *Hard Skool* (which had a handful of differing other tracks, depending on the format); that was a bold choice, considering Rose sang the vocal in a weird haughty accent and one of the only audible lyrics is "pussy full of maggots." "Absurd" didn't get much attention from the mainstream press. *The Star Tribune* called it "trashy."[65] *Stereogum* declared that the lyrics were "ornate in their grossness."[66]

Opinions in Twitter's virtual town square weren't much kinder. "That new Guns N' Roses is MESSY," one user wrote. "It's kind of punk rock in a way," another mused, "having people wait for so long for a new song, and then making it one that no radio station in their right mind would play."[67] In 2024, when *Ultimate Classic Rock* ranked all of Guns N' Roses' songs from worst to greatest, "Absurd" came in dead last, which seems unfair since it's not the one with the vitriolic racism and homophobia or the one written by Charles Manson.⁶⁸

Two other "new" Guns N' Roses songs have been released since then—"Perhaps" and "The General." Like "Hard Skool" and "Absurd," they're both reworking of *Chinese Democracy* era songs massaged over by Slash and McKagan. They're also both pretty unremarkable and made even less of a splash than their immediate predecessors. There was a touch of controversy over the video Guns N' Roses released for "The General" because it featured AI animation.

McKagan made some comments during the press cycle praising AI art for making his skin look great, but ultimately surmised, "I don't know enough about it." As far as AI's potential applications to songwriting, he said, "There's nothing better than sitting down and writing a song on an acoustic guitar. There'll never be anything better than that." Fans have been wondering for about nine years now if McKagan, Slash, and Axl Rose were doing anything like that for a new album. There have been vague promises, all of which have sounded like polite ways of saying, "Don't hold your breath."⁶⁹ ⁷⁰

In 1972, Miles Davis released *On The Corner*, an experimental and expressionistic blend of funk, jazz, rock, and soul that was informed more by Karlheinz Stockhausen than Sly Stone. Serious Miles fans were flummoxed. *On The Corner* prompted an infamous exchange between Davis and a music critic whose name has been lost to time. "Miles, every move you've made musically, I've been there," the critic told him, "but I can't get to where you're at now." Davis retorted, "What the fuck am I supposed to do, motherfucka? Wait for you to get there?"

The years passed and *On The Corner* was reappraised. By 1993, historians were calling it genius, insisting Davis had been ahead of his time.⁷¹ ⁷² *Chinese Democracy* has yet to receive such dramatic reevaluation. This might be because, overall, it was perceived to be simply okay, not egregiously or inconceivably bad. Also, many of the elements Guns N' Roses attempted to fuse on the album—'80s hard rock, '90s rap rock, monster ballads, late '80s guitar shredding—have not yet proven to be as enduringly hip or revered as jazz, funk, or soul. And one should accept the reality that Guns N' Roses will probably never be granted the same benefit of the doubt as Miles Davis (or Lou Reed, or Joni Mitchell) because the breadth and influence of their artistry is much smaller.

Former Guns N' Roses manager Alan Niven has argued that the mystique surrounding *Chinese Democracy* has always been more compelling and valuable than the end product. "I mean, my viewpoint on *Chinese Democracy* was that the biggest mistake was to release it at all," Niven said in 2020. "I would have rather it remained mysterious."⁷³ We see this in practice with Dr. Dre's *Detox*, the *Chinese*

Democracy of hip-hop. Dre spent 13 years working on *Detox*, allegedly his final album, and a concept album on top of that about a contract killer. Anyone who heard *Detox* swore it was genius. Some music dripped out but Dre decided to shelve the project in 2015 because it wasn't meeting his standards. So the fascination never ended.

Allegedly, the beat for 50 Cent's career-making hit "In Da Club" was originally crafted for *Detox*. *Imagine if Dr. Dre had hung onto that beat and done something with it!*[74]

On the other hand, My Bloody Valentine proved it's possible to deliver mind-blowing work after a self-imposed Ice Age. That tale began in 1991, when the Irish shoegaze group issued their sophomore effort *Loveless*, a blistering masterpiece that became one of the most influential rock albums of the decade.[75] Island Records signed My Bloody Valentine the next year and gave them a £500,000 advance for a *Loveless* follow-up. Unfortunately, primary songwriter Kevin Shields had run out of gas. "I lost it," Shields admitted. "I lost what I had and I thought, *You know what? I'm not going to put a crap record out.*"[76] Twenty-one years passed before the next My Bloody Valentine offering, 2013's *m b v*, which the band self-released unexpectedly via their website. *m b v* received nearly universal praise, even from *Loveless* purists.[77] [78]

Of course, Axl Rose is not Dr. Dre or Kevin Shields. He obviously didn't want to shelve *Chinese Democracy*, but he also didn't seem to ever want it to come out. Speaking in 2024 about the push to get Rose to hand over the album, former GNR co-manager Andy Gould remarked, "I think if it didn't come out, he'd still be working on it."[79]

"The moment I wanted to get into music, not even drums, is when I saw *The Song Remains The Same*," Bryan Mantia told *Rolling Stone* in 2022. "There's a scene where Jimmy Page is sitting there with a music box. He turns around and a guy is like, 'We need you. You're going to go play.' The next thing you see, he's at Madison Square Garden. I just loved the fact that I was in [Guns N' Roses], but I was doing other things, like taking golf lessons every day and learning computers and programming and orchestration and music theory.

"And then you get a call like, 'Hey, Axl needs you.' I was like, 'This is the closest I'm going to get to the Zeppelin thing. Who gives a fuck? Make it go forever. This is the coolest thing, that [*Chinese Democracy*] took 10 years.'"

Interviewer Andy Greene replied with a salient point: "The Beatles made *Please Please Me* in a single day, and it's amazing."

Mantia just laughed.[80]

Source: Photo by Kevin Mazur/WireImage via Getty Images.

ACKNOWLEDGMENTS

This book wouldn't exist if it weren't for John Cerullo, the Acquisitions Editor at Backbeat Books, who liked the pitch and pushed it forward to the supreme council of enlightened beings. He also okayed the title, which is great because I really didn't have any other ideas. I must also profusely thank Emily Burr and Chris Chappell, who took over this project after John's departure. Another awesome person at Backbeat is Barbara Claire, who was a tremendous help sorting out all the photos.

I cannot give enough thanks to each and every person who allowed me to interview them for *Magnum Opus*. Whether we spoke for just a few minutes or several hours, my gratitude is king-sized. You all deserve a gold star and a cookie.

Thanks and praise to the Los Angeles Public Library and the New York Public Library, whose vast digital databases are a miracle when it comes to research. I especially appreciate that most of them can be accessed remotely. I'd actually like to thank all public libraries across the nation for providing extremely valuable services to their communities. It breaks my heart that libraries have been under attack in recent years by bigots and fools. Free your minds!

The Internet Archive's Wayback Machine is also an incredible resource. If you're unfamiliar, the Wayback has been taking interactive snapshots of literally billions of websites since the '90s and saving them for reference. It's astonishing how much online journalism has been scrubbed from the Internet. We'd have little way to access it or even know it existed without the Wayback. I understand keeping websites live involves bandwidth, which involves money, but I also know venture capitalists are spending egregious amounts of cash to put AI in toasters. The Wayback Machine is more important.

By the same hand, I must extend gratitude to the long-running Guns N' Roses fan websites/forums *Here Today . . . Gone To Hell!*, *Appetite For Discussion*, *GNR Evolution*, and *My GNR*. These sites have done a tremendous job cataloging every morsel of news, rumor, and innuendo related to this band, along with a remarkable amount of interview transcripts, videos of radio/TV appearances, and general ephemera. Often these sites host sources that even the Wayback Machine missed, so really, hats off to them.

Extra special thanks to Art Tavana, Alan Niven, Joe Gore, Rachel Meyers, Rollie Hatch, Cindy Howle, Kirk Howle, Paul Harries, Chris Ward, Chris Pitman, and Kris Kringle.

The greatest thanks of all goes to my beautiful wife, Amy, our two beautiful kids, Lola and Jason, my beautiful mother, Teddi, and our two beautiful guinea pigs, Beverly and Sonic. I love you all.

If you enjoyed this book and have already purchased several copies but would like to show your support in other ways, please consider donating to one of the following organizations: the Friedrich's Ataxia Research Alliance, the Global Action For Trans Equality, Campaign Zero, the American Friends Service Committee, or the Los Angeles Guinea Pig Rescue.

NOTES

Chapter 1

1. King, Peter B. "Guns N' Roses Albums Score Here." *Pittsburgh Post-Gazette*. September 17, 1991. Section: Entertainment. Pg B7.
2. Watrous, Peter. "Guns N' Roses Albums Use Illusion to Rake in Cash With Huge Advance Sales, Stores Set Midnight Openings." *The Charlotte Observer*. September 12, 1991. Pg 1E.
3. Watrous, Peter; *New York Times* staff writer. "Guns N' Roses Albums Use Illusion to Rake in Cash With Huge Advance Sales, Stores Set Midnight Openings." *The Charlotte Observer*. September 12, 1991. Section: Living. Pg 1E.
4. Scott, Jane. "Area Record Stores Gear Up For Long-Awaited Guns Records." *The Plain Dealer*. September 16, 1991. Pg 5D.
5. Violanti, Anthony. "High Hopes For Guns N' Roses Release." *The Buffalo News*. September 16, 1991. Section: Lifestyles. Pg B1.
6. Shuster, Fred. "Guns Shooting For Success—'Illusion' Sales Start at Midnight." *Daily News of Los Angeles*. September 16, 1991. Section: L.A. Life. Pg L12.
7. "Wax Works Ranked as 9th Largest Record Chain." *Owensboro Messenger-Inquirer*. March 31, 1991. Pg 1D.
8. "Guns Aimed at Michael Jackson." *The San Francisco Chronicle*. September 19, 1991. Pg E2.
9. Toner, Noreen. "No Run on Guns Albums in Region." *Press of Atlantic City*. September 18, 1991. Section: Entertainment. Pg B1.
10. "Industry Banking on New Guns N' Roses." *Press of Atlantic City*. September 17, 1991. Section: Entertainment. Pg C8.
11. Watrous, Peter. "Guns N' Roses Albums Use Illusion to Rake in Cash With Huge Advance Sales, Stores Set Midnight Openings." *The Charlotte Observer*. September 12, 1991. Pg 1E.
12. Mosley, Jim. "Guns N' Roses is Returning . . . Sort of." *The St. Louis Post-Dispatch*. September 12, 1991. Pg 5A.
13. Watrous, Peter. "Guns N' Roses Albums Use Illusion to Rake in Cash With Huge Advance Sales, Stores Set Midnight Openings." *The Charlotte Observer*. September 12, 1991. Pg 1E.

14 Fricke, David. "... And Justice For All/Appetite For Destruction." *Rolling Stone*. Iss. 541/542. December 15, 1988. Pg 201.
15 Duffy, Thom. "Guns N' Roses." *The Orlando Sentinel*. August 7, 1988. Pg 9.
16 Plotnikoff, David. "Guns N' Aeros Topping Music And Video Charts." *The Mercury News*. September 9, 1988. Pg 1E.
17 Holmberg, Mark. "Newest Rude Rockers Display Destructive Hunger." *Richmond Times-Dispatch*. August 9, 1987. Section: Leisure. Pg J3.
18 Barracuda. "Guns N' Roses." *SPIN*. Vol. 3, Iss. 8. January 1, 1988. Pg 61.
19 Love, Katherine; Morgan, Wallace; Hudak, Joseph; Harris, Keith; Johnston, Maura; Epstein, Dan. "50 Wildest Guns N' Roses Moments." *Rolling Stone*. November 24, 2015. https://www.rollingstone.com/culture/culture-lists/50-wildest-guns-n-roses-moments-149883/june-1985-izzy-and-duff-play-hide-the-bass-drum-169025/.
20 "Guns N' Neurosis." *SPIN*. Vol. 7, Iss. 6. September 1, 1991. Pg 77.
21 Beaujour, Tom and Bienstock, Richard. *Nothin' But a Good Time: The Uncensored History of the '80s Hard Rock Explosion*. St. Martin's Griffin, New York. 2022. Pg 279–80.
22 Author interview with Alan Niven. January 15, 2024.
23 Wall, Mick. "Izzy Stradlin: Life And Death, Sex And Drugs And Guns N' Roses." *Louder*. November 7, 2016. https://www.loudersound.com/features/izzy-stradlin-in-too-deep.
24 Booth, Dan. "Public Enemies And Public Relations." *In These Times*. Vol. 13, Iss. 33. September 6, 1989. Pg 21.
25 Pareles, Jon. "Prejudice: American as Mom and Apple Pie." *The Peninsula Times Tribune*. September 10, 1989. Section: Comment. Pg B5.
26 James, Del. "Axl Rose: The Rolling Stone Interview." *Rolling Stone*. Iss. 558. August 10, 1989. Pg 46–7.
27 Mayfield, Geoff. "Between The Bullets." *Billboard*. Vol. 103, Iss. 40. October 5, 1991. Pg 103.
28 Booth, Dan. "Public Enemies And Public Relations." *In These Times*. Vol. 13, Iss. 33. September 6, 1989. Pg 21.
29 Wild, David. "Sinéad O'Connor." *Rolling Stone*. Iss. 599. March 7, 1991. Pg 36, 37.
30 Light, Alan. "Sinéad Speaks." *Rolling Stone*. Iss. 642. October 29, 1992. Pg 80.
31 de la Vina, Mark. "Long Lines an 'Illusion?'" *Philadelphia Daily News*. September 17, 1991. Section: Features. Pg 34.
32 Triplett, Brian McTavishward W. III. "Picking Up Roses After Midnight." *The Kansas City Star*. September 17, 1991. Section: Metropolitan. Pg B3.
33 "Guns N' Roses Fans Wait in Line For Latest Release." *The Orlando Sentinel*. September 17, 1991. Pg A2.
34 Penner, John. "Rushing to 'Illusions.'" *The Los Angeles Times*. September 18, 1991. Pg 2.
35 Burke, David. "Waiting's Over—Early-Rising Fans Scoop Up Latest Releases." *Herald & Review*. September 18, 1991. Pg A3.

36 Burke, David. "Waiting's Over—Early-Rising Fans Scoop Up Latest Releases." *Herald & Review*. September 18, 1991. Pg A3.

37 Watrous, Peter; *New York Times* staff writer. "Guns N' Roses Albums Use Illusion to Rake in Cash With Huge Advance Sales, Stores Set Midnight Openings." *The Charlotte Observer*. September 12, 1991. Section: Living. Pg 1E.

38 King, Peter B. "Hype Hot For Guns N' Roses Discs." *Pittsburgh Post-Gazette*. September 14, 1991. Section: Entertainment. Pg B9.

39 McLeod, Harriet. "'Smokin'—Local Fans Get Up Early For Shot at New Guns N' Roses Albums." *Richmond Times-Dispatch*. September 17, 1991. Section: Entertainment. Pg 30.

40 "Guns N' Roses' Albums Halfway to Gold in Hours." *The Orlando Sentinel*. September 20, 1991. Pg A2.

41 Shuster, Fred. "'Illusion' Sales Hit 1 Million." *The Austin American-Statesman*. September 21, 1991. Section: Time Out. Pg 4.

42 Larsen, Dave. "Guns N' Roses Takes Aim at January Nutter Date." *Dayton Daily News*. December 12, 1991. Section: Arts. Pg 5C.

43 Jolson-Colburn, Jeffrey. "Heavy Mettle: GNR's Dual Discs Sell Million in Day." *The Hollywood Reporter*. Vol. 319, Iss. 14. September 18, 1991. Pg 1–2.

44 "GNR Albums Break a Record." *San Diego Union-Tribune*. September 14, 1991. Section: Lifestyle. Pg C6.

45 Thomas, Cal. "The Band From Hell." *The Richmond Times-Dispatch*. September 26, 1991. Section: Editorial. Pg A16.

46 Hochman, Steve. "Radio 'X.'" *The Los Angeles Times*. October 17, 1991. Pg F3.

47 Holdship, Bill. "Days of Guns N' Roses." *SPIN*. Vol. 4, Iss. 2. May 1, 1988. Pg 34–7.

48 James, Del. "Axl Rose." *Rolling Stone*. Iss. 558. August 10, 1989. Pg 44.

49 Marks, Craig and Tannenbaum, Rob. *I Want My MTV: The Uncensored Story of The Music Video Revolution*. Dutton, New York. 2011. Pg 475.

50 "Guns N' Roses—Estranged." *YouTube*. Uploaded by Guns N' Roses on October 7, 2009. https://www.youtube.com/watch?v=dpmAY059TTY.

51 Fricke, David and Wright, Christian. "Guns n' Roses Blazing: Choose Your Illusion." *Rolling Stone*. Iss. 615. October 17, 1991. Pg 89, 91.

52 Corcoran, Michael. "Delusions of Grandeur—Guns N' Roses Blinded by The Hype." *The Chicago Sun-Times*. September 22, 1991. Pg 5.

53 Mayhew, Don. "Artistry? It's Just An Illusion." *The Fresno Bee*. September 20, 1991. Section: Weekend. Pg E8.

54 Darling, Cary. "A 3-Hour Sweep Through Rose's Thorny Psyche." *The Orange County Register*. September 15, 1991. Pg J21.

55 Considine, J.D. "'Use Your Illusion' Proves Guns N' Roses is Best Rock Band in U.S." *The Baltimore Sun*. September 16, 1991. Section: Features. Pg 1D.

56 Sandall, Robert. "All Mouth And No Taste—Guns N' Roses." *The Sunday Times*. September 22, 1991. Section: Features.

57 Queenan, Joe. "Misfits Metalheads." *TIME*. Vol. 138, Iss. 13. September 30, 1991. Pg 82–3.

58 Eichenberger, Bill. "New Guns N' Roses Albums Are, in a Word, Volatile." *The Columbus Dispatch*. September 16, 1991. Pg 10D.

59 UPI. "An Axl to Grind." *The Toronto Sun*. September 17, 1991. Pg 63.

60 Darling, Cary. "Guns Really Shoot Off Their Mouths." *Orange County Register*. December 16, 1988. Section: Show. Pg P40.

61 Menconi, David. "Trigger-Happy Guns Deliver Scattershot Hits." *The News & Observer*. September 22, 1991. Section: Arts & Entertainment. Pg H1.

62 Rife, Susan L. "'Illusion' Albums Bring Mostly Yawns From Panel." *The Wichita Eagle*. October 4, 1991. Section: Daybreak. Pg 1C.

63 Crumbo, Christine. "Learning The Lessons of War: Teachers Shelve The Classics to Talk About Current Events." *The Wichita Eagle*. January 18, 1991. Pg 5A.

64 Neely, Kim. "Axl Rose: The Rolling Stone Interview." *Rolling Stone*. Iss. 627. April 2, 1992. Pg 34.

65 "Guns N' Roses: Is It All Over? Does Anyone Care?" *Metal Hammer*. November 1995.

66 "Twisted Sister." Universal Music Publishing Group website. Accessed January 22, 2024. https://www.umusicpub.com/us/Artists/T/Twisted-Sister.aspx.

67 Vare, Ethlie Ann. "Twisted Sister's 'Hideous' Road to Success." *Billboard*. Vol. 96, Iss. 38. September 22, 1984. Pg 50.

68 "Appetite For Self-Destruction." *SPIN*. Vol. 15, Iss. 7. July 1, 1999. Pg 87.

69 Fricke, David. " . . . And Justice For All: Appetite for Destruction." *Rolling Stone*. Iss. 541/542. December 15, 1988. Pg 201, 203.

70 Hiatt, Brian. "Filth Sex Cool." *Rolling Stone*. Iss. 1032. August 9, 2007. Pg 58.

71 Parales, Jon, NY Times News Service. "Nasty Boys; Guns N' Roses Prove Raw And Popular." *Leader-Telegram*. September 15, 1991. Pg 4G.

72 Robbins, Ira. "Guns With Punks: Whines and Rose." *Newsday*. November 19, 1993. Pg 91.

73 Healy, James. "Beat Farmers Get Down to Business in Wake of Buddy Blue's Departure." *Omaha World-Herald*. August 9, 1987. Section: Entertainment.

74 Kent, Nick. "Meltdown." *The Guardian*. January 3, 2003. https://www.theguardian.com/music/2003/jan/03/popandrock.artsfeatures.

75 Wilkinson, Peter. "Axl Rose: The Lost Years." *Rolling Stone*. Iss. 840. May 11, 2000. Pg 74.

76 Harris, Steve. "Axl Rose (Guns N' Roses) 1987." *The Tapes Archive*. https://www.thetapesarchive.com/axl-rose/.

77 Muretich, James. "Voxpop: Axl Comes Loose." *Calgary Herald*. July 20, 1989. Pg D2.

78 "The Daze of Swine and Roses." *NME*. June 24, 1989.

79 Hooton, Christopher. "Axl Rose Was Once Late For a Show . . . " *The Independent*. April 18, 2016. https://www.independent.co.uk/arts-entertainment/music/news/axl

-rose-was-once-late-for-a-show-because-he-was-watching-teenage-mutant-ninja-turtles-ii-the-secret-of-the-ooze-a6989076.html.

80 Booth, Philip. "Axl & Friends Make Wait Worthwhile." *The Tampa Tribune*. December 30, 1991. Section: Bailiff. Pg 1.
81 Lanham, Tom. "Wild-Living Rockers Bust Out of L.A. Gutter." *The San Francisco Examiner*. August 30, 1987. Pg 42–3.
82 "Appetite For Self-Destruction." *SPIN*. Vol. 15, Iss. 7. July 1, 1999. Pg 84.
83 Gallotta, Paul and Darzin, Daina. "Axl Rose Speaks Out On . . ." *Circus*. September 30, 1988. Pg 45.
84 Farr, Jory. "Bad-To-The-Bone Rocker." *Daily Press*. August 10, 1986. Pg I1, I4.
85 "Shooting From The Lip." *LA Weekly*. June 16, 1988. Pg 34.
86 "Appetite For Self-Destruction." *SPIN*. Vol. 15, Iss. 7. July 1, 1999. Pg 84.
87 Wall, Mick. *Last of The Giants: The True Story of Guns N' Roses*. Trapeze, 2017. Great Britain. Pg 7.
88 Hilburn, Robert. "Run N' Gun." *The Los Angeles Times*. July 21, 1991. Pg 90.
89 Wall, Mick. *Last of The Giants: The True Story of Guns N' Roses*. Trapeze, 2017. Great Britain. Pg 9.
90 Neely, Kim. "Axl Rose: The Rolling Stone Interview." *Rolling Stone*. Iss. 627. April 2, 1992. Pg 36, 42, 53.
91 Kleid, Beth. "Now Is The Time to Apply to The CSUs." *Los Angeles Times*. November 7, 1991. Pg OCE3.
92 Wall, Mick. "W.A.R.: The Unauthorized Biography of Axl Rose." St. Martins Press, New York. 2007. Pg 22–3, 26.
93 Neely, Kim. "Axl Rose: The Rolling Stone Interview." *Rolling Stone*. Iss. 627. April 2, 1992. Pg 36, 42.
94 Rowland, Mark. "If Guns N' Roses Are Outlawed." *Musician*. Iss. 122. December 1, 1988. Pg 67.
95 Jeremiah, John. "The Final Comeback of Axl Rose." *GQ*. Vol. 76, Iss. 9. September 1, 2006. Pg 388.
96 Tannenbaum, Rob. "The Hard Truth About Guns N' Roses." *Rolling Stone*. Iss. 539. November 17, 1988. Pg 66.
97 "Guns N' Neurosis." *SPIN*. Vol. 7, Iss. 6. September 1, 1991. Pg 77.
98 Gallotta, Paul and Darzin, Daina. "Axl Rose Speaks Out On . . ." *Circus*. September 30, 1988. Pg 45.
99 Sullivan, John Jeremiah. "The Final Comeback of Axl Rose." *GQ*. Vol. 76, Iss. 9. September 1, 2006. Pg 388.
100 Rowland, Mark. "If Guns N' Roses Are Outlawed." *Musician*. Iss. 122. December 1, 1988. Pg 67.
101 Tannenbaum, Rob. "The Hard Truth About Guns N' Roses." *Rolling Stone*. Iss. 539. November 17, 1988. Pg 66.
102 "Guns N' Neurosis." *SPIN*. Vol. 7, Iss. 6. September 1, 1991. Pg 77.

103 "Guns N' Neurosis." *SPIN*. Vol. 7, Iss. 6. September 1, 1991. Pg 75–7.

104 "Ex-Hollywood Rose Guitarist: Axl Rose Was 'Very Ego Motivated.'" *Blabbermouth*. November 19, 2004. Archived at https://web.archive.org/web/20050921111303/http://www.roadrunnerrecords.com/blabbermouth.net/news.aspx?mode=Article&newsitemID=29388.

105 "Guns N' Neurosis." *SPIN*. Vol. 7, Iss. 6. September 1, 1991. Pg 77.

106 Rock, Dr. "Giving It Both Barrels: Dr Rock Takes On Tracii Guns of The LA Guns." *The Quietus*. June 16, 2010. https://thequietus.com/articles/04450-dr-rock-tracii-guns-interview-la-guns-nikki-sixx-poison-guns-n-roses.

107 Beaujour, Tom and Bienstock, Richard. *Nothin' But a Good Time: The Uncensored History of the '80s Hard Rock Explosion*. St. Martins Griffin, New York. 2021. Pg 198–9.

108 Rowland, Mark. "If Guns N' Roses Are Outlawed." *Musician*. Iss. 122. December 1, 1988. Pg 64.

109 "Appetite For Self-Destruction." *SPIN*. Vol. 15, Iss. 7. July 1, 1999. Pg 84.

110 LaSalle, Mick. "Aerosmith and Guns: Battle of The Bads." *The San Francisco Chronicle*. September 10, 1988. Pg C6.

111 "Appetite For Self-Destruction." *SPIN*. Vol. 15, Iss. 7. July 1, 1999. Pg 87.

112 Hiatt, Brian. "Filth Sex Cool." *Rolling Stone*. Iss. 1032. August 9, 2007. Pg 59.

113 "Shooting From The Lip." *LA Weekly*. June 16, 1988. Pg 31.

114 Wiederhorn, Jon. "37 Years Ago: Guns N' Roses Sign to Geffen Records." *Loudwire*. March 26, 2023. https://loudwire.com/guns-n-roses-sign-to-geffen-records-anniversary/.

115 Bryant, Tom. "Six Pack: Slash on Drugs, Dying and Axl Rose." *Louder*. May 1, 2015. https://www.loudersound.com/features/six-pack-slash-on-drugs-dying-and-axl-rose.

116 James, Del. "The World According to W. Axl Rose." *RIP*. April 1989. Archived at http://www.heretodaygonetohell.com/articles/showarticle.php?articleid=2.

117 Morrow, Scott. "L.A. Rocks: The Big Bang Theory." *L.A. Weekly*. July 3, 1986. Pg 32.

118 Wall, Mick. "Inside The Horrific Guns N' Roses 'Hell House.'" *Cuepoint*. January 4, 2017. https://medium.com/cuepoint/inside-the-horrific-guns-n-roses-hell-house-971e20df749c#.pjfvhpyjk.

119 "Appetite For Self-Destruction." *SPIN*. Vol. 15, Iss. 7. July 1, 1999. Pg 84.

120 Wall, Mick. "Inside The Horrific Guns N' Roses 'Hell House.'" *Cuepoint*. January 4, 2017. https://medium.com/cuepoint/inside-the-horrific-guns-n-roses-hell-house-971e20df749c#.pjfvhpyjk.

121 "No Bed of Roses." *Metal Hammer*. February 1990.

122 Slash and Bozza, Anthony. *Slash*. Harper Entertainment. New York, 2007. Pg 125.

123 Cue, Raz. "I Got It Wrong In My Book." RazCue.com. July 2, 2019. https://razcue.com/i-got-it-wrong-in-my-book/.

124 "LittleMichelleLives, her Accusations against Axl Rose for Rape." Posted by Swordfish-Weary in r/Fauxmoi. https://www.reddit.com/r/Fauxmoi/comments/vkmkfu/littlemichellelives_her_accusations_against_axl/.

Axl Rose screaming bloody murder on the comeback trail at the 2002 Video Music Awards. *Source: TIMOTHY A. CLARY/AFP via Getty Images.*

Replacements bassist Tommy Stinson spent 16 years playing in Guns N' Roses; he insisted Axl Rose was easier to work with than Paul Westerberg. *Source: Photo by Robert Cianflone/Getty Images.*

A devotion to studying classical music earned Bryan Mantia the nickname Brain, but he got to live out his Led Zeppelin dreams while in Guns N' Roses. *Source: Photo by Jeff Kravitz/FilmMagic, Inc.*

Chris Pitman was invited to join Guns N' Roses as a multi-instrumentalist and songwriter. On tour, he was the second keyboardist. *Source: Photo by Ethan Miller/Getty Images.*

"I could have never foreseen Buckethead in Guns N' Roses," says friend David Lefkowitz. "He always had visions of grandeur, but always on his own terms." *Source: Photo by Ethan Miller/Getty Images.*

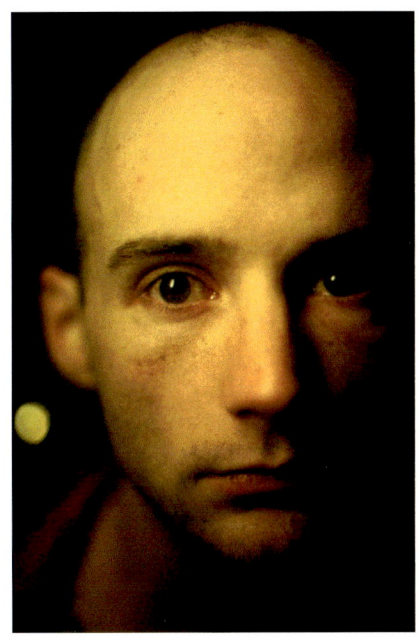 

Clockwise from top left: techno whiz Moby, rapping basketball sensation Shaquille O'Neal, Youth from Killing Joke. They all had brief but memorable stints on *Chinese Democracy. Source: Photos by Martyn Goodacre/ Getty Images; Frazer Harrison/ Getty Images; and Bob Berg/ Getty Images.*

Robin Finck during the Nine Inch Nails Self Destruct Tour in 1994. Little did he know he'd wind up an instrumental figure in Axl Rose's world. *Source: Photo by Ian Dickson/Redferns via Getty Images.*

Ron "Bumblefoot" Thal, seen here with Axl in 2012, can tell you it wasn't all smiles being in GN Effin' R. *Source: Photo by MANJUNATH KIRAN/AFP via Getty Images.*

Nice hat: DJ Ashba on stage with Axl Rose in 2010. *Source: Photo by Neil Lupin/Redferns via Getty Images.*

Axl Rose, 2023. *Source: Photo by Mario Renzi - Formula 1/Formula 1 via Getty Images.*

125 Spurrier, Jeff. "L.A. Beat: Guns N' Roses: Bad Boys Give It Their Best Shot." *The Los Angeles Times*. July 6, 1986. Pg R74.

126 Morrow, Scott. "L.A. Rocks: The Big Bang Theory." *L.A. Weekly*. June 27–July 3, 1986. Pg 32.

127 Rowland, Mark. "If Guns N' Roses Are Outlawed . . . " *Musician*. Iss. 122. December 1, 1988. Pg 113.

128 Hiatt, Brian. "Filth Sex Cool." *Rolling Stone*. Iss. 1032. August 9, 2007. Pg 58.

129 Sciaretto, Amy. "'That Metal Show' Recap: Axl Rose Talks Lateness, Slash + Original 'Appetite' Cover." *Loudwire*. November 12, 2011. https://loudwire.com/that-metal-show-recap-axl-rose-talks-lateness-slash-original-appetite-cover/.

130 Goldstein, Patrick. "Artists You Judge By Their Covers: Exhibit Features Record Albums." *The Los Angeles Times*. December 17, 1987. Pg H1, H4.

131 Goldstein, Patrick. "Pop Eye: Geffen's Guns N' Roses Fires a Volley at PMRC." *The Los Angeles Times*. August 16, 1987. Pg A92.

132 Tiger, J.F. "Realmusic From The Underground—Not The Stuff For Ozzybrats." *Seattle Gay News*. August 21, 1987. Pg 28.

133 Duffy, Thom. "Guns N' Roses." *The Orlando Sentinel*. August 7, 1988. Pg 9.

134 Frost, Deborah and Bouchard, Albert. "Def Lappart; Guns N' Roses." *Creem*. Vol. 19, Iss. 4. December 1, 1987. Pg 15.

135 Lanham, Tom. "Wild-Living Rockers Bust Out of L.A. Gutter." *The San Francisco Examiner*. August 30, 1987. Pg 42–3.

136 Staggs, Jeffrey. "Hot Jesus Jones Aims to Redefine Rock n' Roll." *The Washington Times*. October 2, 1991. Pg E2.

137 "MUSIC: ROCK OVER LONDON: Tragedy Strikes Guns N' Roses." *Radio & Records*. Iss. 752. August 26, 1988. Pg 42.

138 Hilburn, Robert. "Q&A With John Fogerty." *The Los Angeles Times*. January 12, 1993. Pg 1.

139 Wall, Mick. *Last of The Giants: The True Story of Guns N' Roses*. Trapeze, Great Britain. 2017. Pg 478.

140 Sullivan, John Jeremiah. "The Final Comeback of Axl Rose." *GQ*. Vol. 76, Iss. 9. September 1, 2006. Pg 406.

141 Spurrier, Jeff. "L.A. Beat: Guns N' Roses: Bad Boys Give It Their Best Shot." *Los Angeles Times*. July 6, 1986. Pg R74.

142 Trigg, James. "IN YER EAR: Mudhoney's Not So Quiet Ooze Out of America's Great Northwest." *The Bob*. Iss. 38. January 1, 1990. Pg 9.

143 Macdonald, Patrick. "Soundgarden Has Found a Flowering Fan in Axl Rose." *The Seattle Times*. July 21, 1989. Section: Tempo. Pg 10.

144 McCormick, Moira. "New Faces: Soundgarden." *Rolling Stone*. Iss. 569. January 11, 1990. Pg 18.

145 Yarm, Mark. *Everybody Loves Our Town: An Oral History of Grunge*. Three Rivers Press, New York. 2011. Pg 304.

146 AP. "Soundgarden Brings Its Sound to ISU." *The Pantagraph*. February 15, 1992. Pg A7.

147 Valania, Jonathan. "Seattle Soundgarden Is Doing a Balancing Act on The Cutting Edge." *The Morning Call*. December 13, 1991. Section: A.M. Magazine. Pg D1.
148 Yarm, Mark. *Everybody Loves Our Town: An Oral History of Grunge*. Three Rivers Press, New York. 2011. Pg 304.
149 Romandetta, Julie. "Trouble Follows Guns N' Roses." *Boston Herald*. September 10, 1992. Section: Entertainment. Pg 49.
150 Wall, Mick. *Last of The Giants: The True Story of Guns N' Roses*. Trapeze, Great Britain. 2017. Pg 268.
151 Yarm, Mark. *Everybody Loves Our Town: An Oral History of Grunge*. Three Rivers Press, New York. 2011. Pg 305.
152 Author interview with Stevie Rachelle. April 4, 2024.
153 Bisbee, Dana. "Celebrity." *Boston Herald*. December 11, 1991. Pg 17.
154 Jettie, Patricia. "Roses' Rowdy Show About as Subtle as a Gun." *San Diego Union-Tribune*. January 29, 1992. Section: Lifestyle. Pg E1.
155 Bertelson, Christine; Wallstin, Brian; Bell, Kim. "Star, Beer, Guards Blamed For Melee." *St. Louis Post-Dispatch*. July 4, 1991. Pg 1A.
156 Associated Press. "Guns N' Roses Riot Leaves 60 Hurt, Show Site Wrecked." *The Fort Worth Star-Telegram*. July 3, 1991. Pg 12.
157 Bell, Kim. "Police Chief Describes 'Combat.'" *St. Louis Post-Dispatch*. July 4, 1991. Pg 14A.
158 Yarm, Mark. *Everybody Loves Our Town: An Oral History of Grunge*. Three Rivers Press, New York. 2011. Pg 305.
159 Greene, Andy. "Bryan 'Brain' Mantia Was There For Guns N' Roses' Most Unpredictable Era." *Rolling Stone*. August 4, 2022. https://www.rollingstone.com/music/music-features/bryan-brain-mantia-guns-n-roses-tom-waits-primus-1388363/.
160 Fricke, David. "Life After Guns N' Roses." *Rolling Stone*. Iss. 642. October 29, 1992. Pg 26.
161 Shuster, Fred. "A Clean Break From GNR." *The Daily News of Los Angeles*. March 20, 1998. Section: L.A. Life. Pg L20.
162 Young, Charles M. "Izzy Stradlin Loses His Illusion." *Musician*. Iss. 169. November 1, 1992. Pg 40–4, 46, 48.
163 "Snippets." *The Houston Chronicle*. December 23, 1994. Pg 2.
164 Mundy, Chris. "Nirvana." *Rolling Stone*. Iss. 622. January 23, 1992. Pg 41.
165 Rogers, Shelia. "Random Notes." *Rolling Stone*. Iss. 580. June 14, 1990. Pg 10.
166 Rosen, Craig. "Some See 'New Openness' Following Nirvana Success." *Billboard*. Vol. 104, Iss. 4. January 25, 1992. Pg 12.
167 Mundy, Chris. "Nirvana." *Rolling Stone*. Iss. 622. January 23, 1992. Pg 41.
168 Bale, Rockin Jeff. "Rock n' Roll Burnout." *MaximumRockNRoll*. Iss. 103. December 1, 1991. Pg 32.
169 Flanagan, Bill. "Shadow Boxing With Rose." *Musician*. Iss. 164. June 1, 1992. Pg 56.

170 Lewman, Mark. "Nirvana Benefit Show." *Entertainment Weekly*. April 23, 1993. https://ew.com/article/1993/04/23/nirvana-benefit-show/.

171 Yarm, Pg 418.

172 Allman, Kevin. "The Dark Side of Kurt Cobain." *The Advocate*. Iss. 622. February 9, 1993. Pg 39.

173 Lhotka, William C. "Axl Rose Found Guilty, Faces Civil Suit." *St. Louis Post-Dispatch*. November 11, 1992. Pg 3A.

174 Reuter. "AIDS Benefit Unloads Guns N' Roses Offer." *Newsday*. April 8, 1989. Pg 53.

175 Simons, Stephanie L. "Review: Axl Rose Roasts Nirvana During Dramatic Concert." *The News Tribune*. October 8, 1992. Pg F4.

176 Booth, Philip. "Roses' Concert Has Its Thorns." *The Tampa Tribune*. September 4, 1992. Pg 1.

177 Allman, Kevin. "The Dark Side of Kurt Cobain." *The Advocate*. Iss. 622. February 9, 1993. Pg 39.

178 Black, Johnny. "The Story of Axl Rose and Kurt Cobain's MTV Bust-Up, By The People Who Were There." *Louder*. September 28, 2021. https://www.loudersound.com/features/the-story-of-axl-rose-and-kurt-cobains-mtv-bust-up-by-those-who-were-there.

179 Yarm, Pg 186.

180 Yarm, Pg 242–3.

181 Yarm, Pg 300, 316.

182 Yarm, Pg 432.

183 James, Del. "The World According to W. Axl Rose." *RIP*. April 1989. Archived at http://www.heretodaygonetohell.com/articles/showarticle.php?articleid=2.

184 Wall, Pg 224.

185 Hirschberg, Lynn. "Strange Love." *Vanity Fair*. Vol. 55, Iss. 9. September 1992. Pg 296.

186 Swensson, Andrea. "A California Desert Interview With Babes in Toyland." *The Current*. March 11, 2015. https://www.thecurrent.org/feature/2015/03/11/a-california-desert-interview-with-babes-in-toyland.

187 Allman, Kevin. "The Dark Side of Kurt Cobain." *The Advocate*. Iss. 622. February 9, 1993. Pg 39.

188 Cross, Charles R. *Heavier Than Heaven: A Biography of Kurt Cobain*. Hachette Books, New York. 2001. Pg 241.

189 Slash, Pg 336.

190 McKagan, Pg 221–2.

191 Wilkinson, Peter. "Axl Rose: The Lost Years." *Rolling Stone*. Iss. 840. May 11, 2000. Pg 75.

192 Goodman, Fred. "Big Deals: How Money Fever is Changing The Music Business." *Musician*. January 1992. Pg 44.

193 "The David Geffen Company: Geffen Records." *Billboard*. Vol. 270, Iss. 50. March 15, 1982. Pg 20.

194 Sutherland, Sam. "Geffen Maps Massive Push For Kitaro." *Billboard*. Vol. 97, Iss. 33. August 17, 1985. Pg 6.

195 Author interview with Bill Bennet. September 18, 2023.

196 Rosen, Craig. "Geffen Severs Ties With Def American." *Billboard*. Vol. 102, Iss. 39. September 29, 1990. Pg 94.

197 *Reign in Blood*. Slayer. Def American, 1986.

198 Jolson-Colburn, Jeffrey. "Geffen Bars Release of Geto Boys CD." *The Hollywood Reporter*. Vol. 313, Iss. 43. August 16, 1990. Pg 3, 17.

199 Haring, Bruce. "Geffen Nixes Geto Boys." *Variety*. Vol. 340, Iss. 7. August 22, 1990. Pg 79.

200 "Geffen Splits With Def American." *Variety*. Vol. 340, Iss. 11. September 24, 1990. Pg 97.

201 Citron, Alan. "David Geffen Didn't Take The Money And Run." *The Los Angeles Times*. March 7, 1993. Pg 8.

202 Wilkinson, Peter. "Axl Rose: The Lost Years." *Rolling Stone*. Iss. 840. May 11, 2000. Pg 75.

203 Sullivan, Jim. "Guns N' Roses Dips Into History." *The Boston Globe*. November 26, 1993. Pg 79.

204 "Geffen to Pay Manson's Song Royalties to Victim's Family." *UPI Archives*. December 8, 1993. https://www.upi.com/Archives/1993/12/08/Geffen-to-pay-Mansons-song-royalties-to-victims-family/8513755326800/.

205 Philips, Chuck. "Guns N' Roses May Ditch Manson's Tune." *The Houston Chronicle*. December 2, 1993. Pg 22.

206 Grow, Kory. "Red Kross On The Pop Culture Obsessions That Shaped Their Band." *MTV*. August 17, 2012. https://www.mtv.com/news/sl46tq/redd-kross-charles-manson-sofia-coppola.

207 Shuster, Fred. "Guns N' Roses Not Trying to Shock With Manson Song, Singer Contends." *The Daily News of Los Angeles*. December 2, 1993. Pg L7.

208 Jolson-Colburn, Jeffrey. "Rose Downplays Manson." *The Hollywood Reporter*. Vol. 329, Iss 49. December 2, 1993. Pg 17.

209 "Geffen to Pay Manson's Song Royalties to Victim's Family." *UPI Archives*. December 8, 1993. https://www.upi.com/Archives/1993/12/08/Geffen-to-pay-Mansons-song-royalties-to-victims-family/8513755326800/.

210 Philips, Chuck. "Manson Song Stays on Album." *Waterloo Region Record*. December 8, 1993. Pg F3.

211 "Manson T-shirts Are Fad in California." *The Philadelphia Inquirer*. November 25, 1993. Pg B09.

212 Farber, Jim. "'Spaghetti' N' Meatballs." *The Daily News*. November 21, 1993. Pg 34.

213 Philips, Chuck. "Holiday Boom, Diversity Make For Record Year." *The Los Angeles Times*. January 3, 1994. Section: Calendar. Pg F8.

214 Farber, Jim. "Pearl Jam's Whine Steward." *The Daily News*. November 1, 1993. Pg 41.

215 Farber, Jim. "Pearl Jam's Whine Steward." *The Daily News*. November 1, 1993. Pg 41.

216 Yarm, Pg 373–4.

217 Jennings, Rebecca. "Everyone's a Sellout Now." *Vox*. February 1, 2024. https://www.vox.com/culture/2024/2/1/24056883/tiktok-self-promotion-artist-career-how-to-build-following.

218 "1993 Readers Poll." *SPIN*. Vol. 9, Iss. 8. November 1, 1993. Pg 75.

219 Giles, Jeff. "No. 1 With an Attitude." *Rolling Stone*. Iss. 607. June 27, 1991. Pg 41.

220 Graff, Gary. "Into The Pit." *Detroit Free Press*. April 24, 1995.

221 Slash, Pg 377.

222 Jolson-Colburn, Jeffrey. "Miramax Gets 'Highlander III.'" *The Hollywood Reporter*. Vol. 329, Iss. 48. December 1, 1993. Pg 1, 32.

223 Williams, Owen. "Highlander: A History." July 11, 2016. https://www.empireonline.com/movies/features/highlander/.

224 Kirkland, Bruce. "It's Nae Pretty: Immortal Highlander Deserves Quick Death." *The Toronto Sun*. January 30, 1995. Pg 42.

Chapter 2

1 Cover. *Star*. August 24, 1993.

2 Cover. *National Enquirer*. August 24, 1993.

3 Gibbs, Garth. "No Way Cowboy, Axl's Told." *The Daily Mirror*. August 6, 1993. Section: Features. Pg 15.

4 Wall, Mick. *Last of The Giants: The True Story of Guns N' Roses*. Trapeze, Great Britain. 2017. Pg 312–13.

5 "Thorny End?" *Scunthorpe Evening Telegraph*. March 3, 1993. Pg 7.

6 Downey, Maureen, and Harrison, Bette. "Peach Buzz: Talk of Our Town." *The Atlanta Journal*. March 2, 1993. Pg F2.

7 Johnson, Richard. "Richard Johnson." *The Daily News*. March 17, 1993. Pg 12.

8 "Name Dropping." *Lansing State Journal*. September 1, 1993. Pg 8B.

9 Thomas, Karen. "Axl Rose's Thorny Breakup." *USA Today*. August 27, 1993. Section: Life. Pg 2D.

10 "War of The Roses." *The Buffalo News*. November 12, 1993. Section: Lifestyles. Pg C8.

11 Leedham, Robert. "Axl Rose vs. Stephanie Seymour." *The Sunday Times*. September 26, 1993. Section: Features. Pg 8/21.

12 "New Entry in War of Roses." *The Sacramento Bee*. July 11, 1994. Pg A2.

13 Wilkinson, Peter. "Axl Rose: The Lost Years." *Rolling Stone*. Iss. 840. May 11, 2000. Pg 75.

14 Erin I. Everly vs. W. Axl Rose. Verified Complaint for Damages. Case No. SC028980. Filed March 7, 1994. Pg 3–6.

15 "Group Rep's 'Stepping Out' Taps Into Talent of Suzy London." *Los Angeles Examiner*. February 12, 2013.
16 "Nightlife Jazz: Suzie London . . . " *L.A. Weekly*. July 16–22, 1982. Pg 85.
17 "Suzy London." *Actors Access*. Accessed April 25, 2024. https://resumes.actorsaccess.com/suzylondon.
18 "Suzie London." *Remarkable Healings in the Realm of Miracles*. Remarkablehealings.com. Accessed April 11, 2024. http://remarkablehealings.com/suzie_london_bio.html.
19 "Meet The Team." SpiritualPlumbers.com. Accessed May 14, 2024. https://www.spiritualplumbers.com/team.aspx.
20 Smith, Amy. "Controversial Knox Dentist Listed as M.D. by N.C. Clinic." *News Sentinel*. December 3, 1995. Pg A1.
21 Phone call with Suzie London, May 13, 2024.
22 McKagan, Pg 163.
23 DeRogatis, Jim. "Nirvana Vocalist Cobain in Coma After Pills, Booze." *Chicago Sun-Times*. March 5, 1994. Pg 3.
24 "Cobain Expected to Fully Recover." *The Seattle Times*. March 6, 1994. Pg A2.
25 Neely, Kim. "Axl Rose: The Rolling Stone Interview." *Rolling Stone*. Iss. 627. April 2, 1992. Pg 36, 42, 53.
26 Krewen, Nick. "Gunners Just 'Normal Bunch of Guys.'" *The Hamilton Spectator*. August 8, 1992. Pg C3.
27 "Fans Riot at Concert in Canada." *St. Louis Post-Dispatch*. August 9, 1992. Pg 7A.
28 "Riot at Guns N' Roses Concert in Montreal." *UPI*. August 9, 1992.
29 Associated Press. "Montreal Authorities Clean Up After Rock Riot." *Akron Beacon Journal*. August 10, 1992. Pg A4.
30 Associated Press. "12 Arrested in Montreal Guns N' Roses Riot." *Fort Worth Star-Telegram*. August 10, 1992. Pg 3E.
31 Author interview with Alan Niven, January 13, 2024.
32 Author interview with James Barber, June 19, 2023.
33 Barol, Bill and Abramson, Pamela. "Who is This Rama?" *Newsweek*. Vol. 111, Iss. 5. February 1, 1988. Pg 58.
34 Author interview with Alan Niven, January 13, 2024.
35 Wall, Pg 247–8.
36 Author interview with Alan Niven, January 13, 2024.
37 Wilkinson, Peter. "Axl Rose; The Lost Years." *Rolling Stone*. Iss. 840. May 11, 2000. Pg 74.
38 "Proceedings." Superior Court Los Angeles County: Erin I. Everly vs. Axl Rose." SC 28980. Pg 3.
39 "Couples." *The Californian*. April 14, 1995. Pg 2.
40 Blow, Richard. "Moronic Convergence." *The New Republic*. Vol. 198, Iss. 4. January 25, 1988. Pg 26.

41 Barol, Bill and Abramson, Pamela. "Who is This Rama?" *Newsweek*. Vol. 111, Iss. 5. February 1, 1988. Pg 58.
42 Anderson, Lisa. "Getting Cosmic With Shirley." *Chicago Tribune*. August 19, 1987. Section 7. Pg 8.
43 "About." ArcosCielos.com. Captured June 10, 2004, Accessed May 12, 2024. Archived at https://web.archive.org/web/20040610185717/http://www.arcoscielos.com/about.html.
44 Wall, Pg 350.
45 "Electronic Grange Network Receives Ecology Grant." *Sun-Journal*. March 10, 2003. Pg 3.
46 Hausen, Jodi. "Electronic Grange Awarded Grant." *Sun-Journal*. December 22, 2004. Pg B2.
47 Toner, Mike. "Science May Convert Field to Shrimp Farm." *The Miami Herald*. 61st year, No. 14. December 14, 1970. Pg 1.
48 "Sharon Midori Maynard." US Social Security Applications and Claims Index, 1936–2007.
49 Maynard, Elliott. "A Tribute, Thoughts And Observations on Sharon Maynard's Passing." ArcosCielos.com. February 1, 2007. Archived at https://web.archive.org/web/20080907065214/http://www.arcoscielos.com/2007/02/000118.
50 Florida, US, Marriage Indexes, 1822–1875 and 1927–2001. Florida Department of Health. Jacksonville, FL. Archived on Ancestry.com.
51 Province News Services. "Tenerife Jet Collision: $425m in Claims Feared." *The Province*. March 29, 1977. Pg 1, 2.
52 Feaver, Douglas B. "FAA, Insurers Set Up Pool to Pay San Diego Crash Claims." *The Washington Post*. March 27, 1979. Pg A6.
53 Sun News Dispatches. "Crash Survivor Recalls: 'It Was Survival of The Fittest.'" *The Vancouver Sun*. March 28, 1977. Pg 1, 7.
54 Florida, US, Marriage Indexes, 1822–1875 and 1927–2001. Florida Department of Health. Jacksonville, FL. Archived on Ancestry.com.
55 "About." ArcosCielos.com. Captured June 10, 2004, Accessed May 12, 2024. Archived at https://web.archive.org/web/20040610185717/http://www.arcoscielos.com/about.html.
56 Author interview with Wendy Maynard, December 1, 2023.
57 Lambert, Mel. "Insights: Interview With George Massenburg." *Media & Marketing*. July 1997. Archived at http://www.mediaandmarketing.com/13Writer/Interviews/MIX.George_Massenburg.html.
58 Oppenheimer, Jean. "Good Sounds." *The Hollywood Reporter*. Vol. 354, Iss. 2. August 25, 1998. Pg S-24.
59 Author interview with William Malouf, April 11, 2024.
60 Author interview with Chad Blinman, April 20, 2024.
61 Hochman, Steve. "Another GNR Breakup? Yawn." *The Los Angeles Times*. July 17, 1994. Pg 60.

62   Gill, Chris. "Snake N' Bake: Slash's New Band Shakes Up The Ranks." *Guitar* Player, vol. 29, Iss. 5. May 1995. Pg 65-?

63   Rowland, Mark. "Edward Van Halen & Slash." *Musician*. Iss. 196, March 1, 1995. Pg 44.

64   Wake, Matt. "Legendary Rock Band's Ex-Guitarist Says He Was Never Officially Fired." AL.com. March 22, 2024. Section: Life.

65   Slash, Pg 357–8.

66   Author interview with James Barber, June 19, 2023.

67   Author interview with William Malouf, April 11, 2024.

68   Muretich, James and Calgary Herald. "Guns N' Roses Guitarist Talks About What's New, Old." *London Free Press*. January 31, 1994. Pg C8.

69   McKagan, Pg 15–19.

70   Pike, Jeff. "No Recess." *The Rocket*. April 5, 1995.

71   Yarm, Pg 447–8.

72   Roy, Yancey. "Young Area Listeners Spurn 'Greedstock.'" *The Times Union*. June 10, 1994. Pg B7.

73   Schoemer, Karen. "Woodstock '94: Back to the Garden." *Newsweek*. Vol. 124, Iss. 5. August 8, 1994. Pg 45.

74   Blum, David. "Heading Back to Yasgur's Farm." *The Guardian*. September 9, 1993.

75   Harverson, Patrick. "Peace And Percentages." *The Financial Times*. May 30, 1994. Pg 11.

76   Milward, John. "Field of Dreams." *Rolling Stone*. Iss. 688. August 11, 1994. Pg 36.

77   Author interview with John Scher. June 19, 2024.

78   Foege, Alec. "Billie Joe of Green Day." *Rolling* Stone, no. 695, 17 Nov. 1994, Pg 24.

79   Milward, John. "Field of Dreams." *Rolling Stone*. Iss. 688. August 11, 1994. Pg 36.

80   Gold, Jonathan. "The Downward Spiral." *Rolling Stone*. Iss. 678. March 24, 1994. Pg 92.

81   Steinke, Darcey. "Sing The Body Electric." *SPIN*. Vol. 10, Iss. 4. July 1, 1994. Pg 46.

82   Garbarini, Vic. "Pretty Hate Machinery." *Musician*. Iss. 185. March 1, 1994. Pg 52.

83   *Juice* magazine, July 1995.

84   Hochman, Steve. "Another GNR Breakup? Yawn." *The Los Angeles Times*. July 17, 1994. Pg 60.

85   Kaplan, Michael. "Anne Rice Vamps Till Ready." *Rolling* Stone, no. 538, 3 Nov. 1988, Pg 32.

86   McCauley, Mary II. "Oh, Mary!" *The Advocate*. Iss. 575. April 23, 1991. Pg 93.

87   "All About The Signing Game." *Newsweek*. Vol. 121, Iss. 7. February 15, 1993. Pg 70.

88   "Players: Rice Boiling." *Screen International*. Iss. 924. September 10, 1993. Pg 32.

89   Author interview with Pete Rizzo. June 12, 2024.

90   "News Real—Music Devilish Time For Band Members." *Daily News of Los Angeles*. December 27, 1994. Section: L.A. Life. Pg L3.

91. Slash, Pg 379.
92. Parker, Marc and Benefield Parker, Melissa. "Matt Sorum: Guns N' Roses Drummer Creates Chaos." *Smashing Interviews*. November 29, 2022. https://smashinginterviews.com/interviews/musicians/matt-sorum-interview-guns-n-roses-drummer-creates-chaos.
93. Ansen, David. "A Feast of Rats, Blood and Wild Rice." *Newsweek*. Vol. 124, Iss. 21. November 21, 1994. Pg 93.
94. Slash, Pg 379–81.
95. Prato, Greg. "Gilby Clarke." *Song Facts*. October 9, 2013. https://web.archive.org/web/20131123152314/https://www.songfacts.com/blog/interviews/gilby_clarke/.
96. Prato, Greg. "Gilby Clarke." *Song Facts*. October 9, 2013. https://web.archive.org/web/20131123152314/https://www.songfacts.com/blog/interviews/gilby_clarke/.
97. Wake, Matt. "Legendary Rock Band's Ex-Guitarist Says He Was Never Officially Fired." AL.com. March 22, 2024. Section: Life.
98. Ansen, David. "A Feast of Rats, Blood and Wild Rice." *Newsweek*. Vol. 124, Iss. 21. November 21, 1994. Pg 93.
99. Marcus, Greil. "Sympathy For The Devil." *Artforum International*. Vol. 33, Iss. 5. January 1995. Pg 13.
100. Writ, John. "Slash is Coiled to Strike From Snakepit." *The Advocate*. March 31, 1995. Section: Fun. Pg 8.
101. Howell, Peter. "Megadeth's HQ is Hog Heaven for Rockers' Plugged-In Fans." *The Toronto Star*. January 30, 1995. Pg E4.
102. Arar, Cárdena. "Tech Beat—Rockin' The Web." *Daily News of Los Angeles*. March 27, 1995. Section: L.A. Life. Pg L4.
103. Sullivan, Jim. "Reinventing The Rock Of Boston." *The Boston Globe*. May 5, 1995. Pg 57.
104. Eddy, Chuck. "SPINS: Slash's Snakepit." *SPIN*. Vol. 10, Iss. 12. March 1, 1995. Pg 97.
105. Surkamp, David, "Ho Hum! Snakepit Was a Sheer Bore." *St. Louis Post-Dispatch*. May 4, 1995. Pg 3G.
106. Ferman, Dave. "Slash's Rehashed Trash More Slapdash Than Smash." *Fort Worth Star-Telegram*, May 6, 1995. Pg 24.
107. Sculley, Alan. "Guns N' Snakes." *St. Louis Post-Dispatch*. April 28, 1995. Pg 4E.
108. "Zakk Wylde: Waiting For Axl Rose to Release 'Chinese Democracy.'" *Blabbermouth*. March 14, 2005. https://blabbermouth.net/news/zakk-wylde-waiting-for-axl-rose-to-release-chinese-democracy.
109. Lustig, Jay. "Really Hard Stuff." *The Star-Ledger*. April 9, 1995. Section: News.
110. "Guns N' Roses; It It All Over? Does Anyone Care?" *Metal Hammer*. November 1995.
111. McDonald, Sam. "Slash And Burn." *Daily Press*. April 7, 1995. Pg 14.
112. "Zakk Wylde: Waiting For Axl Rose to Release 'Chinese Democracy.'" *Blabbermouth*. March 14, 2005. https://blabbermouth.net/news/zakk-wylde-waiting-for-axl-rose-to-release-chinese-democracy.

113 Slash, Pg 389.
114 Slash, Pg 384–8.
115 Author interview with William Malouf, April 11, 2024.
116 "Slash And Burn: Real GNR Story." *The Daily Breeze*. November 15, 1996. Pg K21.
117 Labrye, Hervé. "Neurotic Outsiders—Timeline." Updated 2021. Accessed June 23, 2024. http://www.philjens.plus.com/kickdown/neurotic_timeline.htm.
118 Howell, Peter. "Neurotic Outsiders, Supergroup." *The Toronto Star*. September 5, 1996. Pg G5.
119 Irwin, Corey. "The Forgotten Sex Pistols, Guns N' Roses, Duran Duran Supergroup." *Ultimate Classic Rock*. September 10, 2021. https://ultimateclassicrock.com/sex-pistols-guns-n-roses-duran-duran-supergroup-neurotic-outsiders/.
120 Author interview with Krys Baratto. July 6, 2024.
121 Author interview with Jeff McDonough. July 5, 2024.
122 Howell, Peter. "Neurotic Outsiders, Supergroup." *The Toronto Star*. September 5, 1996. Pg G5.
123 Stevenson, Jane. "Thinking Man Rockers From Rush." *The Toronto Sun*. September 15, 1996. Pg 54.
124 Smallwood, Dean. "Neurotic Outsiders Supergroup Flops." *The Huntsville Times*. September 26, 1996. Pg D2.
125 Stevenson, Jane. "Roses Are Ready." *The Toronto Sun*. September 4, 1996. Pg 47.
126 Howell, Peter. "Gunners Reloading In Studio." *The Toronto Star*. August 29, 1996. Pg 88.
127 Beck, Marilyn and Smith, Stacy Jenel. "Holly, Carrey Glow On Set Of Her New Movie." *Daily News of Los Angeles*. July 24, 1996. Pg L7.
128 Beck, Marilyn and Smith, Stacy Jenel. "Holly, Carrey Glow On Set Of Her New Movie." *Daily News of Los Angeles*. July 24, 1996. Pg L7.
129 McCollum, Brian. "Guns N' Roses, Anxiety N' Rehearsing." *The Florida Times-Union*. September 26, 1996. Pg D12.
130 Howell, Peter. "Gunners Reloading In Studio." *The Toronto Star*. August 29, 1996. Pg 88.
131 Stevenson, Jane. "Roses Are Ready." *The Toronto Sun*. September 4, 1996. Pg 47.
132 McKagan, Pg 282, 291.
133 "1996.10.30—Fax From Axl." *Appetite For Discussion*. June 22, 2011. https://www.a-4-d.com/t626-1996-10-30-fax-from-axl.
134 "GNR's Blizzard of Acrimony." *MTV News*. November 8, 1996. Archived at https://web.archive.org/web/20220818171807/https://www.mtv.com/news/a8usfj/g-n-rs-blizzard-of-acrimony.
135 Jolson-Colburn, Jeffrey. "Guitar Man Slash Pulls Out of GNR Jungle." *The Hollywood Reporter*. Vol. 344, Iss. 38. November 1, 1996. Pg 8.
136 Hendrickson, Matt. "Slash Leaves Guns N' Roses." *Rolling Stone*. Iss. 749. December 12, 1996. Pg 24.

137 Slash, Pg 391–5.

138 Considine, J.D. "Slash is Touring, Not Leaving Axl N' Guns N' Roses." *The Sun*. April 9, 1995. Pg 1H.

139 Brown, Mark. "GNR Limbo Gives Slash Appetite For Diversity." *The Orange County Register*. January 31, 1997. Pg F47.

140 Author interview with David Dominguez. March 5, 2023.

141 Author interview with William Malouf, April 11, 2024.

142 "Liz Smith Says." *The Chattanooga Times Free Press*. December 6, 1996. Pg D4.

143 Ressner, Jeffrey. "Stand By Me: Inside The World of Rock & Roll Bodyguards." *Rolling Stone*. April 6, 1989. https://www.rollingstone.com/feature/stand-by-me-61186/.

144 Herrera, Dave. "Barry Fey on That Time That He Held a Gun to Axl Rose's Head And How The Business Has Changed." *Denver Westworld Blogs*. November 18, 2011. Archived at https://web.archive.org/web/20111203200038/http://blogs.westword.com/backbeat/2011/11/interview_barry_fey.php.

145 Silverman, David. "Pssssssst . . . If You See Guns N' Roses in Chicago, Just Remember: You Didn't." *Chicago Tribune*. June 26, 1989. Section: Tempo. Pg 1, 3.

146 Slash, Pg 321–3.

147 Wall, Pg 248.

148 McKagan, Pg 221–2.

149 Author interview with William Malouf, April 11, 2024.

Chapter 3

1 "The Complex." Special Advertising Supplement. *Mix*. June 1997. Pg 9.

2 Author interview with William Malouf. April 11, 2024.

3 "2005.09.26—Madagascar88—Interview With Dizzy." September 26, 2005. Archived at https://www.a-4-d.com/t5001-2005-09-26-madagascar88-interview-with-dizzy.

4 "The Unbelievable Truth." *SPIN*. Vol. 15, Iss. 7. July 1, 1999. Pg 82.

5 "2005.09.26—Madagascar88—Interview With Dizzy." September 26, 2005. Archived at https://www.a-4-d.com/t5001-2005-09-26-madagascar88-interview-with-dizzy.

6 Transcript of online chat between Axl Rose and fans. December 13, 2008. Archived at https://www.mygnrforum.com/topic/133108-axl-breaks-silence-on-mygnrforum-message-board/.

7 Author interview with Krys Baratto. July 6, 2024.

8 jomatami. "Manager Recalls Axl's Reaction to Telling Him He Shouldn't Keep Guns N' Roses Name" *Ultimate Guitar*. August 12, 2020. https://www.ultimate-guitar.com/news/general_music_news/manager_recalls_axls_reaction_to_telling_him_he_shouldnt_keep_guns_n_roses_name_after_slash_left_addresses_roses_charles_manson_connection.html.

9 "Informer: Paul Oakenfold." *Vox.* Iss. 51. December 1, 1994. Pg 6.
10 Kemp, Mark. "See Me Feel Me: Moby's Techno Touch." *Option.* Iss. 62. May 1, 1995. Pg 77.
11 Anthem Magazine interview with Moby, June 11, 2009.
12 Panahpour, Nilou. "Random Notes." *Rolling Stone.* Iss. 756. March 20, 1997. Pg 17.
13 "The Unbelievable Truth." *SPIN.* Vol. 15, Iss. 7. July 1, 1999. Pg 82.
14 "Finder: DJ Shadow." *Vox.* Iss. 73. November 1, 1996. Pg 10.
15 Kessler, Ted. "Electric Shadyland." *Vox.* Iss. 73. November 1, 1996. Pg 111.
16 Allstarmag, March 18, 1997.
17 jomatami. "Moby Talks GNR Hiring Him" *Ultimate Guitar.* May 14, 2019. https://www.ultimate-guitar.com/news/general_music_news/moby_talks_gnr_hiring_him_to_produce_chinese_democracy__how_he_angered_axl_with_question_he_was_never_supposed_to_ask.html.
18 Spera, Keith. "Hard-Driving Nine Inch Nails." *The Times-Picayune.* July 12, 1991. Pg L6.
19 "Appetite For Self-Destruction." *SPIN.* Vol. 15, Iss. 7. July 1, 1999. Pg 93.
20 "The Gun Club." *SPIN.* Vol. 15, Iss. 7. July 1, 1999. Pg 83.
21 Rosen, Steven. "Robin Finck: "I've Been Very Blessed With The Opportunities and I've Enjoyed Saying "Yes" to Them." *Ultimate Guitar.* January 17, 2014. Archived at https://web.archive.org/web/20140304064535/https://www.ultimate-guitar.com/interviews/interviews/robin_finck_ive_been_very_blessed_with_the_opportunities_and_ive_enjoyed_saying_yes_to_them.html.
22 Pollack, Marc. "Nine Inch Nails." *The Hollywood Reporter.* Vol. 332, Iss. 1. April 28, 1994. Pg 28.
23 Hendrickson, Matt. "Grapevine." *Rolling Stone.* Iss. 732. April 18, 1996. Pg 32.
24 Rosen, Steven. "Robin Finck: "I've Been Very Blessed With The Opportunities and I've Enjoyed Saying 'Yes' to Them." *Ultimate Guitar.* January 17, 2014. Archived at https://web.archive.org/web/20140304064535/https://www.ultimate-guitar.com/interviews/interviews/robin_finck_ive_been_very_blessed_with_the_opportunities_and_ive_enjoyed_saying_yes_to_them.html.
25 "The Gun Club." *SPIN.* Vol. 15, Iss. 7. July 1, 1999. Pg 83.
26 Author interview with William Malouf. April 11, 2024.
27 "Didn't You Used to Be Axl Rose?" *Q Magazine.* May 2001. Archived at https://heretodaygonetohell.com/articles/showarticle.php?articleid=42.
28 Anderswolleck Blog, April 25, 2004.
29 What's On Dubai, Dec 2010.
30 Wake, Matt. "Why is Nine Inch Nails' Ex-Drummer Teaching College in Alabama?" AL.com. October 24, 2018. https://www.al.com/life-and-culture/erry-2018/10/2b578ecb8a5013/why-is-nine-inch-nails-marilyn.html.
31 Author interview with Dave Abbruzzese. September 6, 2023.
32 Yarm, Mark. *Everybody Loves Our Town: The Oral History of* Grunge. Three Rivers Press. New York, 2011. Pg 476. "Ex-Drummer Claims Pearl Jam Printed

'Tripe' and 'Bullshit Rant.'" *Alternative Nation*. November 15, 2017. https://www.alternativenation.net/ex-drummer-pearl-jam-printed-tripe-bull-rant.

33 Author interview with Dave Abbruzzese. September 6, 2023.
34 Author interview with Dave Abbruzzese. September 6, 2023.
35 Author interview with Jimmy Shoaf. May 1, 2024.
36 Author interview with Dave Abbruzzese. September 6, 2023.
37 "Episode 162 Joey Castillo (drummer—Queens of The Stone Age)." *One Life One Chance Podcast*. Uploaded by Toby Morse One Life One Chance on April 6, 2022. https://www.youtube.com/watch?v=s9SliPPK1K0.
38 Zulaica, Don. "Claiming The Throne: How a 30 Second Audition Led Joey Castillo to Queens of The Stone Age." *Drum!* April 2005. https://drummagazine.com/joey-castillo-josh-homme/.
39 Author interview with William Malouf. April 11, 2024.
40 McKagan, Pg 290.
41 Wake, Matt. "Why is Nine Inch Nails' Ex-Drummer Teaching College in Alabama?" AL.com. October 24, 2018. https://www.al.com/life-and-culture/erry-2018/10/2b578ecb8a5013/why-is-nine-inch-nails-marilyn.html.
42 Katz, Larry. "Remaining Teenagers Just Want Their Due." *The Boston Herald*. November 6, 1992. Pg S19.
43 Cromelin, Richard. "POP MUSIC: Strummer on Man, God, Law—And The Clash." *The Los Angeles Times*. January 31, 1988. https://www.latimes.com/archives/la-xpm-1988-01-31-ca-39596-story.html.
44 Crandall, Bill. "Joe Strummer's Last Words." *Rolling Stone*. Iss. 914. January 23, 2003. Pg 28.
45 Author interview with Bill Bennett, September 18, 2023.
46 "Rosenblatt Appointed Geffen Chairman/CEO." *R&R*. Iss. 1090. April 14, 1995. Pg 1, 13.
47 Philips, Chuck. "Year In Review 1995: A Pressing Time For 'Suits.'" *The Los Angeles Times*. December 31, 1995. Pg 64.
48 Author interview with Bill Bennett, September 18, 2023.
49 Author interview with Robin Sloane Siebert. July 7, 2023.
50 Jolson-Colburn, Jeffrey. "Top A&R Exec Zutaut Exits Geffen Records." *The Hollywood Reporter*. Vol. 335, Iss. 33. January 19, 1995. Pg 8.
51 Rosen, Craig. "Geffen Records Enjoys Best Year." *Billboard*. Vol. 107, Iss. 3. January 21, 1995. Pg 1, 81.
52 Author interview with Bill Bennett, September 18, 2023.
53 Hotten, Jon. "Guns N' Roses: The Real Story Behind Their Reunion." *Louder*. January 5, 2021. https://www.loudersound.com/features/guns-n-roses-the-real-story-behind-their-return.
54 Markel, Howard. "How Groucho Marx Fell Prey to Elder Abuse." *PBS*. August 19, 2019. https://www.pbs.org/newshour/health/how-groucho-marx-fell-prey-to-elder-abuse.

55 Author interview with Bill Bennett, September 18, 2023.
56 Leeds, Jeff. "The Most Expensive Album Never Made." *The New York Times*. March 6, 2005. Pg 28.
57 Phone call with Todd Sullivan. May 2023.
58 "Personality: Howard Hughes, Man of Mystery and Wealth." *The New York Times*, June 24, 1962. Pg 97.
59 "Hughes Extravaganza." *Newsweek*. Vol. 30, Iss. 6. August 11, 1947. Pg 22.
60 "The Hughes Whodunit." *Newsweek*. Vol. 30, Iss. 5. August 4, 1947. Pg 26.
61 "Howard Hughes Sky Leviathan Found Amazing." *The Los Angeles Times*. July 17, 1945. Pg 2.
62 "Hughes Takes Air in Largest Plane." *The Los Angeles Times*. November 3, 1947. Pg 1, 2.
63 "Hughes Plane May Be Sold as Surplus." *The Los Angeles Times*. November 5, 1947. Pg 1.
64 "Saga of The Spruce Goose." *Newsweek*. Vol. 69, Iss. 7. February 13, 1967. Pg 39.
65 Hurst, John. "Spruce Goose May Fly Again." *The Los Angeles Times*. November 20, 1976. Pg B1.
66 Gore, Robert J. "Still No 'Open Sesame' To Hangar For The Spruce Goose." *The Los Angeles Times*. February 10, 1980. Pg SE4.
67 Lariviere, Anne and Belcher, Jerry. "Spruce Goose Finally Lands in New Home." *The Los Angeles Times*. February 12, 1982. Pg D1.
68 Connolly, Mike. "Rambling Reporter." *The Hollywood Reporter*. Vol. 127, Iss. 47. January 22, 1954. Pg 2.
69 "The Howard Hughes Puzzle." *Newsweek*. Vol. 71, Iss. 3. January 15, 1968. Pg 25–6.
70 Dittmann, M. "Hughes's Germ Phobia Revealed in Psychological Autopsy." *American Psychological Association*. Vol. 36, No. 7. July/August 2005. Pg 102.
71 "Howard Hughes." OCDUK.org. Accessed May 30, 2023. https://www.ocduk.org/ocd/history-of-ocd/howard-hughes/.
72 Page, Tim. "Flight of The American Icarus." *The Washington Post*. October 22, 2001. https://www.washingtonpost.com/archive/lifestyle/2001/10/22/flight-of-the-american-icarus/b8a61818-32bb-4f13-9000-a2fe526f6956/.
73 Tennant, Forest. "Howard Hughes and Pseudoaddiction." *Practical Pain Management*. Vol. 7, Iss. 6. July/August 2007. Pg 12–13, 18.
74 Turner, Wallace. "Garbage And Grand Jury Figure in Howard Hughes Controversy." *The New York Times*. November 18, 1971. Pg 41.
75 Sterba, James P. "Howard Hughes Dies at 70 on Flight to Texas Hospital." *The New York Times*. April 6, 1976. Pg 1.
76 Sterba, James P. "Cause of Hughes's Death is Given as Kidney Failure." *The New York Times*. April 7, 1976. Pg 18.
77 Tinker, Jack. "This Was Not Even a Farce, Farces Are Funny." *Daily Mail*. August 21, 2005. Pg 9.

78 Fernandez, Bernard. "Memories of Tyson-McNeeley Still Amaze." *The Sweet Science*. August 14, 2014. https://tss.ib.tv/boxing/featured-boxing-articles-boxing-news-videos-rankings-and-results/19134-memories-of-tyson-mcneeley-still-amaze.

79 Zimmerman, Shannon. "It's Ben Kweller, The Next Big Thing!" *The Washington Post*. April 7, 2002. Pg G14.

80 Miner, Donald and Cannon, Gerald. "Phoenix Police Department Report." February 10, 1998. Pg 1–4.

81 Tarazon, Don. "Phoenix Police Department Report: Supplement." February 10, 1998. Pg 1.

82 Kaufman, Gil. "News Flash: Axl Rose Arrested After Allegedly Threatening Security Guard." *MTV News*. February 11, 1998. Archived at https://web.archive.org/web/20151128104129/http://www.mtv.com/news/3150/news-flash-axl-rose-arrested-after-allegedly-threatening-security-worker/.

83 "Bridging Heaven & Earth Show #288 With Elliott Maynard and Mirabai Ceiba Music Videos." YouTube. Uploaded by bridgingheaven on July 12, 2012. https://www.youtube.com/watch?v=kqEKRbcHwNk&t=1155s.

84 Author interview with Jim Barber. June 19, 2023.

85 Goldstein, Patrick. "David Geffen." *Rolling Stone*. Iss. 655. April 29, 1993. Pg 75.

86 McLevy, Alex. "All Hail Veruca Salt: The Oral History of *American Thighs*." *AV Club*. September 25, 2019. https://www.avclub.com/all-hail-veruca-salt-the-oral-history-of-american-thig-1837988745.

87 Author interview with Jim Barber. June 19, 2023.

88 Author interview with Bill Bennett. September 18, 2023.

89 Leeds, Jeff. "The Most Expensive Album Never Made." *The New York Times*. March 6, 2005. Pg 28.

90 Hochman, Steve. "Atlantic Powers Faltering Warner." *The Los Angeles Times*. December 28, 1997. Pg 63.

91 E-mail from Robbie Fulks, September 17, 2023.

92 Author interview with Chad Blinman. August 30, 2024.

93 Author interview with David Dominguez. March 5, 2023.

94 Author interview with William Malouf. April 11, 2024.

Chapter 4

1 Vida, Herbert J. "People: Boy Drummer's on a Roll; He Hopes It's to Stardom." *The Los Angeles Times*. July 28, 1987. Pg OC A2.

2 Aratani, Lori. "A Career Gets Off to an Upbeat Start." *The Orange County Register*. June 21, 1989. Pg K01.

3 Mitchell, Justin. "Punk's Vandals Are No Slaves to the Writing on The Wall." *Rocky Mountain News*. November 22, 1991. Pg 110.

4   Asch, Andrew. "'Whatever' Makes The Vandals Into a Punk Success." *The Orange County Register*. October 2, 1998. Pg F05.

5   Kane, Rich. "Vandals Incorporated." *OC Weekly*. December 28, 2000. Section: Music.

6   Giffels, David. "Devo-Tees, Your Band is Back in The Game." *Akron-Beacon Journal*. September 3, 1996. Pg A1.

7   Jones, Bill. "Josh Freese of Devo and The Vandals is The Blue Collar Freelance Drummer." *Vice*. August 21, 2014. https://www.vice.com/en/article/r3gevr/josh-freese-interview.

8   Author interview with David Dominguez. March 5, 2023.

9   Author interview with Michael Bland. April 2, 2023.

10 Author interview with David Dominguez. March 5, 2023.

11 Mehr, Pg 420–1.

12 Mustaine, Dave with Selvin, Joel. *Rust in Peace: The Inside Story of The Megadeth Masterpiece*. Hatchette Books, New York. 2020. Pg 79, 97–102.

13 Author interview with David Dominguez. March 5, 2023.

14 Hendrickson, Matt. "Grapevine." *Rolling Stone*. Iss. 781. March 5, 1998. Pg 36.

15 J.C. "Appetite For Procrastination." *SPIN*. Vol. 14, Iss. 4. April 1, 1998. Pg 67.

16 "Producer Steve Lillywhite on Axl Rose's Voice: 'Like Fingers on a Chalkboard.'" radio.com. May 23, 2013. Archived at https://web.archive.org/web/20130609100651/http://news.radio.com/2013/05/23/producer-steve-lillywhite-on-axl-roses-voice-like-fingers-on-a-chalkboard/.

17 Hendrickson, Matt. "Grapevine." *Rolling Stone*. Iss. 788. June 11, 1998. Pg 36.

18 Neilson, John. "Life & Death And Killing Joke." *Creem*. Vol. 13, Iss. 7. December 1, 1981. Pg 18.

19 Gordon, Marsha. "Killing Joke." *The Bob*. Wilmington. Iss. 5. October 1, 1981. Pg 4–5.

20 Neilson, John. "Life & Death And Killing Joke." *Creem*. Vol. 13, Iss. 7. December 1, 1981. Pg 20.

21 "Youth." *Vox*. Iss. 70. August 1, 1996. Pg 46.

22 Author interview with Youth. August 4, 2023.

23 Author interview with David Dominguez. March 5, 2023.

24 Author interview with Youth. August 4, 2023.

25 J.C. "Appetite For Procrastination." *SPIN*. Vol. 14, Iss. 4. April 1, 1998. Pg 67.

26 Author interview with Jim Barber. June 19, 2023.

27 Author interview with Chris Pitman. December 2, 2024.

28 Author interview with Chris Pitman. December 2, 2024.

29 "2013.04.DD.—I'd Hit That Podcast—Interview With Josh." Transcribed by Soulmosnster. *Appetite For Discussion*. May 15, 2013. https://www.a-4-d.com/t2268-2013-04-dd-i-d-hit-that-podcast-interview-with-josh.

30 Farhi, Paul. "Seagram to Acquire Music Firm Polygram." *The Washington Post*. May 22, 1998. Pg D03.

31 "Seagram to Acquire Polygram." *Business Wire*. May 21, 1998. Pg 1.

32 Strauss, Neil. "A Major Merger Shakes Up The World of Rock." *The New York Times (Online)*. December 21, 1998.

33 Philips, Chuck. "Geffen Records Trims Work Force by 10%." *The Los Angeles Times*. May 31, 1997. Pg OCD2.

34 Philips, Chuck. "Interscope Emerges as Star Act For Seagram." *The Los Angeles Times*. December 14, 1999. Pg C12.

35 McNary, Dave. "Seagram Confirms Music Layoffs; Firm Declines to Specify Cuts." *Daily News*. December 11, 1998. Pg B1.

36 McNary, Dave. "Seagram Lays Off Hundreds; Cuts Reduce Area's A&M, Geffen Music Labels to Skeletal Staffs." *Daily News*. January 22, 1999. Pg B1.

37 Hilburn, Robert and Boucher, Geoff. "A&M Records Closes; Geffen Lays Off 110." *The Los Angeles Times*. January 22, 1999. Pg 1.

38 Phillips, Chuck. "The Biz Q&A; Lovine a Key Player in Seagram's New Arrangement For Its Labels." *The Los Angeles Times*. January 22, 1999. Pg 1.

39 Brothers, Michael. "Dishwalla Returns to The Road." *Springfield News Leader*. September 13, 2002. Pg E7.

40 Herron, Mat. "'You're Talking to a Miracle.'" *Louisville Eccentric Observer*. July 16, 2008. Section: Music.

41 Strauss, Neil. "A Major Merger Shakes Up The World of Rock." *The New York Times (Online)*. December 21, 1998.

42 Bleggi, Doug. "'Til Today: 25 Years After Her Solo Debut, Aimee Mann Looks Back." *Stereogum*. November 21, 2018. https://www.stereogum.com/2021942/aimee-mann-early-solo-albums-interview/interviews/qa/.

43 Author interview with Jim Barber. June 19, 2023.

44 "Bush's Gavin Rossdale: 'Nobody Wants The Singer in a Rock Band to do a Solo Record.'" *Blabbermouth*. March 13, 2022. https://blabbermouth.net/news/bushs-gavin-rossdale-nobody-wants-the-singer-in-a-rock-band-to-do-a-solo-record.

45 Marsh, Dave. "Iovine in The Right Place." *Rolling Stone*. Iss. 252. November 17, 1977. Pg 30, 32.

46 Marsh, Dave. "Iovine in The Right Place." *Rolling Stone*. Iss. 252. November 17, 1977. Pg 30, 32.

47 Marsh, Dave. "Iovine in The Right Place." *Rolling Stone*. Iss. 252. November 17, 1977. Pg 30, 32.

48 Fricke, David. "The Man With The Magic Ears." *Rolling Stone*. Iss. 1154. April 12, 2012. Pg 59.

49 Hilburn, Robert and Philips, Chuck. "They Sure Figured Something Out." *The Los Angeles Times*. October 24, 1993. Pg F8, F9.

50 "More Power to Ice Cube and Dr. Dre." *The Los Angeles Times*. February 21, 1993. Pg F62.

51 Hilburn, Robert and Philips, Chuck. "They Sure Figured Something Out." *The Los Angeles Times*. October 24, 1993. Pg F8, F9.

52 Hilburn, Robert. "In The Shadow of Hip-Hop." *The Los Angeles Times*. December 27, 1998. Pg G6.

53 Author interview with Jim Barber. June 19, 2023.

54 Author interview with Jim Barber. June 19, 2023.

55 "Questions of Doom: James Barber, Record Producer." *Poptones*. October 13, 2005. https://web.archive.org/web/20051212181043/http://www.poptones.co.uk/index.php?/questions_of_doom/more/james_barber_record_producer_a_and_r_legand_and_the_man/.

56 Yarm, Mark. *Everybody Loves Our Town: An Oral History of Grunge*. Three Rivers Press, New York. 2011. Pg 375.

57 Author interview with James Barber, January 9, 2024.

58 jomatami. "GN'R Manager Says Fake Audience Noise on Band's Live Album Drives Him Crazy" *Ultimate Guitar*. November 3, 2020. https://www.ultimate-guitar.com/news/general_music_news/gnr_manager_says_fake_audience_noise_on_bands_live_album_drives_him_crazy_talks_how_slash_corrected_live_mistakes_in_studio.html.

59 Author interview with Jim Barber. June 19, 2023.

60 Bream, Jon. "Crow Boosts Image as a Hard (Working) Rocker." *Star Tribune*. April 20, 1999. Pg 01E.

61 "List of 42nd Annual Grammy Awards." *Associated Press Archive*. February 24, 2000.

62 "Rolling Stone Readers Choose The Worst Cover Songs of All Time." *Rolling Stone*. August 18, 2011. https://www.rollingstone.com/music/music-lists/rolling-stone-readers-choose-the-worst-cover-songs-of-all-time-12882/8-avril-lavigne-imagine-154586/.

63 Author interview with Wende Crowley. September 20, 2019.

64 Hay, Carla. "Schur Aims to Revive Geffen." *Billboard*. Vol. 111, Iss. 41. October 9, 1999. Pg 6, 107.

65 Daly, Steven. "Send Porn Stars, Funk and Money: The Limp Bizkit Story." *Rolling Stone*. Iss. 818. August 5, 1999. Pg 34.

66 Gundersen, Edna. "Arnie guns For Axl on Rocker's Video." *USA Today*. June 10, 1991. Pg 1D.

67 Callaghan, Dylan. "Active Rock: Radio's New Heroes Do It For The Movies." *The Hollywood Reporter*. Vol. 360, Iss. 17. November 5, 1999. Pg S–3.

68 "Youth and Sean Bean Interviews." GNREvolution.com Message Board Thread. Accessed August 31, 2024. https://www.gnrevolution.com/viewtopic.php?id=14561.

69 Author interview with Chad Blinman. April 8, 2024.

70 Author interview with Terry Date. May 25, 2023.

71 Layne, Anni and Fischer, Blair R. "November Reign." *Rolling Stone*. November 14, 1998. Archived at https://www.a-4-d.com/t4493-1998-11-14-rolling-stone-november-reign.

72 Goetz, Rick. "Sean Beavan on Mixing, Producing And Music Placement." *Music Consultant.* November 17, 2010. https://musicconsultant.com/music-business/sean-beavan-1/.

73 Sowd, David. "Dial 98.5 For Mad Dogs And a Slice of Humble Pie." *The Plain Dealer.* October 21, 1990.

74 Author interview with Terry Date. May 25, 2023.

75 Skanse, Richard. "Axl Speaks Out." *Rolling Stone.* September 22, 1999. https://www.rollingstone.com/music/music-news/axl-speaks-out-250465/.

76 Callaghan, Dylan. "Active Rock: Radio's New Heroes Do It For The Movies." *The Hollywood Reporter.* Vol. 360, Iss. 17. November 5, 1999. Pg S–3.

77 Pollack, Marc. "Card-Carrying "Pokemon" Fans Collect Soundtrack." *The Hollywood Reporter.* Vol. 360, Iss. 26. November 18, 1999. Pg 4, 20.

78 Pollack, Marc. "A 'Pokémon'-opoly at No. 1." *The Hollywood Reporter.* Vol. 360, Iss. 42. December 9, 1999. Pg 37.

79 Pollack, Marc. "It's 7 Straight For 'Pokémon.'" *The Hollywood Reporter.* Vol. 361, Iss. 6. December 30, 1999. Pg 22.

80 Fusion, Brian. "With $80 Million, 'Toy 2' Goes B.O. Gobble, Gobble." *The Hollywood Reporter.* Vol. 360, Iss. 33. November 29, 1999. Pg 1, 37.

81 Ebert, Roger. "End of Days." November 24, 1999. Archived at https://www.rogerebert.com/reviews/end-of-days-1999.

82 Farber, Jim. "Axl Rose Returns, But Song is No Great Guns." *New York Daily News.* November 9, 1999. Pg 37.

83 "Fiona Blossoms." *Iowa State Daily.* November 10, 1999.

84 Wener, Ben. "POP LIFE—Taking a Movie For a Spin." *The Orange County Register.* November 5, 1999. Pg F47.

85 Boehlert, Eric. "Buzz Been." *Rolling Stone.* Iss. 733. May 2, 1996. Pg 19–20.

86 Blackstar. "1999.11.08—MTV—Axl Rose: A Conversation With Kurt Loder." *Appetite For Discussion.* August 9, 2018. https://www.a-4-d.com/t3074-1999-11-08-mtv-axl-rose-a-conversation-with-kurt-loder.

87 Derogatis, Jim. "The Best Albums We Can't Buy." *The Chicago Sun-Times.* August 5, 2001. Pg 1C.

88 "Guitarist Robin Finck Leaves GN'R to Return to NIN." *MTV News.* August 4, 1999. https://web.archive.org/web/20150518120829/http://www.mtv.com/news/1429780/guitarist-robin-finck-leaves-gnr-to-return-to-nin/.

89 Watson, Vaughn. "MUSIC THIS WEEK" *The Providence Journal.* April 30, 2000. Pg C03.

90 Blackstar. "1999.11.08—MTV—Axl Rose: A Conversation With Kurt Loder." *Appetite For Discussion.* August 9, 2018. https://www.a-4-d.com/t3074-1999-11-08-mtv-axl-rose-a-conversation-with-kurt-loder.

91 Mayfield, Geoff. "Between The Bullets." *Billboard.* Vol. 112, Iss. 5. January 29, 2000. Pg 98.

92 Martin, Gavin. "Reviews: Albums—Guns N' Roses." *Uncut*. Iss. 32. January 1, 2000. Pg 94.
93 "Capsule Reviews." *Fort Worth Star-Telegram*. December 3, 1999. Pg 18.
94 Hurwitz, Matt. "Classic Tracks: Cheap Trick's 'At Budokan.'" *Mix*. August 9, 2017; updated August 12, 2022. https://www.mixonline.com/recording/classic-tracks/classic-tracks-cheap-trick-budokan-430181.
95 "Cheap Trick At Budokan CD Different From Original LP." *Steve Hoffman Music Forums*. Message board thread started by theanalogkidsignals. November 27, 2014. https://forums.stevehoffman.tv/threads/cheap-trick-at-budokan-cd-different-from-original-lp.397292/.
96 "Kiss Starts Recording Their First Live Album 'Alive!'" *KISS TIMELINE*. Accessed September 3, 2024. https://kisstimeline.com/timeline/kiss-started-recording-their-first-live-album-alive/.
97 Bream, Jon. "Carpenter No 'Party Doll,' But Feels Lucky." *Star Tribune*. July 13, 1999. Pg 03E.
98 "LIVE ERA- SONG SOURCE INFOR." Message Board post by IndianaRose. *MyGNRForum*. November 4, 2004. https://www.mygnrforum.com/topic/26028-live-era-song-source-info/.
99 "Why did Axl Record New Vocals for Live Era??" Message board thread started by BaDoBsEsSiOn418. *Here Today . . . Gone to Hell!*. July 10, 2006. https://www.heretodaygonetohell.com/board/index.php?topic=32,969.0;all.
100 "Live ERA 87 -93 YCBM Vocals" Message board thread started by GNRFan87. *MyGNRForum*. August 31, 2014. https://www.mygnrforum.com/topic/208735-live-era-87-93-ycbm-vocals/.
101 "Live Era Revisited." Reddit post in /GunsNRoses by literallawn. Accessed September 5, 2024. https://www.reddit.com/r/GunsNRoses/comments/z2xd0a/live_era_revisited/.
102 Author interview with Jim Barber. June 19, 2023.
103 Stevenson, Jane. "Slash Puts Guns Behind Him." *The Toronto Sun*. August 12, 2000. Section: Entertainment. Pg 40.
104 "Sludge Rewind With Cacophony Guitarist Jason Becker." *Metal Sludge*. March 3, 2009. https://metalsludge.tv/classic/?p=32484.
105 "Zim Zum Turned Down an Offer to Join GNR?" *Here Today . . . Gone to Hell!* November 5, 2000. https://mail.heretodaygonetohell.com/news/shownews.php?newsid=302.
106 "21. SEPTEMBER 1997-NOVEMBER 1999" *Appetite For Discussion*. Accessed April 9, 2024. https://www.a-4-d.com/t5025p30-21-september-1997-november-1999-josh-and-tommy-joins-robin-leaves-live-era-is-released.
107 Author interview with Stevie Salas. August 28, 2023.
108 Author interview with James Barber. June 19, 2023.
109 Author interview with Bill Bennett. December 1, 2023.
110 Author interview with Stevie Salas. August 28, 2023.

Chapter 5

1. Author interview with Joe Gore. October 8, 2024.
2. Gore, Joe. "Profile: Buckethead." *Guitar Player*. Vol. 26, Iss. 12. December 1992. Pg 25.
3. Gore, Joe. "Buckethead: Shredding For The Inner Child." *Guitar Player*. Vol. 28, Iss. 6. June 1994. Pg 45.
4. Rotondi, James. "Destroy All Monsters: Buckethead's Robotic Revenge." *Guitar Player*. Vol. 30, Iss. 11. November 1996. Pg 102.
5. Rotondi, James. "Destroy All Monsters: Buckethead's Robotic Revenge." *Guitar Player*. Vol. 30, Iss. 11. November 1996. Pg 94.
6. Rotondi, James. "Destroy All Monsters: Buckethead's Robotic Revenge." *Guitar Player*. Vol. 30, Iss. 11. November 1996. Pg 100.
7. Buckethead. "Taxidermy Loaf." *Guitar Player*. February 1992. Pg 118.
8. Buckethead. "Giant Robot." *Guitar Player*. July 1992. Pg 114.
9. Buckethead. "1–5 Binge." *Guitar Player*. April 1992. Pg 111.
10. Author interview with Joe Gore. October 8, 2024.
11. Murray, Charles Shaar. "Rock Records." *The Daily Telegraph*. September 18, 1992. Pg XVI.
12. Coleman, Mark. "Praxis." *Vibe*. October 1, 1992. Pg 32.
13. Resnicoff, Matt. "Buckethead, What's in The Bucket?" *Musician*. Iss. 167. September 1, 1992. Pg 87–8, 110.
14. Resnicoff, Matt. "Flea." *Musician*. Iss. 183. January 1, 1994. Pg 28, 30.
15. Resnicoff, Matt. "Buckethead, What's in The Bucket?" *Musician*. Iss. 167. September 1, 1992. Pg 87–8, 110.
16. Author interview with Joe Gore. October 8, 2024.
17. Rotondi, James. "Destroy All Monsters: Buckethead's Robotic Revenge." *Guitar Player*. Vol. 30, Iss. 11. November 1996. Pg 94.
18. Rotondi, James. "Destroy All Monsters: Buckethead's Robotic Revenge." *Guitar Player*. Vol. 30, Iss. 11. November 1996. Pg 100.
19. Gore, Joe. "Profile: Buckethead." *Guitar Player*. Vol. 26, Iss. 12. Dec 1992. Pg 26.
20. Gundersen, Edna. "Boom! The Power Most Definitely Is On—Gearing Up For The Rangers Soundtrack." *The Seattle Times*. April 29, 1995. Pg F1.
21. Christgau, Robert. "Arcana: Arc of The Testimony." *The Village Voice*. November 4, 1997. Pg 74.
22. Author interview with David Lefkowitz. November 1, 2024.
23. Author interview with David Lefkowitz. November 1, 2024.
24. Wild, David. "Axl Speaks." *Rolling Stone*. Iss. 833. February 3, 2000. Pg 21–2, 24.
25. "Axl Rose." *Rolling Stone*. Iss. 836. March 16, 2000. Pg 16.
26. Saidman, Sorelle. "GN'R: Buckethead In, Freese Out." *MTV News*. March 15, 2000. https://web.archive.org/web/20151009215328/http://www.mtv.com/news/1429767/gnr-buckethead-in-freese-out/.

27 Condran, Ed. "Perfect Circle of Friends." *The Record*. Febraury 23, 2001. Pg 16.
28 Condran, Ed. "Perfect Circle of Friends." *The Record*. Febraury 23, 2001. Pg 16.
29 Buchanan, Brett. "Axl Rose Reportedly Didn't Like Maynard James Keenan For Bizarre Reason." *Alternative Nation*. April 2, 2018. https://www.alternativenation.net/axl-rose-reportedly-didnt-like-maynard-james-keenan-bizarre-reason/?fbclid=IwY2xjawFRoztleHRuA2FlbQIxMQABHQyDN7hYA3wbFrLH6vLmaqsEhfyOOtOTl705HoJpLtx60JwRShDo11-tEA_aem_s4oQkLQg0bzGFP2A2MPUEw.
30 Wiederhorn, Jon. "Maynard James Keenan's 7 Favorite Frontpeople." *Revolver*. December 1, 2007. https://www.revolvermag.com/music/maynard-james-keenans-7-favorite-frontpeople/.
31 "Brain Talks About Touring With Buckethead (Fan Questions With Bryan Mantia)." *Natternet*. https://www.natternet.com/touring-with-buckethead.
32 Author interview with Joe Gore. October 8, 2024.
33 Spencer, Lauren. "Limbomaniacs." *SPIN*. Vol. 6, Iss. 9. December 1, 1990. Pg 87.
34 Selvin, Joel. "'Punk Funk' Catches Fire." *The San Francisco Chronicle*. February 8, 1990. Pg E1.
35 Azerrad, Michael. "Does Primus Really Suck?" *Rolling Stone*. October 31, 1991. Pg 81–3.
36 Greene, Andy. "Bryan 'Brain' Mantia Was There For Guns N' Roses' Most Unpredictable Era." *Rolling Stone*. August 4, 2022. https://www.rollingstone.com/music/music-features/bryan-brain-mantia-guns-n-roses-tom-waits-primus-1388363/.
37 Savage, Rod. "Time to Primus." *The Advertiser*. April 9, 1998. Pg 46.
38 Author interview with Joe Gore. October 8, 2024.
39 Savage, Rod. "Time to Primus." *The Advertiser*. April 9, 1998. Pg 46.
40 Phillips, Lior. "Les Claypool Breaks Down The Entire Primus Discography." *Consequence*. September 29, 2017. https://consequence.net/2017/09/les-claypool-breaks-down-the-entire-primus-discography/.
41 Prato, Greg. "Les Claypool: Return of Drummer Jay Lane Has 'Breathed Life' Back Into Primus." *Rolling Stone*. June 10, 2011. https://www.rollingstone.com/music/music-news/les-claypool-return-of-drummer-jay-lane-has-breathed-life-back-into-primus-92178/.
42 Winwood, Ian. "Primus' Les Claypool: "My Daughter Tells Me I'm Weird All The Time."" *Kerrang!*. May 14, 2021. https://www.kerrang.com/primus-les-claypool-my-daughter-tells-me-im-weird-all-the-time.
43 Greene, Andy. "Bryan 'Brain' Mantia Was There For Guns N' Roses' Most Unpredictable Era. Here's What It Was Really Like." *Rolling Stone*. August 4, 2022. https://www.rollingstone.com/music/music-features/bryan-brain-mantia-guns-n-roses-tom-waits-primus-1388363/.
44 "2013.04.DD.—I'd Hit That Podcast—Interview With Josh." Transcribed by Soulmosnster. *Appetite For Discussion*. May 15, 2013. https://www.a-4-d.com/t2268-2013-04-dd-i-d-hit-that-podcast-interview-with-josh.
45 Author interview with Chris Pitman. December 2, 2024.

46 "Episode 27—8mm Interview." *The P.W.A. Show*. August 25, 2012. https://web.archive.org/web/20170423214055/http://www.thepwashow.com/episode-27-8mm-interview/.

47 FIrecloud, Johnny. "Antiquiet's Three-Way With 8mm." *Antiquiet*. August 13, 2008. https://web.archive.org/web/20100301130214/http://www.antiquiet.com/interviews/2008/08/antiquiets-three-way-with-8mm/.

48 Author interview with Tim Palmer. October 16, 2024.

49 Peacock, Ted. "Interview With Nick Blagona." *Journal on The Art of Record Production*. Iss 5. July 2011. https://www.arpjournal.com/asarpwp/interview-with-nick-blagona/.

50 Author interview with Jim Barber. June 19, 2023.

51 Beaujour, Tom and Bienstock, Richard. *Nothin' But a Good Time: The Uncensored History of The '80s Hard Rock Explosion*. St. Martin's Griffin, New York. 2021. Pg 175.

52 Harris, Steve. "Axl Rose Interview Transcription." *The Tapes Archive*. https://www.thetapesarchive.com/axl-rose/.

53 Roy, Lisa. "Surround N' Roses." *EQ*. December 21, 2001. Archived at https://web.archive.org/web/20011221083015/http://www.eqmag.com/1201/feature_baker_113.shtml.

54 Sloman, Larry. "Lou Reed's New Deco-Disk: Sledgehammer Blow to Glitterbugs." *Rolling Stone*. Iss. 144. September 27, 1973. Pg 18.

55 Bonutto, Dante. "Kiss: The Making of Destroyer and The Brutal Boot Camp Genius of Bob Ezrin." *Louder*. November 28, .2021. https://www.loudersound.com/features/kiss-the-making-of-destroyer-and-the-brutal-boot-camp-genius-of-bob-ezrin.

56 Bozza, Anthony. "The Fragile World of Trent Reznor." *Rolling Stone*. Iss. 823. October 14, 1999. Pg 61.

57 thodoris. "Interview: Bob Ezrin (Pink Floyd, Alice Cooper, Kiss, Peter Gabriel). *Hit-Channel*. April 12, 2012. https://hit-channel.com/bob-ezrin-pink-floydalice-cooperkisspeter-gabriel-producer-2508/.

58 Shuster, Fred. "Rock News & Notes—Captain 'N' Tennille 'N' Guns N' Roses." *The Daily News of Los Angeles*. April 13, 1990. Section: L.A. Life. Pg L40.

59 thodoris. "Interview: Bob Ezrin (Pink Floyd, Alice Cooper, Kiss, Peter Gabriel)." *Hit-Channel*. April 12, 2012. https://hit-channel.com/bob-ezrin-pink-floydalice-cooperkisspeter-gabriel-producer-2508/.

60 Author interview with Alan Niven. January 10, 2024.

61 Weingarten, Marc. "Welcome to Studio City." *The Los Angeles Times*. September 27, 1998. Pg 90.

62 Author interview with Matt Marrin, November 30, 2018.

63 Greene, Andy. "Bryan 'Brain' Mantia Was There For Guns N' Roses' Most Unpredictable Era. Here's What It Was Really Like." *Rolling Stone*. August 4, 2022. https://www.rollingstone.com/music/music-features/bryan-brain-mantia-guns-n-roses-tom-waits-primus-1388363/.

64 "GUNS N' ROSES Bassist Talks 'Chinese Democracy.'" *Blabbermouth*. March 20, 2009. https://blabbermouth.net/news/guns-n-roses-bassist-talks-chinese-democracy.

65. Mehr, Bob. *Trouble Boys: The True Story of The Replacements*. Da Capo Press. Boston, 2016. Pg 178.
66. Mehr, Pg 294–9.
67. Rowley, Scott. "Guns N' Roses: The Making of Chinese Democracy." *Louder*. November 23, 2016. https://www.loudersound.com/features/guns-n-roses-the-making-of-chinese-democracy.
68. Kushner, David. "Napster Terrorizes Music Biz." *Rolling Stone*. Iss. 839. April 27, 2000. Pg 25, 29.
69. Evangelista, Benny. "Metallica Suit Rocks Napster." *The San Francisco Chronicle*. April 14, 2000. Pg B3.
70. "Lars Ulrich Admits Delivering Names of Napster Users Was "Maybe Not The Smartest PR Move of All Time."" *Blabbermouth*. November 8, 2017. https://blabbermouth.net/news/lars-ulrich-admits-delivering-names-of-napster-users-was-maybe-not-the-smartest-pr-move-of-all-time.
71. Balaban, David. "The Battle of The Music Industry: The Distribution of Audio And Video Works Via The Internet, Music And More." *Fordham Intellectual Property, Media And Entertainment Law Journal*. Vol. 12, Number 1, Article 6. Published in 2002. Pg 277.
72. Beato, G. "Trading Spaces." *SPIN*. Vol. 16, Iss. 5. May 1, 2000. Pg 118.
73. Saxberg, Lynn. "Hip's Unreleased Disc Available on Internet." *The Kingston Whig-Standard*. April 29, 2000. Pg 33.
74. "Song Leaked to Internet." *The Calgary Sun*. June 2, 2000. Pg G10.
75. "Guns N' Roses Rock Again in Rio." *NME*. October 26, 2000. https://www.nme.com/news/music/guns-n-roses-3561398172.
76. Author interview with Chris Pitman. December 2, 2024.
77. Elfman, Doug. "Long Time Coming." *Las Vegas Review-Journal*. December 29, 2000.
78. Elfman, Doug. "NEON SUNDAY: Get Ready For New Year's Eve." *The Las Vegas Review-Journal*. December 31, 2000.
79. Varga, George. "Guns N' Roses Take The Stage on New Year's." *The San Diego Union-Tribune*. December 6, 2000. Pg F-6.
80. Maddox, Kate. "Columnist Kate Maddox: Electra Has Magical Outlet." *Las Vegas Sun*. January 6, 2001.
81. Abowitz, Richard. "Guns N' Roses: House of Blues." *Rolling Stone*. Iss. 862. February 15, 2001. Pg 34.
82. Strauss, Neil. "Rock Review: Whoever Said Appetite For Destruction?" *The New York Times (Online)*. January 2, 2001.
83. Appleford, Steve. "New Guns N' Roses Gets Right Back in The Jungle." *The Los Angeles Times*. January 2, 2001. https://www.latimes.com/archives/la-xpm-2001-jan-02-ca-7252-story.html.
84. Ashby, Jonathan. "Rio Rockers Can't Tune Out Gulf War." *USA Today*. January 21, 1991. Pg 20.

85 Hankins, Jim. "Gospel Singer Settles Lawsuit." *Austin American-Statesman*. January 23, 1991. Pg A18.

86 Byrne, Louise. "An Awful Lot of Rocking in Brazil." *The Times*. January 22, 1991.

87 Lannert, John. "Rock in Rio an Explosive Music Festival." *The Sun Sentinel*. January 24, 1991. Pg 3E.

88 "Pondran a Brasil ritmo de rock." *Reforma*. January 3, 2001. Pg 7.

89 Lannert, John. "Rock in Rio Solid, Says Acts, But Local Press Differs." *Billboard*. Vol. 103, Iss. 7. February 16, 1991. Pg 31.

90 Cobo, Leila. "Rock in Rio Boosts Spirits, Brands." *Billboard*. Vol. 113, Iss 4. January 27, 2001. Pg 1, 89.

91 Cobo, Leila. "Rock in Rio Boosts Spirits, Brands." *Billboard*. Vol. 113, Iss 4. January 27, 2001. Pg 1, 89.

92 Cobo, Leila. "Rock in Rio Boosts Spirits, Brands." *Billboard*. Vol. 113, Iss 4. January 27, 2001. Pg 1, 89.

93 Nagarajan, Rema and Pyke, Nicholas. "Old Rockers Don't Die: They Tour Brazil and Pakistan." *The Independent*. January 7, 2001. Pg 5.

94 Binelli, Mark. "Axl Ignites Rio Festival." *Rolling Stone*. Iss. 863. March 1, 2001. Pg 16–17.

95 Garcia, Juan Carlos. "Prefieren 'pistolas' a un Oasis." *Mural*. January 16, 2001. Pg 3.

96 Garcia, Juan Carlos. "Saborean buffet de rock 'picante.'" *Mural*. January 23, 2001. Pg 3.

97 Author interview with Chris Pitman. December 2, 2024.

Chapter 6

1 Wall, Mick. *Last of The Giants: The True Story of Guns N' Roses*. Trapeze, Uk. 2017. Pg 344.

2 Vanhorn, Teri. "Guns N' Roses Line Up European Tour Dates." *MTV News*. February 9, 2001. https://web.archive.org/web/20190214002629/http://www.mtv.com/news/1439265/guns-n-roses-line-up-european-tour-dates/.

3 Schumacher-Rasmussen, Eric and Saidman, Sorelle. "Guns N' Roses Cancel European Tour." *MTV News*. May 10, 2001. https://archive.ph/20130129053032/http://www.mtv.com/news/articles/1443523/20010510/guns_n_roses.jhtml.

4 Rush, George and Malloy, Dana. "Axl Hits a Pothole: Band's Tour Called Off." *The Daily News*. May 11, 2001. https://www.nydailynews.com/2001/05/11/axl-hits-a-pothole-bands-tour-called-off/.

5 Saidman, Sorelle. "Guns N' Roses Cancel European Tour—Again." *MTV News*. November 8, 2001. https://web.archive.org/web/20150903130906/http://www.mtv.com/news/1450606/guns-n-roses-cancel-european-tour-again/.

6 Author interview with Alan Niven. February 27, 2024.

7   Rowley, Scott. "Guns N' Roses: The Making of Chinese Democracy." *Louder*. November 23, 2016. https://www.loudersound.com/features/guns-n-roses-the-making-of-chinese-democracy.

8   Rowley, Scott. "Guns N' Roses: The Making of Chinese Democracy." *Louder*. November 23, 2016. https://www.loudersound.com/features/guns-n-roses-the-making-of-chinese-democracy.

9   "Is That Buckethead GNR Story True?—Bryan Brain Mantia Sets The Record Straight!" *Natternet*. https://www.natternet.com/buckethead-gnr-stories.

10 Barton, Geoff. "The New Edition of Classic Rock is Out Today!" *ClassicRockMagazine.com*. February 6, 2008. https://web.archive.org/web/20080208165528/http://www.classicrockmagazine.com/.

11 Wazir, Burhan. "The Most Expensive Album Never Released." *The Times*. March 18, 2005. Pg 24.

12 Rowley, Scott. "Guns N' Roses: The Making of Chinese Democracy." *Louder*. November 23, 2016. https://www.loudersound.com/features/guns-n-roses-the-making-of-chinese-democracy.

13 Author interview with Curtis Laur, July 8, 2023.

14 Rowley, Scott. "Guns N' Roses: The Making of Chinese Democracy." *Louder*. November 23, 2016. https://www.loudersound.com/features/guns-n-roses-the-making-of-chinese-democracy.

15 "Is That Buckethead GNR Story True?—Bryan Brain Mantia Sets The Record Straight!" *Natternet*. https://www.natternet.com/buckethead-gnr-stories.

16 Author interview with David Lefkowitz. November 8, 2024.

17 Author interview with Chris Pitman. December 2, 2024.

18 Rowley, Scott. "Guns N' Roses: The Making of Chinese Democracy." *Louder*. November 23, 2016. https://www.loudersound.com/features/guns-n-roses-the-making-of-chinese-democracy.

19 Sandman, Sorelle. "Krueger Cooks Up Bakery." *The Province*. February 12, 2002. Pg B10.

20 Clark, Rick. "Roy Thomas Baker: Taking Chances And Making Hits." *Mix*. April 1, 1999. https://www.mixonline.com/recording/roy-thomas-baker-taking-chances-and-making-hits-373531.

21 Vineyard, Jennifer. "'I Was Curious,' Slash Says of GN'R Show He Was Banned From." *MTV News*. January 4, 2002. https://web.archive.org/web/20140525224417/http://www.mtv.com/news/1451669/i-was-curious-slash-says-of-gnr-show-he-was-banned-from/.

22 "Slash Barred From Guns N' Roses Show." *ABC News*. December 31, 2001. https://abcnews.go.com/Entertainment/story?id=101,322&page=1.

23 Gamboa, Glenn. "Music Industry Seeks Comeback in 2002." *The Los Angeles Times*. January 5, 2002. Pg F10.

24 Batey, Angus. "Innocence And Experience: Lisa Left Eye Lopes' Supernova Turns 20." *The Quietus*. August 9, 2021. https://thequietus.com/articles/30328-lisa-left-eye-lopes-supernova.

25 Conniff, Tamara. "Virgin Ends Carey Contract." *The Hollywood Reporter*. Vol. 371, Iss. 46. January 29, 2002. Pg 51.

26 Cherry, Robert. "Still Feeding on Frenzy of Guns N' Rose' 15-Year-Old Album." *The Plain Dealer*. July 20, 2002. Pg E1.

27 Mehr, Pg 424.

28 Levitan, Corey. "Wild Wild Westerberg." *The Daily Breeze*. April 19, 2002. Pg K18.

29 Milano, Brett. "Westerberg Gets Back on Track." *The Boston Herald*. April 30, 2002. Pg 44.

30 Author interview with Michael Bland. April 2, 2023.

31 Chestnutt, Fergie. "Paul Westerberg Mentions Axl." *CD Now*. May 4, 2002. Archived at https://www.heretodaygonetohell.com/news/shownews.php?newsid=449.

32 Holdship, Bill. "Off The 'Mats." *The Riverfront Times*. May 22, 2002.

33 Riemenschneider, Chris. "Mano A 'Mono.'" *Star Tribune*. June 28, 2002. Pg 1E.

34 Royston, Reggie. "Replacements Reunion? Stinson Says Westerberg Blew It." *St. Paul Pioneer Press*. November 14, 2002. Pg E2.

35 "Guns N' Roses Spokesperson: No Release Date Scheduled." *Blabbermouth*. June 25, 2002. https://blabbermouth.net/news/guns-n-roses-spokesperson-no-release-date-scheduled.

36 "Guns N' Roses: 'Chinese Democracy' to See Light of Day in November?" *Blabbermouth*. August 12, 2002. https://blabbermouth.net/news/guns-n-roses-chinese-democracy-to-see-light-of-day-in-november.

37 "Axl Rose Stands by Guns N' Roses World Tour." *Breaking News*. August 14, 2002.

38 "For Immediate Release: Guns N' Roses Lauch 'Chinese Democracy' Tour in China." GNROnline.com. August 14, 2002. Archived at https://web.archive.org/web/20020915091434/http://www.gnronline.com/.

39 antiGUY. "Axl Rose Breaks His Silence." *antiMusic*. August 16, 2002. https://www.antimusic.com/news/2002/aug/item30.shtml.

40 Haymes, Greg. "Guitarist Talks About Touring With Guns N' Roses." *Record-Journal*. November 28, 2002. Pg A12.

41 Barr, Greg. "The Sad Tale That is (Was) Guns N' Roses." *The Ottawa Citizen*. December 16, 2002. Pg C2.

42 Haymes, Greg. "Guitarist Talks About Touring With Guns N' Roses." *Record-Journal*. November 28, 2002. Pg A12.

43 Author interview with Chris Pitman. December 2, 2024.

44 "For Immediate Release: Guns N' Roses Lauch 'Chinese Democracy' Tour in China." GNROnline.com. August 14, 2002. Archived at https://web.archive.org/web/20020915091434/http://www.gnronline.com/.

45 Author interview with Joe Gore. October 8, 2024.

46 "Hanoi Rocks Singer: Axl Rose Was Scared of Sharing The Stage With Us." *Blabbermouth*. March 5, 2004. https://blabbermouth.net/news/hanoi-rocks-singer-axl-rose-was-scared-of-sharing-the-stage-with-us.

47 Bartz, Simon. "Summer Sonic: When Dinosaurs Ruled Chiba." *The Japan Times.* August 25, 2002. Pg 13.

48 Perry, Andrew. "LA's Sleaze Merchants Rock On in Bad Hair And Head Buckets." *The Daily Telegraph.* August 28, 2002. Pg 19.

49 Author interview with Salli Frattini. December 18, 2018.

50 Hoffman, Bill. "Biggest Losers at Tonight's MTV Awards: The Cars." *The New York Post.* August 29, 2002. Pg 9.

51 "Guns N' Roses: 'Chinese Democracy' in Stores By June." *Blabbermouth.* November 23, 2002. https://blabbermouth.net/news/guns-n-roses-chinese-democracy-in-stores-by-june.

52 Author interview with Salli Frattini. December 18, 2018.

53 "Artist of The Millennium? MTV Says Jackson Didn't Receive Award." *Associated Press Archive.* August 30, 2002.

54 Moody, Nekesa Mumbi. "MTV Awards Show Lives Up To Reputation." *Akron Beacon Journal.* August 30, 2002. Pg A2.

55 Seymour, Craig. "Getting Freaky—Springsteen, Jackson and Spears Star in MTV's Typically Weird Awards Show." *The Atlanta Journal-Constitution.* August 30, 2002. Pg E1.

56 "Artist of The Millennium? MTV Says Jackson Didn't Receive Award." *Associated Press Archive.* August 30, 2002.

57 Graham, Renee. "An Axl to Grind." *The Boston Globe.* September 10, 2002. Pg F1.

58 DeRogatis, Jim. "Hypefest Turns Into a Snoozer." *The Chicago Sun-Times.* August 30, 2002. Pg 42.

59 Serba, John. "MTV's Always Odd VMAs Are Crash 'N' Burn Spectacle." *The Grand Rapids Press.* August 30, 2002. Pg C1.

60 Author interview with Salli Frattini. December 18, 2018.

61 "Axl Rose—2002 Interview After The VMA's Post Show." Uploaded by Axl Rose on September 2, 2015. https://www.youtube.com/watch?v=omKhZsbk134.

62 "Courtenay Filmmaker Documenting Goodwin." *Comox Valley Record.* July 29, 2015. Pg 1.

63 Marsh, James H. "Bloody Sunday." *The Canadian Encyclopedia.* May 29, 2012. https://www.thecanadianencyclopedia.ca/en/article/bloody-sunday.

64 Mackie, John. "This Week in History, 1966: The Grey Cup Parade Turns Into The Grey Cup Riot." *The Vancouver Sun.* November 25, 2022. https://vancouversun.com/news/this-week-in-history-1966-the-grey-cup-parade-turns-into-the-grey-cup-riot.

65 "Canuck Celebration Turns Into Violence." *The Columbian.* June 15, 1994. Pg D1.

66 Richards, Gwendolyn. "Rose Blames GM Place For Cancelled Concert." *The Vancouver Sun.* November 11, 2002. Pg B3.

67 "Riot in Vancouver After Guns N' Roses Concert Cancelled." *The National—CBC Television.* November 8, 2002.

68 "Vancouver Police Break Up Riot After Guns N' Roses Concert Cancelled." *Canadian Press NewsWire.* November 8, 2002.

69 Derdeyn, Stuart and Keating, Jack. "Guns N' Roses a No-Show, But Trouble Shows Up in Its Place." *The Province*. November 8, 2002. Pg A3.
70 Hume, Mark. "Officers Faced 'Lethal Force' at Riot." *National Post*. November 9, 2002. Pg A14.
71 Newton, Steve. "CKY's Chad I Ginsburg Recalls the 2002 Guns N' Roses Riot in Vancouver." Straight.com. August 11, 2005. Archived at https://earofnewt.com/2013/09/04/cky-is-all-the-rage/#google_vignette.
72 "Riot in Vancouver After Guns N' Roses Concert Cancelled." *The National—CBC Television*. November 8, 2002.
73 "Vancouver Police Break Up Riot After Guns N' Roses Concert Cancelled." *Canadian Press NewsWire*. November 8, 2002.
74 Derdeyn, Stuart; Keating, Jack. "Guns N' Roses a No-Show, But Trouble Shows Up in Its Place." *The Province*. November 8, 2002. Pg A3.
75 Hume, Mark. "Officers Faced 'Lethal Force' at Riot." *National Post*. November 9, 2002. Pg A14.
76 Hume, Mark. "Officers Faced 'Lethal Force' at Riot." *National Post*. November 9, 2002. Pg A14.
77 Joyce, Greg. "Vancouver Police Say They Will Try For More Arrests After Concert Riot." *Canadian Press NewsWIre*. November 8, 2002.
78 Barr, Greg. "The Sad Tale That is (Was) Guns N' Roses." *The Ottawa Citizen*. December 16, 2002. Pg C2.
79 Mervis, Scott. "Axl Rose Brings His Guns to Town." *Pittsburgh Post-Gazette*. November 22, 2002. Section: Weekend Mag. Pg 27.
80 "Axl Rose Didn't Want Show Cancelled." *The London Free Press*. November 11, 2002. Pg D3.
81 "Fans Riot Over Canceled Concert." *Daily Press*. November 9, 2002. Pg A3.
82 "Guns N' Roses Fans Riots in Vancouver." *Akron Beacon Journal*. November 9, 2002. Pg A4.
83 CP. "Guns N' Roses Concert Riot—Thousands Hit Vancouver Streets After No-Show." *The Calgary Sun*. November 8, 2002. Pg 19.
84 Howell, Mike. "Do You Know Any of These Suspects? Police Nab Nine Alleged Guns N' Roses Rioters." *Vancouver Courier*. February 23, 2003. Pg 7.
85 Boucher, Geoff. "Clear Channel Cancels Guns N' Roses Tour." *The Los Angeles Times*. December 13, 2002. Section: Calendar. Pg E2.
86 Jasmin, Ernest A. "Tacoma Dome is First U.S. Stop on Guns N' Roses Tour." *The News Tribune*. November 8, 2002. Pg T04.
87 Jasmin, Ernest A. "Guns N' Roses Rock Tacoma to Star Tour." *The News Tribune*. November 10, 2002. Pg B02.
88 Loder, Kurt. "Axl Blows Out Throat, Dons Chicken Bucket For Glitchy Guns Tour Launch." *MTV.com*. November 9, 2002. https://web.archive.org/web/20021112084239/http://www.mtv.com/news/articles/1458601/20021109/guns_n_roses.jhtml?headlines=true.

89 Esposito, Stefano. "Woman Arrested at Concert." *The News Tribune*. November 11, 2002. Pg B02.

90 Loder, Kurt. "Axl Blows Out Throat, Dons Chicken Bucket For Glitchy Guns Tour Launch." *MTV.com*. November 9, 2002. https://web.archive.org/web/20021112084239/http://www.mtv.com/news/articles/1458601/20021109/guns_n_roses.jhtml?headlines=true.

91 "Rants & Raves." *The Idaho Statesman*. November 15, 2002. Pg 2.

92 "Rants & Raves." *The Idaho Statesman*. November 22, 2002. Pg 2.

93 Nemo, John. "Guns N' Roses Far Off Target." *St. Paul Pioneer Press*. November 16, 2002. Pg B4.

94 Fuoco, Christina. "Rose's Early Exit Doesn't Dampen Show." *The Flint Journal*. November 23, 2002. Pg C2.

95 The Associated Press. "Football Fans Riot After Games." *The Gainesville Sun*. November 25, 2002. https://www.gainesville.com/story/news/2002/11/25/football-fans-riot-after-games/31620379007/.

96 Beck, Aaron. "Riotous Irony." *The Columbus Dispatch*. December 1, 2002. Pg 1F.

97 Rose, Lisa. "Axl Delivers Fresh Donuts, Stale Material." *The Star-Ledger*. December 7, 2002. Pg 19.

98 "Late Night 'In The Year 2000 The Goldblum Edition! 9/5/02." Uploaded to YouTube by Bobblehead Conan on March 11, 2015. https://www.youtube.com/watch?v=jMZy7UrHJxY.

99 "Guns N Roses—Madison Square Garden 2002." Uploaded to YouTube by Guns_N_Roses_Fan on January 2, 2023. https://www.youtube.com/watch?v=WXMZ7Mc91lE&t=5161s.

100 Aquilante, Dan. "Axl's Hired Guns Come Up Roses." *New York Post*. December 6, 2002. Pg 46.

101 Farber, Jim. "Rose Garden." *New York Daily News*. December 7, 2002. Pg 25.

102 Bryan Mantia, *Appetite For Distortion*, March 17, 2019.

103 Caparella, Kitty. "Canceled Rock Show Triggers Melee." *Philadelphia Daily News*. December 7, 2003. Section: Local. Pg 2.

104 Moon, Tom. "No-Shows Cloud Future For Guns N' Roses." *The Philadelphia Inquirer*. December 10, 2002. Pg B4.

105 Condran, Ed. "1210 Guns Roses." *Bucks County Courier Times*. December 10, 2002. Section: Life Local. Pg 3E.

106 "Near-Riot Conditions Reported at Concert." *Delaware County Daily Times*. December 7, 2002.

107 Moon, Tom. "Guns N' Roses Cancellation Truly Hit The Fans." *The Philadelphia Inquirer*. December 15, 2002. Pg H16.

108 Moon, Tom. "Guns N' Roses Cancellation Truly Hit The Fans." *The Philadelphia Inquirer*. December 15, 2002. Pg H16.

109 "An Interview With Axl's Longtime Bodyguard Earl Gabbidon, For Those That Are Curious." Originally published on *Metal-Sludge* in 2002, archived on Reddit by insightful-loaf576. Archived at https://www.reddit.com/r/GunsNRoses/comments/13axvr5/an_interview_with_axls_longtime_bodyguard_earl/.

110 Moon, Tom. "Guns N' Roses Cancellation Truly Hit The Fans." *The Philadelphia Inquiirer*. December 15, 2002. Pg H16.

111 Moon, Tom. "Guns N' Roses Fails to Show in Philadelphia." *Philadelphia Inquirer*. December 7, 2002. Section: City & Region. Pg B1.

112 Wood, Sam. "No-Show Pinned on Rose." *The Philadelphia Inquirer*. December 8, 2002. Pg B01.

113 Valania, Jonathan. "Appetite For Destruction?" *Philly Weekly*. December 11, 2002.

114 Moon, Tom. "Guns N' Roses Cancellation Truly Hit The Fans." *The Philadelphia Inquiirer*. December 15, 2002. Pg H16.

115 Wood, Sam. "No-Show Pinned on Rose." *The Philadelphia Inquirer*. December 8, 2002. Pg B01.

116 "Unloaded." *The Morning Call*. December 11, 2002. Pg E2.

117 Boucher, Geoff. "Clear Channel Cancels Guns N' Roses Tour." *The Los Angeles Times*. December 13, 2002. Section: Calendar. Pg E2.

118 Miller, Kirk and Condran, Ed. "Axl Antics Wreck Tour." *Rolling Stone*. Iss. 914. January 23, 2003. Pg 11.

119 Ferguson, Jon. "Camping Out." *Intelligencer Journal*. February 28, 2003. Pg 2.

120 Kent, Nick. "Meltdown." *The Guardian*. January 3, 2003. Pg 6.

121 Howell, Mike. "Do You Know Any of These Suspects? Police Nab Nine Alleged Guns N' Roses Rioters." *Vancouver Courier*. February 23, 2003. Pg 7.

122 Hall, Neal. "Two Guns N' Roses Fans Sue Police." *The Vancouver Sun*. April 26, 2003. Pg A2.

123 Bridge, Maurice. "Police Officers Watched Helplessly as Rioting Rock Fans Trashed Stadium." *Times—Colonist*. May 19, 2004. Pg A4.

124 Read, Nicholas. "Police Won't Be Charged in Guns N' Roses Riot." *The Vancouver Sun*. May 16, 2003. Pg B1.

125 Hall, Neal. "Two Guns N' Roses Fans Sue Police." *The Vancouver Sun*. April 26, 2003. Pg A2.

126 Hayley, Mick. "Police Officer 'Lost It' During Guns N' Roses Concert Riot: Inquiry Lawyer." *Canadian Press NewsWire*. June 9, 2004.

127 Hall, Neal. "Two Guns N' Roses Fans Sue Police." *The Vancouver Sun*. April 26, 2003. Pg A2.

128 Theodore, Terri. "Computer Tech Says He 'Saw Stars' After Beating By Vancouver Police." *Canadian Press NewsWire*. May 12, 2004.

129 "Officers Used Appropriate Force at Riot, Won't Be Disciplined: Police Chief." *Canadian NewsWire*. June 24, 2004.

130 Terri, Theodore. "Computer Tech Says He 'Saw Stars' After Beating by Vancouver Police." *Canadian Press NewsWire*. May 12, 2004.

Chapter 7

1. Nolan, Tom. "The Beach Boys: A California Saga." *Rolling Stone*. Iss. 94. October 28, 1971. Pg 38–9.
2. Himes, Geoffrey. "The Beach Boys." *Musician*. Iss. 59. September 1, 1983. Pg 70.
3. Kiersh, Edward. "Sly Stone's Heart of Darkness." *SPIN*. Vol. 1, Iss. 8. December 1, 1985. Pg 49.
4. Kiersh, Edward. "Sly Stone's Heart of Darkness." *SPIN*. Vol. 1, Iss. 8. December 1, 1985. Pg 46.
5. Novak, Ralph. "The Decline and Fall of Sly Stone." *People*. June 17, 1996. https://people.com/archive/the-decline-and-fall-of-sly-stone-vol-45-no-24/.
6. "France's Former Vivendi CEO Messier Convicted For Misleading Investors." *France24*. January 21, 2011. https://www.france24.com/en/20110121-former-vivendi-ceo-convicted-misleading-investors-misusing-funds-messier-bronfman-messier.
7. "Re-Visionary." *Time*. March 13, 2008. https://time.com/archive/6684000/re-visionary/.
8. "Vodafone Faces a Challenge as it Covets Vivendi Assets." *The New York Times (Online)*. December 29, 2003.
9. "Vivendi Universal SA: Telephone Revenues Offset Music, Broadcasting Weakness." *The Wall Street Journal*. Eastern Edition. May 16, 2003.
10. Reilly, Dan. "Offspring Reveal Attempt to Steal 'Chinese Democracy.'" *Spinner*. March 12, 2009. https://web.archive.org/web/20130421122401/http://www.spinner.com/2009/03/12/offspring-reveals-attempt-to-steal-chinese-democracy/.
11. "The Offspring Have No Intention of Backing Down From Using 'Chinese Democracy' Title." *Blabbermouth*. March 31, 2003. https://blabbermouth.net/news/the-offspring-have-no-intention-of-backing-down-from-using-chinese-democracy-title.
12. Mervis, Scott. "Come Out And Play—The Offspring Sticks to The Formula of Speed And Power." *The Pittsburgh Post-Gazette*. May 28, 2004. Pg W27.
13. "The Offspring Have No Intention of Backing Down From Using 'Chinese Democracy' Title." *Blabbermouth*. March 31, 2003. https://blabbermouth.net/news/the-offspring-have-no-intention-of-backing-down-from-using-chinese-democracy-title.
14. "The Offspring on 'Solid Legal Ground' in Title-Snatching Stunt." *Blabbermouth*. April 1, 2003. https://blabbermouth.net/news/the-offspring-on-solid-legal-ground-in-title-snatching-stunt.
15. Mervis, Scott. "Come Out and Play—The Offspring Sticks to The Formula of Speed And Power." *The Pittsburgh Post-Gazette*. May 28, 2004. Pg W27.
16. Author interview with Greg Morgenstein. November 16, 2018.
17. E-mail from Caram Costanzo, January 6, 2024.
18. Pullella, Philip. "Mafia Sicily's Largest Employer." *UPI*. September 4, 1982.
19. Author interview with Greg Morgenstein. November 16, 2018.

20 "Weiland to be New Axl Rose." *The Edmonton Sun.* May 16, 2003. Pg WE4.
21 Gorra, Nick. "Get Stoned: The History and Future of Stone Temple Pilots." *The Recorder.* February 8, 2008. https://web.archive.org/web/20081206003057/http://clubs.ccsu.edu/Recorder/entertainment/entertainment_item.asp?NewsID=536.
22 "Stone Temple Pilots Lead Singer Arrested." *The Associated Press News Service.* May 19, 2003.
23 "At The Movies." *The Daily Hampshire Gazette.* June 26, 2003. Pg D1.
24 Alcala, Michael. "News." *The Garden City Telegram.* July 25, 2003.
25 Conniff, Tamara. "Velvet Revolver Draws on 'Hulk' to Make Name." *The Hollywood Reporter.* Vol. 379, Iss. 9. June 19, 2003. Pg 6.
26 "Mike Piazza." Baseball.org. https://baseballhall.org/hall-of-famers/piazza-mike.
27 Schultz, Jeff. "Why Griffey Got My Hall of Fame Vote But Piazza Didn't." *The Atlanta Journal-Constitution.* January 6, 2016.
28 Reilly, Dan. "Mike Piazza: Baseball Hall of Fame's Biggest Van Halen Fan." *Rolling Stone.* August 1, 2016. https://www.rollingstone.com/culture/culture-sports/mike-piazza-baseball-hall-of-fames-biggest-van-halen-fan-249846/.
29 Smith, Lee. "Piazza, With Crust." *GQ.* Vol. 69, Iss. 4. April 1, 1999. Pg 187.
30 "Biography." EddieTrunk.com. Archived at https://web.archive.org/web/20120924140626/http://www.eddietrunk.com/index.cfm/pk/content/pid/400026.
31 Trunk, Eddie. "All The Details on Guns N' Roses, as Eddie Trunk & Mike Piazza" EddieTrunk.com. September 1, 2003. https://web.archive.org/web/20031104062438/http://eddietrunk.com/columns/article.php?columns_id=476.
32 D'Angelo, Joe. "New GN'R Tune Leaked By . . . Mets Catcher Mike Piazza?!" *MTV News.* September 2, 2003. https://web.archive.org/web/20050222153728/http://www.mtv.com/news/articles/1477813/20030902/story.jhtml.
33 Trunk, Eddie. "All The Details on Guns N' Roses, as Eddie Trunk & Mike Piazza" EddieTrunk.com. September 1, 2003. https://web.archive.org/web/20031104062438/http://eddietrunk.com/columns/article.php?columns_id=476.
34 Gitlin, Lauren. "New Guns N' Roses Song Leaked to Radio." *Rolling Stone.* Iss. 932. October 2, 2003. Pg 38.
35 "NTM@NYY: Roger Clemens Beans Mike Piazza." Uploaded by MLB on December 6, 2013. https://www.youtube.com/watch?v=NFScJX1Sf_g.
36 "2000WS Gm2: Clemens Throws Bat in Direction of Piazza." Uploaded by MLB on November 11, 2013. https://www.youtube.com/watch?v=QNTWUPsPrJ8.
37 Morrissey, Michael. "Franco's Return No Sure Thing." *New York Post.* September 27, 2003. Pg 63.
38 "Piazza Responds to Axl (IRS related)." Posted by GypsySoul on HTGTH message board. September 27, 2003. https://www.heretodaygonetohell.com/board/index.php?topic=7699.0.
39 Trunk, Eddie. "All The Details on Guns N' Roses, as Eddie Trunk & Mike Piazza" EddieTrunk.com. September 1, 2003. https://web.archive.org/web/20031104062438/http://eddietrunk.com/columns/article.php?columns_id=476.

40 Jeckell, Barry A. "Stinson Swims in Solo Waters." *Billboard*. June 11, 2003.
41 Rys, Richard. "Naked Ambition." *Philadelphia*. October 2006. Archived at https://web.archive.org/web/20061018190039/https://www.phillymag.com/articles/philadelphia_magazine_naked_ambition/.
42 Miller, Steven. "Vince Piazza Cooperates in The Rizzolo Federal Case." *Inside Vegas*. August 29, 2011. https://www.americanmafia.com/inside_vegas/8-29-11_Inside_Vegas.html.
43 Soulmonster. "2006.05.05—Eddie Trunk's Friday Night Rocks—Interview With Axl Rose and Sebastian Bach." *Appetite For Discussion*. Posted July 8, 2010. https://www.a-4-d.com/t7-2006-05-05-eddie-trunk-s-friday-night-rocks-interview-with-axl-rose-and-sebastian-bach.
44 Lewis, Randy. "Guns N' Roses 'n' Melodrama." *The Los Angeles Times*. April 5, 2004. Section: Calendar. Pg E5.
45 Cohen, Jonathan. "Guns N' Roses Members Sue Label Over Best-Of Album." *Argus-Leader*. March 19, 2004. Pg 10D.
46 Conniff, Tamara. "Record 1.09 Million Buyers Hear Usher's 'Confessions': Best First Week for Male R&B Act." *The Hollywood Reporter*. Vol. 383, Iss. 14. April 1, 2004. Pg 2, 18.
47 Conniff, Tamara. "Hung Howls But Usher Reigns." *The Hollywood Reporter*. Vol. 383, Iss. 23. April 15, 2004. Pg 13.
48 Conniff, Tamara. "New Winans, Prince Discs Fall to Usher." *The Hollywood Reporter*. Vol. 383, Iss. 33. April 29, 2004. Pg 8, 41.
49 Greenwood, Chris. "Guns N' Roses, Greatest Hits (Geffen Records)." *The Evening Press*. April 8, 2004.
50 Liveris, Flora. "Gunners Misfire With Anorexic Set." *NT News*. April 21, 2004. Pg 19.
51 Specker, Lawrence F. "A Sanitized Memento From Guns N' Roses." *The Press-Register*. April 9, 2004. Pg 1.
52 "The Razz: Slashed And Burned: The Ex-Guns N' Roses Guitarist Reveals Why He Will Never Go On Tour Again With Axl Rose." *The Daily Record*. March 5, 2004. Pg 43.
53 Wiederhorn, Jon. "Axl Rose Sued by Ex-Guns N' Roses Bandmates." *MTV News*. May 4, 2004. https://web.archive.org/web/20150214165046/http://www.mtv.com/news/1486792/axl-rose-sued-by-ex-guns-n-roses-bandmates/.
54 Wiederhorn, Jon. "Buckethead's Hand Puppet Says Goodbye to Guns N' Roses." *MTV News*. March 17, 2004. https://web.archive.org/web/20150625230435/http://www.mtv.com/news/1485811/bucketheads-hand-puppet-says-goodbye-to-guns-n-roses/.
55 Greene, Andy. "Bryan 'Brain' Mantia Was There For Guns N' Roses' Most Unpredictable Era. Here's What It Was Really Like." *Rolling Stone*. August 4, 2022. https://www.rollingstone.com/music/music-features/bryan-brain-mantia-guns-n-roses-tom-waits-primus-1388363/.
56 Author interview with Greg Morgenstein. November 16, 2018.

57 Bryan Mantia. "I'd Hit That." March 3, 2015. https://www.podomatic.com/podcasts/idhitthatpodcast/episodes/2015-03-03T09_15_15-08_00.

58 Author interview with Chris Pitman. December 2, 2024.

59 Montgomery, James. "Axl Kicks the Bucket." *SPIN*. Vol. 20, No. 6. June 2004. Pg 29.

60 Leeds, Jeff. "Sanctuary Group Amps Up Manager Roster." *The Los Angeles Times*. April 23, 2001. https://www.latimes.com/archives/la-xpm-2001-apr-23-fi-54555-story.html.

61 Author interview with David Lefkowitz. November 8, 2024.

62 "A Conversation With Buckethead." *Coming Alive*. October 2017. https://www.thetoolsbook.com/blog/a-conversation-with-buckethead.

63 Shapiro, Lila. "Therapy Daddy." *Vulture*. July 30, 2024. https://www.vulture.com/article/phil-stutz-tools-jonah-hill-therapist-interview.html.

64 Goodyear, Dana. "Hollywood Shadows." *The New Yorker*. March 14, 2011. https://www.newyorker.com/magazine/2011/03/21/hollywood-shadows.

65 "A Conversation With Buckethead." *Coming Alive*. October 2017. https://www.thetoolsbook.com/blog/a-conversation-with-buckethead.

66 Leeds, Jeff. "The Most Expensive Album Never Made." *The. New York Times (Online)*. March 6, 2005.

67 Author interview with Greg Morgenstein. November 16, 2018.

68 Author interview with Bob Koszela. May 23, 2023.

69 E-mail from Jordan Schur. March 29, 2023.

70 Author interview with Bob Koszela. May 23, 2023.

71 Author interview with Jeff Leeds. March 25, 2024.

72 Leeds, Jeff. "The Most Expensive Album Never Made." *The. New York Times (Online)*. March 6, 2005.

73 Author interview with Jeff Leeds. March 25, 2024.

74 "Guns N' Roses' Manager Slams NY Times Over 'Rubbish' 'Chinese Democracy' Article." *Blabbermouth*. March 6, 2005. https://blabbermouth.net/news/guns-n-roses-manager-slams-ny-times-over-rubbish-chinese-democracy-article.

75 "Merck Writes Letter to The New York Times." *Here Today Gone to Hell*. March 6, 2005. https://www.heretodaygonetohell.com/news/shownews.php?newsid=1319.

76 "Guns N' Roses' Manager Slams NY Times Over 'Rubbish' 'Chinese Democracy' Article." *Blabbermouth*. March 6, 2005. https://web.archive.org/web/20051105095134/http://www.roadrunnerrecords.com/blabbermouth.net/news.aspx?mode=Article&newsitemID=33807.

77 Zutaut, Tom. "No Compromises." *The. New York Times*. March 20, 2005. Pg 4.

78 "Original Guns N' Roses Drummer Says 'Chinese Democracy' is 'Crap,' Threatens to Punch Axl Rose." *Blabbermouth*. June 4, 2005. https://blabbermouth.net/news/original-guns-n-roses-drummer-says-chinese-democracy-is-crap-threatens-to-punch-axl-rose.

79 "Guns N' Roses: No Reunion With Slash, Duff." *Blabbermouth*. April 1, 2006. https://blabbermouth.net/news/guns-n-roses-no-reunion-with-slash-duff.

80 Sculley, Alan. "Velvet Revolver is Smooth Sailing, Despite Rumors." *The Naperville Sun*. May 10, 2007. Pg 36.

81 "Saul Hudson and Michael McKagan vs. William Bailey et al." Complaint, United States District Court Central District of California. Case No. CV05-6028 CBM-PLA. Filed August 17, 2005. Pg 2.

82 Harris, Chris. "Axl Files Suit Against Slash, Lashed Out as Ex-Bandmates." *MTV News*. March 6, 2006. Archived at https://www.a-4-d.com/t3582-2006-03-06-mtv-news-axl-files-suit-against-slash-lashes-out-at-ex-bandmates.

83 "Scott Weiland Vs. Axl Rose." *Ultimate Guitar*. March 13, 2006. Archived at https://www.a-4-d.com/t3589-2006-03-13-ultimate-guitar-scott-weiland-vs-axl-rose.

84 Rowley, Scott. "There Were No Fists Thrown" *Classic Rock*. June 2008.

85 Makowski, Peter. "Velvet Revolver Are a Band" *Classic Rock*. June 2008. Pg 42–5.

86 "Weiland Blames 'Wives' For Downfall of Velvet Revolver." *World Entertainment News*. March 15, 2010.

87 Hiatt, Brian. "Slash Speaks! Inside The Guns N' Roses Reunion And His New Album." *Rolling Stone*. August 14, 2018. https://www.rollingstone.com/music/music-features/slash-speaks-inside-the-guns-n-roses-reunion-and-his-new-album-710144/.

88 "Guns N' Roses' New Album Out Next Month." *The World Entertainment News Network*. February 12, 2006.

89 Baitlin, Steve. "GNR Mastermind Talks Awaited Album at L.A. Party." *Rolling Stone*. January 18, 2006. Archived at https://www.heretodaygonetohell.com/articles/showarticle.php?articleid=192.

90 Bell, Mike. "Democracy Takes Root? -GNR Disc Set For a March Release." *The Calgary Sun*. January 8, 2006. Pg 39.

91 "Hello my friends" *Matt Sorum's Blog*. April 13, 2006. https://web.archive.org/web/20060614162537/https://mattsorum.com/blog/blogframeset.html.

92 "Steven Adler: Matt Sorum Wouldn't Take Part in Guns N' Roses Reunion Unless I Was Involved." *Blabbermouth*. March 5, 2015. https://blabbermouth.net/news/steven-adler-matt-sorum-wouldnt-take-part-in-guns-n-roses-reunion-unless-i-was-involved.

93 "Guns N' Roses; No Official Release Date Yet For 'Chinese Democracy.'" *Blabbermouth*. January 11, 2005. https://blabbermouth.net/news/guns-n-roses-no-official-release-date-yet-for-chinese-democracy.

94 Associated Press. "Guns N' Roses Leak Could Mean 'Chinese' Release is Near." *Quad-City Times*. February 23, 2006. Section: Go! Pg 4.

95 Journal Culture Staff. "Station Playing Leaked Tracks by Guns N' Roses." *Edmonton Journal*. February 25, 2006. Section: Culture. Pg E2.

96 Hiatt, Brian. "Guns N' Roses: Chinese Democracy Demos." *Rolling Stone*. Iss. 996. Match 23, 2006. Pg 68.

97 "Axl Rose's 'Chinese Democracy' Tirade: Sebastian Bach Tells All." *Rolling Stone*. June 23, 2008. https://www.rollingstone.com/music/music-news/axl-roses-chinese-democracy-tirade-sebastian-bach-tells-all-243936/.

98 Schallau, Bob. "Interview: Ron 'Bumblefoot' Thal on Guns N' Roses, Art of Anarchy And Solo Album." *BobSchallau.wordpress.com*. March 9, 2017. https://bobschallau.wordpress.com/2017/03/09/bumblefoot-interview/.
99 Wall, Pg 408.
100 Author interview with Chris Pitman. December 2, 2024.
101 Wall, Pg 408.
102 Johnson, Richard. "Tommy 'Guns'—Hilfiger Dresses Down Axl in Brawl." *The New York Post*. May 20, 2008. https://nypost.com/2006/05/20/tommy-guns-hilfiger-dresses-down-axl-in-brawl/.
103 Lindner, Tobias. "Så anföll Axl vakten." *Aftonbladet*. June 28, 2006. Archived at https://web.archive.org/web/20060705052431/http://www.aftonbladet.se/vss/noje/story/0,2789,848444,00.html.
104 "AXL ROSE: More Details Revealed About Stockholm Hotel Brawl." *Blabbermouth*. June 28, 2006. https://blabbermouth.net/news/axl-rose-more-details-revealed-about-stockholm-hotel-brawl.
105 Behdjou, Behrang and Kudinoff, Ted. "Axl Rose erkände och släpptes." *Expressen*. June 27, 2006. https://www.expressen.se/noje/axl-rose-erkande-och-slapptes/.
106 Hjertén, Linda; Ekelund, Martin; Sigvardsson, Kajsa; Forsling, Jon; Solfors, Björn. "Här festar han vidare—i planet." *Aftonbladet*. June 28, 2006. Archived at https://web.archive.org/web/20060705045616/http://www.aftonbladet.se/vss/noje/story/0,2789,848443,00.html.
107 Greene, Andy. "Bryan 'Brain' Mantia Was There" *Rolling Stone*. August 4, 2022. https://www.rollingstone.com/music/music-features/bryan-brain-mantia-guns-n-roses-tom-waits-primus-1388363/.
108 Rose, Axl. "An Open Letter From Axl Rose." GunsNRoses.com. December 14, 2006. https://web.archive.org/web/20070106181149/http://web.gunsnroses.com/news/article.jsp?ymd=20061214&content_id=a1&vkey=news&fext=.jsp.
109 "Former Guns N' Roses Manager: 'I Believe in Axl Rose.'" *Blabbermouth*. December 15, 2006. https://blabbermouth.net/news/former-guns-n-roses-manager-i-believe-in-axl-rose.
110 Caro, Mark. "Pop Machine." *Chicago Tribune*. March 18, 2007. Pg 16.
111 Author interview with Dror Mohar. November 18, 2018.

Chapter 8

1 Author interview with Alan Niven. January 13, 2024.
2 E-mail from Angela Treat Lyon. April 20, 2024.
3 Author interview with Chris Kooluris, September 27, 2022.
4 Author interview with Greg Artkop. March 20, 2024.
5 Author interview with Chris Kooluris, September 27, 2022.

6   Varga, George of Copley News Service. "Dr Pepper Woos Axl Rose." *Creators Syndicate*. March 26, 2008.

7   Graham, Adam. "Dr Pepper Coaxes Axl Rose Out of Seclusion." *The Detroit News*. March 26, 2008.

8   Author interview with Chris Kooluris, September 27, 2022.

9   Author interview with Greg Artkop. March 20, 2024.

10 Author interview with Chris Kooluris, September 27, 2022.

11 Graham, Adam. "Dr Pepper Coaxes Axl Rose Out of Seclusion." *The Detroit News*. March 26, 2008.

12 Author interview with Chris Kooluris, September 27, 2022.

13 Skwerl. "Crying Chinese Democracy." *Antiquiet*. June 6, 2008. https://web.archive.org/web/20081219094759/http://www.antiquiet.com/editorials/2008/06/guns-n-roses-chinese-democracy-release-date/.

14 Author interview with Kevil Cogill. June 20, 2023.

15 Skwerl. "The Full Story Behind Our 'Chinese Democracy' Leak." *Antiquiet*. January 6, 2014. https://web.archive.org/web/20140616024406/https://www.antiquiet.com/truth/2014/01/full-story-behind-chinese-democracy/?all=true.

16 Quinn, Michelle and Pandey, Swati. "Man Who Posted Guns N' Roses Songs Online is Charged." *The Los Angeles Times—Washington Post News Service*. August 28, 2008.

17 Author interview with Kevil Cogill. June 20, 2023.

18 Quinn, Michelle and Pandey, Swati. "Man Who Posted Guns N' Roses Songs Online is Charged." *The Los Angeles Times—Washington Post News Service*. August 28, 2008.

19 Haring, Bruce. "Cybermusic Pirates Agree to Stop Pilfering." *USA Today*. January 22, 1998. Pg 1D.

20 "Recoding Industry Sues Napster For Copyright Infringement." *RIAA Press Room*. December 7, 1999. Archived at https://www.crb.gov/proceedings/2006-3/riaa-ex-o-108-dp.pdf.

21 Thigpen, David, and Eliscu, Jenny. "Metallica Slams Napster." *Rolling Stone*. Iss. 841. May 25, 2000. Pg 23.

22 Williams, Stephen. "Metallica Takes Aim at Napster Pirates." *The Hamilton Spectator*. May 3, 2000. Pg E4.

23 "Napster Settles Suit." *CNN Money*. July 12, 2001. https://money.cnn.com/2001/07/12/news/napster/.

24 Beato, G. "Steal This Record And Millions Like It." *The San Francisco Chronicle*. April 27, 2003. Pg M3.

25 Hoffman, Hank. "Will Record Companies Go The Way of The 8-Track?" *Fairfield County Weekly*. February 11, 1998.

26 Gillen, Marilyn A. "Digital Downloads: Will Enough Consumers Care?" *Billboard*. Vol. 112, Iss. 45. November 4, 2000. Pg 5, 78–80.

27 Thigpen, David. "Can Apple Save Music." *Rolling Stone*. Iss. 922. May 16, 2003. Pg 34.

28 Cohen, Warren. "Apple's Big Hit." Iss. 924. June 12, 2003. Pg 20.

29 "24 Songs Cost Single Mother $250,000." *The Australian*. October 6, 2007. Section: World. Pg 17.
30 "Lifetime Download Ban." *Townsville Bulletin*. July 8, 2009. Pg 21.
31 Stodghill, Mark. "Recording Industry's Jury Award Slashed From $1.9 Million to $54,000." *McClatchy-Tribune Business News*. January 22, 2010.
32 Walsh, James. "Music Downloader Ordered to Pay $1.5 Million." *Star Tribune*. November 4, 2010. Pg B2.
33 Walsh, James. "Music Downloader Ordered to Pay $1.5 Million." *Star Tribune*. November 4, 2010. Pg B2.
34 Arango, Tim. "Pirates in Tune—$4.6B Walks Plank In Int'l CD Black Market." *The New York Post*. June 24, 2005. https://nypost.com/2005/06/24/pirates-in-tune-4-6b-walks-plank-in-intl-cd-black-market/.
35 "One-Third of CDs Around World Are Illegal Copies." *Erie Times-News*. October 3, 2000.
36 Author interview with Kevil Cogill. June 20, 2023.
37 Millar, Lindsey. "Wal-Mart Possibly to Release The Most Important Album of The 21st Century." *Arkansas Times (Blogs)*. August 15, 2008. Section: Rock Candy.
38 "Best Buy Snags Guns N' Roses Album Exclusive." *The Tuscola County Advertiser*. September 27, 2008.
39 Szklarski, Cassandra. "HMV Lashes Out as Spate of Retail Exclusives in the U.s. and Canada." *The Canadian Press*. October 18, 2008.
40 "Accused Album Leaker Pleads Not Guilty." *The Associated Press Archive*. October 21, 2008.
41 Raihala, Ross. "Guns N' Roses is Back—But Only at Best Buy." *St. Paul Pioneer Press*. November 23, 2008. Pg A1.
42 Varga, George. "Financial Instruments." *Creators Syndicate*. November 24, 2008.
43 Raihala, Ross. "Guns N' Roses is Back—But Only at Best Buy." *St. Paul Pioneer Press*. November 23, 2008. Pg A1.
44 "Best-Selling Albums of 2007." BestSellingAlbums.org. https://bestsellingalbums.org/year/2007.
45 "For Some Music, It Has to Be Wal-Mart and Nowhere Else." *New York Times (Online)*. June 9, 2008.
46 "Rose Hires Top Svengalis to Manage Guns N' Roses." *World Entertainment News Network*. March 30, 2008.
47 "Andy Gould." *Youbloom*. https://youbloom.com/andy-gould/.
48 "What Really Led to Chinese Democracy's Impending Release?" *Idolator*. 2008. Archived at https://www.gnrevolution.com/viewtopic.php?id=5363.
49 "Order on Stipulation For Dismissal" United States District Court Central District of California. Case 2:07-cv-04894-GW-JC. Document 69. Filed August 25, 2008. Pg 1–3.
50 "Order on Stipulation For Dismissal" United States District Court Central District of California. Case 2:07-cv-04894-GW-JC. Document 71. Filed December 8, 2008. Pg 1–7.

51 "Accused Album Leaker Pleads Not Guilty." *Associated Press Archive*. October 21, 2008.

52 "Blogger Pleads Guilty to GN'R Leak." *Associated Press: Los Angeles Metro Area*. December 15, 2008.

53 McCartney, Anthony. "Blogger Sentenced For Leaking GN'R Album." *Associated Press Archive*. July 14, 2009.

54 Skwerl. "A Lot Can Happen in 15 Minutes." *Antiquiet*. June 29, 2008. https://web.archive.org/web/20081201130704/http://www.antiquiet.com/editorials/2008/06/a-lot-can-happen-in-15-minutes/.

55 Author interview with Kevil Cogill. June 20, 2023.

56 Philipp, Sven. "Guns N' Roses; Chinese Democracy." *Billboard*. Vol. 120, Iss. 45. November 8, 2008. Pg 30.

57 "'Chinese Democracy': Stillborn or Worth The Wait?" *The Kansas City Star: Blogs*. October 23, 2008. Section: Back to Rockville.

58 Cohen, Jonathan. "Guns Blazing: 'Chinese Democracy' Has Strong First Week at Radio." *Billboard*. Vol. 120, Iss. 45. November 8, 2008. Pg 31.

59 "Slash Endorses Chinese Democracy." *World Entertainment News Network*. October 24, 2008.

60 Author interview with Chris Kooluris, September 27, 2022.

61 Author interview with Greg Artkop. March 20, 2024.

62 Author interview with Chris Kooluris. September 27, 2022.

63 "Dr Pepper to Deliver On Its Promise." *PR Newswire*. October 22, 2008.

64 MacDonald, John S.W. "Your Chinese Democracy Will Come With a Side of Dr Pepper." *The New York Observer*. October 17, 2008. Section: Arts and Culture.

65 Author interview with Ryan Corey. November 7, 2018.

66 Author interview with Bob Koszela. May 23, 2023.

67 Author interview with David Dominguez. March 5, 2023.

68 Already, James T. "News in Depth: Guns N' Roses' New Album is Up Against a Chinese Wall." *Wall Street Journal*. November 25, 2008. Pg 20.

69 Bodeen, Christopher. "China State Media Blast New Guns N' Roses Album." *Associated Press Archive*. November 24, 2008.

70 "China's Censore Cool on Guns N' Roses *Democracy* Album." *Agence France-Presse*. November 24, 2008.

71 Already, James T. "News in Depth: Guns N' Roses' New Album is Up Against a Chinese Wall." *Wall Street Journal*. November 25, 2008. Pg 20.

72 Already, James T. "News in Depth: Guns N' Roses' New Album is Up Against a Chinese Wall." *Wall Street Journal*. November 25, 2008. Pg 20.

73 Riemenschneider, Chris. "Best Buy Delighted With Guns N' Roses Exclusivity." *McClatchy-Tribune Business News Service*. November 21, 2008.

74 "Guns N' Roses' Original A&R Man Kicked Out of 'Chinese Democracy' Listening Party." *Metal Sludge*. November 24, 2008. https://metalsludge.tv/classic/?p=32198.

75 Ayres, Chris. "His Album is Here After a Decade. So Where is Axl Rose?" *The Times*. November 22, 2008. Pg 65.

76 Martens, Todd. "Axl Rose Stays Mum." *The Los Angeles Times*. November 22, 2008. Pg E1.

77 Condran, Ed. "Guns N' Roses' November Reign." *AM New York*. November 21, 2008. Pg 20.

78 Smart, Gordon. "Axel Rose—Bizarre." *The Sun*. November 15, 2008. Pg 18.

79 Graff, Gary. "G'n'R: Axl Rose Talks to Gary Graff About His New" *The Oakland Press*. March 2, 2009. Pg 1.

80 Burger, David. "Independent Record Stores Like Utah's Graywhale Banding Together to Sell 'Barred' Albums." *The Salt Lake Tribune*. November 20, 2008.

81 Taylor, Wes and Stickney, Dane. "Does The Love Survive?" *Omaha World-Herald*. November 22, 2008. Section: Living. Pg 01E.

82 Burger, David. "Independent Record Stores Like Utah's Graywhale Banding Together to Sell 'Barred' Albums." *The Salt Lake Tribune*. November 20, 2008.

83 Raihala, Ross. "Guns N' Roses is Back—But Only at Best Buy." *St. Paul Pioneer Press*. November 23, 2008. Pg A1.

84 Varga, George. "Financial Instruments." *Creators Syndicate*. November 24, 2008.

85 Author interview with Stevie Rachelle. April 4, 2024.

86 E-mail from Chris Harris. November 23, 2022.

87 Brouk, Tim. "Fans Grab Long-Awaited Album by Guns N' Roses." *Journal & Courier*. November 24, 2008. Pg C3.

88 Author interview with Chris Koolruis, September 27, 2022.

89 Big Red Boots. "Free Dr Pepper Demands Killing Servers—Thousands Going Thirsty." *Entertainment Examiner*. November 23, 2008.

90 Graham, Adam. "The Good Dr. (With The Bad Web Site) Extends His Hours." *The Detroit News: Blogs*. November 24, 2008.

91 Big Red Boots. "Can't Get Your Free Dr Pepper? Extended Hours And Recorded Phones Help." *Entertainment Examiner*. November 24, 2008.

92 "Axl Rose Demands Apology, Payment From Dr Pepper." *Associated Press Archive*. November 26, 2008.

93 "Guardian Unlimited: Dr Pepper Sweet as Roses With Axl After Giveaway 'Fiasco.'" *The Guardian We Edition*. December 4, 2008.

94 Robinson-Jacobs, Karen. "Dr Pepper Giveaway Lost Its Fizz—Did a Huge Response Leave Some Fans Thirsty?" *The Dallas Morning News*. December 4, 2008. Pg 3E.

95 Winter, Kareen. "Guns N' Roses Lashes Out at Dr Pepper." *CNN*. December 3, 2008. https://web.archive.org/web/20090225234814/https://www.cnn.com/2008/SHOWBIZ/Music/12/02/gunsnroses.soda/index.html.

96 Author interview with Greg Artkop. March 20, 2024.

97 "Dr Pepper: 'No Apology For Guns N' Roses.'" *World Entertainment News Network*. December 3, 2008.

98 Robinson-Jacobs, Karen. "Dr Pepper Giveaway Lost Its Fizz.- Did a Huge Response Leave Some Fans Thirsty?" *The Dallas Morning News*. December 4, 2008. Pg 3E.

99 "Axl Answers Fans' Questions on GN'R Fan Sites [transcripts] [updated Dec 14]." *Here Today, Gone to Hell*. December 13, 2008. https://www.heretodaygonetohell.com/news/shownews.php?newsid=1973.

100 Rocket, Justin. "Throne of Games." *New York Daily News*. June 8, 2014. Pg 9.

101 Author interview with Chris Kooluris, September 27, 2022.

102 Author interview with Greg Artkop. November 15, 2024.

103 "Free DR PEPPER Coupons Begin Arriving In The Mail." *Blabbermouth*. December 17, 2008. https://blabbermouth.net/news/free-dr-pepper-coupons-begin-arriving-in-the-mail.

104 Author interview with Greg Artkop. March 20, 2024.

105 Dawson, N.P. "The Cuttlefish School of Writers." *Forum*. Vol. LXIX. January 1923. Pg 1174.

106 "Are We Witnessing The Break-Up of The Novel?" *Current Opinion*. February 1, 1923. Pg 186.

107 Bennett, Arnold. "Concerning James Joyce's 'Ulysses.'" *The Bookman*. Vol. 55, Iss. 6. August 1922. Pg 567.

108 "Editorial Comment." *The Billboard*. Vol. 34, Iss. 25. June 24, 1922. Pg 44.

109 "James Joyce Dies." *The New York Times*. January 13, 1941. Pg 15.

110 "Improper Novel Costs Women $100." *The New York Times*. February 22, 1921. Pg 12.

111 "Court Lifts Ban on 'Ulysses' Here." *The New York Times*. December 7, 1933. Pg 21.

112 Dawson, N.P. "The Cuttlefish School of Writers." *Forum*. Vol. LXIX. January 1923. Pg 1174.

113 Bennett, Arnold. "Concerning James Joyce's 'Ulysses.'" *The Bookman*. Vol. 55, Iss. 6. August 1922. Pg 567.

114 Rascoe, Burton. "Finnegans Wake." *Newsweek*. Vol. 13, Iss. 19. May 8, 1939. Pg 36.

115 Verschoyle, Derek. "Finnegans Wake." *The Spectator*. Vol. 162, Iss. 5785. May 12, 1939. Pg 820.

116 Lerner, Max. "Open Sesame to James Joyce." *The New York Times*. July 23, 1944. Pg 5, 10.

117 Stewart, Allison. "Axl Rose is Back: No Guns, No Glory." *The Washington Post*. November 22, 2008. Pg C1.

118 Greenman, Ben. "Petal to The Metal." *The New Yorker*. Vol. 84, Iss. 39. December 1, 2008. Pg 13.

119 Derogatis, Jim. "We Waited 17 Years For This?" *The Chicago Sun-Times*. November 23, 2008. Section: Show. Pg D6.

120 Everett-Green, Robert. "A Middle Effort—After 14 Years." *The Globe and Mail*. November 22, 2008. Pg R12.

121 Tarradell, Mario. "An Axl to Grind." *The Dallas Morning News*. November 24, 2008. Pg 1E.

122 Cohen, Howard. "ALBUM REVIEWS: Great Expectations Come With Mild Disappointment." *The Miami Herald*. November 24, 2008. Pg E6.

123 Harvilla, Rob. "Why Chinese Democracy's Fine Print is Way More Fun Than The Record Itself." *The Village Voice*. November 26, 2008. Section: Down in Front.

124 Cohen, Ian. "Chinese Democracy." *Pitchfork*. December 1, 2008. https://pitchfork.com/reviews/albums/12469-chinese-democracy/.

125 Klosterman, Chuck. "Chuck Klosterman Reviews *Chinese Democracy*." AVClub. November 19, 2008. https://www.avclub.com/chuck-klosterman-reviews-chinese-democracy-1798205338.

126 Powers, Ann. "Album Review/Pop Music: Welcome to His Jungle." *The Los Angeles Times*. November 23, 2008. Pg F1.

127 "Dave Navarro Says He 'Pretty Much Loves' Guns N' Roses' 'Chinese Democracy.'" *Blabbermouth*. December 29, 2008. https://blabbermouth.net/news/dave-navarro-says-he-pretty-much-loves-guns-n-roses-chinese-democracy.

128 Kreps, Daniel. "Lars Ulrich Confirms He Appears in Guns N' Roses' 'Better' Video." *Rolling Stone*. January 21, 2009. https://www.rollingstone.com/music/music-news/lars-ulrich-confirms-he-appears-in-guns-n-roses-better-video-243862/.

129 "Metallica's Ulrich, Hammett Name Their Favorite Albums, Songs of The Past Decade." *Blabbermouth*. December 10, 2009. https://blabbermouth.net/news/metallica-s-ulrich-hammett-name-their-favorite-albums-songs-of-past-decade.

130 "Ex-Guns N' Roses Guitarist Gilby Clarke Offers His Opinion of 'Chinese Democracy.'" *Blabbermouth*. February 8, 2009. https://blabbermouth.net/news/ex-guns-n-roses-guitarist-gilby-clarke-offers-his-opinion-of-chinese-democracy.

131 "STEVEN ADLER: I Didn't Like 'Chinese Democracy' One Bit." *Blabbermouth*. June 3, 2009. https://blabbermouth.net/news/steven-adler-i-didn-t-like-chinese-democracy-one-bit.

132 "Slash on 'Chinese Democracy': 'It's a Great Statement by Axl.'" *Blabbermouth*. September 5, 2008. https://blabbermouth.net/news/slash-on-chinese-democracy-it-s-a-great-statement-by-axl.

133 Anthony, James. "Brian May Dropped From Guns N' Roses Album." *The Guardian*. November 7, 2008. https://www.theguardian.com/music/2008/nov/07/brian-may-chinese-democracy.

134 "Brian May Not Feeling Snubbed by Axl Rose." *Ultimate Guitar*. https://www.ultimate-guitar.com/news/general_music_news/brian_may_not_feeling_snubbed_by_axl_rose.html.

135 "Slash Reveals One 'Unnverving' Thing" *Ultimate Guitar*. February 23, 2022. https://www.ultimate-guitar.com/news/general_music_news/slash_reveals_one_unnerving_thing_you_shouldnt_say_when_meeting_your_heroes_remembers_playing_in_front_of_brian_may_and_jimmy_page.html.

136 Christman, Ed. "'Democracy' in America: Disappointing Guns N' Roses Sales Show The Limits of Exclusives." *Billboard*. Vol. 120, Iss. 51. December 20, 2008. Pg 34.

137 Raihala, Ross. "Guns N' Roses is Back—But Only at Best Buy." *St. Paul Pioneer Press*. November 23, 2008. Pg A1.

138 Bustillo, Miguel. "At Best Buy, An Album Sounds a Sour Sales Note." *The Wall Street Journal*. December 16, 2008. Pg B6.

139 Gough, Neil and Shantou. "Zombie Discs." *Time*. January 20, 2003. https://web.archive.org/web/20071102043310/http://www.time.com/time/magazine/article/0,9171,409647,00.html.

140 Umphred, Neil. "The Avid Record Collector #2: 'What is a Cut-Out?'" *Sixties Music Secrets*. July 7, 2021. https://www.sixtiesmusicsecrets.com/the-avid-record-collector-2-what-is-a-cut-out/.

141 "Deemed a Market Flop, Million Copies of Robbie Williams' 'Rudebox' Reportedly Will Aid China's Industrial Project." *Ace Showbiz*. January 17, 2008. https://www.aceshowbiz.com/news/view/00013531.html.

142 Knopper, Steve. "Rock Albums Lead Fall Season, But Record Biz Still Struggles." *Rolling Stone*. Iss. 1066. November 27, 2008. Pg 20.

143 Anderman, Joan. "Finally Pulling The Trigger." *Boston Globe*. November 23, 2008. Pg N1.

144 Bustillo, Miguel. "At Best Buy, An Album Sounds a Sour Sales Note." *The Wall Street Journal*. December 16, 2008. Pg B6.

145 "Axl to Reform Old Band?" *7Days*. December 2, 2008.

146 "Shut-In Axl Irks Music Pals." *New York Post*. December 12, 2008. Section: Page Six. Pg 20.

147 "Axl Answers Fans' Questions on GNR Fan Sites (Transcripts)." *Here TodayGone to Hell!* December 13, 2008, Updated December 14, 2008. https://www.heretodaygonetohell.com/news/shownews.php?newsid=1973.

148 S.K. and Knooper, Steve. "AC/DC vs. Guns N' Roses." *Rolling Stone*. Iss. 1071. February 5, 2009. Pg 17.

149 Cohen, Jonathan. "The Billboard Q&A: Axl Rose." *Billboard*. February 6, 2009. https://www.billboard.com/music/music-news/the-billboard-qa-axl-rose-269462/.

150 Cohen, Jonathan. "The Billboard Q&A: Axl Rose." *Billboard*. February 6, 2009. https://www.billboard.com/music/music-news/the-billboard-qa-axl-rose-269462/.

151 Sculley, Alan. "New Setzer Trio Not Another Stray Cats." *The Post-Tribune*. July 27, 2001. Section: Weekend. Pg D11.

152 Rodman, Sarah. "Trail of Dead Rises, On Its Own Terms." *Boston Globe*. February 27, 2009. Pg G17.

153 Vozick-Ievinson, Simon. "Rivers Cuomo is Trying to Be All Right." *Rolling Stone*. Iss. 1217. September 11, 2014. Pg 50.

154 Hiatt, Brian. "Josh Homme Talks New Queens of The Stone Age LP, Parenting, Hangovers." *Rolling Stone*. August 24, 2017. https://www.rollingstone.com/music/music-features/josh-homme-talks-new-queens-of-the-stone-age-lp-parenting-hangovers-204754/.

155 Marchese, David. "The SPIN Interview: Queens of the Stone Age's Josh Homme." *SPIN*. June 13, 2013. https://www.spin.com/2013/06/queens-of-the-stone-age-josh-homme-like-clockwork-interview-2013/.

156 Firecloud, Johnny. "Josh Homme of Queens of The Stone Age: Interscope Sucks My Dick." *Antiquiet*. December 2, 2007. Archived at https://web.archive.org/web/20081118172205/http://antiquiet.com/interviews/2007/12/antiquiet-interviews-josh-homme-of-queens-of-the-stone-age/.

157 Frere-Jones, Sasha. "High Fidelity." *New Yorker*. September 14, 2009. Pg 83.

158 Cohen, Jonathan. "The Billboard Q&A: Axl Rose." *Billboard*. February 6, 2009. https://www.billboard.com/music/music-news/the-billboard-qa-axl-rose-269462/.

159 Hilburn, Robert. "Ears Wide Open." *The Los Angeles Times*. November 30, 2006.

160 Tavana, Art. "The Divisive Legacy & Surprising Future f Guns N' Roses' 'Chinese Democracy.'" *Billboard*. December 12, 2018. https://www.billboard.com/music/rock/guns-n-roses-chinese-democracy-album-legacy-8490842/.

161 Author interview with Chris Pitman. December 2, 2024.

162 Cohen, Jonathan. "The Billboard Q&A: Jimmy Iovine." *Billboard*. Vol. 120, Iss. 49. December 6, 2008. Pg 16.

163 Author interview with Robin Sloane Seibert. July 7, 2023.

Chapter 9

1 Lewis, Randy. "A Long Wait, A Fast Fall." *The Los Angeles Times*. December 13, 2008. Pg E1.

2 Skllings, Jon. "Music Sales For 2008 Ride Digital Coattails." *CNET*. January 1, 2009. https://www.cnet.com/tech/services-and-software/music-sales-for-2008-ride-digital-coattails/.

3 Sisario, Ben. "Music Sales Fell in 2008, But Climbed on Web." *The New York Times*. December 31, 2008. https://www.nytimes.com/2009/01/01/arts/music/01indu.html.

4 Lewis, Randy. "A Long Wait, A Fast Fall." *The Los Angeles Times*. December 13, 2008. Pg E1.

5 Author interview with Chris Pitman. December 2, 2024.

6 Traken, Roy. "Record Reviews: Post-Lobotomy Van Halen Go On With Half a Mind." *Musician*. Iss. 7. June 1, 1986. Pg 75.

7 McCormick, Moira. "Van Hagar." *Rolling Stone*. Iss. 475. June 5, 1986. Pg 13.

8 Vozick-Ievinson, Simon. "Rivers Cuomo is Trying to Be All Right." *Rolling Stone*. Iss. 1217. September 11, 2014. Pg 50.

9 James, Del. "Axl Rose Insists Original Guns N' Roses Lineup is Dead and Buried." *Spinner*. February 27, 2009. https://web.archive.org/web/20090310194946/http://www.spinner.com/2009/02/27/axl-rose-insists-original-guns-n-roses-lineup-is-dead-and-burie/.

10 "Axl Rose Signs Sixx's DJ For Summer Shows." *World Entertainment News Network*. March 23, 2009.

11 Roberts, Randall. "Axl Rose's Appetite is For Today's Guns N' Roses." *The Los Angeles Times*. December 21, 2011. https://www.latimes.com/entertainment/music/la-xpm-2011-dec-21-la-et-12-20-axl-rose-interview-20111221-story.html.

12 Montgomery, James. "Axl Rose sued by Management Company For Nearly $2 Million." *MTV News*. March 26, 2010. https://web.archive.org/web/20150518083534/http://www.mtv.com/news/1634771/axl-rose-sued-by-management-company-for-nearly-2-million/.

13 Vozick-Levinson, Simon. "Axl Rose Sues Former Manager Over Alleged 'Sabotage.'" *Entertainment Weekly*. May 19, 2010. https://ew.com/article/2010/05/19/axl-rose-manager-lawsuit/.

14 Ryan, Joel. "Axl Rose's Top Five Conspiracy Theories." *E! Online*. May 18, 2010. https://www.eonline.com/news/181678/axl_roses_top_five_conspiracy_theories.

15 Sciarretto, Amy. "Axl Rose Settles Lawsuit Against Former Manager Irving Azoff." *Ultimate Classic Rock*. June 16, 2011. https://ultimateclassicrock.com/axl-rose-settles-lawsuit/.

16 "Guns N' Roses' Axl Rose Lawsuit Gets Off To a Touchy Start." *Daily Breeze*. July 23, 2010.

17 "Flying Files in Axl Case." *New York Post*. August 2, 2010. Section: Page Six. Pg 12.

18 "Doc McGhee on Guns N' Roses." *Inside The Music*. Podcast. Posted May 12, 2020. https://podbay.fm/p/inside-the-music/e/1589320917.

19 Roberts, Randall. "Axl Rose's Appetite is For Today's Guns N' Roses." *The Los Angeles Times*. December 21, 2011. https://www.latimes.com/entertainment/music/la-xpm-2011-dec-21-la-et-12-20-axl-rose-interview-20111221-story.html.

20 Martens, Todd, and Roberts, Randall. "Axl Rose Says No to Rock Hall." *The Los Angeles Times*. April 12, 2012. Pg D1.

21 Nissim, Mayer. "Slash Talks Axl No-Show at Guns N' Roses Hall of Fame Induction." *Digital Spy*. February 17, 2024. https://www.digitalspy.com/music/a549549/slash-talks-axl-no-show-at-guns-n-roses-hall-of-fame-induction/.

22 Michael, Sean. "Guns N' Roses Lead Rock and Roll Hall of Fame Inductions." *The Guardian*. April 16, 2012. https://www.theguardian.com/music/2012/apr/16/guns-n-roses-rock-roll-hall-fame.

23 Nissim, Mayer. "Slash Talks Axl No-Show at Guns N' Roses Hall of Fame Induction." *Digital Spy*. February 17, 2024. https://www.digitalspy.com/music/a549549/slash-talks-axl-no-show-at-guns-n-roses-hall-of-fame-induction/.

24 Hochman, Steve. "These Guys' Bad Moon Rose a Loooong Time Ago." *The Los Angeles Times*. January 31, 1993. Pg 55.

25 Greene, Andy. "John Fogerty: My Anger Towards Creedence Bandmates Has Faded." *Rolling Stone*. October 25, 2011. https://www.rollingstone.com/music/music-news/john-fogerty-my-anger-towards-creedence-bandmates-has-faded-236086/?stop_mobi=yes.

26 "Cook and Clifford Rule Out Creedence Revival." *World Entertainment News Network*. January 3, 2012.

27 Hotten, Jon. "Guns N' Roses: The Real Story Behind Their Reunion." *Louder*. January 5, 2021. https://www.loudersound.com/features/guns-n-roses-the-real-story-behind-their-return.

28 Lifton, Dave. "Tommy Stinson Speaks About Leaving Guns N' Roses." *Ultimate Classic Rock*. January 23, 2016. https://ultimateclassicrock.com/tommy-stinson-guns-n-roses-reunion/.

29 "Tommy Stinson: Axl Rose 'Didn't Appreciate' Me Leaving Guns N' Roses." *Blabbermouth*. May 29, 2023. https://blabbermouth.net/news/tommy-stinson-axl-rose-didnt-appreciate-me-leaving-guns-n-roses.

30 "Ron 'Bumblefoot' Thal On His Exit From Guns N' Roses: 'I Needed to Go.'" *Blabbermouth*. July 6, 2016. https://blabbermouth.net/news/ron-bumblefoot-thal-on-his-exit-from-guns-n-roses-i-needed-to-go.

32 Author interview with Stevie Rachelle. April 4, 2024.

33 Buchanan, Brett. "Slash & Duff McKagan Lobbied For Axl Rose to Bring Back Ex-Guns N' Roses Member." *Alternative Nation*. May 13, 2016. https://www.alternativenation.net/slash-duff-mckagan-lobbied-for-axl-rose-to-bring-back-ex-guns-n-roses-member/.

34 Greene, Andy. "Guns N' Roses Drummer Matt Sorum On His Tell-All Memoir, Getting Shut Out of Their Reunion Tour." *Rolling Stone*. September 14, 2021. https://www.rollingstone.com/music/music-features/matt-sorum-guns-n-roses-book-interview-1215822/.

35 "Matt Sorum Gets Honest in This Rolling Stone Interview." Posted in r/GunsNRoses by Haunting Mortgage. https://www.reddit.com/r/GunsNRoses/comments/po9y2a/matt_sorum_gets_honest_in_this_rolling_stone/.

36 "Is Anyone Buying the 'Sorum Leak?'" Posted by badapplemp3 in r/GunsNRoses. https://www.reddit.com/r/GunsNRoses/comments/pp2nst/is_anyone_buying_the_sorum_leak/.

37 "Matt Sorum Says He Looks at His Exclusion From Guns N' Roses Reunion Differently Now: 'I'm Not Supposed to Be There.'" *Blabbermouth*. May 27, 2024. https://blabbermouth.net/news/matt-sorum-says-he-looks-at-his-exclusion-from-guns-n-roses-reunion-differently-now-im-not-supposed-to-be-there.

38 Magnotta, Andrew. "Izzy Stradlin Finally Addresses Absence From Guns N' Roses Reunion." *Q104.3*. May 29, 2018. https://q1043.iheart.com/content/2018-05-29-izzy-stradlin-finally-addresses-absence-from-guns-n-roses-reunion/.

39 Greene, Andy. "Welcome to The Jungle: How Melissa Reese Broke The Guns N' Roses Glass Ceiling." *Rolling Stone*. June 10, 2020. https://www.rollingstone.com/music/music-features/guns-n-roses-melissa-reese-interview-1003943/.

40 "So What Happened with Pitman?" Posted by username05 on mygnrforum.com. October 5, 2019. https://www.mygnrforum.com/topic/222834-so-what-happened-with-pitman/.

41 Childers, Chad. "Axl Rose Settles Lawsuit With Former Guns N' Roses Instrumentalist Chris Pitman." *Loudwire*. November 27, 2016. https://loudwire.com/axl-rose-settles-lawsuit-guns-n-roses-instrumentalist-chris-pitman/.

42 Varga, George. "Axl Rose Breaks Foot; Guns N' Roses Tour Still On." *The San Diego Union-Tribune: The Web Edition*. April 8, 2016.

43 Nass, Daniel. "Guns N' Roses Rock Vegas . . . With a Loan From Dave Grohl." *Minnesota Public Radio*. April 10, 2016.

44 Reilly, Nick. "Axl Rose Bought Dave Grohl 'The Nicest Fucking Guitar' After Borrowing His Throne." *NME.* January 8, 2021. https://www.nme.com/news/music/axl-rose-bought-dave-grohl-the-nicest-fucking-guitar-after-borrowing-his-throne-2852191.

45 Colophon, Scott. "22 Reasons Why Dave Grohl is The Nicest Guy in Rock." *Rayo.* September 3, 2023. https://hellorayo.co.uk/absolute-radio/music/news/dave-grohl-nice-guy/.

46 Starkey, Arun. "Why William Goldsmith Hates Dave Grohl." *Far Out.* January 16, 2024. https://faroutmagazine.co.uk/why-william-goldsmith-hates-dave-grohl/.

47 Wilson, Abi. "There Goes My Hero: Dave Grohl's History of Infidelity." *The Good 5 Cent Cigar.* September 26, 2024. https://rhodycigar.com/2024/09/26/there-goes-my-hero-dave-grohls-history-of-infidelity/#:~:text=The%20musician%20has%20had%20a,newborn%20child%20that%20is%20involved.

48 McKenzie-Murray, Martin. "The Foo Fighters' AIDS Denialism Should Be On The Record." *The Monthly.* February 19, 2021. Archived at https://medium.com/the-monthly/the-foo-fighters-aids-denialism-should-be-on-the-record-6e33666fdc3c.

49 Stutz, Colin. "Read Axl Rose's Letter to Indonesian President Asking For Execution Pardons." *Billboard.* April 28, 2015. https://www.billboard.com/music/rock/axl-rose-letter-pardon-andrew-chan-myuran-sukumaran-indonesia-6546294/.

50 Schaffner, Lauryn. "19 Times Axl Rose Directly Called People Out on Twitter." *Loudwire.* November 22, 2022. https://loudwire.com/times-axl-rose-called-people-out-twitter/.

51 Schaffner, Lauryn. "19 Times Axl Rose Directly Called People Out on Twitter." *Loudwire.* November 22, 2022. https://loudwire.com/times-axl-rose-called-people-out-twitter/.

52 Byrne, Suzy. "Fans Shocked That Axl Rose is 'The Voice of Reason' After" *Y! Entertainment.* November 5, 2018. https://www.yahoo.com/entertainment/fans-shocked-axl-rose-voice-reason-comes-obscene-trump-white-house-204537591.html?guccounter=1&guce_referrer=aHR0cHM6Ly93d3cuZ29vZ2xlLmNvbS8&guce_referrer_sig=AQAAAIcDiZG-I-x4GLqrKnFYZg357vJbXW0MSefVgU-r2GuAZnKS23Jy5b2cuQBX7vLk26Ac8jQPKS4yiKrWZ6I0EeDAWo7lQv-fhRfy_CtkRhEKLAOeFccgzDXxTZ8aHqMJVq2ihulMnxd8U_pTgsswfo4BW45RfOxzKAgpnTgNIhLh.

53 Moyers, Bill D. "What a Real President Was Like." *The Washington Post.* November 13, 1988. https://www.washingtonpost.com/archive/opinions/1988/11/13/what-a-real-president-was-like/d483c1be-d0da-43b7-bde6-04e10106ff6c/.

54 Vain, Madison. "Coachella 2016: Guns N' Roses Bring Out AC/DC's Angus Young." *Entertainment Weekly.* April 15, 2016. https://ew.com/article/2016/04/15/guns-n-roses-coachella-2016/#:~:text=The%20group%20played%20a%20mostly,the%20band's%20designated%20start%20time.

55 Weiss, Jeff. "Watch The Throne, Literally: Guns N' Roses Show Their Age at Coachella." *Vice.* April 17, 2016. https://www.vice.com/en/article/guns-n-roses-coachella-2016-reunion-review/.

56 Frankenberg, Eric. "Billboard Boxscore Top 10 Tours of All Time: Beyoncé Breaks Ground." *Billboard.* October 13, 2023. https://www.billboard.com/lists/billboard

-boxscore-top-10-tours-all-time-elton-john-harry-styles/roger-waters-the-wall-live-2010-13/.

57 Magnotta, Andrew. "Slash Reflects On How He Reconciled With Axl Rose Years After GNR Breakup." *iHeart*. January 6, 2022. https://www.iheart.com/content/2022-01-06-slash-reflects-on-how-he-reconciled-with-axl-rose-years-after-gnr-breakup/.

58 Hiatt, Brian. "Slash Speaks! Inside The Guns N' Roses Reunion And His New Album." *Rolling Stone*. August 14, 2018. https://www.rollingstone.com/music/music-features/slash-speaks-inside-the-guns-n-roses-reunion-and-his-new-album-710144/.

59 Peisner, David. "The Search For Guns N' Roses' Lost Masterpiece." *Rolling Stone*. December 23, 2022. https://www.rollingstone.com/music/music-features/guns-n-roses-chinese-democracy-fans-leaks-axl-rose-1234645804/.

60 Beaugez, Jim. "Rick Dunsford Leaked a Trove of Unreleased Guns N' Roses Music. Now He's Exiled For Life." *Magnolia Tribune*. August 28, 2024. https://magnoliatribune.com/2024/08/28/rick-dunsford-leaked-a-trove-of-unreleased-guns-n-roses-music-now-hes-exiled-for-life/.

61 Peisner, David. "The Search For Guns N' Roses' Lost Masterpiece." *Rolling Stone*. December 23, 2022. https://www.rollingstone.com/music/music-features/guns-n-roses-chinese-democracy-fans-leaks-axl-rose-1234645804/.

62 "Pissed at Fan Over Leaked Music . . . WELCOME TO THE LEGAL JUNGLE!!!" *TMZ*. January 2, 2020. https://www.tmz.com/2020/01/02/guns-n-roses-pissed-superfan-leaked-music-leak/.

63 Peisner, David. "The Search For Guns N' Roses' Lost Masterpiece." *Rolling Stone*. December 23, 2022. https://www.rollingstone.com/music/music-features/guns-n-roses-chinese-democracy-fans-leaks-axl-rose-1234645804/.

64 Peisner, David. "The Search For Guns N' Roses' Lost Masterpiece." *Rolling Stone*. December 23, 2022. https://www.rollingstone.com/music/music-features/guns-n-roses-chinese-democracy-fans-leaks-axl-rose-1234645804/.

65 Beaugez, Jim. "Rick Dunsford Leaked a Trove of Unreleased Guns N' Roses Music. Now He's Exiled For Life." *Magnolia Tribune*. August 28, 2024. https://magnoliatribune.com/2024/08/28/rick-dunsford-leaked-a-trove-of-unreleased-guns-n-roses-music-now-hes-exiled-for-life/.

66 Riemenschneider, Chris. "Lots of Social Distance at Guns N' Roses Show." *The Star Tribune*. September 21, 2021. Pg 2B.

67 Breihan, Tom. "Guns N' Roses—'ABSURD.'" *Stereogum*. August 6, 2021. https://www.stereogum.com/2156544/guns-n-roses-absu%D1%8Fd/music/.

68 Trapp, Philip. "Fans React to Guns N' Roses' New Studio Recording of 'Absurd.'" *Loudwire*. August 6, 2021. https://loudwire.com/fans-react-guns-n-roses-absurd/.

69 Wilkering, Matthew. "All 84 Guns N' Roses Songs Ranked Worst to Best." *Ultimate Classic Rock*. January 17, 2024. https://ultimateclassicrock.com/guns-n-roses-songs-ranked/.

70 Hudak, Joseph. "Axl Rose Empathizes, Apologizes in New" *Rolling Stone*. August 18, 2023. https://www.rollingstone.com/music/music-news/guns-n-roses-perhaps-axl-rose-1234808408/.

71 Koe, Crystal. "For a Rock Band Like Guns N' Roses" *Guitar*. July 24, 2024. https://guitar.com/news/music-news/duff-mckagan-ai-guns-n-roses/.

72 Woodard, Josef. "Miles Davis: On The Corner." *Musician*. December 1993. Pg 95.

73 "The Complete On The Corner Sessions." MilesDavis.com. Accessed December 2, 2024. https://www.milesdavis.com/albums/the-complete-on-the-corner-sessions/.

74 Erel, Eray. "Manager Reveals The Biggest Mistake" *Metal Castle*. November 15, 2020. https://www.metalcastle.net/manager-reveals-the-biggest-mistake-of-guns-n-roses-i-would-have-rather-it-remained-mysterious/.

75 Maxwell, Tom. "Shelved; Dr. Dre's Detox." *Longreads*. March 16, 2021. https://longreads.com/2021/03/16/shelved-dr-dres-detox/.

76 Azerrad, Michael. "The Sound of The Future." *Rolling Stone*. Iss. 623. February 6, 1992. Pg 20.

77 Lester, Paul. "I Lost It." *The Guardian*. March 12, 2004. https://www.theguardian.com/music/2004/mar/12/2.

78 Dombal, Ryan. "Kevin Shields." *Pitchfork*. August 9, 2013. https://pitchfork.com/features/interview/9192-kevin-shields/.

79 Leas, Ryan. "*m b v* Turns 10." *Stereogum*. February 2, 2023. https://www.stereogum.com/2211268/my-bloody-valentine-m-b-v-turns-10/reviews/the-anniversary/.

80 Meyers, Danny. "Artist Manager, Producer, Andy Gould—Panda Off The Charts." *Panda*. January 26, 2024. https://pandamembers.org/artist-manager-producer-andy-gould-panda-off-charts/.

81 Greene, Andy. "Bryan 'Brain' Mantia Was There" *Rolling Stone*. August 4, 2022. https://www.rollingstone.com/music/music-features/bryan-brain-mantia-guns-n-roses-tom-waits-primus-1388363/.

INDEX

A&M Records 68, 69, 71, 72, 80, 86, 152
AC/DC 37, 161, 162, 169, 170
Abbruzzese, Dave 47–51
Abrams, Elliott 2
"Absurd" 188–9
Adler, Steven 9, 11, 15, 91, 142, 143, 168, 177, 179, 180
Aerosmith 4, 10, 19, 53
...And Justice for All 8
Antiquiet 151–2, 155
Appetite for Destruction 1, 12, 33, 39, 53, 91, 94, 102, 116, 142, 177, 180
  continued popularity of 111
  controversy over cover art 13
  cowbell on 49
  Geffen's initial lack of faith in 8, 175
  guitar work on 114
  re-recording of 60, 65, 76
  style and sound of 4, 6, 60, 149
  unexpected success of 4
Apple, Fiona 77
Animal Rights 45
Arcos Cielos 27
Ashba, DJ 177–8
Azoff, Irving 124, 155, 178

Bach, Sebastian 134, 144, 161
Baratto, Krys 38–9, 43, 44
Beethoven, Ludwig Von 1
Beyoncé 175
Barr, Roseanne 5
Bailey, William. See Rose, Axl
Baker, Roy Thomas 66, 93–5, 96–8, 109, 129

Barber, Jim 26, 29, 58, 59, 70–2, 78, 80–1
Beach Boys, the 127
Beavan, Sean 74, 92, 149, 168–9
Beck 87, 101, 109
Bennett, Bill 19, 53–5, 59, 81
Best Buy 2, 154–5, 160, 162, 169–70, 178
"Better" 143, 165, 168
Black Ice 161, 169, 170
Bland, Michael 62–3
Blinman, Chad 29, 59, 73–4
Bonham, John 27
Bowie, David 4, 31, 45, 125
Brain. See Mantia, Bryan
Bridenthal, Bryn 4, 30, 58, 66, 72
Brydon, Rob 2
Buckethead 1, 81, 90, 96, 99, 114–16, 122, 123, 129, 132, 144, 145, 151, 168, 188
  ability to see out of the bucket 137
  departure from Guns N' Roses 135–6
  difficulties in Guns N' Roses 98, 108, 135
  friendship with Bryan Mantia 89, 90
  health problems of 105, 106, 136–7
  joining Guns N' Roses 86, 88, 91
  nicknaming friends 92
  origins of 83–5
  obsession with Disney 84, 85, 88
  personality of 89, 130
  pikes 136
  use of chicken coop in studio 108–9
  use of puppet 135–6
Bumblefoot 144–5, 148, 151, 161, 168, 181

CKY   120, 124
Caged Heat   25
Carroll, Brian. *See* Buckethead
"Catcher in the Rye"   86, 168–9
Castillo, Joey   51–2
Caudieux, Eric   66, 138
Clash, the   53
Claypool, Les   89, 90
Clear Channel   119, 123, 124
Clink, Mike   33, 59–60, 64
Cobain, Kurt   16–19, 25, 30, 54, 73
Cogill, Kevin   151–2, 154, 155
Corgan, Billy   67
"Chinese Democracy"   156, 157, 159–60
Chinese Democracy   1
   aborted 2011 relaunch   178
   alternate titles for   77
   amount of material recorded for   76–7, 87
   artwork for   157–8
   Chinese fan reaction to   159–60
   Chinese government reaction to   159
   cost of   59, 80–1, 127, 140
   critical reaction to   165–7, 189
   Dr Pepper promotional tie-in   150–1, 156–7, 162–4
   disagreements about completion   92, 95, 148, 171, 172, 190
   fan reaction to   160
   first and second week sales figures   169, 170
   leaks from   132–4, 143–4, 151–5
   Music Monitor disruption   161–2
   production under Sean Beavan   74, 92
   production under Roy Thomas Baker   93–8
   production under Youth   65–6
   re-recording drums   97–9
   re-recording guitars   98
   reasons for commercial failure   175–6
   release of   2, 154–5, 162
   removal of Brian May from   168–9
   unmet release dates   39, 58, 59, 68, 71, 77, 87, 92, 103, 105–6, 109, 112, 133, 134, 138, 143, 147
   unreleased material from   181, 185–8

Chotiner, Isaac   2
Clarke, Gilby   15–16, 29, 33, 35, 37, 99, 168, 179, 180
Coogan, Steve   2
Cornell, Chris   14, 63
Costanzo, Caram   130, 135, 138, 139, 157
Crawdaddy   2
Crow, Sheryl   69, 72–3, 78

DGC   16, 53
Dr Pepper   150–1, 156–7
Dr. Dre   71, 172, 189–90
Danzig   19, 52
Date, Terry   74
Davis, Miles   91, 122, 189
Depeche Mode   9
Dead Kennedys   1
Devo   61, 62
Dominguez, David   41, 59–60, 64, 66, 157
"Don't Cry"   6, 25
Downward Spiral, the   31, 46, 74
Dragon, Daryl   65, 95
Dunsford, Rick   186–7

ELO   10
Eagles, the   54, 154–5
Eminem   71, 117, 172
End of Days (soundtrack)   73, 75, 77
Everly, Erin   23–5, 27, 106–7, 180
Ezrin, Bob   95

Fallon, Jimmy   117, 118
Fat Boys, the   1
Ferrar, Frank   145, 161, 182, 185
Finck, Robin   45–6, 49, 55, 63, 74, 77, 78, 88, 99, 109, 120, 136, 145
Flood (producer)   54–5
Fogerty, John   13, 180
Foo Fighters, the   62, 101, 183
Fortus, Richard   113–14, 115, 120, 145, 168, 182, 185
Freese, Josh   1, 61–2, 63, 68, 74, 79, 86, 88, 97, 129
Front Line Management   155, 178

Gabbidon, "Big" Earl   62, 123
Gates of Hell (Rodin)   2

Germs, the 1
Geffen, David 8, 17, 19–20, 32, 53, 58–9
Geffen Records 3, 6, 8, 13, 29, 32, 34, 36, 40, 58, 66, 72, 73, 80–1, 106, 134, 138, 143–4, 148, 152, 155, 160, 170, 171, 173, 185
   acquiescence to Guns N' Roses 4, 19–20, 54, 140, 142
   attempts to push *Chinese Democracy* forward 54–5, 59
   cultish vibe of 58–9
   decline of 53–4, 59
   fold into Interscope 68–70, 71, 80–1
   signing Guns N' Roses 12
Gersch, Gary 54, 106
Geto Boys, the 19–20
Glover, Martin. *See* Youth
Goldstein, Doug 23, 26, 37, 40, 44, 48, 51, 52, 66, 72, 88, 111, 179
   final dispute with Axl Rose 105–6
   management style of 41–2
Gore, Joe 83–5, 89, 90, 105, 115
Gould, Andy 155, 161, 190
GNR Lies 4, 5, 177
Greatest Hits (GNR album) 134, 138
Green Day 31, 168
Greenberg, Jeff 97, 137
Grohl, Dave 19, 107, 183
Guiccione, Bob Jr. 7
Guns N' Roses, after 1993
   2002 *Chinese Democracy* tour 112–16, 119–25
   2006 *Chinese Democracy* tour 144–6
   2006 original lineup reunion rumors 142
   at 2002 VMAs 117–19
   with Buckethead 86, 88, 91, 98, 99, 108, 135–6
   at the Complex 28–30, 36–7, 43–4, 46–7, 49–52, 59–60, 62, 73–4
   cancelled 2001 European tour 105–6
   departure of Duff McKagan 52, 76
   departure of Slash 40–2
   departure of Matt Sorum 46–7, 76
   with Dave Abbruzzese 48–51
   Greatest Hits injunction 134
   at Interscope studio 138–9
   lawsuit over catalog licensing 134
   lawsuit over publishing copyrights 142, 155
   loudness of 79
   with Paul Huge 29–30, 33, 37, 43, 46, 49, 50, 74, 79, 99, 113–14
   Philadelphia riot 123–5
   relationship with Geffen 54, 58–9
   relationship with Interscope 138–9, 171–2
   return to live performance 99–103
   at Rock in Rio 99, 101–3, 105
   at Rumbo Recorders 59–60, 62, 63, 65–8, 95, 96
   "Sympathy For The Devil" 32–4
   with three guitarists 99, 144–5
   Vancouver riot 119–21, 125
   at the Village 96–8, 108–10, 137
   with Zakk Wylde 36
Guns N' Roses, after *Chinese Democracy*
   2011 tour 178, 179
   difficulties getting booked 181
   induction into RRHOF 179–80
   reunion of original lineup 180–5
Guns N' Roses, before 1993
   Charles Manson controversy 20–1
   drugs, use of 12
   early success of 4, 8, 12
   formation of 11–12
   Montreal riot 25–6
   "One in a Million" controversy 4–5
   objectification of women 15
   popularity in China 158
   profitability of 19
   rape charges against 12–13
   relationship with Geffen 8, 12, 19–20
   St. Louis riot 5–6, 15–17, 125
   as sellouts 21–2
   Steven Adler lawsuit 15, 19
   stylistic changes of 7–8
Guns, Tracii 11

Hamilton, Vicky 13, 106
Hanoi Rocks 115–16
"Hard Skool" 188, 189
Heavy D 1
Highlander III 22
Hip-hop 76, 77
Hole 54, 59

Hollywood Rose   11
House of Blues   99–101, 110–11
Howerdel, Billy   67, 88
Hudson, Saul. *See* Slash
Huge, Paul   43, 49
   attitude and abilities of   29–30, 33, 37, 46, 50, 74, 79
   departure from GNR   113–14
   joining Guns N' Roses   29
   as Paul Tobias   99, 103, 136, 168
Hughes, Howard   56, 184

"I.R.S."   86, 132, 133, 134, 143
Interscope Records   68–71, 107, 137, 139, 148, 152, 169, 170, 171, 173, 187
Interview with the Vampire   32, 33, 34
Iovine, Jimmy   56, 73, 92, 95, 106, 139, 151–2, 157, 171, 172
   early career of   70–1
   relationships with artists   69, 70
Isbell, Jeff. *See* Izzy Stradlin
It's Five O'Clock Somewhere   34–6
"It's So Easy"   102, 114, 166
iTunes   153, 176

Jackson, Michael   6, 86, 87, 109, 111, 117, 124–5
James, Del   72, 78, 157, 177
Jane's Addiction   15, 77, 167
Johnny Crash (band)   38
Jones, Steve   37
Joyce, James   164–6

Kalodner, John   54, 106
Keenan, Maynard James   88–9
Kid Rock   117
KISS   78, 95
Kitaro   19
Kmart   6
Kooluris, Chris   150–1, 156–7, 162–4
Koszela, Bob   138–9, 157

L.A. Guns   11
Laswell, Bill   84, 85, 89
Leeds, Jeff   139–41
Lewis, Leona   176
Lil Wayne   176
Lilywhite, Steve   64–5

Litt, Scott   54–5, 65
Little Michelle   11–12
Lebowitz, Fran   2
Lefkowitz, David   86, 108, 136
Leggs (band)   25
Lebeis, Beta   55, 103, 152, 157, 158, 179
Lennon, John   70, 148
Lenz, Frederick   26
Limbomaniacs, the   84, 86, 89
Limp Bizkit   68, 73, 188
Live Era: '87-'93   72, 76–8
Loder, Kurt   76–7, 102, 118–20
London, Susie   24–5
Lopes, Lisa "Left Eye"   111, 117
Los Angeles Times, the   19, 32, 61, 69, 100, 111, 163, 167, 179
Love Spit Love   113, 145
Love, Courtney   17, 18, 54, 72
Lymon, Frankie   52–3

McGhee, Doc   178–9
"Madagascar"   67, 118, 167
Madonna   21, 38, 53, 73
Malouf, William   28–30, 37, 41–3, 46, 51–2, 59
Manson, Charles   20–1, 188
Mantia, Bryan   15, 115, 129, 135, 144, 145, 182, 190
   complaints about Tom Zutaut   107, 108
   with Limbomaniacs   89
   origin of Brain nickname   90
   performing with Guns N' Roses   91, 100–1, 123
   re-recording drums for *Chinese Democracy*   97–8
Marilyn Manson (band)   77, 78
Marrin, Matt   96–7
Maverick Records   53, 38
Massenburg, George   28
May, Brian   168–9
Maynard, Elliott   27–8, 58, 149
Maynard, Sharon   25–8, 55, 88, 149
McKagan, Duff   4, 8, 11, 19, 22, 25, 33, 39–40, 42, 49, 58, 63, 74, 100, 114, 134, 142–4, 155, 176, 179–82
   departure from Guns N' Roses   52, 76
   early performing career   12

exploding pancreas of   30
in Neurotic Outsiders   37–9
opinion of AI   189
in Velvet Revolver   130–2
Medicina Alternativa   25
Megadeth   64, 75
Mercuriadis, Merck   140–1, 147–8
Metal Sludge   162, 178, 182
Metallica   8, 21, 25–26, 77, 98, 99, 153, 170
Moby   44–5, 47, 65, 117
Monroe, Michael   116
Morgenstein, Greg   129–30, 135, 137
Mother Goose. *See* Chris Pitman
Mötley Crüe   115, 178
MTV   1, 8, 17, 21, 40, 41, 44, 55, 75, 76, 117–19
MTV Music Video Awards   17, 117–19
Mudhoney   14, 17
My Bloody Valentine   190

Naked Cage, The   25
Napster   98–9, 153
Navarro, Dave   77, 167
Neely, Kim   7, 51
New York Mets   1
Nevermind   16, 107
New York Times, The   100, 103, 139–41, 163, 165, 170
Nine Inch Nails   30, 31, 44, 45, 47, 68, 74, 76, 77, 111, 166, 171
Nirvana   16–19, 53, 54, 107, 183
Niven, Alan   4, 26, 42, 106, 149, 189
"November Rain"   6, 94, 101, 122

O'Connor, Sinéad   5
O'Neal, Shaquille   1, 43–4
Oakenfold, Paul   44
Oasis   101–3
Offspring, the   34, 128–9
"Oh My God"   73–7, 86
"One in a Million"   4–5, 20, 142, 167, 184

Palmer, Tim   92–3
Pantera   74, 155
"Paradise City"   101, 103, 118
Pearl Jam   21, 29, 47–8, 51, 130
Piazza, Mike   132–4

Pitman, Chris   67–8, 91–2, 99, 103, 108–9, 114, 123, 136, 145, 168, 172, 176, 181, 182
Praxis   84, 89
Presley, Elvis   66, 102
Primus   86, 89–91, 100
Prince   62, 91

Queen   22, 93, 168, 169

Rage Against the Machine   50, 96, 130, 139
Ramones, the   8
Reed, Dizzy   37, 38, 43–4, 49, 79–80, 120, 145, 182
Reese, Melissa   182
Red Hot Chili Peppers, the   21, 84–5, 96, 101, 116
Red Kross   20
Replacements, the   62, 63, 98, 111–12
Reznor, Trent   31–2, 87, 95, 171
Riggs, Sid   38–9, 43
Rock and Roll Hall of Fame   127, 179–80
Rodin, Auguste   2
Rogers, Roy   23
Rolling Stone   5–8, 25, 31, 51, 65, 73, 86–7, 100, 130, 133, 171, 182, 185, 187, 190
Rolling Stones, the   4, 32–4, 41, 99, 111
Rollins, Henry   21, 31
Rose, Axl   1, 43
  2016 foot injury   182–3
  abuse of romantic partners   12–13, 23–4, 106–7, 180
  alleged animal murders   9
  alleged resistance to addiction   12
  altercation with Tommy Hilfiger   145
  arrests and convictions of   10, 16, 57–8, 125, 145–6, 178
  bigotry of   4–5, 115, 184
  complaints about Interscope   170, 171
  detente with Slash   180, 185
  dispute with Merck Mercuriadis   147–8
  early life of   9–11
  erratic behavior and temper of   4, 9, 50, 51, 63, 73–4, 65, 109, 117, 119–21, 123–4, 127–9, 138, 139, 144

exorcism of   9, 26
feud with Conan O'Brien   122
feud with Kurt Cobain   16–17
friction and disputes with Slash   21–2, 29, 33, 36–7, 76, 87, 114, 134, 179
friction with Buckethead   130, 136
friction with Matt Sorum   46–7, 114–15
guitar playing of   28, 39, 168
interest in electronic music   44–5, 46
inability to commit to new material   65, 93, 190
as joke teller   49, 92, 122
lawsuits against   23–4, 26–7
New Age practices and beliefs   24–7, 58, 72, 88, 108
refusal to give up GNR name   44, 52, 87
refusal to promote *Chinese Democracy*   160–1, 170–1
refusal to reunite with original GNR lineup   176–7, 179
refusal to be inducted into RRHOF   179
relationship with Beta Lebeis   55
relationship with Geffen   54, 55
response to Dr Pepper fiasco   153
return to live performing   99–103
songwriting with Chris Pitman   67–8
similarities with Kurt Cobain   17, 18
unspecified issue with Bob Marley   138
unspecified issue with Mario Van Peebles   22
vocal ability and style of   4, 9, 59, 64, 129–30, 166
withdrawal from public life   55–7, 185
"Woke Axl"   183–4
Rudebox   170

Saints, the   1
Salas, Stevie   79–81
Sanctuary Group   136, 140, 141
Santos, Fernando   152, 179, 186
Schur, Jordan   73, 75, 138, 139
Seymour, Stephanie   23, 24, 27, 107
Sex Pistols, the   4, 37, 179
Siebert, Robin Sloane   54, 173

Slash   8, 11, 12, 19, 20, 30, 37, 46, 72, 75, 100, 102, 113, 114, 144, 150, 155, 168, 169, 176, 177, 179–82, 189
attempt to see Guns N' Roses in 2001   110–11
departure from Guns N' Roses   40–2
detente with Axl Rose   180, 185
friction and disputes with Axl Rose   21–2, 29, 33, 36–7, 41, 76, 114, 134, 142, 179
friction with Paul Huge   29, 33
involvement with *Live Era*   78
opinions of *Chinese Democracy*   156, 168, 185
opinion of Kevin Cogill   152
opinion of Saddam Hussein   101
in Slash's Snakepit   34–6
in Velvet Revolver   130–2, 142–3
Slayer   19
Smashing Pumpkins   47, 96
Snoop Dogg   71, 172
"The Spaghetti Incident?"   20–1, 28, 116
Spears, Britney   101, 117
Springsteen, Bruce   71, 111
Soriano, Laurie   48, 49, 163
Sorum, Matt   15, 29, 45, 49, 58, 66, 74, 79, 114, 143, 144, 168, 179, 180
departure from Guns N' Roses   46–7, 76
absence from GNR reunion   182
in Neurotic Outsiders   37–9
in Velvet Revolver   130–2
Soul Asylum   1
Soundgarden   14, 15, 32, 74, 135
SPIN   4, 7, 21, 31, 35, 66, 89
Star Wars   176
Stinson, Tommy   1, 74, 79, 90, 91, 109, 114, 120, 145, 160–1, 172
2002 feud with Paul Westerberg   111–12
departure from Guns N' Roses   181
joining Guns N' Roses   63–4
in the Replacements   63, 98, 112
Stone, Sly   127
Stone Temple Pilots   28–9, 32, 130–1
Strummer, Joe   53
Suede   115, 116
Sullivan, Todd   55
Summer, Donna   19

"Sweet Child O' Mine"   4, 72–3, 116
Swift, Taylor   65, 72–3, 162, 175
Stradlin, Izzy   11, 12, 15, 22, 78, 114, 142, 168, 177, 182
Supertramp   10
"Sympathy For The Devil"   32–3

Tate, Patty   20
Technotronic   1
Teenage Mutant Ninja Turtles II: The Secret of The Ooze   10
Tenerife airport disaster   27
Tennille, Toni   65, 96
Thal, Ron. *See* Bumblefoot
This Boy's Life   23
The Trip   2
"There Was a Time"   86, 143, 165
Tobias, Paul. *See* Huge, Paul
Tool   67, 88
Transmutation (Mutatis Mutandis)   84, 89
Trunk, Eddie   132–4
Twisted Sister   8

U2   21, 64, 71, 92
Ugly Kid Joe   1
Ulrich, Lars   153, 167–8
Universal Music Group   68, 69, 127, 171, 186, 188
Use Your Illusion   1, 16, 20, 21, 40, 41, 53, 64, 72, 74, 113, 116
    critical appraisal of   6–7
    release of   3, 5–6, 78
    tour to promote   14, 15, 33
    videos from   6, 25, 75

Vs.   21, 45
Van Halen   34, 122, 176
Van Halen, Eddie   61
Van Peebles, Mario   22
Vandals, the   61, 62, 86
Vedder, Eddie   21, 32, 48, 51, 83
Velvet Revolver   130–2, 142–4
Vrenna, Chris   47, 52
Veruca Salt   58, 59
Vitalogy   47, 130

Waits, Tom   89–91
Wallace, Andy   73, 172
Wallin, Axel   119
Walmart   6, 154–5, 161, 162, 169
"Welcome to the Jungle"   4, 8, 59, 94, 102, 109, 114, 118
Weezer   54, 115, 171
Weiland, Scott   29, 130–1, 143
West, Kanye   175
Westerberg, Paul   62, 98, 111–12
Woodstock '94   30–1
White Zombie   44, 50, 54, 76
Williams, Robbie   170
Wylde, Zakk   36, 40

Yankovic, "Weird Al"   1
Yoda. *See* Maynard, Sharon
Youth   65–6

Zapata, Mia   16
Zombie, Rob   59, 156
Zutaut, Tom   8, 12, 54, 106–10, 140–2, 160, 186, 187